SCHOOLBOY Legends

SCHOOLBOY Legends

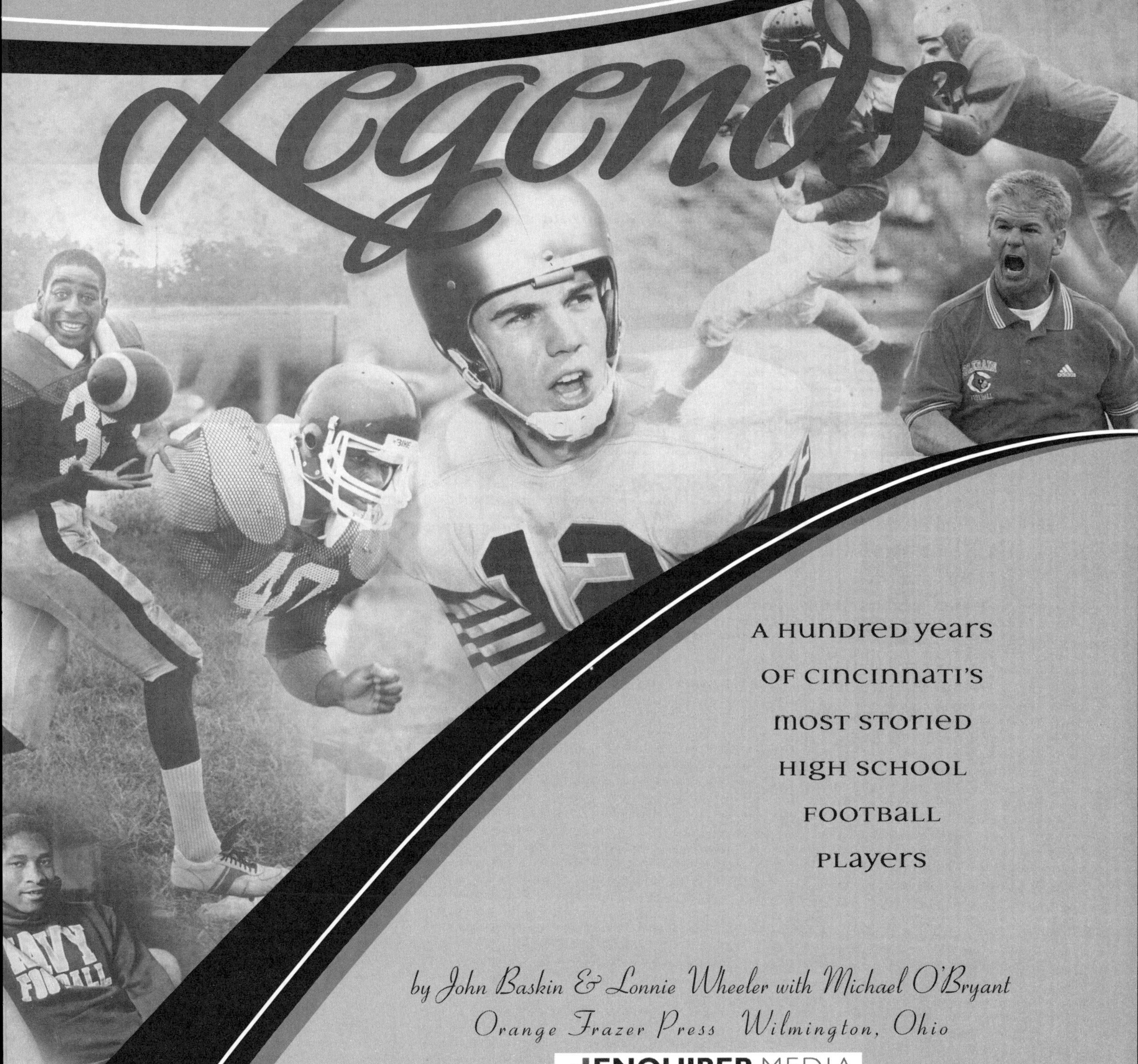

A HUNDRED YEARS OF CINCINNATI'S MOST STORIED HIGH SCHOOL FOOTBALL PLAYERS

by John Baskin & Lonnie Wheeler with Michael O'Bryant

Orange Frazer Press Wilmington, Ohio

ENQUIRER MEDIA
YOUR GOALS. OUR SOLUTIONS. GREAT RESULTS.

ISBN 978-1-933197-55-5

Additional copies of *Schoolboy Legends* may be ordered directly from:
Orange Frazer Press
P.O. Box 214
Wilmington, OH 45177

Telephone 1.800.852.9332 for price and shipping information.
Website: *www.orangefrazer.com*

Art direction and cover: Jeff Fulwiler
Interior design: John Baskin

Library of Congress Cataloging-in-Publication Data

Wheeler, Lonnie.
Cincinnati schoolboy legends : a hundred years of Cincinnati's most storied high school football players : the feats, tales, quotes, and otherwise superlative moments / by Lonnie Wheeler & John Baskin ; with Michael O'Bryant.
p. cm.
Includes bibliographical references and index.
ISBN 978-1-933197-55-5 (alk. paper)
1. High school football players--Ohio--Cincinnati--Biography. 2. Football--Ohio--Cincinnati--History. I. Baskin, John. II. O'Bryant, Michael, 1948- III. Title.
GV939.A1W44 2009
796.3320922--dc22
[B]

2009007273

ACKNOWLEDGEMENTS

The following were prominent among many who helped: Sherry Sheffield, Wyoming Historical Society; Joe Hammond; Tom and Tim Lichtenberg; Roger Koepfle; Steve Imhoff; Bob Kramer; Bob Goodridge; Ben Hubbard; Jack Flaherty; Tom Barr; Russ Hutchins; Rod Russell, Mason High School; Karen Mooney, Sycamore City Schools; Bob Wallace, Alumni & Development Director, Purcell Marian High School; Linda Hilsinger, Roger Bacon High School; Jackie Colville; Stu Eversole, Lakota Schools; Tom Crosby, Madeira High School; Otis Williams; Jim Stoll, Sycamore High School; Curt Stevens; Gary Popovich, Mason High School; Phyllis Hegner and Patricia Van Skaik, Public Library of Cincinnati and Hamilton County; Dick Ballard, Ross Local Schools; Keith L. Klinefelter, Ross Local Schools; John Hamstra, Harrison High School.

Harry Andreadis, Erbil Barkley, Ron Bird, Jim Bolger, Sandy Bowles, Ken Brater, Jack Brennan, Dave Creech, Dr. Barrry Cromer, Tom Groeschen, Jim Herbstreit, Jim Kelly, Jim Lippincott, Pat Mancuso, Ken Minor, Mike Paolercio, Enos Pennington, Phil Redrow and Tiny Jim Vickers, Rodney Roberts, Glenn Sample, Jim Schottelkotte, Will Stargel, Jeff Wallner, and Michael Wiethe.

Notable among the Hamilton folks (many of whom are now elsewhere but still at heart Hamilton folks) were Cliff Wilkie in Chicago; Lou Florio in sunny Florida; John Martinkovic and wife Clare in not-so-sunny Green Bay; Nathaniel Lampley, late of the Second Ward; Jack Young, Jim Blount (particularly for his research on Paul Sarringhaus), and Dr. Jim Carr, the local historians; the former Linda Thomas and cheerleader captain (for both her thoughts and her scrapbooks); Joe Arminio and Kim Nuxhall; Dan Reid; Joni Copas of the Hamilton City Schools; Tony Lamke; Terry Malone; and Mike Townsend.

Special thanks to the folks who create and maintain websites for Elder and St. Xavier. Elder has scores, game summaries, and rosters of virtually every team and game in its rich history, and St. X provides wonderfully written biographies for its Hall of Fame. A particular nod to Sean Kelley; Bob, Craig, and Dave James; and the good folks at Elder for information, interviews, contact information, and photographs. More thanks to Jason Helfrich's Colerain site, *WeAreColerain.com.*, and especially these Colerain folks: Al Gabriel, Don Goodman, Gary Schatz, and Joe and Marcy Smith.

Thanks to the sports information guys all over, but particularly, Pat McKenna at Xavier University, Mike Pearson at Miami University, Michael Clark at Eastern Kentucky University, and Lee Bowman, Wilmington College archives.

—Linda Deitch, Archive and Collections Manager at the *Columbus Dispatch.*

— Carolyn Ellison, who generously provided background on her father, Tiger Ellison, and permitted us to quote from her own book, *Coach the Kid, Build the Boy, Mold the Man, The Legacy of Run and Shoot Football*, which is available through *www.Xlibris.com.*

—Mark Huber, sports editor of the *Wilmington New Journal*, for some sharp-eyed emendations.

—Kevin Grace and the Archives and Rare Books Library, University of Cincinnati, for its collection of public relation stills, yearbook photographs, related memorabilia, and its committment to the disssemination of Cincinnati information.

—Michael Perry of the *Cincinnati Enquirer*, who really made the book possible; along with Michael McCarter, the *Enquirer's* director of Visuals; and Jeff Seuss, archivist, who did the heavy lifting, as well as supplying an aesthetic eye in the quest for photographs.

A special debt to these books and articles: Denny Dressman's *Gerry Faust, Notre Dame's Man in Motion*, A.S. Barnes & Company, Inc., New York, 1981; Bill Koch's books on Elder, *The Pride of Price Hill* and *The Color of Victory*, Orange Frazer Press, 2002 & 2003; Bob McKay's piece on Norwood football, "Fourth and Long," *Ohio* magazine, September, 1982; *Hamilton Football: 100 Years*, by Seth Morris and Kristen Kreidenwels; George Ratterman's book (with Robert Deindorfer), *Tales of a Gypsy Quarterback*, Coward-McCann, Inc., New York, 1962; and Roger Staubach's *Time Enough to Win*, Word Books, Waco, 1980.

Contributing writers:

MICHAEL GRAHAM, who wrote the profile on Napoleon McCallum (page 59), and *On playing big Moe, a true-life adventure* (page 266).

CATHY MALONE, who contributed to *Hamilton, tough house* (page 232); the profiles on her father, Terry Malone (page 277), and Pat Mancuso (page 283); and wrote *No practice with losing* (page 280), which is excerpted from her forthcoming book, *T-Bone, a coach's life.*

PHIL REDROW, who wrote the essay *Waiting for the Big Time* (page 24).

TABLE OF CONTENTS

Joe Thesing, Elder, class of 1936, scored five times against Western Hills and went on to become an honorable mention All-American at Notre Dame.

Introduction

Who's legendary?

For starters, somebody has to remember you by saying something like this: "There ain't ever been a fullback like him. When he come downhill on you, he looked just like a big ole boxcar (*page 88*), which is how he got his name...."

If there isn't a story, a game on the line, a deciding play, well, you might have been a wonderful athlete—but not a legend.

Legendary is Tom Fouchey showing up for a Reading preseason scrimmage, and—with each team getting seven possessions from the 30-yard line—Fouchey reeling off seven straight 70-yard scoring runs. That was when one of the coaches, Kenny Minor, recovered enough to suggest it might be wise to save Fouchey for the regular season (*page 69*).

Legendary is the story of Clyde Murrell's father, driving from Kentucky and showing up in the Hamilton athletic offices where he offered to trade the football skills of his gigantic son for a job he desperately needed (*page 239*). Legendary is a recruiter offering Cris Carter's mother a horse if she'd steer her multitalented son into his basketball program (*page 113*). Legendary is the referee taking pity on the defensive tackle across from Connor Smith during Colerain's state championship game in 2004 and suggesting that since the game was safely put away, would Kerry Coombs mind taking the Smith kid off the field before he killed somebody (*page 162*).

It's the number of times the names Ray Nolting (*page 93*) and Steve Niehaus (*page 159*) still come up in football conversations even though Nolting played in the 1940s. It's the stories of T-Bone Malone spitting his false teeth into the turf during a moment of animated sideline instruction (*page 279*), and it's the replays of the 1959 Elder-

Purcell game (*page 34*) in which Roger Staubach won the game on a long sideline scamper (Purcell's story),although he just may have stepped out of bounds in front of the Elder bench (Elder's story).

Legendary is the play Country Day's Barry Cromer almost—but not quite—stopped in the 1982 Stanford-Cal game, which—with its five laterals and a trampled trombone player—was called "the wildest kickoff return in history (*page 299*)." Legendary is Middletown producing Ohio's first bonafide All-American and a coach who left town to win five Rose Bowls (*page 272*). It's Wyoming High's astounding season in which not one single point was scored on the Cowboy defense (*page 273*), and it's Gerry Faust creating one of America's first national prep teams, winning five national titles in seven years (*page 260*). It's Elder's Bob Hoernschemeyer, who scored so many points so quickly he ended up in the *Guinness Book of Records* (*page 54*), and it's two of the winningest prep coaches in America (*pages 246 and 277*).

Not content with mere records, the area guys also helped remake the national game. There was, for instance, Tiger Ellison's "lonesome polecat," the trademark play of a high school formation that altered offenses all the way into the pros (*page 257*). There was the flinty linebacker Socko Weithe who taught linebackers how to blitz (*page 170*), Roger Staubach who taught quarterbacks how to play like halfbacks (*page 28*), and Cris Carter who taught receivers to play like, well, they'd never played the position before (*page 112*).

We had a Heisman (*page 28*), one Maxwell Trophy (*page 114*), a host of NCAA records, the CFL's TD leader (*page 130*), too many All-Americans to count, and the highest paid offensive lineman in pro football history (*page 148*).

Along the way, we talked to as many people as we could, combed through old newspapers, magazine archives, yearbooks, programs, and media guides. After more than a year of research, we came up with some 250 area players in nearly 150 profiles varying in length from 50 words to 2,000. There are nearly 400 players and coaches referenced in the games, teams, scores, and plays inside. In short, it's a huge reference work spanning the entire history of prep football in the greater Cincinnati area, but it's designed to read like a hybrid of *Sports Illustrated* and *Friday Night Lights*, with just a dash of a good smart-mouth internet blog.

We're aware that there's a huge area discrepancy between Cincinnati's national-class large schools and some of the smaller county programs. There's also the difficulty of adequate records—who, for instance, can post a site such as Elder's, which accurately references every game in its 85 years of playing football? (On the site, for instance, you'll learn that its first team of 23 players, in 1923, was unbeaten until the final game when it lost to St. Xavier.) St. X's own site is less detailed as to records, but no school has a better hall of fame site, in which the biographies are small pieces of genuine sportswriting.

You may also note that we didn't cross the river, into that hotbed of gridiron excellence found in Northern Kentucky. Our decision was to look north, into the surrounding counties and the schools of Hamilton and Middletown, all the Ohio rivalries that compete for the same championships, awards, and lists. Otherwise, our imperfections are meant to be mitigated by our numbers and our devout considerations of players, coaches, and teams. In normal projects, the lists stop at fifty, perhaps a hundred. We've tripled that and are still chagrined because we've missed a lot of guys who belong here. Statistics have been troublesome, too, because even media guides sometimes print figures that don't add up. So while we've done the due diligence, we still need your help. Let us hear about any inaccuracies, and make your own nominations for a second volume.

We didn't run out of stories. We only ran out of time and space.

—John Baskin, Lonnie Wheeler, and Michael O'Bryant,
summer, 2009

This is the West, sir.
When the legend becomes fact, print the legend.
—newspaper editor, *The Man Who Shot Liberty Valence*

CAPTAIN TOMILSON, WALNUT HILLS TEAM

Prologue

A world apart: Football begins in the Queen City

It was a world so different that looking back, we might be watching a tribal ritual. The only familiarity is the number of players—although at half the size. Equipment was largely nonexistent, plays rudimentary. There was no forward pass. (The shape of the ball itself, which resembled a Findlay Market melon, almost forbade it.) Early Cincinnatians on the field wore heavy sweaters, canvas pants more suitable for duck hunting, and sometimes farmers' brogans to which cleats were attached by a shoemaker. The players grew their hair long in the crude belief it afforded some protection when, in truth, they were protected only by the Divine Providence that was prayed to by each side.

The first murky accounts of football in the Queen City begin to emerge in the mid-1880s with newspaper accounts of the University of Cincinnati playing a Mt. Auburn team in 1885 and 1886, then in 1887 the University played a single game with Woodward High School, defeating it 8 to 4 (in those days a touchdown was worth 4 points). That 1887 game may have been the first time a high school—or a team purporting to represent a high school—played football in Cincinnati. (The word was hyphenated, "foot-ball," since the foot was still predominant in the game.)

For points of comparison, students at OSU played some football as early as 1881, only a dozen years after Princeton and Rutgers played the first official college football game. (A Rutgers professor, watching that 1869 game, saw in its unalloyed aspects the decline of civilization, or what passed for it at the time. Pedaling madly away on his bicycle, he was heard to shout, "You men will come to no Christian end!" Truth be told, the early teams—and those who would come after, high school or college—were less interested in a Christian end; it was a pagan the coaches wanted at the position.)

We point out the college game because, in truth, football was mightily egalitarian in those days. Everybody played anybody, anybody played anywhere. In 1890—a year after Ohio State students took up a collection to buy themselves a football—Woodward actually beat the University of Cincinnati, 16-8, which, as far as we can tell, makes it the only Cincinnati high school to ever officially beat a college team.*

Woodward may have had the city's first genuine high school football star, too—Frank Thompson, who was called by the papers "the finest half back in the city." In late November of 1890, Thompson was a spectator as UC played a local club team, White and Sykes. Recognized on the sidelines, he was pressed into service by the club team, then had his ankle dislocated.

"I wouldn't care if I had only been hurt fighting for Woodward, but it's tough to be knocked out in a scrub game," he said, unintentionally maligning the university, which would suffer such indignities off and on for the next century.

Thompson's Woodward team went undefeated and had already beaten White and Sykes 18-0. At the end of the season, even with Thompson out, Woodward

** When the Buckeyes' football arrived, they were befuddled as to its shape and debated returning it, although by this time it already had scuff marks. Reading through the rule book, they were pleased to discover their ball was not defective after all.*

pummeled UC 38-0 in what the paper called "a practice game."

Between those two beatings UC was twice victorious over a team from Wyoming. The second Wyoming game, played at League Park, the home of the Cincinnati Reds (who shared, incidentally, a birthday with college football 1869), was the city's first Thanksgiving Day game. Five hundred spectators watched players slog through the rain and the mud as UC won 6-0 despite the presence of experienced players from the University of Pennsylvania and Lehigh University on the Wyoming team.

The development of the local game was aided by Eastern players who brought their game back to the city. One of them was Dan Loewenstein, who returned after graduating from Harvard. Besides his enthusiasm for the game, he also brought the city's first rugby ball. He had been on the Crimson football team (although by his own admission played little) and now back in his hometown he helped organize and coach the UC team, on which he sometimes played as a "ringer."

His passion spread to the sports editor of the *Times-Star*, Ren Mulford. In 1890, Mulford used the paper to explain and promote the game. Explanations were sorely needed because two somewhat different games were competing for the name "football." In one game, played by "Association" rules, kicking was emphasized, and only the goal keeper was allowed to use his hands. It closely resembled soccer, although the paper described it as "football,

The local lads at play: a scene at League Park, the 1890s.

and simple." This was the game played during Woodward High's famous annual "kicks," when the school alumni gathered each fall. In later years it would be called "old time football."

The game that Mulford promoted, although little known in Cincinnati, was well established in the East. While it was evolving under the leadership of Yale alumnus Walter Camp—with annual rule changes—it still resembled English rugby and was referred to as "Rugby football." The difference was that in rugby football "everything goes," meaning primarily that players could run with the ball.

The games themselves were pickup affairs with the organization of a bar fight. High schools, college, neighborhoods, and teams representing gyms and YMCAs all played one another. Players often had only passing connections with the teams for which they played, and teachers and graduates played on their school teams. (An 1895 account reporting on the Ohio Military Institute's fine tackle, Cotton Henshaw, also cast some doubt about whether he was actually a College Hill cadet or not. "They say he takes music lessons there," wrote the paper with an air of suspicion. "It is open for debate, however.")

Team captains usually served as coaches. Otherwise, there were none. There seemed to be no preseason scheduling in Cincinnati, but each September teams were organized and challenges issued.

By the mid-1890s, football was gaining popularity in Cincinnati and the game was losing its rugby components, evolving into the passably modern game. The rules changed constantly, although by 1895 the T-formation appeared, tackling below the waist was allowed, and linemen could no longer block with extended arms. The open rugby-soccer aspects began to coalesce into the power and physicality that would be—*eureka!*—trademarks of a rapidly industrializing, dynamic young buck of a country.

The year 1895 was notable in Cincinnati for another reason: a new school—Walnut Hills—was added to the public mix, and it played football. Cincinnati's premier egghead school of a century later would begin as the essential School of Hard Blocks. One of its students, John Tomlinson, organized the team. Tomlinson, by even the scarce accounts of the day, was one of Cincinnati's first great schoolboy athletes, an end who had played for Woodward in 1894; then he and several of his teammates learned that the new district lines put them at Walnut Hills.

The new school was not without its athletic growing pains, and an early crisis occurred when the players rejected the school color, white, which had been selected by the girls and teachers. The fellows thought white was lacking in both body and inspiration. It was not a color, it was the *absence* of color. They needed a color with presence, something to fight for. A compromise was reached and the new colors were navy blue and cream, and new navy-and-cream sweaters were specially made, emphasis on the navy.

A quarterback candidate at Walnut Hills that autumn had one of the city's first great nicknames—"Weary" Walters. "With 50 or 75 pounds more of weight and an additional two inches of hair," wrote the school paper, "he would have a cinch on the job." It is therefore safe to speculate that Weary saw the playing field most often from the sidelines.

Walnut Hills practiced at the Norwood baseball park every day but Saturday, and Captain Tomlinson almost missed their first game, which occurred October 19, 1895, with the Technical High School at League Park, the home of the Cincinnati Reds (who shared, incidentally, a birthday with college football—1869).

Tomlinson had committed to participate in the Norwood Field Day before the game had been scheduled (such was scheduling in those days), so as his game began at League Park, he was at Norwood winning the Field Championship Medal by placing first in the 50-yard dash, the high jump, the hop-step-and-jump, and second in the 100-yard dash. He then rushed over to League Park in time to play the final nine minutes of the Technical School game as Walnut Hills won, 26-18.

Wonderful phrases appeared in the newspapers, which would give rise to an entire lexicon. "Lovers of the oval ball," they wrote of Hughes High enthusiasts, and this inspired bit of early sporting doggerel:

Now Woodward and Hughes have a very good team,
And Technical School's not the worse, it would seem;
But to think they can beat Walnut Hills is a dream . . .

The signal note of the year 1895 in the Queen City was that, late in the season, the first semblance of organization was applied to school football. Professor C.M.

Bartlett proposed a championship to be decided among the high schools and the business colleges. The winner would receive an engraved silver service set (valued at $100) as a trophy. The trophy would be retained by any school that won the championship a second time.

On November 21st, the managers from Walnut Hills, Hughes, Technical, and Woodward High met with those from Franklin, Nelson, and Bartlett business schools, and they agreed on a set of conditions upon which the championship would be contested.

The teams would consist of only pupils—all teachers or ringers were barred. The champions of the high school teams would play the champions of the business school teams to decide the winner. (Other customs were evolving, as well, to wit, Woodward placed its players on a diet, and the practice quickly spread to other

WOODWARD '95 FOOTBALL TEAM.

schools, which led to the unspecified downfall of the Walnut Hills quarterback, Innes, who was caught eating apple pie during the season.)

Tomlinson's Walnut Hills team entered the competition as the favorite. The team was described as "the best drilled of any in the city." Its first game following the agreement was against Woodward on December 7, 1895, and the newspapers called the game "the most exciting and scientific ever played by any scholastic team on the local gridiron." There were "running bucks," "criss crosses," and "end runs." The magnificent Tomlinson, they wrote, "sailed through the line like a Viking through the ocean."

Walnut Hills won going away, 28-0, and the next week beat the business school division champion, Franklin, 10-4. That was Cincinnati's first football championship, and Walnut Hills the city's first champion.

The next year, Walnut Hills successfully defended its title. Its team was somewhat lighter (an average of 147 pounds per player as opposed to the walloping 164 of 1895) but with better "tricks and team play." Walnut Hills dispatched both Hughes and Woodward, then met Bartlett College at League Park in the championship game. After winning 30-0, headlines read: *The Hilltop Boys, They of the Shaggy, Chrysanthemum Hair, are the Champions Now* and *Bartlett Trophy Theirs by Force of Muscle*.

By winning twice in a row, Walnut Hills took possession of the Bartlett Trophy. It was not offered again, but the Bartlett Trophy marked the beginning of a structure for the city's high school football programs. By giving city schools some official measure, as well as providing organization, the Trophy had made the seasons become more meaningful, and its early attempts would serve as a model for the future.

These periodic sepia accounts make us yearn for more details of those early boys and their gridiron encounters. And yet we can see them still, cavorting across green fields towards winter as the earth cools around them, warming themselves with their new passion for a game that would grow ever larger. They could not know it, but in the new century it would become—for better or worse—*our* game.

A Western Hills High film session in the late 1940s.

"Cincinnati is the one city where everyone relates to you by their high school. In other cities they say what college they went to. In Cincinnati they say what high school. I've never seen so many guys hang onto their high school football days. These guys remember every play. They remember the weather on game day. Two guys run into each other at Kroger and one says, 'Hey,' then, 'Where'd you go to high school?' And the other dude's like, 'Princeton! We whooped your ass back in '76."

—*Comedian/actor Gary Owen, explaining Cincinnati sports*

Purcell practices in Eden Park.

SCHOOLBOY *Legends*

When the one-time Purcell quarterback, Roger Staubach, led the Dallas Cowboys, they were never shut out. That's Princeton's Johnny Mattress at far right.

QB

Quarterbacks

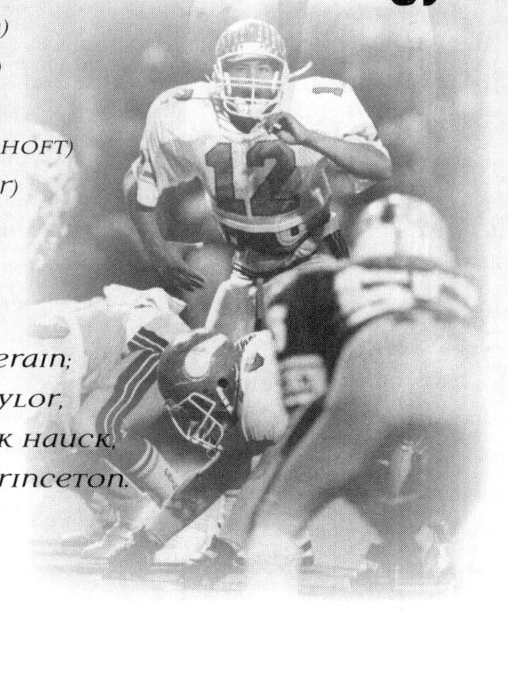

bench strength—TIM CLIFFORD, COLERAIN; BRYAN CUPITO, MCNICHOLAS; MICHAEL TAYLOR, PRINCETON; ROGER FRANZ, PURCELL; CHUCK HAUCK, WILLIAMSBURG; and JOHNNY MATTRESS, PRINCETON.

Mike Daniels

Princeton quarterback class of 20*03*

03

There was the game in 2002 when Colerain, the empire of the Greater Miami Conference, pulled out to a 21-0 lead against Princeton and then held to win 35-34 after Mike Daniels, the Vikings' itty-bitty quarterback, threw five touchdown passes in defiance of the fact that the exceedingly talented Cardinals devoted the vast majority of their attention to him.

Afterwards, Colerain coach Kerry Coombs, in what would just barely qualify as being facetious, told the *Cincinnati Enquirer* that, you know, "It's tough playing the best player in the world."

That was pretty much the consensus around the Northern suburbs. Sycamore coach Tom Adams testified that, "In my twenty-seven years of coaching, I've never seen anything like him. He's a phenom." Moeller coach Steve Klonne gushed that Daniels was one of the most dynamic players he had seen in thirty years on the scene. And the kid was 5-7.

At that size, Daniels wouldn't have been nearly so tough if only the defenses could have laid a hand on him. But therein lay the colossal problem.

Due to his elusiveness and general resourcefulness afoot, Daniels is remembered as primarily a running quarterback. Princeton employed a spread, shotgun, no-huddle offense that enabled him to scoot and improvise at will. Doing so, his 1,387 rushing yards as a senior (leading to 24 touchdowns) ranked him second in the metropolitan area.

But here's the thing. In passing yards—2,569 (with another 19 touchdowns)—he was *first*. And they were actually fewer than he threw for as a junior (2,769). Daniels was the *Enquirer's* Player of the Year, Ohio Offensive Player of the Year, and All-State as a senior, while breaking most of the Princeton records put up by versatile Michael Taylor, who started for three years at Michigan, and passing specialist Johnny Mattress.

"He's the most productive athlete we've had here as far as numbers," said Princeton coach Scott Miltenberger, paying his dues in the Mike Daniels Fan Club, "but what was most important was what he did for us spiritually, and for team chemistry. It's the intangibles—that knack for seeing and doing things nobody else can."

All of that, as it turned out, was what Daniels later brought to the University of Cincinnati. At UC, his size prevented him from playing quarterback, and it didn't help him much at running back or wide receiver, either. He had his moments but was never the irrepressible player he had been in high school. As a senior under new UC coach Brian Kelly, Daniels, coming off ACL surgery, rarely played.

And yet, he was the one whom Kelly brought to meet the media late in a very successful season. He was the kind of player the program could be proud of, and clearly was.

"You don't need to be an impact player to be a leader," pointed out his admiring teammate, Haruki Nakamura. "He's a great motivator, always energetic. He's a guy who's always bouncing around, trying to get everybody ready during practice and games. That sort of impact you don't get from everybody."

Daniels himself got it, in part, from the Princeton tradition that he grew up with. Taylor, who quarterbacked the Vikings' 1983 state championship team, is his cousin. The noseguard on that team, Reggie Hunter, is Daniels' father.

And yet, Daniels didn't start out at Princeton. As a freshman at Lockland, he rushed for close to 1,100 yards. After transferring to Woodward as a sophomore, he *passed* for more than 1,000 and rushed for nearly as many. As a junior at Princeton, he led the Vikings to the playoffs for the first time in eight years.

Utilizing his running skill to overburden the secondary, the plucky playmaker passed so fruitfully that one of his 2001 receivers, Darren Barnett, set a Cincinnati record with 81 catches. In 2002, *another* Princeton receiver, Johnny Long, broke Barnett's record with 85. Over those two years, Daniels averaged nearly 370 yards a game of total offense, more than two-thirds of it through the air.

The other third was through whichever poor suckers stood in the way, groping.

Greg Frey

St. Xavier | quarterback | class of 19**86**

86

He came out of St. Xavier with so much gridiron decoration that he needed his own insert in the media guide. He rewrote the St. X record book, was Cincinnati's Player of the Year, the Ohio Back of the Year, honorable mention All-American, a National Football Hall of Fame Scholar Athlete, and he played a game against Moeller that ended up in the national high school record books.

All of that, and yet it seemed as if Greg Frey were always having to prove himself. He did, of course. You could count on that.

With Frey, there was always proof, usually arriving in the Large Offensive Moment (*both* meanings of the word "offensive" were used by victimized secondaries).

First, there was that Moeller game, in which he completed 28 of 55 passes for a then-state record 487 yards. It was the greatest high school passing show the city had ever seen. Unofficially, said *Sports Illustrated*, it was the ninth-highest total ever at a U.S. high school. Okay, St. X lost, 56-42. Give the man a break. His impressive total might have been higher if it hadn't been for the play of Moeller defensive back Vada Murray, who picked off three Frey passes.

(Lost in the Frey aerial assault was *Moeller's* offensive production: Tony Jackson rushed for 216 yards and Frey's counterpart, Scott Schaffer, threw for 216 yards. Moeller went on to win the state championship; Frey set the city passing record with 2,970 yards.)

Headed for OSU, there was a change in coaches and suddenly Frey was quarterback *non grata*. Finally, his father called the school to find out why, and two weeks later Frey was signed. Soon, he began addressing such issues as his height (at 6-1, too short), his speed (at 5.1 for the 40, too slow), and his arm (too weak).

As a sophomore, he led the Big Ten in interceptions, but he also threw for 2,000 yards. As a junior, his passing efficiency ranked 10th nationally, which made

His greatest accolade came from the coach who didn't recruit him, OSU's John Cooper, who inherited Frey. "The best thing he does is play from the eyebrows up," Cooper said.

his additional 2,000 yards look even better. He was the first OSU quarterback with three 2,000-yard seasons. And there were the L.O.M's (Large Offensive Moments), as well. As a sophomore in 1988, OSU scored 16 points in the last five minutes to beat LSU, 36-33, and Frey threw the game-winner with 47 seconds left. The *real* L.O.M. came his junior year against Minnesota in Minneapolis, a game they still talk about in two states.

The Buckeyes started so badly, they might have been playing in snowshoes. Minnesota took a 31-0 lead, and coach John Cooper said it was the worst half of football he'd ever been associated with. Then Frey began to work the Bucks back into contention. He ran an option keeper into the end zone to cut the lead to 37-34, and with 1:52 left, hit Carlos Snow (the Cincinnati connection, literally) for 18 yards. Three passes later, he was in the end zone with a 41-37 win.

Frey had thrown for 327 yards in the second half alone, pulling off OSU's greatest comeback. It was almost the greatest college comeback ever, tying Maryland's 1984 win over Miami.

As a senior, he beat Number 2-ranked Iowa in Iowa City, moving the Bucks 48 yards with 59 seconds remaining. When he threw a TD strike to wideout Bobby Olive for the 27-26 win, there was one second left on the clock. Frey left OSU with 6,316 passing yards and 37 TDs—second only to Art Schlichter. Nearly two decades after the fact, he's still among OSU's top five passers in at least half a dozen categories.

His football career almost obscured the fact that he was also among the handful of major college players in the modern era to become two-sport stars. At St. X., he was a two-time All-City baseball player, batting .400, setting the school strikeout record two years in a row, and sharing the GCL Player of the Year title with, as the school put it, "some kid named Griffey." At OSU, he helped the Bucks win the Big Ten title in 1991, and in the Big Ten tournament against Minnesota, he had three hits with two home runs and five RBIs. "All my best games came against Minnesota," he said.

His greatest accolade came from his football coach, John Cooper, who hadn't recruited him but along the way became a convert. "He does a lot of things well," said Cooper of his quarterback, "but the best thing he does is play from the eyebrows up."

Dominick Goodman

Colerain quarterback class of 2005

05

By the time Dominick Goodman was in the third grade, he was already confounding everybody—coaches, fans, the opposition.

He could play anywhere, it seemed, and do most anything with a football. He started out as a pee-wee linebacker and tight end, then he was a receiver. Then a quarterback. All the way into college, it was a toss-up: where was he better, receiver or quarterback? For a time, the logical answer seemed to be, let the kid play *both*; he could throw the ball to *himself*, which seemed only so far-fetched to those who'd seen him play.

As a Colerain sophomore, he was the junior varsity quarterback, the varsity receiver. It was difficult to keep an athlete like Goodman off the field. He was going to be *somewhere*. Then as a senior on one of the most talent-laden teams to ever come out of Cincinnati, he was the driver. The man. The QB. His father, Don, had always told him it didn't matter where you played but wherever it was, don't follow. *Lead*. And so he did.

The Transformer

St. Xavier receiver **Mike Healey**, who had been Greg Frey's go-to guy, underwent a wondrous seasonal transformation by becoming Frey's successor at quarterback, proving that he was adept at either end of the field.

By the time he graduated in 1988, he had thrown for 3,260 yards and 29 TDs, was named Cincinnati's Player of the Year (by both newspapers), and made second-team All-State.

He was also team captain in three sports, something that hadn't occurred at X for a quarter of a century. He

Colerain went through its 2004 season vengefully. In the previous five years Colerain had lost just one game in the regular season before hitting one playoff impediment or another. The Cardinals had, as someone pointed out, lived with the label of the best team in Ohio never to attain that title officially. But this was the year the stone would be rolled from the door. Colerain, with Goodman leading, waltzed into the state championship game with a 40-point average margin of victory against one of the meanest schedules in the country.

Then, opening against Canton McKinley in the grand finale, Dominick fumbled. Not once. *Four* of Colerain's first six snaps.

Up in the stands, Mr. Goodman's friends eyed him warily. "What's wrong with Dominick?" they asked. "Nothing," he said. "Bad read. Life . . . ."

There was a little signal between father and son, a

Where was Dominick (above) better? Anywhere with the ball. The pitcher at right is Mike Healey of St. Xavier, another QB who could also catch.

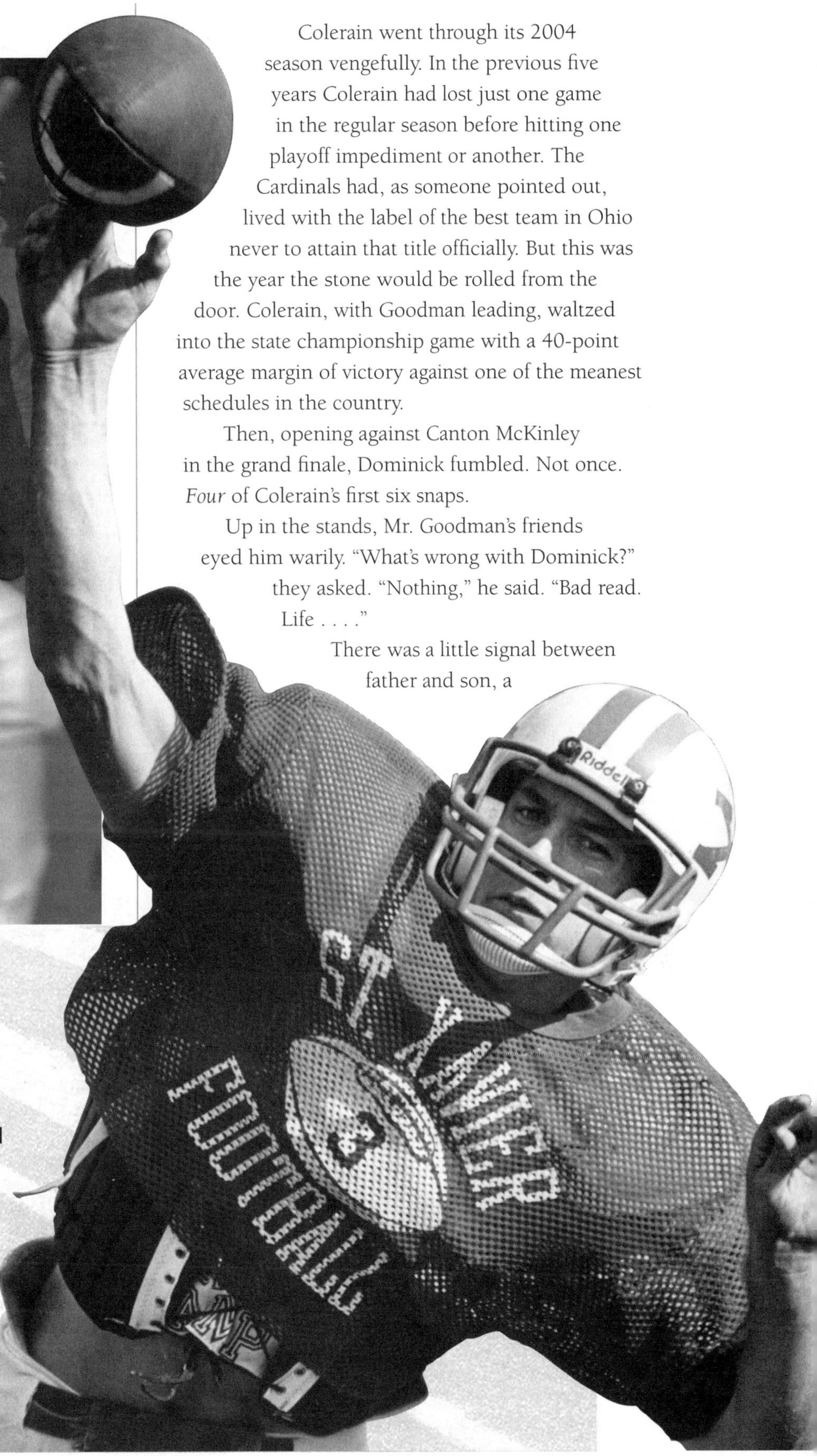

left town for Vanderbilt where he was the top-rated passer in the Southeastern Conference in 1990.

"Despite playing for the eternally disadvantaged Commodores in the eternally over advantaged Southeast Conference," wrote St. X in Healey's Hall of Fame bio, he still holds Vandy's all-time record for lowest interception percentage (0.77 in 1990) as well as two of the top ten all-time longest pass plays in school history, 86 and 78 yards.

whistle. The kid looked up from the field, caught his father's eye. It was a bit of telepathy between them, the elder Goodman saying, *Relax. Have fun....*

He may have been thinking about his own big game in 1983, when as UC's captain and fullback he'd turned the ball over on the Penn State nine. UC was decidedly the underdog, playing the defending national champions at hostile Beaver Stadium. It was no place to fumble. It was no place to *visit*. But one play later, UC intercepted and Goodman redeemed himself by catching a 22-yard pass to the 11, which set up UC's first score. Then he scored on an 8-yard draw play. That afternoon, in a stunning 14-3 upset, Goodman had 61 yards on the ground and caught eight passes for another 69 yards. A man's philosophy is developed on such afternoons.

So the kid faced his own moment. And by the time the game was over, Dominick *had* relaxed. He and his Colerain teammates turned in the most dominant performance the state finals had yet seen. Their 50-10 win was the most one-sided victory in the history of the Ohio title game, and Dominick was its MVP. His 259 rushing yards and four TDs were records, too.

There was one more moment between fatheer and son. After the game, they were walking up the stadium steps in Canton's near-deserted field and Dominick said, "Dad, am I as good as you were?"

Mr. Goodman was glad the stadium was darkened, only a few lights left on.

"Dominick," he said, his eyes glistening, "you're way better than I was...."

For the season, Dominick had gained 2,047 yards, scored 30 TDs, and *USA Today* had named him its national player of the week. Colerain, meanwhile, was the Number 5 team in America.

Now consider that *basketball* may have been the kid's first love. All that on the football field, and he may have been better as a basketball player. He was a three-year starter, Colerain's all-time leading scorer with 1,082 points (a 21.5 average), and had signed a letter of intent to play basketball for the University of Findlay. Even the Findlay coaches couldn't believe their fortune. They came to his football games, stared at the kid on the field, and said, "I can't believe this."

In time, it *did* prove too good to be true. Dominick sat down with his dad and said, "I've changed my mind, Dad. I want to play football."

His dad sighed. He'd have to call the Findlay recruiter, a guy he really liked, and tell him.

"I knew it was going to be hard for Dominick," the long-suffering recruiter said when he heard.

So the kid stayed at home, attending Mr. Goodman's school, and moved himself back to receiver so he could get himself on the field quicker. He established himself as a sophomore when he was the team's leading receiver, had a 25.8 yard average in kickoff returns, and was MVP of the International Bowl when he had seven catches for 109 yards and two TDs, converting his new coach, Brian Kelly, who had voiced doubts about Dominick fitting into his no-huddle spread offense.

But there was Dominick again, *becoming* Kelly's offense, much like he had been doing, in one way or another, since the third grade. Kelly was gracious about it, too. "Coach, he made me smart," he said to Kerry Coombs, Dominick's old coach, now a UC assistant.

Coombs could have told him as much. "It doesn't matter what position he plays," Coombs said. "When the lights come on, Goody makes the plays."

Dominick's father, a quiet man who didn't say much, could have told Kelly, too, but talking wasn't his way. Besides, he knew from experience—his own and Dominick's—that all he had to do was be patient. He remembered himself at Penn State and his son at Canton. Look how *that* turned out.

And then there was Cincinnati's amazing 2008 season, with Dominick in the middle of it, teaming up with UC's quarterback surprise, Tony Pike. Pike had started out so far down on the depth chart his relatives had to bring binoculars to games. Lightly recruited out of Reading High School, in spite of a lively arm, nifty feet, and 6-6 size, he spent three seasons on the UC bench until, as a redshirt junior in 2008, he was pressed into emergency service and—playing with a soft cast on a broken left forearm—he led UC to the Orange Bowl, the program's first-ever BCS bowl appearance.

And downfield was Goodman, called "the Wizard" for his contortionist's ability to catch impossible balls. Sure enough, before the near-miraculous year was out, the Wiz had become UC's all-time leader in receiving yards (2,512) and his 22 career TD receptions broke—by one—Jim O'Brien's record.

Not bad for a reformed quarterback who'd learned to catch all those years ago in his old man's driveway.

Rob Florian

and friends—Bradley Glatthaar, Bill Poland, and Tony Carvitti

Elder | quarterback | class of 20**04**

04

WHILE THEY WOULD NOT OCCUPY THE CANONICAL PEAK OF ELDER'S GRIDIRON ANOINTED, THEY WOULD DO SOMETHING NONE OF THE OTHERS could do—win Elder's first state title. And—*mirabile dictu!*—two of them turned around and did it twice. It was as if, among them, they had decided to make up for that noticeable Price Hill drought where titles had been won—almost flagrantly—by most every other sport including, of all things sacred, *volleyball*.

They might have been called a mixed foursome—three glamour positions framed against the backdrop of Carvitti, the agile defensive lineman. But as school began in 2002, the boys weren't glamorous yet; they were still underclassmen, and Florian was fresh off the junior varsity farm, all 5-9, 164 pounds of him. The thing his coaches quickly saw, though, was that Florian could control the huddle (even if *couldn't* see over it) and he could run. He was an undersized overachiever in the weighty GCL universe, small but not small-time, and he had ample survival instincts.

He had, one of the writers noted, "a preternatural, I'm-in-control calm," a trait derived from his mother, who tells the story of when Rob was a fourth-grader. The Florians were returning from a family vacation, about to miss a plane connection in Salt Lake City, and Rob ran to another terminal and asked for the plane to be held.

Said the sportswriter: "He hasn't missed a connection since."

So the prospects were a junior varsity graduate, the relatively untested Glatthaar and Poland, and the oft-tested Tony Carvitti, Mr. Bulwark. But they were coming off a 2001 season in which Elder beat three teams ranked Number 1 in Ohio at the time before losing a heartbreaking regional final to St. Xavier, 24-21.

Since state playoffs began in the 1970s, Elder had three undefeated regular seasons and six one-loss seasons. Where, they asked themselves, *was* the Promised Land? That thought in mind, Elder set off on its most spectacular season ever. By game seven, when the Panthers beat up perennial spoiler, Moeller, 47-21, they had also toppled Ohio power St. Ignatius and Indianapolis Roncalli (which would eventually

Florian was another in a long line of tough undersized Elder QBs. The difference was that only one of them won back-to-back titles.

win the Indiana state title), and they'd gotten the St. X monkey off their backs, 21-17. It was one of only two games in which the Panthers had failed to score at least 42 points, and they'd lost only to powerful Louisville Trinity (16th nationally).

When the dust had settled and Elder beat Oak Hills for the 17th consecutive time, running back Glatthaar had 1,479 yards and 22 TDs, new school records. The offensive linemen were so pleased they shaved their heads, making them appear even more formidable for their run through the playoffs.

In the opening round, the four Bossmen of the Apocalypse—Florian (195 passing yards), Glatthaar (101 yards, three TDs), Poland (107 receiving yards), and Carvitti (assorted mayhem) led Elder over St. X again, 20-14. Then the Panthers beat Wayne, Colerain (number two in the city), and Findlay, to reach the title game in Canton against Ohio's number one team, Warren Harding (11th in the nation).

They'd beaten Warren—and running back Maurice Clarett—the year before in The Pit, and now they were off to try it again, on less favorable turf. On game day, the faithful lined Vincent Avenue to see their guys off in two buses. Carvitti and guard Marty Bauer —whose brother, Matt, was a co-captain on the 1993 Elder team and whose father, Ed, was Elder's MVP in 1970—kicked the coaches out of their seats up front where *they* always sat, and the coaches deferred, no doubt recognizing the tribal practices of their more primitive charges.

There was a police escort to the beltway consisting of three motorcycles, two fire engines, an ambulance, and the long-denied aspirations of the entire Elder Nation.

By the time the buses reached Canton at 3 p.m., the snow was blowing sideways. At the 8 p.m. kickoff, "it was like playing football in a snow globe," noted a sportswriter, and the windchill was near zero. Florian played with a sore shoulder, Poland a sore knee, and Glatthaar a sprained ankle. Deep in the third quarter, Florian couldn't get his arm over his shoulder. He could still run, however, and he did: a 41-yard draw play to the Harding one, scoring on the next play (21-7, Elder). Even though Harding's great receiver, Mario Manningham, brought his team back, Carvitti and his defense held. The final: 21-19.

Florian, with his 116 passing yards and another 120 on the ground, was the game's MVP. The Panther linemen, at midfield in the snow, did their victory dance, and Elder Nation—most of whom had followed the team, at least 10,000 strong—fogged the Canton night with a frosty exhalation eighty years in the making.

The repeat in 2003 was almost predestined. Elder barreled through the season, 9-1 (topped only by another out-of-state powerhouse, Indianpolis Warren Central this time). Other than hometown Colerain (a 24-23 Elder win at UC), no opposition showed up for any of the playoff games—five in all. The Panthers returned to Canton as if they owned real estate there, obliterating Lakewood St. Edward 31-7. Glatthaar's 252 yards was a new Division I title game record, and earned him the game's MVP award. He was first team All-State, too (along with teammate Tony Stegeman), and Florian was named Cincinnati's Player of the Year.

They went off to college ball, but except for Carvitti, it must have seemed a bit anticlimactic. Three of them played for UC and Florian was a University of Dayton backup, relegated to more of an observer than he would have preferred, and yet in his first varsity start, he demonstrated his old magic. Stepping in for the injured starter, Florian, who had never thrown a collegiate pass, tossed for 411 yards, three short of UD's record. Glatthar was UC's outstanding back in 2005 as the team's leading rusher, then became a short-yardage specialist for the rest of his collegiate career.

It was Carvitti, however, who ultimately carried on the old Elder lunch pail tradition. When one reporter wrote, "Crowded and classic old-school, Elder's style is more chili than Chipotle, more orange barrel than Crate and Barrel," he really meant Carvitti. At the major college level, the lineman became as much an undersized overachiever as Florian had been.

Carvitti left Elder as Division I Tri-defensive Player of the Year. He was All-State, had 109 tackles his senior year, and set three school records—sacks in a season (18), sacks in a career (27), and most career tackles for loss (29). (Asked a local wag, "Where does he shop? Sacks Fifth Avenue. Where else?")

But Division I said he was both too short and too small, and his answer was to walk on at UC and show them. As a freshman, a Bearcat upperclassman took one look at the unimposing speciman before him and burst out laughing. Such stereotypical humor was put to rest by Carvitti's play, even if not immediately; he was the very personification of Cincinnati Catholic school tough guys.

"Size is only something that's in your head," he said. "If those guys are big, I'm going to have to *play* big—at least in my mind. If I *think* I'm big, I'm going to *play* big."

The 6-2, 235-pound Carvitti—as a senior, and not much bigger than his old Elder mate, Glatthaar—worked his way into the starting lineup, and when he tore his anterior cruciate ligament in September of 2006, he worked so hard that he was back for the last two games of the season. His coach said he was "the heart and soul of this team."

Of course, he'd been that since the fifth grade at Our Lady of Victory, when he'd first begun to believe that no one could block him.

It was the attribute of any good defensive lineman, of course, but it was a particular attribute of Elder. As Paul Daugherty said, after long observation, "If you live only once, it might as well be purple."

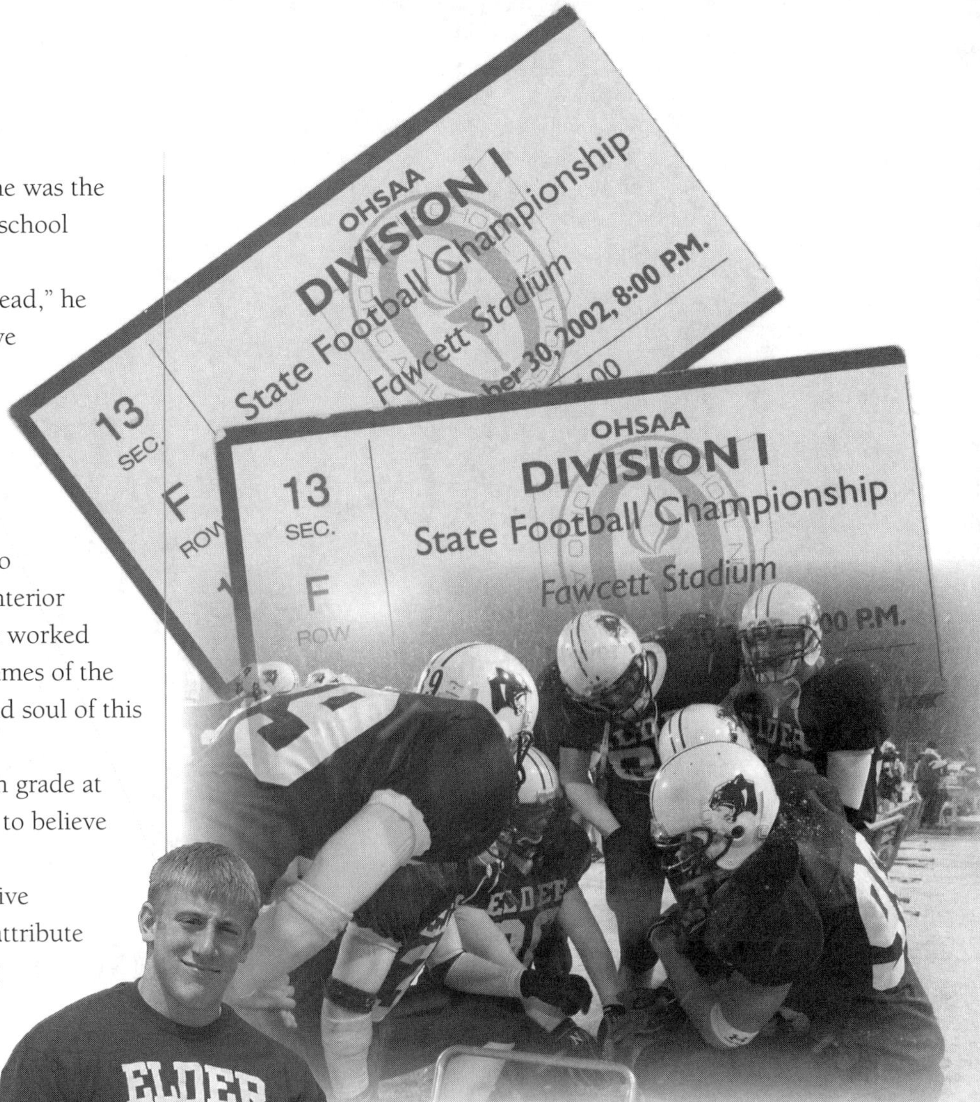

Tony Carvitti, left, superimposed over his guys as they celebrate first state title in 2002. For Carvitti, superimposition was the correct verb for his style.

37

Receiver Bill Poland was an offensive mainstay, and defenses around the state became too familiar with his bread-and-butter play—diagrammed above by his coach, Doug Ramsey.

Tim Koegel and his parents, Mr. and Mrs. Paul Koegel, at the time of Tim's signing with Notre Dame. At far right: a Koegel handoff at Moeller.

THE WEEPING IRISH

The same year **Harry Oliver**, the little kicker, moved on from Moeller to Notre Dame, so did Bob Crable, the big linebacker. **Tim Koegel**, the golden quarterback, had already been wearing the Irish colors for a year. Of Oliver's signing, needless to say, not much was made.

And yet, three years later, on a Sunday in September, 1980, Dan Devine, the Notre Dame coach, was calling Gerry Faust, the Moeller coach, and thanking him for sending Oliver to South Bend.

The day before, time had been running out at Notre Dame Stadium with the home team trailing Michigan 27-26. The Irish were at their own 39-yard line, from which

Tim Koegel

Moeller | quarterback | class of 1977

77

THESE DAYS, TIM KOEGEL IS KNOWN NATIONALLY AS THE EXCEPTIONAL PRESENTER, WHICH WAS THE NAME OF THE BOOK HE WROTE THAT DEBUTED at Number 4 on *The New York Times* bestseller list for advice and how-to guides. It's about communication, about crafting one's message in the most effective manner. Among other clients, Koegel works with Congress and the White House on such stuff, and now and then appears on television critiquing Presidential debates and the like, pointing up such fatal gaffes as Al Gore rolling his eyes or George (no W) Bush glancing at his watch.

But back in the day—back when Moeller High was crafting its message as the best football school in the country—Koegel was known as The Exceptional Passer, without the capitals, perhaps. He was known as the quarterback who carried the Crusaders to their first national championship, and their first two state titles.

Surely, there was help in greater supply than what was available to any other local quarterback, maybe ever. The great Bob Crable dominated the defense. The offensive line was held down by Jim Brown, a 270-pound *Parade* All-American. But ask another Brown—Mike, the president of the Bengals, and a Moeller fan going way back—who was the best Crusader ever, and he'll say Koegel without skipping a beat.

Officially, Koegel was an All-American, the school record-setter in passing yards (3,737) and touchdowns (46, still the standard), and the best player in Ohio in 1976, when Moeller nosed out Gahanna Lincoln in the state championship game, 43-5. Those 43 points

Blair Kiel, a freshman quarterback, found tight end Tony Hunter—who had kept the Moeller pipeline pumping the year after Oliver and Crable had followed Koegel and receiver Dave Condeni to the great Catholic school—on the sideline, at the Michigan 34. Four seconds remained. Koegel entered the game and knelt down at the 41. Oliver—a cross country runner persuaded by his high school friends to come out for football because he had a strong left leg—lined up behind him. The wind was howling. Oliver had already missed an extra point. "Harry," said Koegel, his words buffeted by the gusting crosscurrents, "I have a better chance of running this in from 51 yards than you do of kicking it."

Notre Dame lore has it that the 15-mile-an-hour gale stopped dead the moment Oliver strode toward the ball in Koegel's grasp. The kick soared against the breathless Irish backdrop and slipped between the uprights as time disappeared from the clock. Notre Dame had won. Harry Oliver had become a legend.

"It's probably what's going to be on my tombstone instead of when I was born or when I died," Oliver told *The New York Times*. "This is by far the greatest moment of my life. Getting a scholarship to Notre Dame is a close second."

Twenty-seven years later, Oliver passed on quietly in Cincinnati. Irish eyes wept.

exceeded the total that the Crusaders gave up all year.

Koegel, whose older brother Vic had been a star defensive end at Moeller and Ohio State, actually lost a game his sophomore year at Moeller. It would be the last until he got to Notre Dame. Dan Devine recruited him and Gerry Faust, his high school coach, inherited him. Faust's first year was Koegel's last, and Fuzzy couldn't figure out whether to start his fifth-year senior or sophomore Blair Kiel. All season long, he fudged. It worked out for none of the above.

When he graduated from Notre Dame, Koegel's professional prospects abounded; but not in football. His study of personal communications was so thorough and successful that he ultimately started his own consulting company in the Washington, D.C., area.

It's called the Koegel Group, which could also be used to describe Moeller High School, circa 1976.

Leon Murray

North College Hill quarterback class of 1974

74

Bruce Baarendse, the North College Hill football coach, was also a North College Hill football player, back in the late 1970s, and one good enough to be considered by Ohio State.

He made a recruiting trip to Columbus to see a game, and the Buckeyes lost, which meant that Woody Hayes was not in the most accommodating of moods afterwards. He did, however, assemble the prospects and ask each of them to state his name and high school. When it was Baarendse's turn, and he reported "North College Hill," the great coach interrupted and said, "Stop right there. You're from the school that that Murray kid came from, aren't you? And we didn't get him."

That would have been Leon Murray, the greatest athlete that NCH has ever produced. Say what you will about O.J. Mayo, the itinerant basketball icon who spent three seasons at the Hill; or about Dwayne Crutchfield, who was Murray's bigger, meaner, younger cousin, and led the Big Eight in rushing before plowing ahead to the NFL. Mayo and Crutchfield acquired more national renown than Murray. Their talents converted more directly into dollars.

But if you're talking athlete, you're talking Murray, especially if you're talking to anyone around North College Hill in, say, 1973 or 1974, when Murray was leading the city's basketball players in scoring at 33 points a game (one game against Taylor: 49 points,

Leon Murray: the legend said he was NCH's greatest athlete.

Old Times with Mark and Tom

Tom Waddle hoped it would be like old times. He and **Mark Kamphaus** had grown up on the same street in Cincinnati, wouldn't play in pickup games unless they were on the same team, became high school teammates at Moeller, and again at Boston College. (They completed their high schools days with gaudy statistics: Kamphaus passed for a school record 1,947 yards and 40 touchdowns; Waddle caught 50 passes for 14 TDs and 724 yards.)

And now, early in September of 1988, they were playing the University of Cincinnati in Boston. In BC's opener the previous week against Southern California, Waddle scored

15 steals, 13 rebounds, 7 assists) and scoring 39 touchdowns of every conceivable stripe as an All-State running back, which is what they called him even though he was actually a quarterback.

"Leon Murray is still my favorite athlete of all time," said Mike Ball, an *Enquirer* sports department operative known to his friends and colleagues as Flea. Ball was a Trojan manager back in Murray's day. "He's the guy who named me Flea. One day he said, 'Hey, come over here and tape my ankle, you little flea.'" And even with that, Flea still loves the guy.

So does Joe Nickel, the longtime NCH athletic director. Nickel started assistant coaching in football when Murray was a 5-10, 170-pound junior with moves that couldn't be taught. "He could do whatever he wanted," Nickel recalled. "He was phenomenal.

"We used him as a quarterback, running back, whatever. He did most of his damage running the ball, but some of it came off flea-flickers, where he'd pass to the wideout and the receiver would pitch it back to him. Or we'd just give him the ball and let him go. He didn't run people over, and he wasn't the type to just run up the middle, but he was so quick, and the way he moved sideways and changed speeds, they just couldn't get him. He was devastating as a punt returner. He actually even punted for us, and sometimes you didn't know what to expect then, either. All the sudden he'd be running up the sideline for a touchdown."

That's why Woody wanted him. So did Michigan. So did Kansas, for basketball. Fran Curci got him, for Kentucky. Murray's brother, Robert, one year older, had gone to Kentucky as a defensive end.

on a 60-yard pass from his old neighborhood quarterback, and said, "I think the last time we got together for a touchdown was in the last regular-season game of our senior year in high school. I had three TDs from Mark in that game. So I guess the last time we did it, I had three and we just took three years to get one touchdown. I hope the next one doesn't take that long."

The week before the Cincinnati game, the Boston papers pointed out that it would be a long haul for the Bearcats to go halfway across the country just to get beaten by a couple of hometown boys.

Long haul it was, too. The boys from Moeller collaborated for two TD passes—the next one *didn't* take long—and BC beat Cincinnati 41-7. Waddle wanted it to be like old times, and, shades of Moeller, so it was.

When Waddle went to Da Bears, they called him "the Ultimate Grabowski," and said he was a working class hero.

Curci harbored big plans for Leon, but as a freshman in 1974 the younger Murray injured his knee and was reduced to holding for placekicks. The next season, he was expected to challenge Derrick Ramsey for the starting quarterback job. Ramsey became an All-American and played nine years in the NFL. Murray became a minor-league baseball player.

Before he had tossed a pass or pitched to a trailing halfback, he signed with the Baltimore Orioles, which ticked off Curci and surprised the folks back home, seeing as how Mr. Everything had played only one year of baseball for the Trojans. On the other hand, whatever Leon wanted to do . . .

As it happened, between the bad knee and whatever else, Murray never made the big leagues, and his name ceased to echo much beyond Hamilton Avenue. The Leon Murray who occasionally pops up now and then is his son, who grew up in Louisiana and starred as a quarterback at Tennessee State and had some good years in the Arena League and World League but not with the Washington Redskins or New York Giants, with whom he had a sip of espresso.

For a spell, Leon Sr. moved back to North College Hill, where another son, Justin, played basketball with Mayo and Bill Walker and helped win a state championship even after they were gone.

While he was back, Leon spoke at the school a time or two as a lay minister, and as a legend. Then he returned quietly to the South, where nobody could have possibly known that he was the greatest athlete who ever played at O.J Mayo's high school.

Freddie Ratterman

Withrow quarterback class of 1930

30

AT WITHROW HIGH, TOWARD THE END OF THE 1920S, THERE WAS A HEARTENING TRANSFER WHO WOULD BRIGHTEN EVEN THE LOOMING DEPRESSION. LAWRENCE Fred Ratterman arrived just ahead of his celebrated reputation at St. Mary's. Reputations in grade school are one thing; maintaining one is the proof.

There was something about him, though, a handsome, dark-haired kid gazing a bit sullenly at the camera in his class picture, as if he had better things to do. He might have been an athlete, or he may have been a cornet player. But before he left Withrow, his music was all on the field.

Brad Maurer's Double Life

Before his junior year at Kings High School, **Brad Maurer**, the Knights' intellectually curious quarterback, did a little summer reading. He chose the book about wide-open offense by former Middletown coach Tiger Ellison. By the fall, Kings was running it and Maurer was showing up in headlines. The biggest of those, unfortunately, came when he broke his leg halfway through the season. That gave him plenty of time for reading, at least, and it happened that, the next year, which was 2002, when Maurer was passing for 2,620 yards and 29 touchdowns and being named the state's co-Player of the Year in Division II, he was also becoming valedictorian and a National Merit scholar finalist and Ohio's top football scholar-athlete. All of that took him to Lafayette, where he set school records for completion percentage, carried his team to the I-AA playoffs and was the Patriot League's Scholar-Athlete of the Year, all the while majoring in neuroscience. "I lead a bit of a double life," he said. When he was named a Lafayette Marquis Scholar "for academic excellence and intellectual curiosity" —the college's highest scholarship—some of his teachers were unaware that he was a football player. But then, learned as they were, they hadn't read Ellison.

The background illustration is from Tiger Ellison's book, Run and Shoot Football*—a formation he called "the Live Polecat."*

The entire Public League danced to his tune, and he made headlines even in Hamilton where he was positively atonal to Dana King, the Big Blue coach.

King was a legend in his own right. He had an unparalleled tenure at Hamilton and before he hung up his resumé he had coached the University of Cincinnati and the old Cincinnati Bengals—they played a pickup schedule at Xavier University's field in 1938, upset the Bears 17-14, knocked off Pittsburgh 27-0, and finished 7-2-2. So he knew a player when he saw one, and he was sorry he'd ever seen Ratterman.

Lawrence of Withrow . . .

Meeting Hamilton, Freddie Ratterman proved to be a team of one, reeling off elegant runs of 60 and 70 yards, and when King went to the chalkboard to diagram how to beat Withrow, he wrote Ratterman's name in capital letters.

When the latter part of 1929 rolled around and Wall Street's Black Thursday devastated the country's economy, Ratterman and his Withrow teammates countered with Black Fridays of their own, making Public League coaches want to leap out of windows.

Odd that it was Withrow's most eventful football season to date. The coach began practice that autumn with only six returning lettermen and, as he put it, "a thorough search for promising new material."

But he had Ratterman, and he moved his veteran All-City guard, Ed Moeller, into the backfield. It was all Withrow needed.

The Tigers beat Hillsboro 64-0, rolled over Columbus' East High, Dayton's Oakwood (31-6, pronounced "uninteresting except for the wonderful running of Ratterman"), topped Woodward 31-19, Walnut Hills 66-0, and clinched the city title with four second-half scores against Hughes. They ended an extraordinary year with a 50-0 recreational outing against Western Hills. The only blemish on the season was a scoreless tie with Xenia.

Ratterman and Moeller had become part of the most productive backfield the school had ever assembled. Withrow had scored 325 points against 51 and it came about, wholly unpredictably, on the footwork of a converted guard and a kid from grade school.

By the time Ratterman graduated and headed off to Michigan, he was being heralded as the greatest Cincinnati football player of the past twenty years. And, before that, well, who knows? It was exalted company Ratterman was keeping with himself.

But on his first day with the Michigan varsity in 1931, he sustained a knee injury that put him in the hospital. Complications set in, followed by rumors that he'd never walk again. He was back in uniform in the autumn of 1932, reinjured the knee, and underwent more surgery. The former Michigan All-American, Benny Oosterbaan, who worked with a trainer trying to rehab Ratterman, called Freddie "the gamest football player at the University of Michigan."

He never saw the field again, his promise only a sepia moment in time. He was one of Cincinnati's legends, though, both for his early brilliance, as well as for his poignant departure from the game, leaving us with one of local sporting history's more intriguing "What if?" moments.

George Ratterman

St. Xavier quarterback class of 19**44**

44

GEORGE RATTERMAN WAS ONE OF THE MOST UNUSUAL ATHLETES THE CITY HAD EVER SEEN—OR HEARD. IN HIGH SCHOOL, HE WAS EQUALLY GOOD in four different sports, repeated himself at Notre Dame, and by the time he launched a ten-year career in professional football, he'd added a fifth sport—the perfectly spiraled retort.

His sporting fortunes seemed destiny: he was born early on the morning of the traditional Ohio State-Michigan game, which allowed his father to stop by the hospital for a moment before venturing on to Columbus and the big game, his view being, George would later point out, "that even childbirth was incidental to football."

By the age of 5, young George was being tutored by the old man, who announced to one of George's playmates, "George is going to be a quarterback."

"No, he isn't," said the unconvinced playmate. "George is going to be a bum."

Recalling the moment much later, George allowed as how they were *both* right. "By the time less partisan authorities could see for themselves," he said, "I was a bum quarterback . . . ."

The truth is, he was a very good quarterback, although one with a timing problem. The timing had nothing to do with his mechanics; it was that throughout his career, he always found himself standing beside—or behind—a *great* quarterback.

So at St. Xavier, he quarterbacked the football team to a GCL title (1943), captained the basketball team, made All-State in both sports, played baseball, and was the Junior Amateur Tennis Champion of Southwestern Ohio. He kept St. X in one game by throwing an unheard of 62 passes, thus the school's nickname was changed from the Conquerors to the Bombers. The opposition, in virtually everything, was glad to see him head off to Notre Dame where he found himself standing beside Johnny Lujack.

"SUCCEEDING IN FOOTBALL WITHOUT PLAYING IS AN ART FORM," GEORGE SAID, "LIKE CARVING PEACH PITS INTO WATCH FOBS."

Lujack had just returned from the war and was about to become one of Notre Dame's all-time legendary quarterbacks— Heisman winner and twice All-American. In 1946, when the Irish won the national championship, Lujack usually played the first and third quarters and Ratterman occupied the second and fourth. Still and all, in the spring of 1947, the world lay beneath Ratterman's cleated feet. He was heading into his senior year with a national championship, and he, too, knew how to play quarterback (the Irish players called him "Snake," because of his nifty ball-handling).

The family convened in Chicago that spring, and there was a photograph of the Rattermans posing in front of Chicago's famous Palmer House—George, an older brother who was a priest, and their parents. Years afterward, George's own son would explain the picture and its significance. "If you were a Catholic parent in 1947 and you have one son who is a priest and the other one is a quarterback at Notre Dame," Tim Ratterman said, "that's better than sitting next to the Pope."

There are two stories as to why George ended up forfeiting his senior year at Notre Dame. The columnists said that George asked Frank Leahy, the Irish football dean, to shift Lujack to running back so that *both* of them could do what they did best. George not being a shy lad, the writers could picture this conversation. George himself said he had been banished over a bottle of sarsaparilla. Or rather the drinking of it after hours, when undergraduates were supposed to be safely ensconced in their dorms.

Whatever George had done, he was about to convert tragedy into triumph. It might have been his finest gridiron moment, and it, too, had something of the legendary about it. In late August, Ratterman, for once, was not the understudy; he led the College All-Stars to a thumping of the mighty Chicago Bears, 16-0, and the NFL champs never got beyond the All-Star 30-yard line. Buddy Young, the flashy Illinois halfback, shared the spotlight with George, but it was George's show.

He had outplayed the great Sid Luckman, pro football's top quarterback, and his ball-handling was spectacular. Young was named MVP—by four ballots—but the experienced writers gave it to the baby-faced Cincinnatian. The players said George had diagrammed impromptu plays in the turf. Red Grange called Ratterman the greatest T-formation passer of the last thirty years. The final word was by a sportswriter for the *Davenport Democrat*. "The fact is," he wrote, "the kid good enough only to be a sub in his college days stood the football world on its ear Friday night, and the way he doublecrossed them Bears up was awful."

When George reported to the Buffalo Bills of the All-America Conference, he showed up in sneakers and flannel pants. The publicity man asked, "What's a skinny fellow like you doing out here with all these big brutes?"

"Isn't this where the tennis team works out?" George asked, for at a robust 175 pounds, he barely outweighed the practice dummy. (When he appeared at Notre Dame weighing 149 pounds, the dismayed team trainer said he had to wear a single-digit number. “You aren’t wide enough to carry two digits on your back,” he said.”)

One of his Bills’ teammates was the infamous Chubby Grigg, who was exactly twice George’s size. He was so big that the coach liked to say at the conclusion of practice, “Run that last play again, boys, then everybody take two laps around Chubby.”

In the opening game, George and his virtual unknowns upset the fabled New York Yankees 28-24. One of the sportswriters, noting George’s background, wrote, “You get a pretty fair idea of how good the Notre Dame *first* stringers are.” George led the league with 22 TD passes, put Buffalo in the AAFC title game with the Browns, and when the old league folded in 1949, he, too, became a Yankee. Then when his interceptions rose, he played with Montreal for a year (“the only city where I’ve ever been booed in two languages”), and in 1952 ended up in Cleveland, once again the understudy for yet another great quarterback.

“My itinerant nature did not go unnoticed by teammates, who often stuffed bus schedules and travel folders in my locker,” he said.

“It was Ratterman who

. . . and George of St. X

brought the forwarding address to pro football," said Ed Modzelewski.

It was in Cleveland that George grew finally inured to his role as America's most famous substitute. Here, he fully developed what proved to be an abiding talent for recognizing the foibles of life as lived through football. "During my rococo career," he said, "I took the view that while quarterbacks might not be able to solve Blaberski's Equation or assemble a nuclear weapon, they, or more accurately we, happened to be inordinately bright and gifted and our value to the team was beyond any calculation. Nobody disputed this except centers, guards, tackles, ends, and fullbacks."

Paul Brown, the emperor of Cleveland, took the general position that almost *everyone* was over-valued. His man, Otto Graham, however, was not only a great QB, he was a great competitor. And he rarely needed relief. But in 1953, near the end of the first half against the 49ers, Graham was knocked cold, and George found himself the relief.

"Do you want me to go in or should we forfeit?" George said to Brown.

George played out the remaining minute or two, Graham got ten or fifteen stitches in his mouth, and played the entire second half.

On one uncharacteristic afternoon with Graham struggling, the fans began to yell for Ratterman. Finally, Brown beckoned. George grabbed his helmet, thinking, *Any moment I'll be in the midst of the bloodletting*.

"George, your friends are calling for you," Brown said. "Maybe you'd better go up there in the stands and sit with them awhile."

In 1956, George participated in the ill-fated experiment in league electronics; he wore football's first radio helmet. The experiment concluded when George discovered the local police department was using the same frequency.

Said Brown: "Didn't I tell you to throw a pass on that last play?"

Replied George: "I don't know, coach, but some guy just got stabbed over on Fifth Avenue."

In 1956, with Graham's retirement, George appeared on the cover of *Sports Illustrated*, then—classic cover jinx—he blew out a knee. This time, he'd had four games as Number 1.

There would be one more turn in the limelight:

An Ear for the game

George Ratterman liked the story told by Jimmy Phelan, his coach when he played for the New York Yanks.

A roughed up old pro showed up one day, wanting an audition, and Phelan asked him what he played.

"The line," the player said.

"What position?" asked Phelan.

"Oh, sort of bent over like this," the oldtimer answered, showing Phelan his stance.

Ratterman was persuaded to run for sheriff of Newport on a reform ticket. The campaign, with threats of violence, reminded the ex-quarterback of the league's old "educational plays," such as "the 48-Undertaker," or the "Say Good-bye to the Wife and Kids" play. He'd already been threatened by some of the best.

There was one more famous Ratterman moment. It featured a photograph of George in bed with a stripper named April Flowers. The compromising photograph seemed to have come via a mickey with enough chloral hydrate in it "to kill a normal person." As usual, George proved to be other than normal. National headlines brought a grand jury investigation into what was regarded as a frame-up, George was elected sheriff by a landslide, and U.S. Attorney General Robert Kennedy dispatched the FBI to Kentucky. George was credited with breaking up organized crime in Newport (which implied it would then be returned to the unorganized where it more properly belonged).

The old quarterback had come off the bench a final time, proving, really, that he was nobody's understudy. He'd never started a game at Notre Dame, but he'd still become legendary, and he'd done it the hard way. He had been football's first standup quarterback, working the small houses of his teammates who appreciated him even when management didn't. He played his entire career hearing footsteps, but when you took a close look, you saw how good he'd always been, at every level.

He'd known, though. And nobody ever beat him one-on-one at repartee. There, he had *really* dazzled 'em.

Phil Redrow

Williamsburg quarterback class of 19**68**

68

He's on the west coast now, but they still speak of him reverently (and otherwise) in and around Williamsburg, remembering those Ken Osborne teams when it seemed that any play might put a spiraling football forty or fifty yards downfield. The ground game still ruled high school football in the 1960s, although a few cocky guys with high-caliber arms were popping up here and there, testing the thinner upper atmosphere of local stadiums.

Redrow was one of them, although Osborne, his coach, should get equal billing, for coaches were a conservative lot in the 1960s, believing largely in the holy high school trinity: a good little guard, a hardnosed halfback, and a bulldozing fullback. The other coaches found Osborne a little odd; he'd forego the system (*gracious!*) and build his team around a player. Redrow may have been the first one he built a team around, but he wouldn't be the last (flash-forward to the year 2000 and a kid named Jason Bainum).

> *"Sometimes I see myself as* **Robin Hood** *out there. And these are my merry men." —Phil Redrow, Quarterback*

Redrow would much later recall how his sophomore year began, pressed into duty after the veteran QB went down: "Ozzie told me to relax and go out there and throw the ball to the guys with the same colors as I had on. I raised my hand to throw the ball and the ref tossed a flag and asked who the hell I thought I was. I explained that I'd heard of schools where, contrary to the Woody Hayes doctrine on the ground game, balls spiraled in the cool autumn nights and crowds cheered. 'Oh yeah,' he said, 'but if you don't watch it you'll end up a Democrat or a....*homosexual*."

Understand that Redrow had by this time become a songwriter with a renowned sense of hyperbole, but the underlying truth of it was accurate. And so Redrow—and lest we forget, Ozzie—lit up Clermont County. That was the year Redrow threw for six TDs against Felicity, an area mark that stood for nearly thirty years (until another Osborne protégé, Bill Brewer, tossed seven against Hillcrest in 1994). Even today, only a dozen or so guys have thrown more.

"It's this simple: we threw when most of the rest of Ohio was running. I had quite a few 300-plus yard games but I didn't think I was anything special, just *different*. My answer to every situation was roll-out pass. It floods an area and allows cowards to run like a bitch. Once, in a critical situation, Lenny Toft, who was known for understatement, ran in the play. He got to the huddle and was annoyingly silent. I said, 'What the hell's the play, Lenny?' And he said, 'Red, I can't really say but is there a play like green two hundred something?'

"I called a roll-out pass right. What's a guy to do?"

For a time, Redrow and Osborne were Butch and Sundance. The Redrow household was missing a father, and Osborne became Redrow's father-figure. Redrow lived behind the school, and when he'd skip school, Osborne would come over and yell at him through his bedroom window. "Ozzie invented the word 'chickenshit,'" Redrow said. "I know he did...."

Here's Redrow's description of Osborne arriving in Williamsburg: "He blew into town from somewhere in Kentucky, a Johnny Unitas-loving, flattop-wearing country boy, equal parts Charlemagne, Swamp Fox, and drill sergeant. By the time I graduated, I wanted to *be* him. He spoke concisely and properly, but it was rounded off by that unmistakable Kentucky drawl. You were a *frashman* and you *wrastled*. He was hard core strict and unreadable, but his gift was adaptability, and no one ever informed him he was in Woody Hayes country.

"After a good crop of seniors in '64 and a co-championship, the autumns of '65 and '66 were like the plague years. Only historians will be able to extricate what happened to the children born in 1948 and 1949 in the small town of 1,500 people, and it gives further credibility to the phrase that God works in mysterious ways. God, however, loves irony. Why else would my gardener be named Jesus? So Osborne decided there was

Waiting for the Big Time

The Browns spotted me warming up one of their receivers in summer camp. Odd that I was even on the field because while they practiced at Wilmington College, I didn't hang out much when they were around. I didn't like seeing guys getting paid to sweat. I always had to sweat for nothing.

They were breaking camp, so Mike Brown told me to come down to Spinney. It was a gloomy day as I pulled into Spinney Field in my old Falcon. There were nicer cars in the lot for sure, but you couldn't downshift them into first gear from the column.

There wasn't a lot going on that morning, and minutes later I was on the field, alone with Bill Walsh, Paul Brown, and his sons. My first throw to Walsh was about 15 yards away and it hit him in the hands about throat high and exploded out of them like so many had done with my college receivers. (If you're reading this, Kenny Minor, I don't mean you. But you were a tight end. I never thought of you as a receiver. You were my contract man for every defensive end in the league.)

I apologized and sent another missile at him, with the same results. He could coach but he couldn't catch.

'Back up about ten yards,' he said.

This kept up until I was 45 yards away, although I do believe he snagged a few in the interim.

They huddled for a moment then asked if I wanted to come to the weekend rookie camp. I told them with the rain and all, I might have to get a ride down with someone.

They asked if my car was having problems, and I told them that my windshield wipers were shot. Pete Brown pulled out a fifty-dollar bill and said, "That ought to get you some wipers."

So this is that big bonus money I've heard about, I thought to myself. I had arrived.

Now you have to remember that times were hard and my monthly rent at Mary Farquar's house across from the college was five dollars, and I was delinquent. I'm not ashamed to say that I paid two or three bucks for the wipers and told my girlfriend that we were going to Kings Island with the rest of it.

So off we went on the Bengals' dime. The reason I bring this up is that in the world of magnificent coincidence, which would dazzle me my entire lifetime, this was a classic: At Kings Island, I was goaded into throwing a football through a tire. I refused the wager at first because I had suffered mightily and forever the disappointment of throwing to things with no hands.

I unloaded the first two balls effortlessly. They went through the hoop without touching rubber but nearly took out the back of the tent. The third one caught rubber and spun around the tire and fell to the ground.

Then just as I turned I ran—face to face—into my new coach. Paul Brown didn't grin or fumble for a nicety as he and his wife walked past me. He Clint Eastwooded me.

So here I was at Spinney, literally his turf, no glimmer of recognition. I did my Wilmington drop back (part All-Conference, part post-hippie) when I set up to throw to Isaac Curtis, an All-American sprinter.

I threw the ball so hard that it hurt my fillings. It hit the Number 1 draft pick on his fingertips 60 yards downfield. Walsh ordered more posts and flag patterns from other receivers. The same results occurred. It was joy in Mudville, for

Redrow on Walsh: 'He could coach but he couldn't catch...' (In background is Redrow at the WC Steinway.)

after that weekend, I was an official Bengal rookie. Paul Brown only said two things to me in camp and years later I was golfing with the legendary Jim Brown. He asked me how I found Paul to be.

I said, 'Heck, Jim, I'm just Phil Redrow. You're Jim Brown. He only said a couple of things to me.'

'He never said much more to *me*,' Jim said.

Me and Jim Brown, peas in a pod.

Summer camp came. One morning we ran sprints and I was having bad dizziness. I suffered from this affliction my entire career. I had been in a bad car accident and my head had been turned into a Denny's omelette. One game in college I went to the wrong huddle and was baffled by our new uniforms. I spent the evening in the hospital being observed.

I tried to fake it. I was hurt and I knew it, but in those days you just lowered your head and went again.

Funny thing, when you have pro football camp at your own school, they have access to your medical records and mine revealed the truth.

I was called over to the table at lunch where Bill Walsh and Paul Brown informed me that it would be a big mistake for me to continue the game that had given me an identity in high school, as well as a college diploma.

Later, recruited by the WFL, I was told again the danger of playing that stupid game. 'There's not enough money to risk your head for,' Pete Brown said.

It took me awhile to get over not playing. Throwing a football was the one thing that was perfect to me, the one thing that never deserted me. I didn't shine like a light but deep inside I will always remember when Bill Walsh told me: *You have one of the best arms I've ever seen.*

It's a shame it didn't come with a head.

—Phil Redrow

"THE GOOD THING ABOUT ALZHEIMER'S IS, EVERY DOWN IS FIRST DOWN."

—KEN OSBORNE, PONDERING RETIREMENT.

no way in hell that his sophomores and juniors were gonna run the ball because that required beef and we had spaghetti. So he came up with the idea of throwing the ball—a whole lot. We had no blockers, no real runners, one receiver, no beef, but plenty of sauce. I was the sauce, prepared cold to rushers polite enough to give me about 1.9 seconds to throw the ball. We won three games one year and two and a tie the other. We still threw for over 2,000 yards those years.

"So while Ozzie had two daughters, he would father legions of boys for years to come, a sign of true greatness. And now his first boys had grown up and wanted to be Vikings, pillaging those who had been taking from them. And there were now two boys on his team who wore extra large and he positioned them so that they anchored an offensive line that flip-flopped their strength from left to right. Earl Toft and Tiny Jim Vickers—all 280 pounds of him. So it was Tiny left, and Tiny right . . . ."

By the time Redrow was a senior, Williamsburg had its best team ever. It was a school of fewer than 300 students playing schools with student bodies of 2,000. The only blemish on the year was a tie with powerful Covington Catholic. Tiny Jim went off to UC and as a sophomore letterman, blew out his knee. Redrow went to Morehead, ran afoul of a coaching change, and ended up at Wilmington College where he was three times All-League.

His career as songwriter began at Wilmington after he discovered an old Steinway in the arts building. He could be found there after football practice, startling frail and reedy musicians walking in on the 6-2, 200-pound quarterback working on his songs. He shrugged at the disparity. "They let me use their piano," he said. "I let them use my goalpost . . . ."

He went into the Cincinnati Bengals' camp as a free agent, looked promising in early workouts, then flunked his physical, the result of an old head injury. Seeing as how it was Redrow, there was a story in that, too. Maybe he'll tell you about it . . . .

Dick Selcer

Elder | quarterback | class of 1955

FIFTY YEARS AFTER THE FACT OF HIS OWN YOUTH, JIM GLATTHAAR WOULD WATCH HIS GRANDSON, BRADLEY, WIN A STATE FOOTBALL CHAMPIONSHIP at Elder. The kid, one of the best backs Cincinnati had ever seen, ran for 252 yards in the title game alone and came away from his career with so many trophies the family considered adding a room onto the house. But the old man was still one up. He'd played on the 1954 Elder team that was unbeaten and untied—the only such team in all of Elder's fabled history.*

Ironically, the team leader was a bantam quarterback, Dick Selcer, and he was much like the Florian kid (Rob) who would help Glatthaar win that future title for Elder. Selcer could run as well as throw but what he did best was *think*. Virgil Scardina, in only his second year as head coach, had counseled with that UC offensive mastermind, Sid Gillman, and Gillman enticed Scardina with Oklahoma's split-T, a run-oriented option offense.

Scardina bought a book on it, studied it, then handed the system to Selcer. "We gave Dick a free hand in calling plays," Scardina said. "Every once in a while, I'd call a player off the bench and start telling him about a play I wanted called. By the time he was ready to go in, I'd look up and Dick would be calling the same play."

Elder held Chillicothe to four first downs, blanked Hamilton, Portsmouth, and Dayton Chaminade (intercepting Chaminade *seven* times), and handed city power Purcell its first GCL loss in four years. Say what you will, the boys of '54 have remained inviolable to comparisions over time. They *still* hold a handful of school records, including most rushing TDs in a season—39 (they scored nine in one game). They scored 319 points to the opposition's 65, put three guys on the All-State team, and sent at least four guys on to major colleges.

Selcer was UPI first team All-State, along with center Dan James, and when the Ohio sportswriters chose their team, Selcer made that one, too (James was second team). Dick Royer was first-team defensive end. Selcer and Royer went off to Notre Dame; James starred at OSU, was captain of the College All-Star team, then played for Pittsburgh and Chicago in the NFL. Joe Schaffer was a three-year starter and team captain at Tennessee, then played for Buffalo.

Selcer and Royer were teammates when Notre Dame pulled off one of college football's biggest upsets, beating Oklahoma to stop a 47-game winning streak (a small and unnoted example of ingratitude, as this was the vaunted split-T offense Selcer and Royer used so efficaciously back at Elder).

Not unnaturally, Selcer went on to a long career in coaching, both collegiately and in the pros. He coached Xavier in the game made famous by the movie, *We are Marshall*, the school's second game in 1971 after the devastating 1970 plane crash that killed most of the Marshall team. (XU lost in the last minute, prompting XU fans to nickname their coach "Alka" Selcer.) He was linebackers coach with the Bengals when they went to the Super Bowl in 1989, and he also coached defensive backs for Detroit.

On the West Side of the Cincinnati, though, he's still the baby-faced quarterback who took Elder to its only unbeaten, untied season.

**Elder's 1989 and 1991 teams went undefeated during the regular season before playoff losses, and even the state title teams of 2002 and 2003 were once-beaten. The boys of 1954, unburdened by a postseason, stayed wholly and singularly undefeated.*

To Air Is Human: A Fable

When **Rob Schoenhoft** graduated from St. Xavier in 2005, he was one of the biggest, most ballyhooed quarterbacks ever to come out of the Queen City. He was one of the top pro-style quarterback prospects in America and at 6-6, 240, built like a tight end with a commercial wingspan.

He'd had an arm, even in grade school. Playing baseball as an elementary school kid, he'd thrown a fly ball from the fence to home plate. There was a joke in the St. X locker room about how many fingers he had broken with his passes. For a time, they were thinking of adding broken fingers as a statistical category in the school records. Schoenhoft thought his personal best was 22.

In the prestigious Elite 11 quarterback camp in California in 2004, Schoenhoft was voted most likely to win a national college title, which seemed an omen for title-hungry Ohio State, which wanted him badly. First, though, he led St. X to a 10-0 regular season in 2004 and into the second round of state playoffs. He was Ohio's MVP in the Big 33 Classic between Ohio and Pennsylvania after he broke the game's record for passing yardage (267 yards along with two TDs, one of them a 74-yarder).

In the spring of his sophomore year at Ohio State, he was the Number 2 QB. He played sparingly, though, and before long he transferred to Delaware. Now here's where the story takes a fabled turn. His former St. X teammate, a kid named **Dominic Randolph**, was just coming into his own at another eastern school, Holy Cross. Randolph had been Schoenhoft's St. X backup, playing receiver just to get on the field. As someone said, he found Holy Cross as much as the school found him.

His dad wrote HC a letter and the school said bring a medical waiver and a helmet. Right away, HC saw fate had dealt it a good hand—with a passing arm attached.

"This is one of the great stories in college football at any level," his coach, Tom Gilmore, would say.

The spring before Randolph was a soph, Gilmore put in a spread offense—the same system St. X used. In 2007, tri-captain Randolph was the Pioneer League's Player of the Year, throwing for 30 TDs. At Fitton Field with 19 seconds on the clock, he threw a 40-yard TD to beat Harvard, wowing the homecoming crowd, in addition to those already wowed.

In early November of 2008, as a senior, he was a top candidate for the Walter Payton Award (I-AA's MVP award) and led the country in total offense. He finished ninth in the Payton Award voting, but he was league MVP again. He'd thrown 83 TDs in his Holy Cross career, he was just shy of 10,000 passing yards, and he was in the school record book so many times it looked as if his relatives had written it.

Schoenhoft had a remarkable prep career, and at OSU—before moving on—he played on two national title teams, even though neither had been his to win. If his old St. X understudy seemed to have one-upped him, look at it this way: when had a Cincinnati high school—a high school *anywhere*—had two such guys wearing the same uniform?

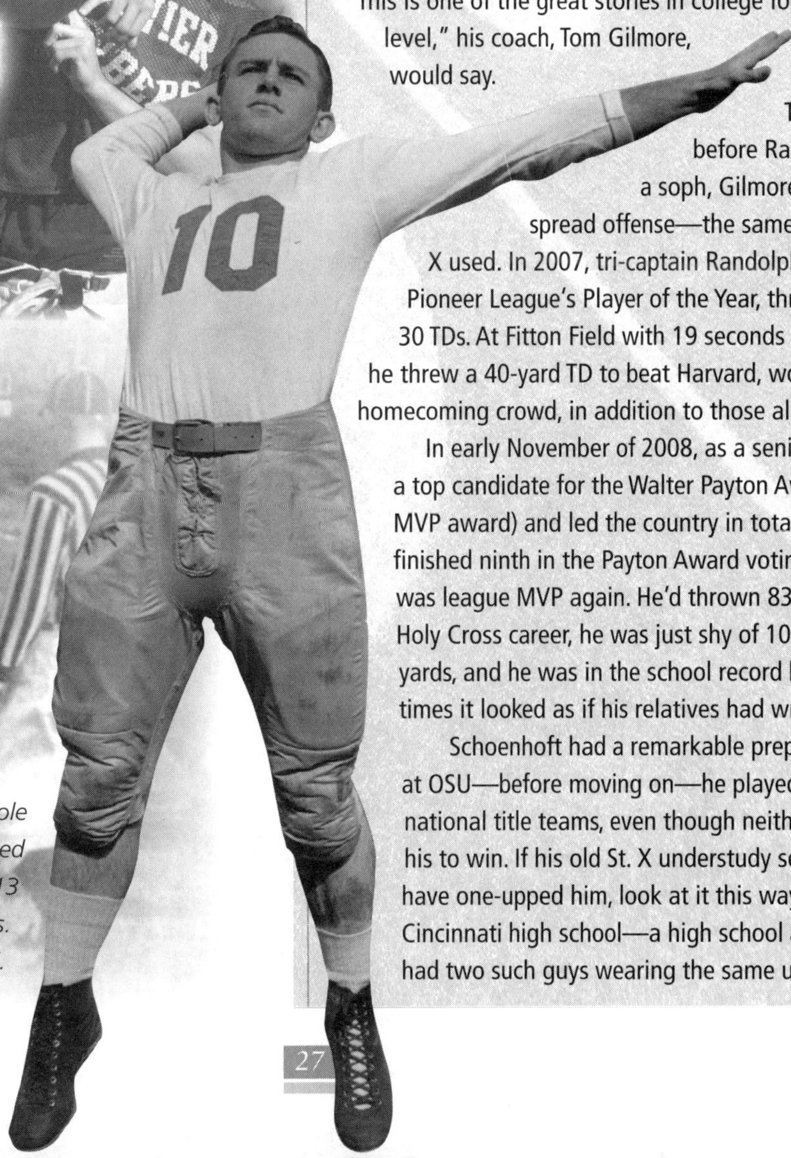

Making Bacon: Selcer finds manhole vs. Roger Bacon in 1954. He scored twice,giving Elder first GCL title in 13 years. And, yes, he had two numbers. Above is Rob Schoenhoft of St. X.

Roger Staubach

Purcell quarterback class of 19***60***

60

LONG BEFORE HE WAS A QUARTERBACK, ROGER STAUBACH WAS AN ALTAR BOY AT ST. JOHN THE EVANGELIST, WHERE, IN THE EIGHTH GRADE, HE ALSO PLAYED running back and endeavored to impress a cheerleader called Pidge. The subsequent marriage would suggest that he succeeded.

His career as a halfback, however, was aborted at Purcell High School. When 100 guys showed up for football his freshman year, Staubach decided to try out for end, since that line was shorter. Either way, he wouldn't be touching the ball for a few years. Jim McCarthy, the veteran coach of the Hackberry Street Assassins, followed a rigid system by which underclassmen played rarely, juniors played defense, and seniors scored the touchdowns. Later, as the latter, Staubach looked to be the best athlete at McCarthy's disposal, which made him—*surprise!*— the quarterback.

For his part, Staubach saw to it that his new position would deviate as little as possible from his old ones. He was not an unskilled passer, but a reluctant one, choosing instead—in the absence of quarterback keepers in McCarthy's playbook—to drop back and run the ball at the slightest provocation. His teammates called him Roger the Dodger. And Ostrich.

Unlike the players today of his caliber, Staubach had not been raised with a football future foremost in mind. His parents had directed him toward the piano, actually, and when the time arrived for his recital, young Roger cut a handsome figure in his tuxedo. His number was the *William Tell Overture*, but apparently the boy had not watched enough episodes of *The Lone Ranger*. He forgot his notes almost totally, and resorted to pounding the keyboard with an indiscriminate vigor that at least left them laughing.

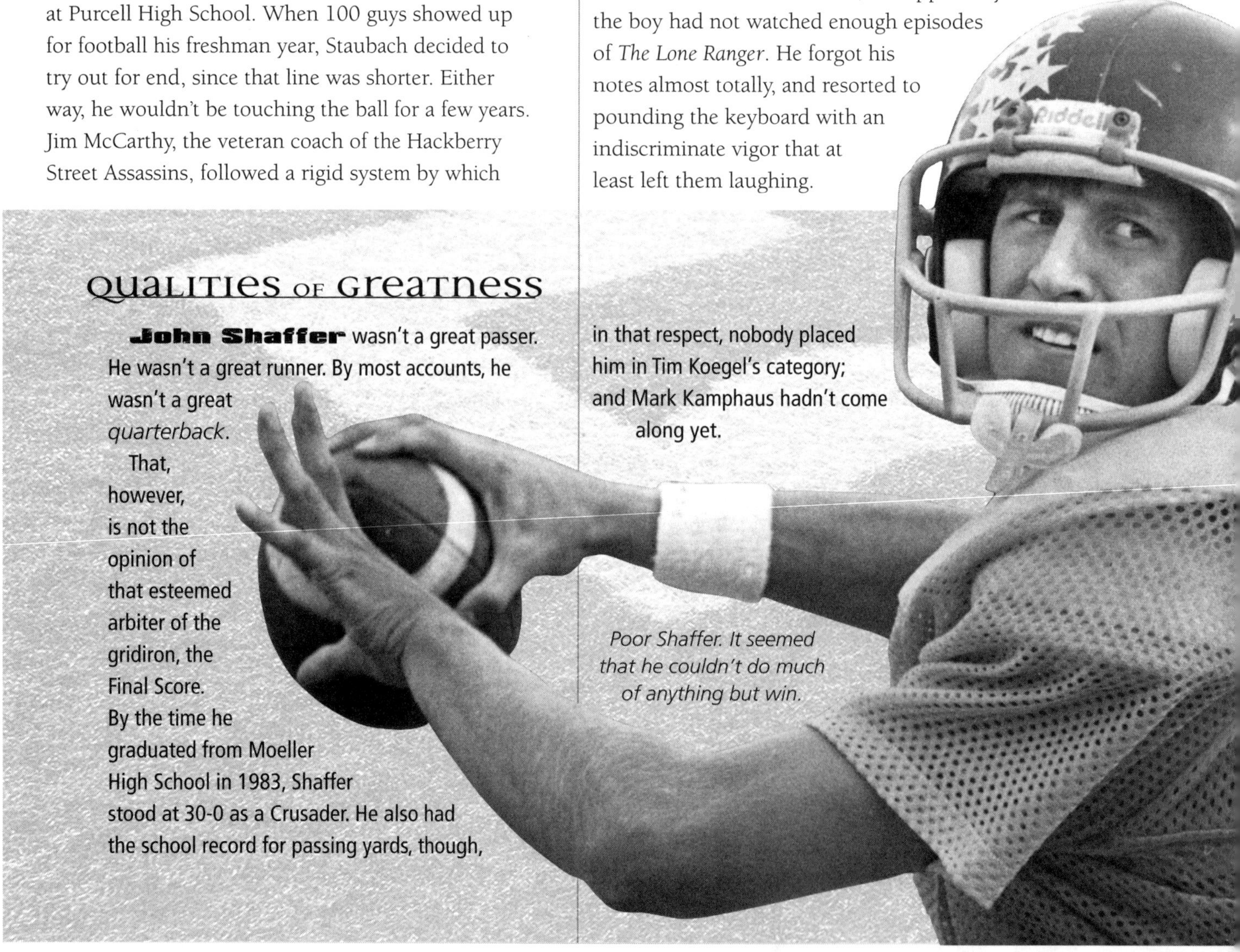

QUALITIES OF GREATNESS

John Shaffer wasn't a great passer. He wasn't a great runner. By most accounts, he wasn't a great *quarterback*.

That, however, is not the opinion of that esteemed arbiter of the gridiron, the Final Score. By the time he graduated from Moeller High School in 1983, Shaffer stood at 30-0 as a Crusader. He also had the school record for passing yards, though, in that respect, nobody placed him in Tim Koegel's category; and Mark Kamphaus hadn't come along yet.

Poor Shaffer. It seemed that he couldn't do much of anything but win.

Even after he was liberated from his scales, football was just another thing in Staubach's ample life. He enjoyed playing basketball across the street from his Silverton home with the Brannen family, to which that game became important. And there was plenty to keep him busy in his own house, where the kid shared a room with his ailing grandmother.

An only child, it was his father's health, however, that was on Staubach's mind in November of 1959, before the scrambling senior led Purcell into the Pit for a GCL match with title implications. Robert Staubach had developed gangrene in his foot and had to have part of it amputated. In his father's absence at the big affair, Roger dedicated the game to him. It was the best one he ever played as a high schooler.

Elder's quarterback was Steve Tensi, who would also show up in the NFL one day and who took more delight than Staubach in throwing the ball. But Purcell's student body president had other designs. Late in anybody's game, he told his running back and lifelong friend, Vince Eysoldt, to act as though he had been handed the ball. With his blockers uninformed, Staubach kept it for a naked reverse that worked for 60-something yards, a 20-14 win, and a three-way share of the title with Elder and Roger Bacon.

He had hoped that such performances would attract the attention of Notre Dame. They did not. Cincinnati and Xavier courted him madly, but he preferred to leave town. He crossed Michigan off his list when he visited Ann Arbor and the players dragged him to bars and burlesque shows. Woody Hayes phoned him for seven consecutive nights, but by then Staubach had made up his mind in favor of Purdue. When he excelled in the Ohio All-Star game, Notre Dame was suddenly enamored of him. Confused, he opted for the plan suggested by the Naval Academy, which involved spending a year at New Mexico Military Institute.

It wasn't easy for him at Navy. An inveterate prankster, he collected enough demerits in his first few months that expulsion wasn't far off. But he adjusted, and he played, and in 1963, Staubach—who by that time had warmed to the concept of the forward pass—beat Notre Dame and won the Heisman Trophy.

He would become, of course—after four years of military service, including a stint in Vietnam—an icon of the Dallas Cowboys and one of the most decorated

As a starter, in fact, Shaffer hadn't lost a game dating all the way back to seventh grade. And when he got to Penn State—apparently, Joe Paterno was of the same mind as the Final Score—the trend continued. He was still undefeated when, on New Year's Day of 1986, as a junior, he led the Nittany Lions against Oklahoma in the Orange Bowl. Penn State, like Shaffer, had a perfect record, and another victory would mean a national championship.

Oklahoma, it turned out, was not Massillon. Shaffer lost. His winning streak had ended at 54.

But he would get another chance, this time in the Fiesta Bowl, which in 1987, for the first time, was being played after New Year's Day. Again, Penn State was undefeated, ranked Number 2 in the country. Its opponent, Miami, was Number 1.

And Miami had Vinny Testaverde as its quarterback. And Michael Irvin as his leading receiver. Penn State didn't *believe* in a leading receiver. It believed in defense and fundamentals and not screwing up. For Paterno, Shaffer was just the right quarterback.

And he proved it against Miami. He proved it even while completing only 5 of 16 passes for 53 yards, while Testaverde was hitting 26 of 50 for 285. But Testaverde also threw five interceptions. They were the difference.

Penn State won, 14-10. Shaffer had quarterbacked his team to the national championship.

For his efforts, and for his 66-1 record as a starter since he was 13, he was not drafted by the NFL. He tried out briefly with the Dallas Cowboys but *asked* to be cut. He was an Academic All-American with a degree in finance.

He took his game to Wall Street, where the winning continued and nobody questioned his arm strength.

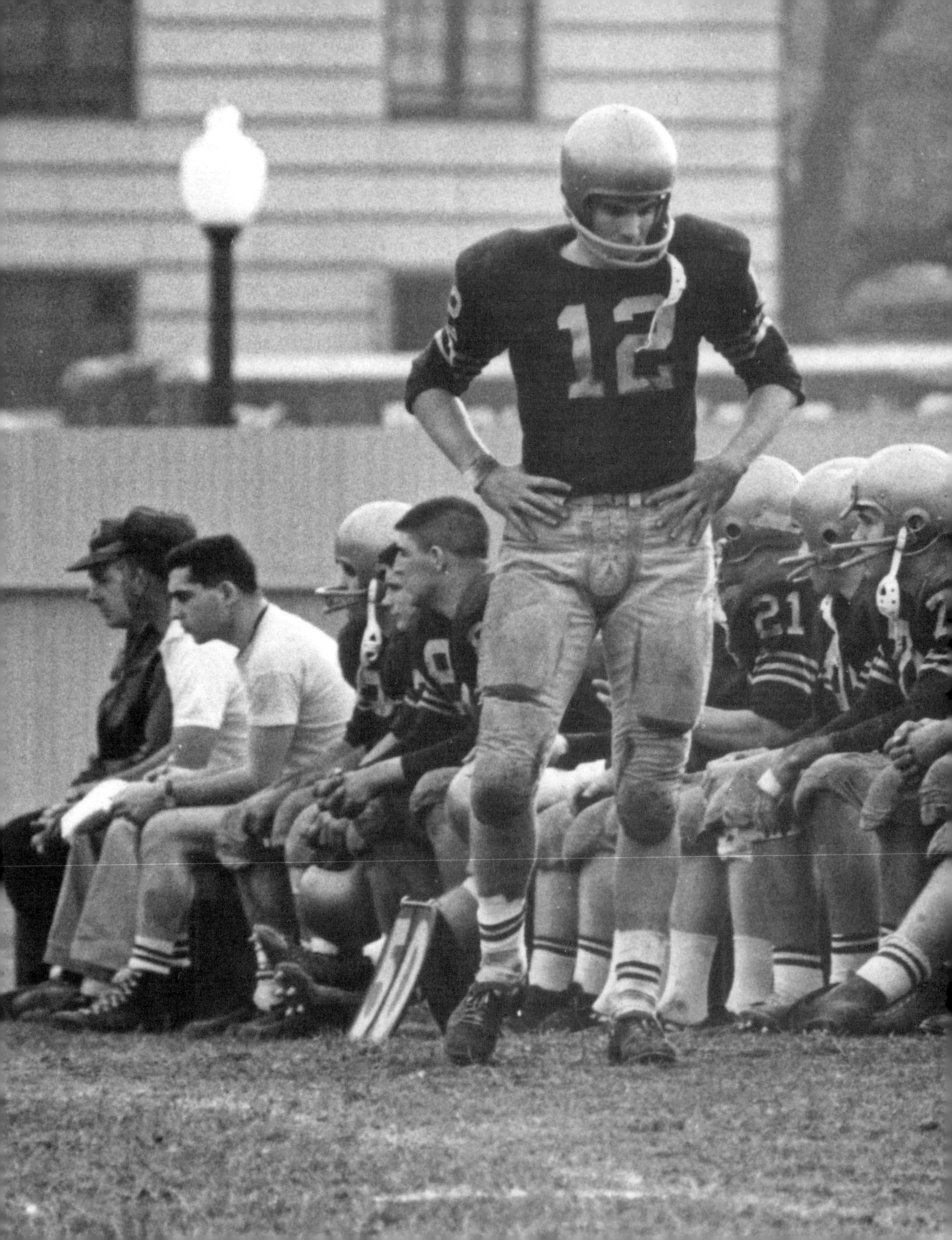

At Purcell, Staubach was a lanky kid who thought he'd be a receiver. His coach, Jim McCarthy, had other ideas. But even McCarthy couldn't keep the kid from running. Staubach would, it seemed, always be a runner.

quarterbacks in NFL history. At the time of his retirement in 1979, Staubach—in spite of his ground-hugging tendencies in the beginning—was the league's all-time leader in passer rating. He was also a six-time Pro Bowler, four-time conference champion, two-time Super Bowl champ, and one-time Super Bowl MVP.

Just as he did at Purcell, the Dodger also took advantage of the running potential that his position offered. He had a special knack for breaking loose late in a game, which contributed famously to the 23 come-from-behind victories to which he led the Cowboys, including 14 in the final two minutes.

His election to the Pro Football Hall of Fame, in 1985, was a foregone conclusion. Staubach remains the only Cincinnati product in the Canton shrine; and yet, as it turned out for him, getting there was significantly easier than getting the ball at Purcell as a junior.

Bob Timberlake

Franklin quarterback class of 19***61***

61

A normal fellow might not have been found in Franklin, Ohio. But what was that to Bob Timberlake?

He was spotted from Michigan, being, as he was, "a man among boys," according to his teammate, Dave Creech, who later became Franklin's athletic director. "At that time, having a 6-4 quarterback, with the physique he had, was unbelievable."

Also among the un-words involved was undefeated, in both football and regular-season basketball, led in the respective seasons by the big and bright All-Stater. Of course, it couldn't have happened without a deep, gifted class that included Bobby Worrell, maybe the second most accomplished athlete in Franklin history (unless you count golfers, in the interest of Frank Lickliter).

But it was Number 60—the digits since retired—

Staubach, a Chronology

1942—On February 5, Elizabeth Staubach, wife of Robert, a shoe and leather representative, gives birth to a boy who forty-three years later will become the first—and so far only—native Cincinnatian inducted into the Pro Football Hall of Fame.

1963—Roger Staubach wins the Heisman, which, given the Purcell High School grad's typical modesty, is stored in trunk of the Navy publicist's wife's car. That made for unusual trips to the supermarket. "I'd tell the bag boys," said the publicist's wife, "'Put the groceries in there, right next to the Heisman Trophy.'" It ended up in Cincinnati, in the custody of Staubach's mother.

1975—Roger Staubach, the former Cincinnati altar boy, playing for Dallas against Minnesota in the playoffs, who attracted the attention of Michigan and, in 1964, led the Wolverines to their first Big Ten championship in fourteen years. Timberlake was the son of a schoolteacher and an engineer, in a well-known family of smart folks, although there were plenty of Buckeyes who questioned the intelligence of his college choice.

At first, Bump Elliott deployed him as a hard-running halfback. The switch back to quarterback, specializing in the option, was an unqualified success, and almost an unbeatable one by the time Timberlake was a senior.

That year, Michigan lost only to Purdue (led by Bob Griese) by one point. And one foot. The pride of Franklin had carried the ball 54 yards for the near-tying touchdown, and instead of kicking the extra point—those honors would have been his, as well—the Wolverines ran the ball for a chance to win, only to see Timberlake stopped twelve inches short of triumph.

He was not stopped at Ohio State, however, scoring all 10 of the game's points as Michigan, in a showdown between two Top 10 teams, won by a shutout.

The victory assured that Timberlake would be chosen by the *Chicago Tribune* as the Big Ten's Most Valuable Player, and also that the Maize and Blue would play Oregon State in the Rose Bowl. That victory came easily, 34-7.

Running the option, Timberlake was a man among boys.

throws 50-yard touchdown pass to Drew Pearson with time running out—his favorite career moment—and says, "I just closed my eyes and said a Hail Mary."

This is widely reported as the origin of the Hail Mary pass. Teammate Drew Pearson caught the pass after pushing Viking safety Nate Wright to the ground, a pass inteference, which, according to *Sports Illustrated*, "brought that phrase into the sports lexicon, killed the father of Vikings quarterback Fran Tarkenton (whose name was Dallas and who died of a heart attack in front of his TV in Savannah) and sent the Cowboys on their way to the Super Bowl."

The referee, said *SI*, "oblivious to Pearson's pass intefer-ence—was brained by a whiskey bottle, which toss is still regarded, in the Twin Cities, as the game's *true* Hail Mary."

1985—Roger Staubach, Purcell High's reluctant quarterback, goes into the Pro Football Hall of Fame in Canton. Afterward, there is a reunion with Staubach's high school teammates. "The more we talked," said Staubach, "the better we got. It ended up we won the Purcell-Roger Bacon game last night, the one we really lost in 1960."

2008—Roger Staubach, who rose from humble running back origins in Cincinnati to a Hall of Fame career, returns to Cincinnati, speaking at St. Xavier High's annual Hall of Fame induction dinner. Says Staubach, "When I talked to Jack Cassady he said, 'You're a man who served in the Navy, who believes in our rights, our right to free speech, so we'd like you to do a free speech, and here I am."

All-American honors followed for the rugged quarterback, and they underwhelmed him. During his Michigan years, Timberlake had committed himself to Christianity, teaching Sunday School in Ann Arbor and declaring his intentions to become a Presbyterian minister. In all of that, he found room for football, but not for the trappings that attended it.

"There's a great deal of loneliness in being an All-American," he said in an interview circulated by Newspaper Enterprises Association. "I get sick of it. They all want to shake your hand, but they don't really know you. All they do is stick out the glad hand.

"I don't mind talking to anyone who is interested in ideas, but nothing makes me sicker than having my name dropped by people who don't know anything about me except that I'm an All-American."

The experience sent Timberlake to the New York Giants as a third-round draft choice with reservations. Y.A. Tittle was gone, and the rookie was expected to compete for the starting quarterback position; but his heart simply wasn't in it.

> "There's a great deal of loneliness in being an All-American."
>
> —Bob Timberlake

He was relegated to kickoffs and later, through an injury to a teammate, field-goal and extra-point attempts. He had previously converted a 43-yard field goal, but in the more regular role he missed all 14 of his attempts. Eleven of them came from beyond 40 yards, and the other three were blocked, but the stigma stuck, nevertheless. Years later, one football publication described Timberlake as "the worst kicker ever."

And that was it for him as a football player. He participated in the 1966 preseason, but couldn't climb the depth chart and was cut in late August.

Timberlake was thus free to become ordained as Presbyterian minister, which he did. He also caught on as a hospital administrator in Milwaukee and a teacher at Marquette University, which doesn't play football—a notion that the old quarterback can appreciate more than most.

Elder-Purcell, 1959: The Untold Story

When Purcell met Elder in 1959 it was the only game in Cincinnati high school football history when two future NFL quarterbacks opposed each other on the field, although only one of them—Elder's **Steve Tensi**—truly resembled a quarterback. The skinny Staubach kid from Purcell galloped around like a colt and his thoroughbred tendencies were first revealed as a runner.

It wasn't that he couldn't throw, just that he was—by his own admission—wild and inefficient. He trusted his feet, not his arm, and Purcell succeeded "not because I bombed anybody's secondary," he said. "I made more yardage from the *threat* of passing than actually putting the ball in the air."

He ran for over 500 yards that year, then said, "You only have to know one thing to grasp my early tendencies: we didn't have any running plays for the quarterback."

In contrast, Elder's offense depended on the strong arm of its junior quarterback, Tensi, and behind him, the Panthers had lost only once—to a strong Steubenville Central Catholic team.

Tensi, like many good quarterbacks, had a bit of the showman about him, amusing his teammates with a dead-on Elvis, complete with lip curl. So instead of mourning the loss, Tensi led some of his teammates on a tour of downtown Steubenville, which ended when they walked into a bar inhabited by the Elder coaching staff.

The next week during practice, center **Bob James** inadvertently missed Tensi's signal and hiked the ball directly into Tensi's crotch. Tensi collapsed to the ground, groaning.

"So," said James, "Coach Scardina comes over, looks down at him, and says, 'I've been thinking all week what I was going to do to you for that Steubenville stunt but now I don't have to. James just did it for me.'"

The Purcell-Elder tilt was classic GCL bigtime. The game was played the Sunday afternoon before Thanksgiving at The Pit, SRO, and Purcell took a 14-8

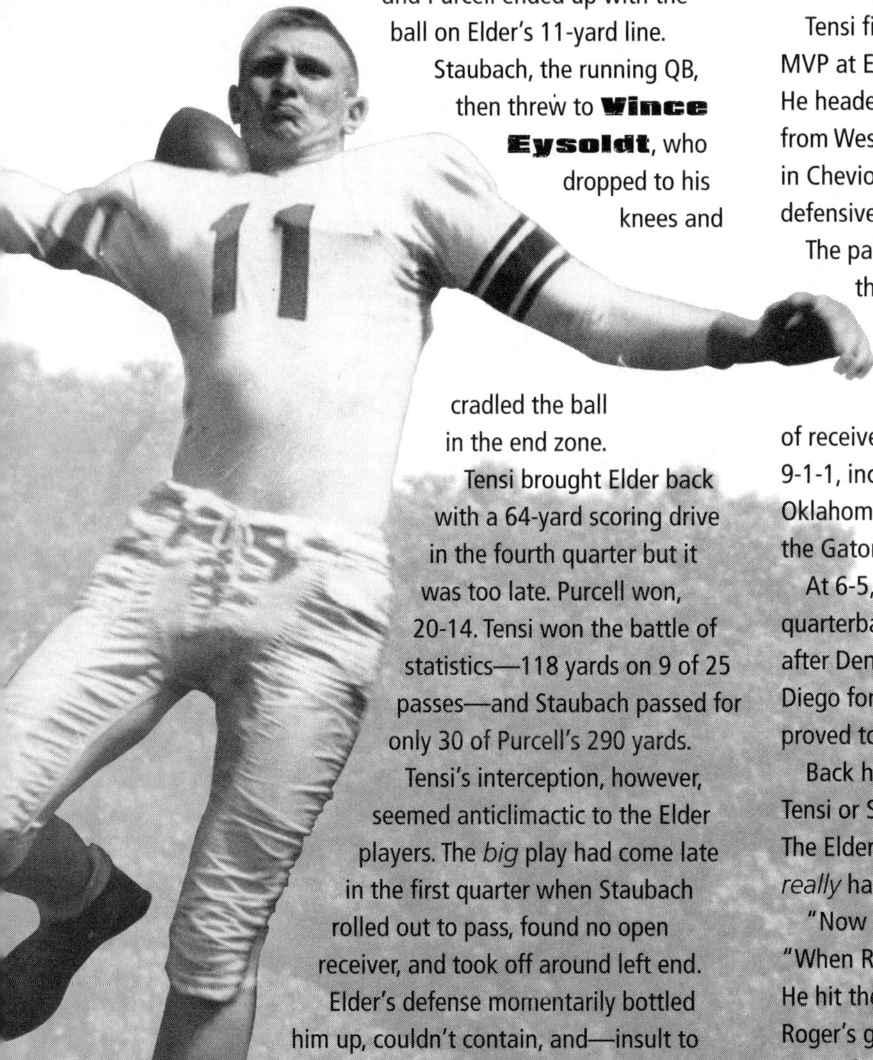

lead into halftime. Ironically, the passing quarterback, Tensi, threw a fatal interception late in the third quarter and Purcell ended up with the ball on Elder's 11-yard line. Staubach, the running QB, then threw to **Vince Eysoldt**, who dropped to his knees and cradled the ball in the end zone.

Tensi brought Elder back with a 64-yard scoring drive in the fourth quarter but it was too late. Purcell won, 20-14. Tensi won the battle of statistics—118 yards on 9 of 25 passes—and Staubach passed for only 30 of Purcell's 290 yards.

Tensi's interception, however, seemed anticlimactic to the Elder players. The *big* play had come late in the first quarter when Staubach rolled out to pass, found no open receiver, and took off around left end. Elder's defense momentarily bottled him up, couldn't contain, and—insult to injury—Staubach scampered directly past the Elder bench on his way to a 69-yard score. He would later say that it was his longest high school run.

"The big blond guy," they called him. And he was—one of the first truly big quarterbacks. That's Tensi's college teammate, Maury Bibent (33), in the inset.

Tensi finished his high school career as a two-time MVP at Elder, All-City, and honorable mention All-State. He headed for Florida State, along with an old adversary from Western Hills, **Maury Bibent**—they lived in Cheviot, half a mile apart—who was converted into a defensive back.

The pair of Cincinnatians were actually present at the creation, when FSU's fledgling program—no winning tradition or conference affiliation—stepped into the big time. Tensi was a bigtime quarterback, aided by the outrageous skills of receiver Fred Biletnikoff. In 1964, Florida State went 9-1-1, including its first victory over Florida and a win over Oklahoma in the Gator Bowl. Tensi threw five TD passes in the Gator Bowl, still a record.

At 6-5, 215 pounds, he was one of the first big pro quarterbacks ("the big blond guy," they called him), but after Denver gave up two Number 1 draft choices to San Diego for his services, he was oft-injured and his best days proved to be historic.

Back home in the Queen City, the big game for either Tensi or Staubach remained the 1959 West Side encounter. The Elder veterans, though, had a different story about what *really* happened.

"Now here's the story," said Bob James, Tensi's center. "When Roger comes past our bench, I see the chalk fly up. He hit the out-of-bounds line. But the ref doesn't see it. Roger's gone for 60-something yards and the score. We'da won otherwise.

"So years later, he's back in town for a GCL banquet and he gets up and says, 'Now before I begin I want to say to all you Elder people out there, I did NOT step out of bounds.'"

Bob James shakes his head sadly. He can *still* see the chalk dust, as if there were out-of- bounds lines in his living room.

"After all these years," he said, "he just had to turn the knife...."

Don Zimmer

Western Hills quarterback class of 19 *49*

49

Never mind what you know about Don Zimmer from recent years, sitting next to Joe Torre in baseball threads he outgrew a few decades ago, with arms folded on a well-fed ledge and a hamster cheek full of tobacco. The old Boston skipper whom the Red Sox referred to, not entirely fondly, as The Gerbil, or the doddering, roly-poly Yankee coach who thought he could take on Pedro Martinez, have nothing to do with the slim, dashing athlete who did it all at Western Hills High School.

And then again, the two are very much one, at heart.

The West Side, in those days—the middle of the 20th century—spawned guys who loved to play games, and played them in a fashion that was found nowhere else. Zimmer and his pals were national American Legion baseball champions, and the day they put down their gloves was the day they put on their pads. They seldom lost at football, either.

Zimmer's senior season, 1948, West High was beaten but twice, by Elder and Purcell. Both times, Zimmer was injured in the first half and missed the rest of the game. Both times, it was probably an accident; but the story got around, true or not, that at Elder—the ferocious neighborhood rival—they were selling T-shirts that said *Get Zimmer*.

He was the quarterback, at about 5-8, 150 pounds. That's right, 150. "I'm not exaggerating," said Harry Andreadis, a rival at Withrow, "Zimmer could hide behind a broom handle when he was in high school." (Even then, however, there was a rodent theme. His high school buddies called him "Rat," although not in the least disrespectfully.)

Zimmer had "Itchy" McKinley for his junior year English class, a fortuitous choice as "Itchy" gave the football players a B-plus for each touchdown they scored in a big game. He also had the football-sympathetic Mr. Ehler for math.

"Plane geometry," Zimmer said in a later interview. "I never even knew how to spell it. I still don't. I convinced Frey (his classmate and fellow jock) to take it, and I'm

sitting in the back and he's sitting in the front. I'm doing fine. I'm getting my B's. Then one Saturday night, Mr. Ehler drops dead. I hear it on Monday morning, and my first thought is, *Phew! I ain't got a chance.*

"This young woman appears and she puts a problem on the board. Calls on me. First one out of the chute. 'Mr Zimmer, can you explain this problem?' I don't even try to fool her. I say, 'No, ma'am, I can't.' I sit down. Class ends. I go straight to the principal's office and transfer to shop."

As far as Jim Frey was concerned, Zim deserted. "I'm still sitting up there," he said, ruefully, "studying geometry and Zimmer is in the basement making lamps...."

"Don was one of the best athletes that ever came out of Cincinnati," said his center, Glenn Sample, who saw most of them. "And that goes for football, very much.

"We had a multiple offense—some T-formation, a single wing, a spinning type of thing—and Don was a great runner, a great thrower, a smart ballplayer. He called a lot of the plays on his own, and he also did the kicking for us. I'd put him up there with just about anybody. Maybe Staubach."

Bear Bryant flew Zim to Lexington for a workout. Zim went, then he told The Bear, 'Thanks, but no thanks.' He was off to play baseball and collegiate sports lost one whiz of a quarterback.

In a game with Sidney his senior year, Zimmer made the wire services by throwing himself a pass—then catching it and scoring. It happened this way: Western Hills was down 12-0 when Zim tossed a short pass to one of his receivers, the ball hit a Sidney player, bounced high in the air—and when it came down Zim was under it. He got another score by returning a punt 50 yards, and Western Hills won 14-12.

Of Zim's modest 150 pounds, a disproportionate amount was forearm, honestly acquired. At about 2 in the morning, Zimmer and any number of his brothers would regularly head down from their house at 777 Sedam Street to the family's wholesale produce business on what is now Pete Rose Way, named for yet another Sedamsville ballplayer. There were boxcars to unload. School was then reached by streetcar. Practice ran late. There was no offseason.

In his lovable years, Zimmer has enjoyed telling people that he never worked a day out of baseball. There was a part of a day, though. It was when he got up on a roof at his uncle's behest to hammer in some sheet metal, and on the fourth swing smashed his thumb.

Of course, that was nothing compared to when his head was smashed in Triple-A ball. At the time, having signed with the Dodgers right out of West High as the kid who would replace Pee Wee Reese at shortstop, he was, according to some, the most celebrated prospect since Ted Williams. In 1950, he had led his league in home runs while *stealing* home ten times. And on July 7, 1953, he was leading the American Association in homers, with 23, when a curveball caught him in the skull. Zimmer was unconscious for thirteen days. He is the reason ballplayers started wearing helmets.

Three years later, Elder's favorite quarterback was enjoying a visit to his hometown when the Reds' Hal Jeffcoat found his cheekbone with a fastball. It's ironic that, for Zimmer, football may have been a safer alternative. Bear Bryant wanted him at Kentucky. Everybody wanted him. But the Dodgers paid the best.

On top of that, baseball offered tobacco.

The 1948 Lettermen of Western Hills—First row: Howard Mills, Harold Mills, Huestler, Bassett, Tierney, Stormer. Kruse, Sachs, Schnell, Rhien, Peters, Bludau. Second row: Botuchis, Flake, Harris, Gussett, Miederhelman, Starman, Young, Greenfield, Ott. Third row: Johnson, Mundstock, Kiradjieff, Stevenson, Zimmer, Adams, Williams, Sinks. Fourth row: Fissel, Schutte, Rabenstein, Wolff, Rennich, Frey, Loughry, Wiese, Hoinke. Fifth row: Gamble, Prafka, O'Neal, Renner, McCreadie, Beck, Stegner, Klein.

FOOTBAL

Tim Clifford was a chubby sophomore guard in 1974 when the Colerain players were playfully tossing the ball around the field before a preseason practice. Coach Ben Hubbard and his staff encouraged them to do that, and Clifford was the reason why. One of the assistants spotted him winging hard spirals and suggested to Hubbard that they ought to take a look at the kid as a quarterback. Over the next three years, Clifford set the school passing records for completions and touchdowns. Five years later, after setting more records at Indiana U., Clifford was named MVP of the Big Ten . . . **Bryan Cupito**, McNicholas quarterback (1998-2001), is still in the Ohio record book for throwing six TDs in a game (twice), his 92 career TD tosses, and his 8,386 total yards. He once threw 64 passes in a game with Roger Bacon and Moeller coach Steve Klonne (who coached Penn State's John Shaffer) called Cupito the best quarterback he'd ever seen. Cupito broke his thumb just before the Ohio All-Star Classic, then went out and outplayed OSU's much-lauded recruit, Justin Zwick. At Minnesota in 2005, facing Ohio State's top-shelf defense, he passed for a career-high 396 yards, even though it was in a losing cause (the Gophers posted 578 yards of total offense, the second-highest total ever allowed by the Bucks). He played through injuries (after hurting his shoulder his girlfriend had to brush his teeth for him), and finished his career as Minnesota's all-time top passer—most TD passes (55), most yardage (7,446), and best pass efficiency rating (138.34) . . . **Michael Taylor** took Princeton to a state title in 1983. "I always told Pat Mancuso that Michael Taylor wasn't fair, because he could pass *and* run," said former Moeller athletic director Jim Lippincott. "He was strong and smart with the ball." As a starting quarterback at Michigan, Taylor broke his collarbone late in the 1988 season, depriving him of a victory over Ohio State and another against Southern Cal in the Rose Bowl. The next year, as a senior, he did engineer a triumph over the Buckeyes in Ann Arbor. But in Bo Schembechler's last game as head coach, Taylor was unable to lead the Wolverines past USC in Pasadena . . . **Roger Franz** was overshadowed at Purcell, where he handed the ball to Jim Bolger and threw it to Ron Beagle. But not so at Fordham University, where he made All-American and the school's Hall of Fame. To quarterback the Rams, Franz passed up an opportunity to play at Notre Dame . . . In 1975, **Chuck Hauck** of tiny Williamsburg was Class A Back of the Year in Ohio, capitalizing on the run-and-shoot offense that coach Ken Osborne installed just for him. He later started at Miami, where the offense was *not* installed just for him . . . Princeton won another state title in 1987 behind junior **Johnny Mattress**, perhaps the purest passer the Vikings had produced. As a senior, Mattress was a *Parade* All-American, a hot prospect headed for Ohio State. But he didn't qualify academically and instead played the 1990 season at Coffeyville Community College in Kansas, leading his team to the national junior-college championship. Eventually, he ended up at California (Pa.) University and became the starting quarterback. Then in the summer of 1994 he and a teammate were wounded in a shooting incident. Mattress was hit in the stomach. He returned to the field but struggled and was later suspended for academic and disciplinary reasons. After the season, he left school. In 1999, the former prep All-American and another man were sentenced to ninety days at the Hamilton County Justice Center for hitting a guy in the head with a softball bat during a local game that took on racial overtones . . . And, finally, this item, which we call "Short in the Pocket:" Clean-cut Walnut Hills lad, **Jerry Rubin**, keeper of football statistics for local newspapers in 1955, forewent his early ambition as sportswriter to become quarterback of the Yippies and the 1960s anti-war movement. In Berkeley, Chicago, and other playing fields of the revolution, his abandon-the-pocket scramblings and untraditional signal-calling helped define the century's noisiest decade. Even At 5-6, 130 pounds, he stood tall in the pocket of the decade, although his height may have caused him to try and ban the bomb rather than throw it.

Mattress

RB

Running backs

JASON BAINUM—*williamsburg/class of 2002*

ERBIL BARKLEY—*central/class of 1952*

JIM BOLGER—*purcell/class of 1950*

THE FRANCISCOS, HIAWATHA & D'JUAN
—*moeller/classes of 1983 & 1985*

RICHARD HALL—*wyoming/class of 1998*

THE HARKRADERS, JERRY, MIKE & ROB
—*middletown, fenwick/classes of 1952, 1976, 1979*

BOB HOERNSCHEMEYER—*elder/class of 1943*

DEHART HUBBARD—*walnut hills/class of 1921*

NAPOLEON MCCALLUM—*milford/class of 1981*

THE ROECKERS, BERNIE & WALT
—*roger bacon/classes of 1948 & 1957*

PAUL SARRINGHAUS—*hamilton/class of 1940*

CARLOS SNOW—*cape/class of 1987*

THE SOLLMANNS, SCOTT & STEVE
—*st. xavier/classes of 1993 & 2000*

THE TAFT BACKFIELD, WALTER JOHNSON, AL NELSON, CLEOPHUS EDWARDS & CARL WARD
—*classes of 1961-1963*

OTIS WILLIAMS—*withrow/class of 1954*

JORDAN TO THE RESCUE (*paul jordan*)

WHY BILL KUNTZ HAS HIS OWN STADIUM *(jim "red dog" daugherty, jim dole, jim kater, ted harless & charlie key)*

THE MASON-LEBANON RIVALRY *(kelton lindsay, brady merchant, jeff bentley, greg richards, craig adkins, david linville & dave brausch)*

KEN MINOR AND THE READING YEARS *(tom fouchey & deshawn wynn)*

ROSE AND THE OTHER GAME (*pete rose*)

THAT CHAMPIONSHIP SEASON *(alan degraffenreid, ron carpenter, markus thomas, william reese & craig thompson)*

bench strength—freddie jacobs and steve fletcher, wyoming; mike gayles, princeton; eric ellington, moeller; larry parker, elder; harry and jake andreadis, withrow and anderson; dick ernst, withrow; jeff "chill" hill, mt. healthy; darius ashley, st. xavier; chris cionni, st. xavier; walter gruber, st. xavier; craig english, goshen; nick wilson, ross; donald "the tree" oglesby, batavia.

Jason Bainum

Williamsburg running back class of 2002

02

FIRST, YOU HAVE TO UNDERSTAND HOW SMALL WILLIAMSBURG HIGH SCHOOL IS. ITS VETERAN FOOTBALL COACH, KEN OSBORNE, SURELY DID. LUCKY TO HAVE thirty boys out for the team most years, Osborne developed the practice of identifying his most talented or versatile or something-or-other athlete, and building an offense around him.

In Jason Bainum, he was fortunate to have a fellow who could throw well, run better, and do it all night. So Osborne, who had learned a thing or two during thirty-six seasons on the job, put him back in short-punt formation, and watched the records fall.

As a sophomore, Bainum ran for 1,473 yards and 24 touchdowns, which was excellent but nothing like the numbers he would put up as a junior. As a junior, the 6-footer rushed for a ridiculous 3,042 yards, setting a Cincinnati-area record with two weeks to spare, then breaking the state mark the following Friday. That was remarkable and unprecedented. But it wasn't his best effort.

Late in September of 2001, his senior season, in a Southern Buckeye Conference game against Clermont Northeastern—which, like every school that played Williamsburg, had considerably more boys enrolled—the humble Clermont Countian hit the mother lode. Baimum carried the ball 56 times that night for an unheard-of 532 yards, breaking the single-game state record of 529 set in 1956 by Bob Ferguson, an Ohio State All-American from Troy. He also accounted personally for all 46 of Williamsburg's points.

Running behind grade-school pals whom Osborne called the best blockers he'd ever coached, Bainum finished the year with 44 touchdowns and 3,386 rushing yards, breaking his own single-season state record. With 8,216 yards all told, he routed the career record of CAPE's Carlos Snow by 455. During his time at Williamsburg, Bainum also completed 58 percent of his passes for 1,433 yards and 14 touchdowns.

Jason Bainum was the center of Williamsburg's offense, at once tailback and quarterback. And just before he broke Ohio's career rushing record, he shrugged and said, "It's just a number. Let's win the game."

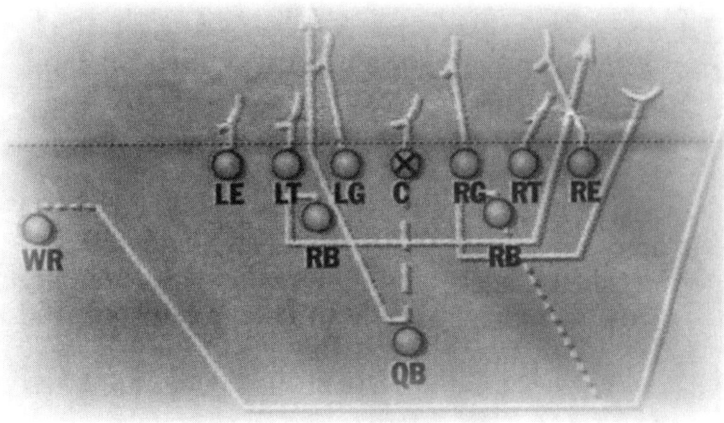

Williamsburg's offense puts the QB in a shotgun formation with no backs behind him. The backs, primarily blockers, are positioned behind the linemen on either side of the QB. There's one wide receiver, and two ends. With the shotgun, says Coach Osborne, "Jason can see the holes better."

His exploits as a senior got him into both *Sports Illustrated* and the Division VI playoffs. They did not, however, get him into a Division I football program.

He wasn't too small, at 208 pounds, but insufficiently speedy for the big time. That worked to the advantage of Capital University, where Bainum became a starting tailback but not an extraordinary one.

Now, maybe if they'd given him the ball 56 times a game . . .

Erbil Barkley

Central | halfback | class of 19**52**

52

AT ABOUT 5-9, 140 POUNDS, ERBIL BARKLEY ENTERTAINED NO ILLUSIONS ABOUT HIS FUTURE IN FOOTBALL. ON THAT SCORE, he tended to agree with Woody Hayes.

In 1950, when Barkley was a junior at Central High School—a vocational institution that typically didn't attract a lot of attention from college recruiters—Hayes, enamored of the little fellow's speed, had courted him for the Miami Redskins. The next year, however, Hayes took the Ohio State job and delivered to Barkley a sober dose of reality. Too small, son.

The new coach at Miami was Ara Parseghian, and size notwithstanding, Parseghian followed through with the scholarship offer. It helped Barkley's case—it helped him make All-State, as well—when he ran for 300 yards in a startling rout of St. Xavier. That didn't count the opening kickoff, which he returned 85 yards for a touchdown, only to have it called back. The next time, he went 90.

Barkley led the city in rushing that year, putting his relative smallness to full advantage. Central's offensive line was anchored by a 6-6, 300-pounder named Tom Jones, who would ultimately play with the Cleveland Browns.

"I hid behind him," Barkley said.

Jones, a shotputter, moved on to Miami for both football and track, and the same deal was extended the scatback who grew up in the East End and often hiked through the woods to work out on Withrow's track (or jump into whatever pickup game was going on).

And, yes, as a state champion in the 220—and after leading Central to back-to-back team titles—he wished to continue his track career after high school. But he didn't care to do it in Ohio.

He opted for North Carolina A&T, a traditionally black college where he was joined by another high school chum, Harold Horn. He and Horn ran on the same 400 relay team that won the prestigious Penn Relays. Ultimately, Barkley made it into A&T's Hall of Fame; and he did it on legs that were never quite right.

The problem cropped up originally at the North-South All-Star game in the summer of 1952. "We ran a lot of 40-yard sprints," recalled Barkley, long retired from his job as an engineer at General Electric.

"I wasn't really warmed up enough, and they wanted to see if this one fellow could beat me—Jerry Harkrader from Middletown. He went to Ohio State and played halfback for Woody. He was something special. Anyway, I beat him in the sprint, but I pulled a muscle in my thigh. It wasn't too serious, but I had a lot of muscle trouble after that."

Of course, it might have had to do with all the weight he was hauling around in college. By then, he was up to nearly 150.

Jim Bolger

Purcell | halfback | class of 1950

THE OLD-TIMERS WILL TELL YOU THAT ROGER STAUBACH WAS NOT THE GREATEST FOOTBALL PLAYER WHO EVER WORE THE COLORS of Purcell High School—at least, while he was wearing them. Eventually, in the larger scheme, yeah; sure. He was the Hall of Famer, the Super Bowl hero, America's Quarterback, all of that. And he was good at Purcell, as well—as a senior. But not *that* good. He scarcely threw the ball.

He was no Jim Bolger.

Well, Bolger *never* threw the ball; but then, his coach, Jim McCarthy, didn't go much for that sort of thing. McCarthy ran the T-formation, and he wanted a guy who could carry home the bacon in his hands and sizzle up a crisp, delicious victory; a guy like Dutch Bolger, as he was called, like his dad.

They say that Bolger was the fastest fellow around, patently uncatchable, but that's mostly the legend, according to the man himself. "I wasn't a speed guy, but I knew how to run the ball," he said, somewhat uncomfortably. "I just had the instinct to run the ball to open spaces."

It was 1949 when he was a Purcell senior. Ed Kluska had fashioned the Cavaliers into the powerhouse of Cincinnati, one undefeated team after another, and then he had moved on to Xavier University, making room for McCarthy, who was dead serious about maintaining Purcell's preeminence. McCarthy was dead serious about most everything, in fact.

He was a former lieutenant commander in the Navy, white-haired and Irish and possessed of different notions. He didn't believe in scrimmaging once the season started. And he didn't believe in wearing his boys out once the game started. Locally, at least, McCarthy was the originator of the platoon system—in part because Purcell had the manpower to do it. While he was at it, the stern coach involved not only large numbers of student-athletes, but parents as well, inviting them to Wednesday night film sessions. The result was an average home crowd of 10,000.

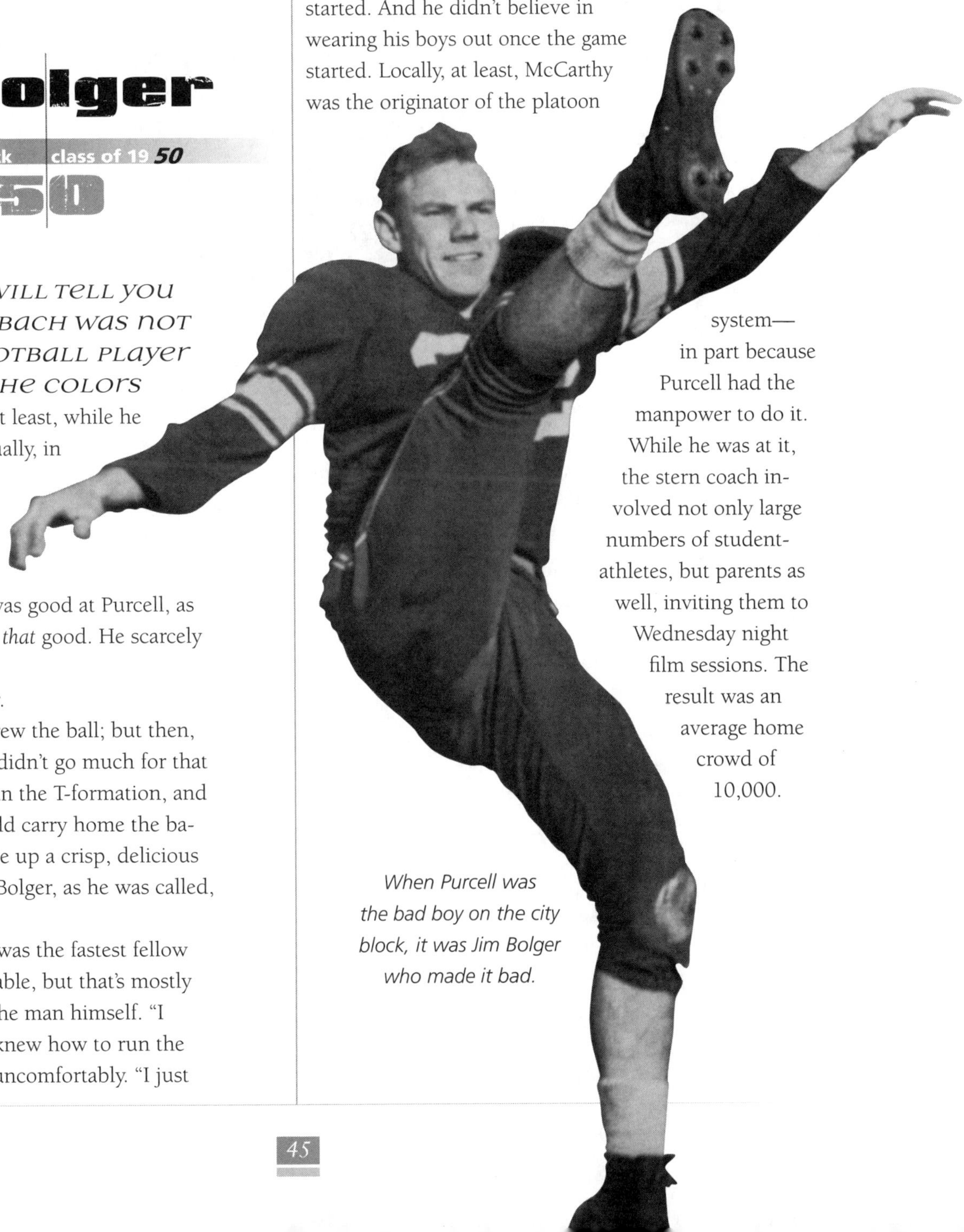

When Purcell was the bad boy on the city block, it was Jim Bolger who made it bad.

So it was that the word spread about the Cavaliers, and about Bolger in particular. In 1949, he averaged more than 14 yards a carry, scored 20 touchdowns, punted like a pro, made All-State, and left a lot of people thinking he was the best player that Cincinnati had ever seen.

The same people thought Purcell was the best team that Cincinnati had ever seen. Ron Beagle, a future All-American at Navy, was a junior end that year. Roger Franz, the quarterback, later made All-American at Fordham. The Cavalier defense was called the Hard Rocks, and not undeservedly.

Purcell's biggest challenge in 1949 figured to come from Withrow, which featured running backs Dick Ernst, who later played at Ohio State, and Harry Andreadis, who went on to the University of Cincinnati.

"We made the mistake of beating them my junior year," recalled Andreadis. "Well, they beat us 49-0 that night. That's how I learned Purcell's fight song. They played it every time they scored a touchdown. I got to learn that song very well."

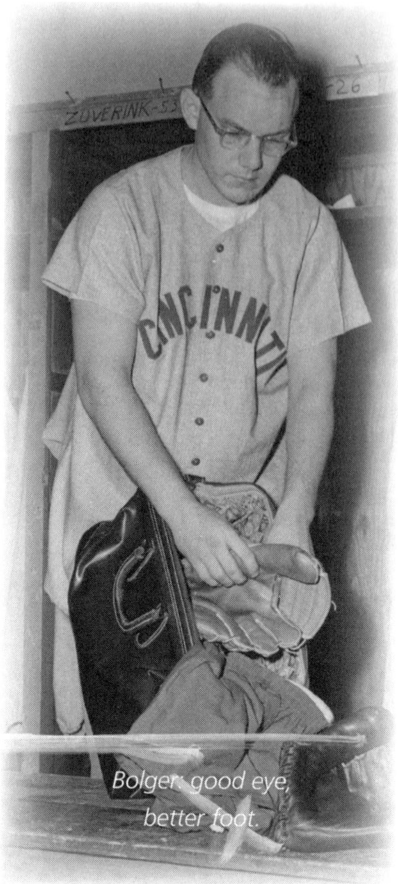

Bolger: good eye, better foot.

The Cavaliers proceeded to complete another undefeated season, and in doing so viewed themselves as state champs. But so did Massillon. The Northern voters, as usual, saw it Massillon's way. In the final *AP* poll, Purcell ranked fourth.

Phooey.

At that, the pollsters considered themselves uncommonly open-minded. The wire service identified McCarthy's team as "the first Queen City club to ever threaten the northeastern sector's dominance of the interscholastic grid picture."

Truth be told, though, the slight was fully expected and didn't cause much of a stir about town. Not like the decision that Bolger made when school was out.

He had done all of the high-profile visiting that befitted a star of his stature—one who was among the first class of five players inducted into the Greater Cincinnati Sports Hall of Fame. Frank Leahy had summoned him up to Notre Dame. Wes Fesler wanted him for the Buckeyes. Even Miami, Florida, was after Bolger. Instead, he signed with the Reds.

He was, apparently, a better athlete than outfielder. After coming up to the big leagues in 1950—just a few months after he graduated—Bolger shuttled back and forth and managed only one hit in a Cincinnati uniform. In 1954, he was traded to the Cubs for Johnny Klippstein. He did a bit better there, but was out of the game by the end of the decade.

"I've looked back on it," Bolger said, hinting at regret but not surrendering to it. "But what can you say? I did what I wanted to do. It wasn't a hard decision. I had been playing baseball since I was seven or eight years old."

More than half a century later, Bolger's twin grandsons would make a similar kind of decision. Keith and Brett Bolger were stars of Elder's 2002 state championship football team. Brett was the captain and a record-setting punt returner. Keith was the team MVP and GCL Player of the Year. They opted to play baseball at Eastern Kentucky University, where Brett led the Ohio Valley Conference in batting.

Their father, Tom—Dutch's son—had gone the football route, Elder to Notre Dame, where he was a guard on the 1973 national champions. Jim's father had also pursued football for a while. The *real* old-timers will tell you that Dutch Junior had nothing on Dutch Senior as a football player; if anything, it was the other way around. The elder Bolger—Cyril was his real name—went to high school at St. Mary's in Hyde Park and played there in a leather helmet before the St. Mary's boys were shifted over to Purcell in 1927.

Cyril Bolger then played two strong years at Xavier, as a running back, before he went to work in the family coal business. And got married. And moved to Mariemont. And raised the best high school football player in the history of Purcell.

The Franciscos

Hiawatha and D'Juan

Moeller running backs classes of 1983,1985

83, 85

HOW DO YOU SMUGGLE IN A 185-POUND RUNNING BACK WHO HAS CAN'T-CATCH-ME SPEED, CUTS LIKE A PERFECT INSULT, AND ANSWERS TO A NAME LIKE HIAWATHA FRANCISCO?

You just don't, and Gerry Faust knew it better than anyone. Faust knew the things that were being whispered about the Moeller program —about players coming over from Northern Kentucky and wherever he could allegedly recruit them from. It was 1979, and the Crusaders were already tucked tightly into their roll of state and national championships. The envy was bitter and spreading.

And then the Franciscos—an attentive mom and two swift boys of Spanish and Native American heritage —moved into a house in the Moeller district that happened to belong, in part, to the head coach. Didn't look good.

Undeniably, the Moeller *program* had, by virtue only of its station, recruited Hiawatha and his little brother D'Juan. The program was the best around, and a local football player with swerving hips and soaring ambition would very possibly want to play there. A nurturing mother of said fellow would very possibly try to make it happen.

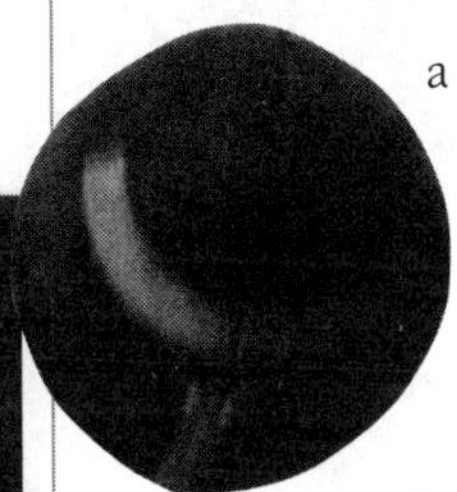

So Mrs. Francisco, needing to leave a neighborhood that was giving way to an industrial park, had come to Faust with her plans to move closer to Moeller, and asking about places to rent. Faust, of course, knew of one, since it belonged to him and his business partner. But before he offered it, he contacted the OHSAA to inquire about the propriety. Assured that there was no violation involved, the arrangements were made and the Crusaders had themselves a pair of

Hiawatha to the left, D'Juan to the right —Moe's unbeatable brother act.

Hiawatha Francisco was Moeller's best back until his little brother, D'Juan, came along. Then Moe had TWO best backs. Between them, they copped four straight Cincinnati Player-of-the Year awards.

The family Francisco—at back, Hiawatha, Donna, and D'Juan. Dwayne is just below Donna, and Shaun in front.

record-breaking runners.

In his four years at the Montgomery school, Hiawatha, in spite of knee surgery after his sophomore season, would win 50 games and lose only the state title match in 1981. Moeller brought home the rest of the Ohio titles when he was there, and each was accompanied by a mythical national championship. A bursting back, Francisco ran for 3,319 yards and 37 touchdowns, twice being named as the local Player of the Year and once—in his senior season of 1982, when he was honored as an All-American—as the state's.

He was the best runner Moeller had ever produced—until his brother came along two years later. D'Juan broke Hiawatha's records for rushing yards, with 4,070, and as a senior scored 26 touchdowns. For his incredible Crusader career, he averaged 8.6 yards per carry, and, in concert with his big brother, ran the Francisco streak to four straight Cincinnati Player of the Year awards. Unlike Hiawatha, he was *twice* a high school All-American.

D'Juan and Hiawatha also ran together in the spring, on the Moeller track team. They would arrive at the meets with the horn blaring "Dixie" on the 1967 Chrysler they called the General Lee, because it looked like it belonged on the *Dukes of Hazzard*. Then, being proficient at both sprinting and handoffs, they'd hunker down with the 400-meter relay squad that won a state championship.

After Moeller, the Franciscos played together at Notre Dame, as well—under Faust, who this time could fairly be accused of recruiting them.

Richard Hall

Wyoming running back class of 1998

98

WHEN HE WAS IN THE FIFTH GRADE, RICHARD HALL ENROLLED AT THE CINCINNATI ACADEMY OF PHYSICAL EDUCATION, BECAUSE THAT'S WHERE his idol, Carlos Snow, had cut his swath. But before Hall was in the eighth, the school had closed down.

In 1997, Hall was Ohio's best player.

So he went to Wyoming, broke Snow's area record for touchdowns, finished second to Snow in Ohio history for rushing yards, like Snow was named the state's top player as a senior, and accepted a scholarship to play at Ohio State because that's where his role model had gone. Apparently, though, it just wasn't meant for Hall to follow in the tracks of Snow.

OSU never admitted him. There was an academic issue, and some bad advice about attending a branch campus, and basically a regrettable mess that caused Hall to miss two entire years of football—three if you take into account the season he had to sit out after he transferred to the University of Cincinnati.

By that time, Hall was no longer the gust of wind that, in his legendary high school career, had opposing coaches comparing him to Gale Sayers and Barry Sanders. The former Cowboy was UC's leading runner by his senior season, but inertia, injuries, and inactivity had intercepted his sprint to greater things.

His plight was not unlike Snow's, in the end. Snow had succeeded at Ohio State, but, interrupted by ailments, not at the level that his high school heroics would have portended. He wasn't the back that Hall had watched so excitedly as a 5-year-old, sitting next to his grandfather until the CAPE icon touched the ball, at which point both would be standing in eager expectation of still another score. "Aw, that's a touchdown," the boy would say to his ancestor.

Often enough, it was. And more often than that, Hall found the end zone for Wyoming. Snow's local record fell on the last night of October in 1998, when, against Indian Hill, his successor-in-spirit took the first handoff 90 yards for his 108th touchdown.

When the season ended with a loss to Coldwater in the state semifinals, Hall had scored a staggering 46 touchdowns and run for 2,855 yards, a measly three feet off the Ohio record set the same year by Ryan Brewer of Troy (and broken three years later by Jason Bainum of Williamsburg). Like his rushing yardage, Hall's career total of 121 touchdowns stood second in the state.

He did it all with an elusive genius that was more than most high school tacklers could cope with. "Basically in the open field—and I'm not trying to be cocky or anything—I'm unstoppable in the open field," Hall said. "When I get the ball in the open field, it's lights out."

Without being cocky or anything, he might have called it a white-out, as well.

Like a lot of Snow.

the Harkraders
Jerry, Mike, and Rob

Middletown running backs class of '52, 76, '78

52, 76, 79

THE HARKRADERS, JERRY, THE OLD MAN, AND SONS MIKE AND ROB, WERE MIDDLETOWN'S ROYAL FOOTBALL FAMILY. JERRY WAS MIDDIE CAPTAIN AND HALFBACK FOR A TIGER ELLISON team that was ranked as high in the state as Number 6. He averaged seven yards a clip that season, played safety and linebacker, and was the best player on the field when the Middies beat a good Alliance team quarterbacked by none other than Len Dawson, who presaged his MVP trophy in Super Bowl IV by throwing for 204 yards against the Middies—and he did it with a wet ball.

Jerry was named the Number 2 gridder in the Greater Cincinnati area in 1951, behind Don Nuxhall, Hamilton's captain, as the blue collar boys

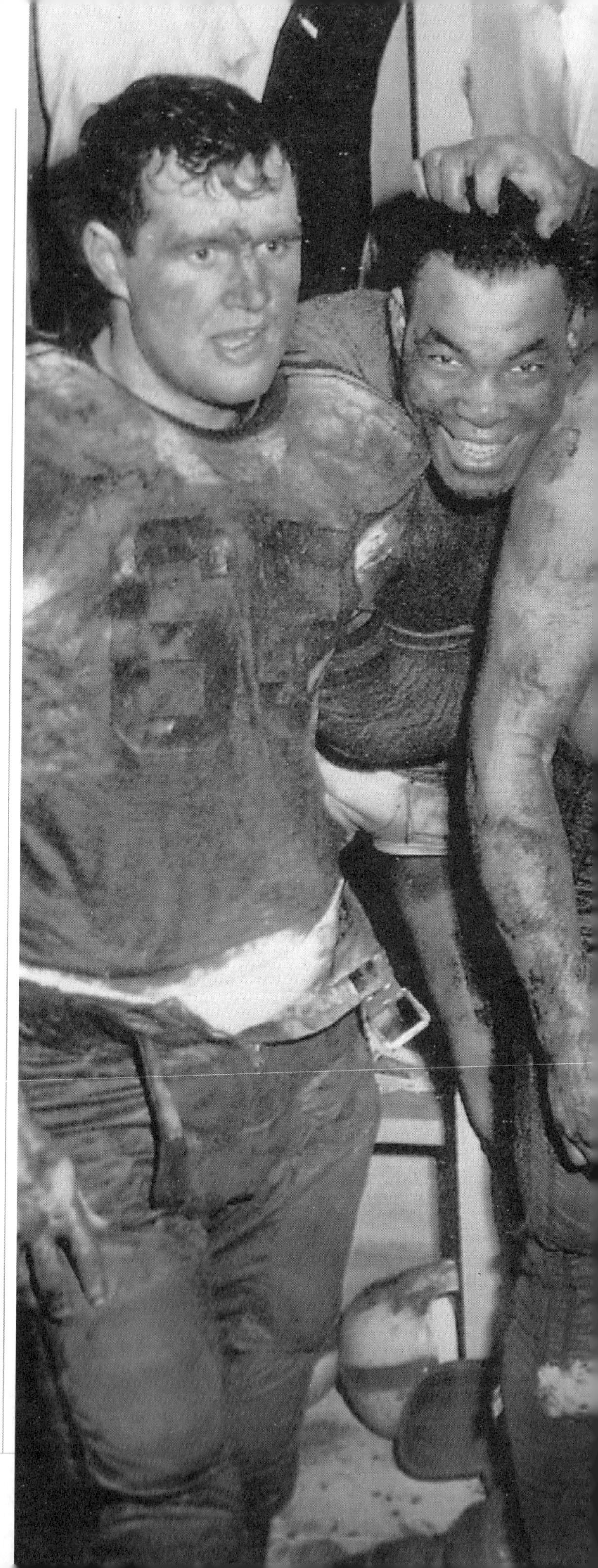

The Rose Bowl win of early 1955 was one of Harkrader's great moments. The celebratory OSU posse included Jim Reichenbach, Jim Parker, Hubert Bobo, Dave Liggett, Hopalong Cassady, Harkrader, and (seated) Bobby Watkins.

from Hamilton and Middletown completely locked Cincinnati out of the All-State berths. (First-teamers were Nuxhall's quarterback, Bob Lakes, who made the team as a linebacker, and Hamilton Catholic's big Notre Dame-bound center, Jim Mense. Nuxhall and Harkrader made the second team, along with Dorsie Blankenship, Hamilton's offensive guard.)

In the North-South High School All-Star Game, Jerry was a "sensation at halfback," running for 104 yards on 14 carries, including three straight carries in the third quarter for 53 yards and a touchdown as the South won, 21-19.

Jerry was second-team *UPI* All-State, as well as making the Chic Harley All-Star High School Football Team, along with a Columbus halfback named Howard "Hopalong" Cassady, who would ultimately win the Heisman. Keen prescience by the All-Star judges—and Ohio State, which got both of them.

In OSU's spring practice of 1953, Jerry was called "the best sophomore since Vic Janowicz" and a sure starter, but he injured his knee, which plagued him throughout his career. Some observers said the knee was the only reason Harkrader was Cassady's backup. Even so, in the Rose Bowl of January, 1955, "the wettest, muddiest in 21 years," he set up OSU's final TD with a 15-yard pass reception in a heavy downpour that put the ball on the USC 9, then scored on a pitchout for the 20-7 win—and the national championship.

He went to the New York Giants in the 1956 draft, but the next phase of his life was coaching not playing. At Middletown Fenwick, Jerry was known for foot-racing his players and beating them while running backward. In 1972, the first season of the state playoffs, Fenwick raced into the 1972 semifinal (losing 18-0 to Lorain), then won back-to-back Class A titles in 1973 and 1974. Under the playoff system, Jerry was the first coach to win two state titles. He missed a third straight championship in 1975 when Fenwick lost 11-0 to Newark Catholic in the semifinal (a game that avenged Fenwick's 34-6 semifinal thumping of Newark in 1974 when Jerry's son, Mike, scored four TDs).

His Fenwick boys went deep into the playoffs three more times (losing the 1984 final to Newark 14-6), but for once, the old halfback was having timing problems: his teams had run athwart one of Ohio's all-time small-school dynasties, Newark Catholic, in the finals every year between 1970 and 1978, and winning all but two.

The 1974 season might have been Fenwick's pinnacle, what the *Associated Press* called "the year of the Harkraders"—Jerry was named Class A Coach of the Year, and son Mike became the first junior to win Class A Back of the Year honors. In 1975, Mike repeated as *UPI* All-Ohio and was the small school Back of the Year a second straight time. His three-year totals, said the *AP*, were 4,203 yards and 50 TDs.

His brother, Rob, was Ohio's Back of the Year in 1977 as a junior, gaining 1,000-plus yards and scoring 23 TDs. He was also in the state track 100 and 200-dash finals, and in 1978, when Fenwick lost to Newark 20-6 in the state semifinal, Rob was second-team All-Ohio.

Mike and Rob both went on to play at Indiana, but Mike set the records. In November of 1976, the 5-7 tailback with near 10-second speed became the fourth freshman in NCAA history (and the first Big Ten back) to rush for 1,000 yards. In 1980 he became the seventh player in Big Ten history to surpass 3,000 yards, rushing 18 times for 117 yards in a 27-17 October loss to OSU.

His seriously ill father looked on, as he had almost every Saturday of the season. But he was so ill that on the trip back to Middletown he could not recall his son's 36-yard run halfway through the fourth quarter, the run that pushed him over 3,000 yards.

By the time Mike graduated, he was Indiana's all-time career rushing champ—3,257 yards, a mark unbroken until 1988.

The school tradition at Fenwick today is the stadium's victory bell, rung after each victory and in memory of Jerry Harkrader, unlikely to be forgotten in Middletown, for his courage both on and off the field.

Bob Hoernschemeyer

Elder running back class of 19**43**

43

The game was simpler then. You had an athlete like Bob Hoernschemeyer, you just lined him up in the single-wing formation,
a few yards behind the center, snapped him the ball, and started knocking people down.

Hoernschemeyer's prowess was such that one Sunday afternoon game against Purcell, when he scored 27 points in six minutes, landed him in the Guinness Book of World Records. His six passing TDs against Nebraska in 1943 is still first in Indiana's record book (and his 817 yards in punt returns, 1943-'44, is second).

It worked for Elder. Babe Bartlett knew what he had in Hoernschemeyer, although that required no particular genius. While Bartlett was an illustrious coach, even the Price Hill schoolboys knew that Hunchy was something special. In the summer, they'd steer their bikes over to the cemetery where Hoernschemeyer worked, just to watch him paint the fence.

As a sophomore, two years removed from the death of his father, the versatile *wunderkind* carried Elder to its first undefeated football season (marred only by a scoreless tie with Withrow). By the time he was a senior, Hunchy's legend was well-established. And yet, nobody could imagine that, against Purcell, *in the final six minutes* of the 1942 game, the Panthers' triple-threat tailback would run for two touchdowns, pass for another, score another off an interception, and kick all the extra points. (He would have done the punting, too, had there been occasion for it.)

Nor was it foreseeable, even by his most ardent West Side admirers, that Hoernschemeyer would start the next season at Indiana University as a 17-year-old freshman quarterback and lead the nation in total offense. Along the way, Bill and Emma's boy beat Ohio State and scorched Nebraska for 458 yards, most of it with a passing game that produced six touchdowns. Just a few months after leading the Elder baseball team to its first state championship, Hoernschemeyer was an All-American.

But it was wartime, and just like that, he was off to the Navy. He came back as a pro, the object of a bidding war won by Chicago Rockets of the All-America Football Conference. Hoernschemeyer spent four years in the AAFC, until it folded, then signed on with the Detroit Lions, where he shared the backfield with all-time greats Doak Walker and Bobby Layne. Behind that historic group, the Lions won two NFL titles. Two was also the number of Pro Bowls played in by the former star of St. Teresa grade school.

As a pro, Hoernschemeyer was a short-yardage specialist who nevertheless managed to reel off the longest ground gains in the league on three separate occasions. He also managed to lead the Lions in rushing for four years running, all the while earning the reputation as "the best third-down back in pro football."

To top it off, he passed for nearly as many yards as he ran for, while also—at various times—punting, returning kicks, and playing defense. After just four years in the more enduring league, Hoernschemeyer's rushing yardage stood second all-time to Steve Van Buren's—ahead of Bronko Nagurski—the problem being that AAFC yards were not included in NFL records. Also not included was the plain fact self-evident to most of Hoernschemeyer's hometown—that Hunchy was something special.

He was, in the final analysis, perhaps the best all-around player to ever come out of Cincinnati.

DeHart Hubbard

Walnut Hills sprinter class of 19**21**

21

DEHART HUBBARD'S CRIME WAS EXCESSIVE SPEED. THE YOUNG FELLOW WAS SO FAST THAT WHEN A NEW BOY WOULD TURN UP AT WALNUT HILLS High School, purporting to be an athlete, the coach would send him outside to race Hubbard. The new lad would take his stance 40 yards from the finish line, but when he looked around for his opponent, there was Hubbard *behind* him, set to run 60 yards—*and over hurdles*. It was the only way the contest would be at all sporting.

Searching unremittingly for competition, Hubbard would run wherever he was invited or challenged. As a high school junior, he sprinted and jumped for a couple of track clubs in Pittsburgh and also, reportedly, in the Penn Relays. That was evidently the complaint during the following football season when, as Hubbard practiced with his Walnut Hills team between 1920's first game and its second, a car of self-important administrators rolled up to the field with grim tidings. By whatever scholastic ordinance, Walnut's only black player was ruled ineligible.

That, however, was unacceptable to Hubbard's teammates. Shortly thereafter, captain George Mason gathered them together with a recommendation. Mason felt that if Hubbard were not allowed to play, the rest of them shouldn't either. They unanimously agreed.

Hubbard was curiously reinstated in time for baseball season, and history will never know what he might have accomplished with a football in his mitts. It's safe to say, though, that he wouldn't have been caught from behind.

At the University of Michigan, which he attended as a result of winning a scholarship contest, Hubbard embarked on a track and field career that would bring him seven Big Ten championships and world records in the 60-yard dash, the 100, and the long jump.

It was in the latter, though, that the scholarly superstar left his most enduring mark. At Paris in 1924, representing the United States in the famous Chariots of Fire games, Hubbard became the first African-American to win an Olympic gold medal.

For that great distinction, he was eminently eligible and impeccably suited. Hubbard was the worthiest sort of champion, the type unwilling to rest on his renown. Back in Cincinnati, he organized baseball and basketball teams and worked fifteen years for the Cincinnati Recreation Commission, leaving only when he felt stymied in his attempts to make a more significant difference. Repairing to Cleveland, he was appointed racial relations advisor for the Federal Public Housing Authority.

When he died in 1976, Hubbard was nineteen years a member of the National Track Hall of Fame and more than half a century removed from his leather helmet. "In retrospect," Mason reflected in the Walnut Hills alumni newsletter, at the age of 96, "I'm really glad DeHart didn't play football that season. He might have been hurt and his career would have been ruined. Maybe things do turn out for the best."

On that score, his old teammates would have unanimously agreed yet again.

Jordan to the rescue

In 1971, and hanging on to a four-point lead with less than a minute to play, the Sycamore Aviators' first undefeated season was on the line. Their opponent, Wyoming, dropped back to pass—and the ball was picked off by Sycamore junior **Paul Jordan**. His 40-yard return seemed to put the game away, but a penalty gave the Cowboys one more chance.

Again Wyoming dropped back to pass.

Again Paul Jordan stepped in and intercepted.

Again he returned it for a touchdown.

This time, it was a 60-yard return, and it stuck.

Jordan had scored his 35th touchdown—his 241st point of the season—to lead the city and—more important to Paul—Sycamore had its first undefeated season.

Jordan had grown up in the Sycamore district, playing with most of his teammates since pee-wee football. While a few of them succumbed to the lure of Moeller, Paul and his friends stayed in the public school where, early on, he made an impression.

"We went through a week of practice before we realized he was only a freshman," recalled Sycamore coach Dave Hurst. "And right then we knew he was no ordinary freshman."

This extraordinary freshman broke into the varsity where he made such an impression as a defensive back that after the last game of his freshman year, a college scout—checking out some of the team's seniors—wanted to offer him a scholarship.

"Somehow Paul had worn number 82 in that game and wasn't in the program," Hurst recalled. "I said to this coach, 'Hold onto your coffee. The kid's only a freshman.'"

By his junior year in 1971, the 5-10, 180-pound halfback was playing both ways and did the placekicking, as well. He gained 1,537 yards on the ground and picked up an additional 216 yards receiving. While leading the city, he scored nearly a quarter of his team's points—personally outscoring 34 of the Cincinnati area's 40 football teams.

Sycamore went 7-3 in 1972 and Jordan's rushing totals slipped to 1,170 yards, but he successfully defended his city scoring title, scoring all 23 points in the team's final game against Wyoming, edging Princeton's Mike Gayles, 175-174.

He showed up in *Sports Illustrated's* "Faces in the Crowd," where the magazine pointed out that in Jordan's four years, he, personally, had scored 522 points while opposing teams in the aggregate totaled 253. After graduation, Jordon went to West Virginia where he was a three-year letterman for Bobby Bowden's Mountaineers.

BILL KUNTZ AND HIS STADIUM

Every school has one fan who seems to know about —or has seen—every great play, every great player, and every great game in the school's football history. But only one of them has **Bill Kuntz**. Out in Harrison, a few steps from Indiana basketball territory, Bill has been announcing the school's football games since Harry Truman was the decider. Bill, who played the six-man version of the game for Harrison, was asked to take over the mike in 1947. Since he owned the local newspaper, the *Harrison Press*, and had to cover the game anyway, it was an easy decision.

A few years later, in 1950, the school hired **Jim "Red Dog" Daugherty** to coach. His tenure was a high point in Harrison football: his teams won 57 games in the seven seasons he spent on the edge of Ohio, losing only eight, and tying three others. He had two undefeated seasons and a 26-game winning streak.

Charlie Key on the run

As Kuntz recalls it, the strength of Daugherty's teams was a trio of running backs who each led the city in scoring. The first was **Jim Dole**, a slick, shifty runner who scored at least one touchdown in 21 straight games. He went on to Louisville where his brush with fame was that he caught passes from Johnny Unitas.

Kuntz was at XU's field when Dole and the Cardinals came to town and battled the Musketeers. They returned downriver 27-13 losers but Dole accounted for six of the Cardinal points with a TD catch from Johnny U. (He confessed later to Kuntz that he'd thrown his hands up in self-defense, and no one was more surprised that he actually caught the ball than he was.)

Two years later, **Jim Kater** was finishing up a career at Harrison that would see him score 360 points. To Kuntz's experienced eye, Kater was the best athlete of the bunch. He excelled at basketball and baseball and was a big, bruising fullback-type runner who led the team to its first undefeated season.

The third of Daugherty's backs, **Ted Harless**, is the only Harrison football player to have his jersey retired. Known for his speed and long runs, Harless scored four touchdowns in a game against Indian Hill on runs of 45, 47, 55, and 60 yards. He later had a 99-yard run against Sycamore in which Harless was described as taking two tacklers with him for several yards before he broke clear.

So for nearly sixty years, Bill Kuntz has watched, announced, and written about the football players of Harrison. He'll tell you about Dole's elusiveness, Kater's strength, and Harless' speed. He'll rattle off the names and exploits of a dozen other players who played in front of him.

For those who weren't there, he's a walking encyclopedia of Harrison football. The attention spans of most fans, when it comes to high school football, are limited. They remember their teams and perhaps they followed the teams when their own kids were in high school. They might remember Harrison's **Charlie Key** and the night he scored six touchdowns against Mason or his 31 touchdowns and his more than 2,000 yards rushing in the year 2000 and think he's the best there ever was.

But they don't really know.

And if they really want to know how Key, or anybody else, stacks up, they only need to ask Bill Kuntz. He knows, for instance, that Charlie Key is most like Harless, and he's all over the Rose-Hulman Institute's record book (Charlie is first in rushing TDs—38—and first in all-purpose yards—4,400—and he's in the top ten in at least another half dozen categories.)

And if your school has a Bill Kuntz you might just do what Harrison did—name the football stadium after him.

Nap McCallum

Milford | running back | class of 1981

81

YOU CAN GOOGLE "NAPOLEON MCCALLUM" TO WATCH A VIDEO OF HIS LAST RUSHING ATTEMPT. WARNING: THIS CLIP CONTAINS EXPLICIT CONTENT. Viewer discretion is advised. Running backs are strongly cautioned.

"Nap" McCallum, an All-Ohio running back at Milford High School and two-time All-American at Navy, took his last hand-off at Candlestick Park in San Francisco in 1994 during a *Monday Night Football* game between the 49ers and the Los Angeles Raiders. When the play was over, he lay on top of 49ers linebacker Ken Norton, Jr., who knew, instantly, something was horribly wrong.

"Don't move!" said Norton. "Don't move!"

The replay showed Norton grabbing McCallum from behind and falling against his left leg—still planted, unfortunately, in the turf. Frank Gifford urged viewers to turn their heads, while his partner, Dan Dierdorf, was at a stunned loss for words.

"Oh Lord," groaned Dierdorf. "Oh Lord . . ."

The leg was as bad as it looked. Complete hyperextension and dislocation of the knee. Damage to three ligaments. Ruptured artery. Severed tendons. Calf and hamstring, ripped from the bone. They put horses down with lesser injuries.

McCallum was airlifted to a hospital where surgeons told him they might have to amputate. Football players know when they put on the pads they're just one injury away from retirement. They just don't expect to lose a limb. The doctors saved Nap's, although he underwent multiple operations and spent months unable to lift his foot due to the nerve damage.

Nap believed he would play again, but after losing a footrace to one of the neighborhood kids—a little girl who didn't look much older than a pre-schooler—he decided to walk away from the game while he still could.

You can go to websites such as *Extremesportclips*, *Manlyweb*, or *20minutestokill* and watch what happened to McCallum that night in San Francisco. His physical trauma occupies a gothic chamber in the Football Injury Hall of Fame alongside the compound fractures that disabled Tim Krumrie of the Cincinnati Bengals and Washington Redskins quarterback Joe Theismann.

McCallum's personal filmography is better served by plays that turned the head rather than the stomach, and they began sixteen years earlier in Milford, Ohio, when his high school coach, on the first day of summer practice, took one look at his lanky sophomore and knew he needed a promotion.

When George Carl, the coach, informed his young defensive back that he was being moved up from the JV squad to the varsity, effective immediately, Nap wasn't sure how his father would feel about him cracking pads with the older boys. "My daddy might not like that," he said to the coach.

Napoleon Sr. coached the wrestling team at Princeton High School (in addition to his teaching duties), so he never objected to his son's athletic aspirations. But on the McCallum eleven-acre farmstead in Milford, work always trumped play. You had chores and homework done or you didn't go to practice. Nap helped his father log, clear and fence-in their property, build two barns, and remodel the house. He was out of bed at 6:30 a.m., feeding cows and goats, working in the fields, and maintaining his 3.0 grade point average through high school.

McCallum played three years on the defensive side of the ball for Milford, unused at running back until his senior year when he rushed for 1,625 yards (fourth best in Greater Cincinnati) and scored 17 touchdowns while continuing to make a menace of himself on defense with 12 interceptions. He was All-League, All-City, and All-State.

Nap was a three-sport star, and football wasn't even his favorite. Wrestling was. In track, he had personal bests of 13-6 in the pole vault, qualifying for the state meet, and 6-8 in the high jump—strong indicators of his natural athleticism.

None of it changed his career plans. Nap went to the Naval Academy to become a pilot and an astronaut, turning down offers from Syracuse to Georgia Tech and points between.

Napoleon Sr. was pleased by his son's choice among

post-secondary schools. Annapolis was a good place, he said, for his "sheltered kid." Midshipmen had to get up early. They had to follow orders. They had study hours and a curfew. They also had a military obligation—five years of active duty—which Nap was less inclined to fulfill the more his gridiron stature grew.

After rushing for over 700 yards as a sophomore, he considered transferring to another school—one where they didn't blow reveille at that godawful hour in the morning, no white-gloved officers conducted surprise room inspections, and the only formation in which he had to pass muster would be on the football field.

His breakout came when he was a junior in 1983. That was the year he led the nation in all-purpose yardage (rushing, receiving, and returning punts and kicks) and finished sixth in the Heisman balloting. His coach, Gary Tranquill, attributed Nap's performance to hard work and physical maturity. Off-season weight-training, along with some timely assistance from Mother Nature, transformed the "skinny and under-developed" player McCallum had been at Milford High School—his words, by the way—into a rangy 6-2, 220-pound consensus All-American and NFL prospect.

Nap could have dropped out of the academy, done a two-year hitch as an enlisted man, and set sail in the NFL at the still young age of 23. That other Cincinnatian with Navy credentials, Roger Staubach, advised Nap against it. When he decided to stay the course, Navy gave McCallum the full Heisman treatment, posing him in an 18th century naval uniform in front of the cannons on the *U.S. Constellation* in Baltimore's Inner Harbor.

The legend on his promotional poster read: "I have not yet begun to run," which, unfortunately, turned out to be true; in the second game of the 1984 season he went down with a broken leg. Nap returned the following fall after the Naval Academy granted his request for a fifth year of eligibility under the NCAA's hardship rule.

It was the first such special dispensation ever given an athlete in the service academies, and it resulted in another All-American season and another all-purpose national title. Even so, it didn't thrill Nap's mother, Virginia, who was a schoolteacher and wanted to see her son graduate on time.

The decision to "redshirt" McCallum didn't get a pass from the dress gray folks at West Point, either.

McCallum, said Sports Illustrated, "IS Navy...a phenomenon found only once every 20 years or so at a service academy." He left with 26 Navy records, was twice All-American, and the NCAA record holder for all-purpose yardage.

The editor of the *Armed Forces Journal*—a West Point grad—fired a shot across the bow at the academy for being more interested in producing another Heisman winner than preparing Midshipman McCallum for his duties as a professional naval officer.

That drew a response from Navy Secretary John Lehman, Jr. "I should have hoped for a more benevolent attitude," wrote Lehman after the Midshipmen, without McCallum, lost to Army in 1984 for the first time since the 1977 season, "inasmuch as West Point has just won—with a very fine performance—its normal allotment of one game in every eight."

The midshipman McCallum sets sail.

It was Lehman who allowed Nap to play in the NFL after the Raiders selected McCallum in the fourth round of the 1986 draft despite his impending service commitment. Ensign McCallum gained 536 yards for the Raiders that season, changing his sailor whites each day and commuting between LA and Long Beach, where he was stationed aboard an aircraft carrier in dry dock.

His schedule was so tight he took his wife to the team movies on Friday nights so they could spend time together.

Lehman's replacement, James Webb, Jr., was not impressed by McCallum's time management skills. He revoked Nap's playing privileges after his rookie season and ordered him out to sea, where he earned his combat pay escorting oil tankers through the Strait of Hormuz. He stayed in shape by running laps on the decks of warships and worked out on his SoloFlex in his cramped stateroom.

Returning to the Raiders in 1990, McCallum saw limited action over the next four seasons on special teams and in short-yardage situations before his catastrophic injury. The payoff came, finally, in 2003 when Nap was enshrined in the College Football Hall of Fame with some slouches named Marino, Lott, Winslow, and Reggie "The Minister of Defense" White. That year Navy also began handing out The Napoleon McCallum Award to the graduating varsity football player with the most all-purpose yards during his career at Annapolis.

Nap's Hall of Fame biography reads: "When it came to advancing the football, few players did it as well as Navy's Napoleon McCallum. As the French emperor gained territory across Europe, this Napoleon gained ground in football stadiums across the nation . . . ."

Through the 2007 season, no McCallum recipient at Navy had surpassed the 7,172 total yards of the award's namesake and only two players in NCAA Division I history—DeAngelo Williams of Memphis and Ricky Williams of Texas—had accumulated more all-purpose yardage in their respective college careers.

McCallum didn't have the stopwatch speed that keeps defensive coordinators up all night. His best clocking in the 40 was just under 4.6. What he *did* have was deceptive speed. Tacklers were fooled by his long, smooth stride, which made him faster and quicker than he appeared to his pursuers. Tranquill, his coach at Navy, described Nap as a "glider" who had what all great backs possess: vision.

Nap didn't realize his dream of becoming an astronaut, but after football he launched a successful business career in Las Vegas, and, at last report, was ambulating around the golf course with nothing worse than a 16-handicap.—*Michael Graham*

KELTON LINDSAY AND THE MASON-LEBANON RIVALRY

Great rivalries are defined by great performances—and the amount of ire they provoke in the breasts of the vanquished. Great games stick in the minds of their fans. Or perhaps the eye. Talk to any Mason player from 1965 and it isn't Mason's nine victories that stand out; it's the one loss to Lebanon. The score was 14-8, at the end of the season, in the rain, as though even nature conspired against the Comets. Forty years later, the team's fullback, Keith Carter, confessed, "I think about that loss every day."

The competition between the two schools may have been more cultural phenomenon than athletic, where the dislike one felt for the other was best expressed once each year on an autumn Friday night. It was a kind of border dispute, actually. Picture Mason's bucolic locals standing alongside Route 42 and tugging at their forelocks as Lebanon's commercial aristocracy drove past on their way to Cincinnati. Mason quietly occupied the forlorn approaches to historic, well-settled old Lebanon. It was barely visible to the naked eye, an insignificant little moon in Lebanon's outer orbit. Surely it was natural that the parvenu wished to trounce their betters up the road. And just as natural that Lebanon wanted to thump the upstarts, relegating them always to cornfields that would not produce corn forever.

And so the rivalry was a kind of tug-of-war, not a brawl. Even Mason's football team was recent—1962—and when Lebanon deigned to schedule its country cousin, Mason seemed to hear Lebanon's lip curl. Lebanon expected to win, and it did. It won every game for the first ten years. When Mason finally broke through in 1974, it was on a mud-soaked field in a game that had been postponed for a day. To earn the 18-13 victory, the Comets blocked two punts for touchdowns, then won the game when **Jeff Bentley** passed six yards to **Greg Richards** for the winning score. The next year, Richards quarterbacked the team to its second victory over the Warriors, and Bentley went to the University of Cincinnati on a football scholarship. (In an unusual twist for the time, Bentley dropped football and played basketball for Ed Badger's 'Cats, finishing his athletic career as captain of the basketball team.)

It was an eternity until the 1990s, when the rivalry began to turn. The country to the south was no longer country; it was a wealthy, sprawling suburban enclave, no longer a hamlet of less than 1,800 people. The size was showing on the football field, too. By 1997, Mason had won five of the last seven games. The plantation next door would have one last moment, though, largely because of a kid named **Kelton Lindsay**, who may have been the finest running back to ever come out of Warren County. (Lindsay and his quarterback, **Brady Merchant**, would be named by the *Western Star* as co-athletes of the century, beating out Jeff Bentley, which proved nothing to Mason except the newspaper's traditional bias.)

The 1997 game was an early-season showdown, as

Bentley could throw, but he liked shooting better and turned to basketball at UC.

highly anticipated as any the two teams ever played. Lindsay began with a 91-yard TD on the game's opening kickoff, an auspicious moment for parity. But on Mason's first play from scrimmage, Mason's **Craig Adkins**—who would graduate with more than twenty scoring plays of over 20 yards—broke a 57-yard scoring run of his own. By the third quarter, however, Lebanon had built a 32-13 lead. One of the scores came on Lindsay's 66-yard interception run. While the night seemed to belong to Lebanon, the quick-footed Adkins did not go gently into it. He led a comeback—228 rushing yards to Lindsay's 79—that got Mason within five points. When Brady Merchant's 51-yard pass play set up a Lindsay score from the 2, it was all over, and Lebanon had a 40-27 win.

Behind Lindsay and Merchant, Lebanon—the Number 1 ranked Division II team in Ohio—went to the state semifinals before losing 28-20 to Defiance, the eventual state champion. It was quite a year for Lindsay. He was the top junior prospect in Ohio and D-II's co-player of the year, a 190-pound back with 4.4 speed and 2,194 newly acquired yards on his resumé, along with 41 TDs. He'd gained 9.5 yards every time he touched the ball, and college recruiters from everywhere were carrying his photograph in their wallets. Said his coach, **Dave Brausch**, "He's the type of kid you might only get the chance to coach once."

Lebanon would be even more balanced in 1998, when the Mason rivalry was again such that Lindsay would say, "We knew this was going to be the best game we would play all season." Lebanon won that one, too, and Lindsay was true to his word: he had runs of 63 and 69 yards—174 yards on 20 carries—and two interceptions.

Not much went right for Mason; everything did for Lebanon, as it did all season. The Warriors steamrolled most of the opposition, averaging over 50 points a game. Lindsay's totals were a mere 1,500 yards—but Lebanon had two other backs who gained 1,422 between them. Together, they trashed Wilmington 88-7, Little Miami 56-0, Norwood 74-0. Down to earth against Chardon in the state final, they won the title 27-21, with a sleeper known as "the hook and ladder," in which a receiver runs

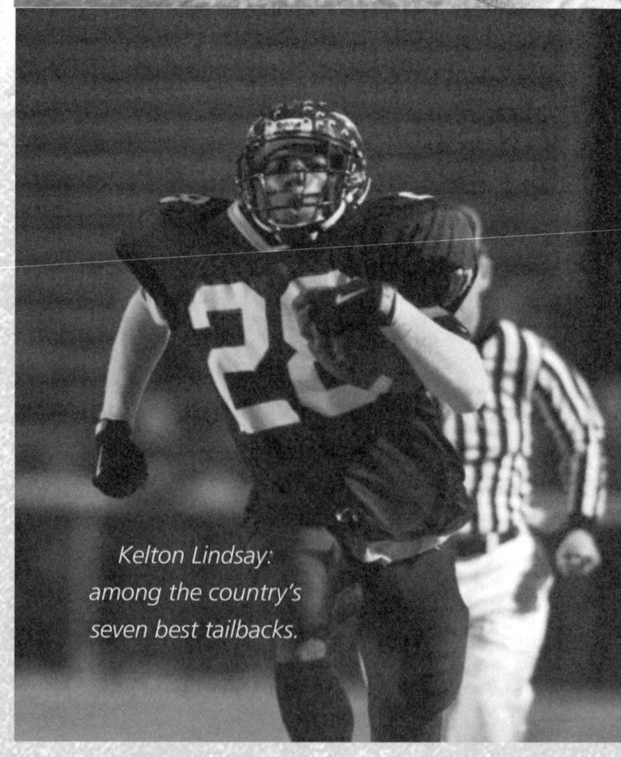

Kelton Lindsay: among the country's seven best tailbacks.

a hook pattern, then pitches to a trailing back.

With the score tied 21-all and less than a minute left, Merchant threw to receiver **David Linville**, who curled in, caught the pass, then lateraled to Lindsay circling out of the backfield. Lindsay went down the sideline for the score. It might have been a trick play, but Lebanon practiced it every day, had run it several times during the season, and Chardon was aware of it. This time it worked perfectly.

Lindsay was an All-American, twice All-State, and ranked among the country's seven best tailbacks. In his four-year Lebanon career, he'd rushed for 5,483 yards and scored 76 TDs, headed for OSU in a college class rated Number 2 in the country.

The Mason-Lebanon games continued for only four more years, split evenly between them. Just as the rivalry had truly become one on the field, it was over. Oddly, the two games with Kelton Lindsay were the last hurrah for Lebanon within the rivalry, and for Lindsay, as well. Even as fans recalled him as the fastest, most powerful high school back they'd ever seen, he began his college career as a defensive back, lettered in 1999, then tore up his knee in a pickup basketball game. He never played again.

Odd, also, that for so much time Lebanon had been largely unaware of Mason's existence. And now the cleats were on the other foot. Mason, reinvented as the hottest residential spot in Greater Cincinnati, had grown out of its infrastructure *and* the rivalry.

Mason was no longer preoccupied with its neighbor to the north. Many of its amazing influx of new residents were unaware there'd ever *been* a rivalry. Rivalries were articles of faith, of course. If one of the rivals no longer believed, then the rivalry didn't exist.

And so it didn't.

Beating Lebanon: A long time coming. That's Biehle (70), toweriing over both teammates and opposition.

65
77

This scene is from Walnut Hills in 1942, featuring Jack Beyersdorfer, a 6-1, 170-pounder who was the team's punter, play-caller, and in spite of being the fullback, did a lot of the passing. It explains why he was the team's MVP, although here he's aided magnificently by the textbook blocking of his end.

THE READING YEARS: KEN MINOR, TOM FOUCHEY & DESHAWN WYNN

His senior year at Reading High, **Ken Minor's** defensive coordinator was **Jerry Glanville**, already polishing his eccentricities for his years in the NFL where he would be known for the Houston Astrodome's "House of Pain," will-call tickets for Elvis, and a mouth timed at a legitimate 4.2.

The year before, coaching at Lima, Glanville passed equipment over the dutch doors, asking, "Do you believe in pain and misery?" And underclassman, their reedy voices cracking, would answer, "Yes, sir. I *do* believe in pain and misery." At Reading, Glanville did not allow players to speak to him except on the field. When Minor ended up with a helmet that didn't fit, he couldn't tell Glanville, and therefore ended up hatless at tackling practice.

"Well, Minor," said Glanville, speaking at last—and about to send Minor into the drill—"let's see how tough you are."

Minor was a tough kid, but he wasn't Bronko Nagurski. Fortunately, Reading's head coach, **Bill Atsalis**, stopped Glanville, who was soon off to Western Kentucky and the helmeted world of the NFL. Contemplating his own life in football, Minor grasped that such eccentricity might be best held in check.

Although Reading had its moments, it was not known as a neighborhood for the exporting of football players into the college ranks. Minor, though, was one of them, reunited at Wilmington College with his old coach, Atsalis, who—along with Minor, a hotshot Williamsburg quarterback named Phil Redrow, and a handful of topflight small-college athletes—laid the groundwork for 20 straight winning seasons at WC. Previously, there hadn't been a winning season since 1955 and a meager 17 wins in the 15 intervening years.

By this time, Minor was a tight end and a good one. "If you threw it he caught it," said his QB, Redrow, "then he took a bite out of it. If you didn't throw it, he took a bite out of *you*. He had a great instinct to follow the QB on a scramble. I knew he would always be there as an option, unless he took time to chew on a DE's leg. He thought they were tasty...."

Minor was back at Reading in the fall of 1973, on

Minor, back in the day: first he was a good tight end at Wilmington, then an assistant.

Jerry Daugherty's staff. Daugherty, who had been a standout quarterback at Anderson High, was putting together his second unbeaten season at Reading (and a 25-game winning streak) but fell gravely ill. He was in the hospital when his team went into the playoffs, losing eventually to Ironton, 7-0 in the Ohio AA semifinals.

Daugherty was Ohio's AA Coach of the Year, and his QB, **Randy Christophel**, was first team All-State. (Randy's father, Bob, was a single-wing quarterback for Reading in 1944 when the Blue Devils had their first unbeaten season.) But Daugherty, at age 31 and considered one of Ohio's most promising coaches, died before Reading's next season.

Reading, traditionally a farm team for the powerful mid-century teams of Roger Bacon, now found itself under the gravitational pull of newly built Moeller, which had superseded the older inner-city dynasties of Bacon and Purcell.

(The country of Reading was said to have furnished

ten of Moeller's first twenty-two starters. It was like a fiefdom in which the vassals paid an annual tribute in livestock to the overlord. With the advent of Moeller, though, there was a small rebellion: the Reading parish of Sts. Peter and Paul sent a petition to the archbishop asking that it remain part of Bacon's district, rather than being assigned to Moeller, even though Moeller was only ten or fifteen minutes away. The implication was, of course, that Reading preferred the thief it knew, as opposed to the new thief it *didn't* know.)

In spite of all this, Reading in 1976 put together another unbeaten season, and it was built around a kid that stayed at home, **Tom Fouchey**.

A diminutive 5-8 and 160 pounds, Fouchey played as if he were twice the size. He was such a fierce athlete—at both middle linebacker and running back—that on game day Reading trundled him onto the field in a circus wagon. He was a tireless 4.6 guy who could run 20 sprints in a row, all at speed. Everything he did was at 4.6, the speed and intensity leveraging his weight upwards. Minor had never seen a player like him.

The first thing Minor saw of him was a Reading scrimmage with New Miami. Each team got the ball for seven plays, run from the 30. Fouchey ran a 32 Trap seven times and scored each time—from 70 yards out. "I thought, *My God, we better save some of those for the regular season*," Minor said.

His teammates had a slogan: "The Fouch is loose." Playing favored North College Hill, Fouchey went after Dwayne Crutchfield, a 220-pound running back who would go on to Iowa State and become the Big Eight's leading rusher. "The undisputed heavyweight champ of the gridiron," the *Enquirer* called him. Fouchey, however, was full of dispute. He was on Crutchfield every play, making virtually every tackle as Reading upset NCH. It was another amazing performance by Fouchey.

> "We had only 17 kids. I used to holler, 'Punt team!' and one guy went in. We beat schools that had 100 guys on the other sideline..."—Jerry Glanville, Reading assistant, 1966

Once, Fouchey nearly lost three fingers in an accident, had himself sewed back together, and played that night's game. When Reading reached the end of the regular season, only Wyoming—also unbeaten—stood in its way. With 4:01 left in the fourth quarter, game tied 8-8, the ball was on Reading's 36-yard line. But when Blue Devil quarterback Randy Anderson handed the ball to his meal-ticket running back, Fouchey ripped off 50 yards.

DeShawn Wynn, the unholy roller, from Reading to the Pack.

On the next play, he got the other 14 yards—the finishing touch on Reading's undefeated season.

Reading was ranked Number 1 in the state all year, but that last night, eight of the ten teams Reading had played lost. By the penurious system of the early playoff years, Reading missed the playoffs by a fraction of a point. Minor was in Akron's Rubber Bowl for the AA finals, watching Elyria Catholic beat Brookville for the title.

"I'm not a homer," he said, "and I know we were

three TDs better than Elyria. Man, that was hard. The next Friday night, I was wandering around, feeling kind of lost, and I went out to the field. I just wanted to sit in the bleachers for a while. When I got there half the team was there. So we moped a bit, then we talked about our season, and that was it...."

Fouchey's was the finest one-man show in Reading's history. As a senior, he'd gained 1,830 yards, which was then the second highest total in Cincinnati prep history, and he was named Ohio's AA Player of the Year. Fouchey went to Fort Eustis Junior College (Virginia) where his career was ended by a knee injury.

In 1979—his first as head coach—Minor went unbeaten in the league, 8-2 overall, and among other very good players, Minor would have one more supernatural player: **DeShawn Wynn**. The difference between Fouchey and Wynn was that Wynn had big time size.

Wynn gained 1,915 yards and scored 34 TDs in 1998 as a Lockland freshman and made first team All-State. After being injured for most of his sophomore year—and his best friends and coach leaving for elsewhere—Wynn transferred to Reading where he'd played little league football. His eligibility was questioned by the Reading school superintendent who finally gave Wynn clearance to play four games into the season, after the Blue Devils had lost two close games.

In his first game, against Finneytown, Wynn went 80 yards the first time he touched the ball. He scored seven TDs and gained 464 yards on 22 carries as Reading won 49-35.

Reading went 11-3 in that 2000 season, losing 7-0 in the semifinals to the eventual state champion, Amanda-Clearcreek.

"Before a game," said Minor, "I'd say to DeShawn, 'Now I need at least four TDs and 220 yards.' And he'd be on the dot. I'd never seen anything like it. One night, I asked for something like six TDs and 400 yards.

"'Coach,' he said, 'I ain't Superman.'"

Most of the opposition thought he was, though. Before DeShawn arrived, Reading's longest run from scrimmage was 87 yards. He broke that five times. He ran for 2,000 yards and 30 TDs twice—2,283 as a senior, along with a 9.3 average—and his 467 yards against Finneytown in 2000 is still among the top ten rushing games in Ohio schoolboy history. He was a *Parade* All-American, considered by many as the best back in the nation.

Almost every major school east of the Mississippi recruited him, including every Big Ten school. The one school that didn't was the school he wanted: the University of Florida. Who'd have known? The kid from blue collar Reading was a Gator at heart. So Minor sent film. No word. Finally, he called. "You might want to take a look at DeShawn," he said, "because the teams that have been kicking your butt are all after him."

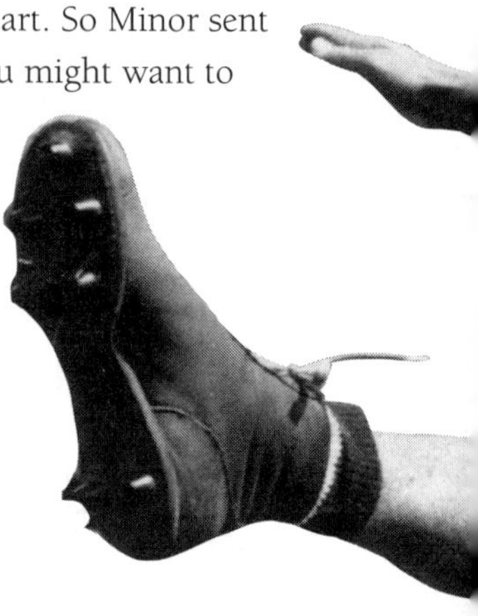

Florida immediately called back.

"Where has this kid been?" they asked.

As a redshirt freshman in 2002, Florida's first road game was against Miami in the Orange Bowl, 70,000 screaming fans.
Ron Zook, the Florida coach who had gotten married in Reading, went over to DeShawn and put his arm around him.

"This ain't Reading, is it?" he said.

Wynn grinned, then rushed for 100 yards on eight carries, including an electrifying 65-yard run on national television.

His four TDs against Florida A&M was the first time in Gator history that a freshman had scored so many times in a single game. The rest of his time at Florida wasn't as beguiling—coaching change, injuries—but he finished his college career in the 2007 BCS Championship game, the Gators' leading rusher, and his 2-yard TD against Ohio State in the second quarter put the Gators up 21-7. He went to Green Bay in the seventh round of the NFL draft.

Minor was moving to a new home, as well, taking a stellar 170-129-1 record to North College Hill where he spent a year as offensive coordinator before becoming head coach at Summit Country Day in 2009. He'd coached in a tough place, he'd coached a pair of the best schoolboys to ever come out of Cincinnati—as well as a few hundred other guys he'd never forget—and he'd spent most of his time on the winning side of the game.

And the best part? He wasn't done yet. Not by a long shot. He was an offensive-minded guy, and long shots were his specialty.

Brother Bernie at XU, and in background, breaking a 45-yard trap against Purcell.

The Roeckers
Bernie and Walt

Roger Bacon halfbacks classes of 1948 & 1957

48, 57

IN HIS LATER YEARS, THE GREAT BRON BACEVICH USED TO SAY THAT WALT ROECKERS WAS THE BEST HIGH SCHOOL FOOTBALL PLAYER HE EVER SAW. Bavevich being the best *coach* that a lot of Cincinnatians ever saw, his judgment must be taken seriously. And yet, his objectivity comes into question.

Could it be that Roeckers simply meant more to him than any other player, and for Bacevich the lines were blurred between importance and preeminence? The two of them, after all, rose together at Roger Bacon; and Roger Bacon rose with *them*. In 1954, Bacevich showed up at the St. Bernard school after twenty years of coaching in Illinois. The same year, Roeckers surfaced as a sophomore maker of headlines.

Backing up a bit, Roeckers was not the first of his family to distinguish himself at the boys-only Franciscan institution. Brother Bernie, a 1948 graduate, had been a wiry, 150-pound running and punting sensation, his reputation resting largely upon his surpassing ability to boot a football far and forever. He averaged 46 yards per punt, and that wasn't the half of it. "What made him such a great punter," recalled Glenn Sample, "was that he kicked the ball so high that you couldn't get a return." In 2000, the *Enquirer* made Roeckers the punter on its All-Century team.

Bernie took his multiple skills to Xavier University, where he scored touchdowns, intercepted passes, buried opponents in their own territory, stood out on the undefeated Salad Bowl champions of 1950, batted over .300 as a shortstop, and was referred to in the papers as "the former Roger Bacon flash." By the time Walt made himself known at Bacon, little big brother, after a military stint in Korea, had embarked on a teaching and coaching career at Amelia, McNicholas, and Milford high schools. He also starred on a world championship softball team—staying with the game into his seven-ties—and for decades refereed football and basketball games. He was, in fact, returning home from a long day of officiating in October, 2004, when he was involved in an automobile accident and died at the age of 74.

The Roeckers boys were raised in a big white house overlooking the University of Cincinnati's Nippert Stadium. When Sample played at UC in the early 1950s, Bernie was doing the same at Xavier, which made the Bearcats just a little nervous. "You could look right down on the field from that house," Sample recalled. "We'd be practicing and we'd look up there and see all kinds of people at the house watching us, people in the windows. We thought, gosh, maybe they're taking movies up there."

On that count, however, Walt was not suspected. The younger Roeckers wasn't yet a teenager, and he and his playful friends were known to the UC athletes as "the Corryville rats. They were always hanging around all over the place," said Sample. "Walt used to climb up on the light stanchions and then jump down into the wire platform that was used to catch the glass if a bulb shattered. They'd shag balls for the kickers, and occasionally take off with one. But they always brought them back. They thought that was funny."

Walter was never slender like his older brother, but stout and powerful and ornery enough to complete the combination. He was just the rugged kind of runner Bacevich needed for the single-wing offense he brought to Roger Bacon. As a sophomore, Roeckers delighted the new coach with 73 points over a five-game stretch, including five touchdowns against Newport Catholic. His exploits were trumpeted in newspapers all across Ohio.

"Walt was one tough cookie," attested Sample. "He was the real deal. Bron told me often that, pound for pound, he was the best."

The 1954 season would be the only losing one in Bacevich's twenty-one years at Roger Bacon. By 1956, he would already have, in Bernie Roeckers' big little brother, his single-season (1,331 yards) and career (3,100) rushing leader, not to mention his top touchdown producer. He would also, thanks to Roeckers, have a head start on the longest stretch of serious winning the city has ever seen.

True to the tradition, Roeckers, in spite of his boyhood ties to UC and a preliminary commitment to LSU, moved on to Xavier. It was what the priests in the local Catholic schools urged their best students and athletes to do—if not Xavier, then Notre Dame or Dayton or Holy Cross, etc.

Not being the scholastic type, however, Roeckers wasn't long for XU. There was an opportunity at Procter and Gamble that suited him better. Bacevich helped him land it. The old coach owed that much, at least, to the most important player he ever had; and perhaps the best.

On that score, as it turns out, there is actually corroboration. Roeckers graduated from Roger Bacon the same year Jim Herbstreit graduated from Reading. Herbstreit went on to captain Ohio State and play in the East-West Shrine Game with Bob Lilly and Mike Ditka. He coached at OSU and Miami. He remains connected to the game by working with his son, Kirk, on the prep classic that brings in many of the best teams in the nation. He also grew up in Silverton with Roger Staubach. And yet, in Herbstreit's view, "The greatest football player I ever saw was Walt Roeckers.

"I mean pure football, in the spirit of Princeton and Columbia, where you go out and beat on each other and then go have a beer. Walt was like out of Boys Town. He was a tough son of a gun, I tell ya. He was similar to Pete Rose, but more. I've seen All-Americans at Ohio State, and I loved Roger Staubach, don't get me wrong—but for the pure spirit of football, Walt Roeckers was the best football player I ever saw."

Like Bacevich said.

Paul Sarringhaus

Hamilton | halfback | class of 19**40**

40

FAME MAY BE FLEETING BUT SO WAS PAUL SARRINGHAUS, WHO AFTER SEVENTY YEARS STILL GETS MOST OF THE BACK-IN-THE-GRIDIRON-DAY VOTES as Hamilton High's best ever running back. Sarringhaus, a dash man on the track team, was big and powerful, the captain of Coach Ray Tilton's unbeaten 1939 team that laid claim to the state championship (a loose affair in those days when the downstate victor did not always—or *ever*—get the spoils). Then—seemingly unsatisfied with his inconclusive prep title—he was the mainstay in OSU's splendid 1942 season when as an All-American

Rose and the Other game

The All-City team of 1959, while finding room for Roger Staubach, was otherwise distinguished by stars of another season: future big-leaguers Jimmy Wynn, Eddie Brinkman and—as an honorable mention—a feisty Western Hills halfback named **Pete Rose**. In 1958, His Scrappiness helped Western Hills engineer one of its best seasons, when the Mustangs were ranked as high as 11th in the state. They set a single-game mark by scoring 60 points against Withrow, thrashed their Turkey Day Day rival, Elder, 31-14—"to prove why they had been called the best offensive team in the city"—and finished as Public League co-champs. Rose scored on an interception on Thanksgiving Day, then traded the yard markers for base paths.

tailback he helped the Buckeyes to their first national title—this one *was* official—and himself to the cover of *LIFE* magazine.

At Hamilton, he was a 185-pound six-footer with, as one local sports scribe put it, "hula hips and the ability to send would-be tacklers out into space as if hit by a truck." In his three high school seasons, Hamilton won all but two of its games. In one of those losses (a 20-0 loss to Portsmouth in 1937) he played only a minute; in the other (an 18-7 loss to Cincinnati Hughes in 1938) he played none at all.

The 1939 unbeaten team scored 229 points in nine games and allowed only 47. Sarringhaus's 18 touchdowns was almost half of Hamilton's total, and he saved his best game for last—a 20-13 win over arch-rival Middletown. A formidable opponent, the Middies came into the game with six wins and two ties, and no one had scored more than one touchdown on a Middie defense that had permitted but 26 points all season.

Sarringhaus torched the Middies' inviolability on the fourth play from scrimmage, going 61 yards to score. He scored the Big Blue's third TD from 76 yards out, and kicked the points after. His 1940 class was the school's first class to graduate without a loss to Middletown, and Sarringhaus was heralded as Ohio's outstanding high school footballer, sought after by nearly every major program east of the Mississippi.

At Ohio State, Sarringhaus was princely in an imperial lineup that featured seven All-Big Ten players, the Big Ten's scoring leader—Gene Fekete, Sarringhaus's fullback, led with 92 points and Sarringhaus was second with 72—and four All-Americans, including Sarringhaus himself.

The Buckeyes rolled up 337 mostly one-sided points—a record that would stand for nearly thirty years—with only one blemish: the infamous "bad water" game with Wisconsin in which players and coaches came down with a bad case of the Wisconsin Quick Step after drinking from a contaminated drinking fountain. They lost 17-7 in what Sarringhaus and teammates considered their "asterisk" game, and to prove it, came back to wallop Michigan 21-7 and end the season as the *Associated Press's* Number 1 team in the country.

Sarringhaus's Michigan game still ranks among the very top OSU-Michigan contests, and Sarringhaus accounted—in one way or another—for all three OSU

When Sarringhaus was at Ohio State there was no Sports Illustrrated. He had to settle for the cover of LIFE.

scores: he caught a pass for the first one, then tossed two passes himself for the final scores—a 60-yarder and another for 32 yards.

The next year, Sarringhaus joined the army, as did most of his OSU teammates. He returned in 1945 to appear on the cover of *LIFE* magazine, but nagging injuries throughout the season kept him from his old form. ("Paul Sarringhaus is one reason why college football play will be far better this fall than it has been since the war began," wrote the magazine, proving that cover jinxes existed before *Sports Illustrated* did.)

Even with injuries and weak eyesight—he was one of the first football players to wear contact lenses—he played two more years in the NFL before injuries claimed the schoolboy who was considered Butler County's greatest running back.

Carlos Snow

CAPE running back class of 1987

87

The Cincinnati Academy for Physical Education was a magnet school specializing in just what it sounds like, and when the Crusaders won back-to-back state football championships in 1985 (Division IV) and 1986 (Division III), folks complained that it wasn't fair.

And it wasn't. Because CAPE had Carlos Snow.

What wasn't fair was a high school kid trying to tackle a guy too strong to stop, too quick to grab, and too fast to catch. There was only one way to slow Snow: wait until the second half. By then, nearly always, CAPE had such a big lead that the transcendent tailback could take the rest of the night off.

His speed was such that he won the 100-yard dash at the state track meet, and he probably could have done it with a football in the crook of his elbow. In four years of running track, Snow never lost a sprint in Greater Cincinnati.

He rarely lost a collision, either. Snow was a low-slung runner, 5-8 and 195 pounds, a thick-legged *Parade* All-American who gave a lot better than he got. And yet, his feet were light enough to elude a linebacker and tightwalk a sideline.

When all his half-games had been totaled, Snow, averaging more than 10 yards a carry, had run for 7,761 yards, which at the time placed him third in high school history behind Ken Hall and Emmitt Smith. His 106 touchdowns ranked second.

In fact, Smith, who graduated from high school the same year as Snow and became the NFL's all-time leading rusher, is the player with whom the CAPE icon might be and has been compared. Vinnie Clark, Snow's old College Hill buddy and a teammate at both CAPE and Ohio State—a defensive back who was a first-round draft choice of the Green Bay Packers and played six seasons in the NFL—has assured that, with healthy hips and knees, Snow would have produced professionally at a level quite like Smith's.

Even with the issues he endured at OSU, Snow left Columbus as the fourth-leading ground gainer in Buckeye history. That was in spite of a tumor in his hip and grinding knees that made him considerably less than the runner who, in high school, rushed for more than 2,000 yards for three consecutive seasons.

But he had his collegiate moments. As a freshman, OSU

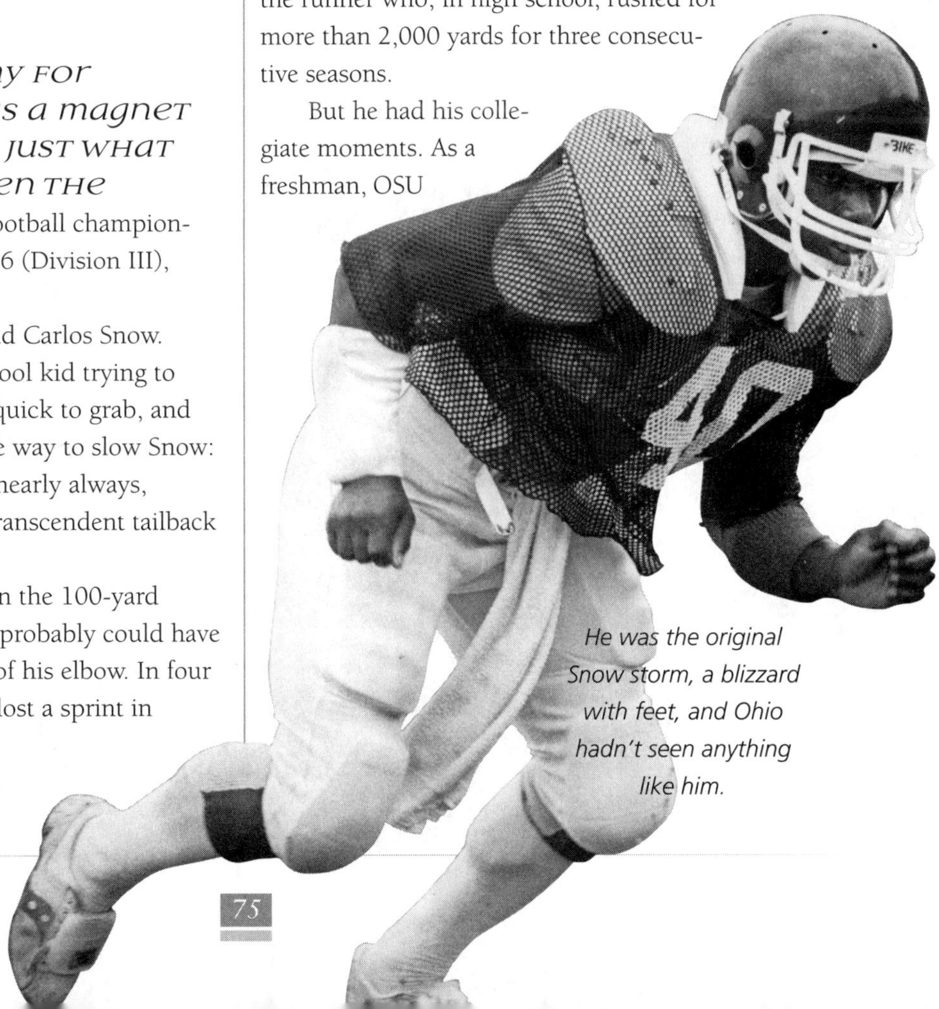

He was the original Snow storm, a blizzard with feet, and Ohio hadn't seen anything like him.

Snow was so good that he left Ohio State as its fourth-leading ground gainer, in spite of his bad knees and hip.

trailing in the third quarter at Michigan, Snow nabbed a swing pass from Tom Tupa, swerved to the edge of the field and booked 70 yards for the touchdown that won Earle Bruce's last game as Ohio State's head coach. The next Michigan game, under John Cooper, was less successful for the Buckeyes but nevertheless memorable for Snow, who ran 25 times for 170 yards, the most by an OSU player in more than sixty years of college football's richest rivalry.

The former prodigy missed 1990 for hip surgery and somehow toughed out more than 800 yards as a fifth-year senior. His leg strength, however, never returned to NFL standards, and as a result, Snow's legacy revolves around his halcyon days of high school, when he was so good it wasn't fair.

The Sollmanns

Scott and Steve

St. Xavier running backs class of 1993 & 2000

93, 00

In their own ways, the Sollmann brothers, Scott and Steve, were the quintessential Cincinnati athletes—undersized, gifted with grit, and chronically conflicted between the two sports that seem so organic to the city.

First came Scott. *Fast* came Scott. As he once put it, drawing a distinction between himself and his slightly larger successor at St. Xavier High School, "I ran away from guys, but he seems to run *at* them or *over* them."

Scott had no choice, really. He was but 5-8, 150-something pounds, so physically unimposing that his wispy coach at Notre Dame, Lou Holtz, had this to say in 1995, when Holtz underwent back surgery after a collision with Sollmann on the sideline: "When Scott Sollmann bumps into you and you notice it, you know you're in trouble."

The real trouble, for those who played against Sollmann in high school, was that few people *could* bump into him. As a senior, he piled up 2,512 all-purpose yards and scored 34 touchdowns, *nine* of them on kick or punt returns. Most memorable was the punt return against Piqua in the 1992 state semifinals. In what is considered the most sensational play in St. X history, Sollmann, according to witnesses, ran about 150 yards and avoided nearly as many tackles, encountering every last member of Piqua's coverage team. The TD put the Bombers in the title game against Cleveland St. Ignatius, and Sollmann kept St. X in that rugged affair, as well, despite an injury to quarterback Jamie Doxsey in the second quarter. At year's end, he'd averaged 8.2 yards and set the school's career record (1,794) for return yardage, which still stands. Sollmann was appropriately feted as the local Player of the Year, Co-Player of the Year for all of Ohio, and honorable mention All-American.

And yet, his scholarship to Notre Dame was awarded for baseball. Sollmann was a sizzling center fielder, a Freshman All-American and three-time All-Big East player who set Irish single-season records for triples and stolen bases. Irrepressible, he also walked-on to the football team and found his way to the field, catching a few passes and returning more than a few kicks. He left after his junior year, when the Detroit Tigers drafted him in the seventh round. Scott stole 216 minor-league bases and played for the Reds' AA team in Chattanooga before he retired in 2001, completed his law degree and joined a Cincinnati firm.

By that time, little brother—but not *that* little, at 5-11, 180—had scored 60 touchdowns at St. Xavier, breaking Scott's school record by two. Steve Sollmann had the advantage of starting every game from the time he was a freshman, the only player to do so in the long tenure of coach Steve Rasso. As a junior in 1998, he racked up 316 rushing yards in a regional game against Colerain, plowing over people in a way that Scott, watching closely, could only admire.

When he was finished, Steve had also set the St. X records for career rushing and all-purpose yards. He was a tailback, like his predecessor, and in that role was able to exact a little revenge for Scott's championship loss to St. Ignatius seven years earlier: In October of his senior season, Sollmann tallied six touchdowns in a 50-33 comeuppance of the Cleveland power.

Like Scott, Steve played in and lost a state championship game, his 1998 Bombers falling to Canton McKinley. Like Scott, he was a first-team All-State player and Cincinnati Player of the Year. Unlike Scott, he led his large private school to a state championship in basketball, starting at point guard for St. Xavier's triumphant 2000 team.

In baseball, the younger Sollmann played centerfield, just like Scott; but that's not what Notre Dame needed. The Irish were convinced they needed *him*, however, and converted him into a second baseman. He took to it. Sollmann was a Freshman All-American—need we say, like his brother—and in 2003 made both All-American and Academic All-American. The Milwaukee Brewers drafted Steve in the tenth round of 2004, changing his position again. This time, it was first base. He was voted Best Defensive First Baseman in the Southern League (AA) in 2007, and selected as an all-star. That earned him an advancement to AAA in 2008; but suddenly, less than two months into the season, Sollmann did as his brother had done before him at the same age of 26.

He moved on.

The Taft backfield

Walter Johnson, Al Nelson, Cleophus Edwards, & Carl Ward

Taft backs classes of 1961, 1962, 1963

61, 62, 63

THIS goes TO SHOW YOU HOW GOOD ROGER BACON WAS IN 1960. HOW GOOD PURCELL WAS THAT YEAR—THE YEAR AFTER ROGER STAUBACH.

Both of them beat Taft.

Taft Schmaft, you say? No respect for the city league? Fair enough. Other than Cincinnati Academy for Physical Education, in its short and singular life, no state football champion has ever come out of the Cincinnati Public Schools system. None of the old, traditional, surviving institutions—Taft, Hughes, Withrow, Woodward, Western Hills, Walnut Hills, or even Aiken—has so much as won a playoff game, ever. By 1960, their day was pretty long gone.

And yet, behold this backfield. Introducing your Taft Senators:

There was a quarterback, of course. His name was Dennis Whitehead, and while he must surely have been a gentleman and scholar, the most memorable aspect of young Mr. Whitehead's high school football career was who he pitched or handed the ball to.

There was his senior fullback, first off; Walter Johnson stood 6-4 and weighed 230-something pounds, on his way to 270; on his way to becoming an All-Pro defensive tackle for the Cleveland Browns. He was also a professional wrestler for fifteen years, wearing his number 71 as part of the schtick, and the fellows he faux-fought with will tell you that as a wrestler, Johnson was a whale of a defensive lineman. His signature move was a flying tackle off a three-point stance. The other guys—the real pros—said that Johnson never really understood the finer points of big-time wrestling. He hurt people.

There was also Whitehead's senior left halfback. Al Nelson was smaller than Johnson but conspicuously faster. He won both the 220 and 440 at the Public High League track meet. The 440 (now the 400 meters) is considered perhaps the most grueling race in the sport, which suggests that Nelson outgrew the asthma he battled in grade school, when his mother wouldn't let him play football. In fact, he became quite accustomed to sprinting significant distances. At the University of Cincinnati, he finished third in the nation in rushing, all the while succeeding in staying close to his attentive mom. "I could have gone to a bigger football school," he said, "but I preferred to stay home. Besides, at that time, we got $15 a month for laundry. I took the money and brought the laundry home to my mother."

THAT CHAMPIONSHIP SEASON

Princeton's championship team of 1987 may have been its finest. Its coaching staff would point to twelve guys going on to Division I ball, with three of them—**Alan DeGraffenreid**, **Ron Carpenter**, and **Markus Thomas**—playing in the NFL. It featured one of the quickest defenses Princeton ever had—tackle **William Reese** was Ohio's Division I Lineman of the Year and eventually team captain at Michigan State. And it had the biggest offensive line in school history.

In practice, when D went against O, the two 1,000-yard backs were sent out for water because the staff didn't want them running into those lines. In that 14-7 championship win over Boardman, running back Thomas scored the first TD, and

Later, in a nine-year career with the Philadelphia Eagles, Nelson was a defensive back and breakaway kick returner. He holds the NFL record for the longest return (101 yards) off a missed field goal. He also holds the record for the *second* longest return (100 yards) off a missed field goal. Crazy, huh?

But back to Whitehead's astonishing alternatives. At the quarterback's disposal there was, in addition, his junior right halfback. Cleophus (Cid) Edwards was about 6-2, 210, which frankly wasn't sporting in the same alignment as Johnson and Nelson. Edwards, who grew up on the riverbank next to the spot that Riverfront Stadium would occupy, made All-City as a runner the next year, when he moved up a spot or two among the options. After the North-South All-Star Game he reported to Tennessee State, stayed a year, and then joined the military, where he kept his legs churning and made the All-Asian team. The experience was not quite as foreign as it sounds, and apparently put Edwards in good stead when he tried out with the St. Louis Cardinals as a 230-pound fullback. For eight NFL seasons, his gig was mostly blocking; although in 1972, his first in San Diego, Edwards saw the ball enough to rack up 679 rushing yards and another 557 in pass receptions, a healthy 1,236 altogether.

And finally, as the Senators' fourth prospect for carrying the ball, there was the sophomore halfback who couldn't crack the starting lineup, at least on offense. Carl Ward played plenty of defense the autumn JFK was elected, and was happy, as well, to take Whitehead's handoff whenever Nelson or Edwards needed a break.

By the time Ward graduated two years later, a local sportswriter was calling him, at just 5-9 and 170 pounds, the best all-around back the city had produced in a decade.

He was almost certainly the speediest on the scene, placing third

a kid named **Craig Thompson**—he later became a record-setting kick returner at Eastern Michigan—broke a long punt return on the ice-covered field to set up the other one.

Thomas, largely ignored by major schools, became Division I-AA's all-time leading rusher on his way to making the 1992 Kodak All-American football team. In his four collegiate years, Thomas rushed for 5,556 yards and 52 touchdowns. He also set an NCAA record for yards-per-carry—6.57. He rushed for 100 yards in 30 of 47 games, even though injured through most of his sophomore year.

The rap on Thomas coming out of Princeton was that he did not have breakaway speed, an incentive, no doubt, to Thomas' 16 collegiate runs of 50 or more yards, including a 90-yarder, an 80-yarder, and four others of over 70 yards.

"I've been known to go outside," he said, demonstrably laying his critics to rest.

Thomas on a Division I-AA tear.

at the state track meet in both the 100- and 220-yard dashes. During practice for the North-South All-Star Game in 1963, he dropped jaws by sprinting 100 yards in 9.7 seconds. But it was more than just speed that he possessed: In spite of a bad loss at Massillon that year, Ward so impressed Tigers coach Leo Strang that he called the little scatback "the best opposing player I've seen at Massillon since I've been here." Massillon even invited Ward to its own post-season banquet, honoring him as the season's top opponent.

But when the Taft star got to the Michigan varsity in 1964, he found, again, that one of the backfield positions was occupied, this time by Mel Anthony of Roger Bacon, an old nemesis from the 1960 Bron Bacevich team that had bested the Senators. Meanwhile, the Wolverine quarterback was Bob Timberlake of Franklin, Ohio, who was a first-team All-American that stellar season—which, at Michigan, describes any season that entails a victory over Ohio State.

This one, though, also included a resounding Rose Bowl triumph over Oregon State. In Pasadena, Ward broke loose for a 43-yard touchdown. But Anthony, wouldn't you know, scored one from 84 yards, two more besides, and took home the MVP award.

Ward's time was yet to come. By the time he was finished at Michigan, Al Nelson's former substitute had led the Big Blue in rushing and produced four games of more than 100 yards on the ground—only to find himself back on defense in the NFL. In three seasons there, he managed just one touchdown; but it was spectacular —a 104-yard kickoff return for the Browns in 1967.

After Ward and Edwards settled into their Sunday routines, it was thought and written that the 1960 Senators were the only team ever to send four players to the NFL from its backfield; and they may still be. The best of the lot, as a pro, was Johnson, known in Cleveland as "Zoom," for his startling acceleration, which explains why Taft coach Will Stargel had him playing fullback.

Although he ended his thirteen-year career in Cincinnati, with a bad back, his first dozen seasons were spent in Ohio's other NFL city, and there he retired into private business. When Art Modell spirited the team out of town in 1995, Johnson lamented, "It's as if someone went into my personal biography and took eleven years of my life and ripped it right out of the book." A few months later, he died of a heart attack.

By that time, Taft had produced two more NFL players, safety Neal Craig and defensive end Vaughn Booker. Both of them spent three years with the Bengals, among other stops, playing next door to Edwards' old stomping ground.

All in all, it's quite a heritage for a school that, at the turn of the century, was having a hard time getting games because its opponents were never quite sure if the Taft bus would show up. The Taft coaches, at the same time, were never quite sure they'd have enough players at practice *to* practice; sometimes, there were six.

Football, it seemed, wasn't cool on Ezzard Charles Drive. When the Senators played a game, observed Dave Dierker, athletic director for CPS, "There's a league championship team standing outside the stadium heckling them."

But then came the new Stargel Stadium, and new uniforms, and a new coach—Mike Martin, a former Bengal—and a fresh new atmosphere. Suddenly, football at Taft was about as cool as it had ever been.

Except for 1960, of course. Nothing was as cool as *that*.

Otis Williams

Withrow scatback class of 19 **54**

54

"Back up, back up, this guy can kick!" The Withrow coach yelled at his star running back. Otis Williams thought his coach was crazy.

I play pool with the guy, he thought. *He can't kick it over MY head.* Then the Woodward player put his foot into it, the ball arced into the stratosphere, and Williams began to backpedal furiously. Finally, at the last possible instant, he managed to field the ball in the very back of the end zone. And then the defense was all around him.

"It seems like I bounced around for five or six seconds while half the team was hitting me," he said. "One guy would just about knock me over and another would come along, hit me, and straighten me up. Finally, I saw a hole and broke loose." He got a key block on the 25, side-stepped the pool player on the 40, and 109 yards later, he was in the end zone. "No one was going to catch me," he said.

The newspapers couldn't agree on the distance; one said he ran 103 yards, the other 105. Williams disagreed with their disagreement. He remembered that he and the ball were almost on the back stripe. The Ohio high school records list runs of 109 and 108 yards, which meant, unofficially, at least, that Williams tied the state record. (No one in the city has ever come close; three Cincinnati-area players are in the state records for kick returns, among 13 players tied for 10th with 99-yard runbacks—Tom Lefker of Williamsburg in 1982, Michael Larkin of St. X in 1999, and Matt Ghere of Turpin in 2003).

Early on, Williams didn't even care much for football; baseball was *his* sport (he'd come by it naturally; his mother had played professional softball). His middle school didn't even have a football team, so when he got to Withrow as a sophomore he had played only one year. That summer, Leon "Buster" Macklin took the fast little kid down to the park and taught him how to play the game. Macklin was five or six years older, and he

Either way—on the field or behind the microphone—Otis was Charmed.

showed Williams how to block, as well as how to use his speed and quickness.

When it came time to play for real, Macklin gave Williams a pair of low-cut shoes. Williams had never seen anything like them. "Back then everyone wore those big high-tops," he said, "but these were light and I could move faster in them." Buster told him the shoes would take three seconds off his hundred times, and Williams believed him. The shoes made him feel like he might be able to leap tall buildings in a single bound.

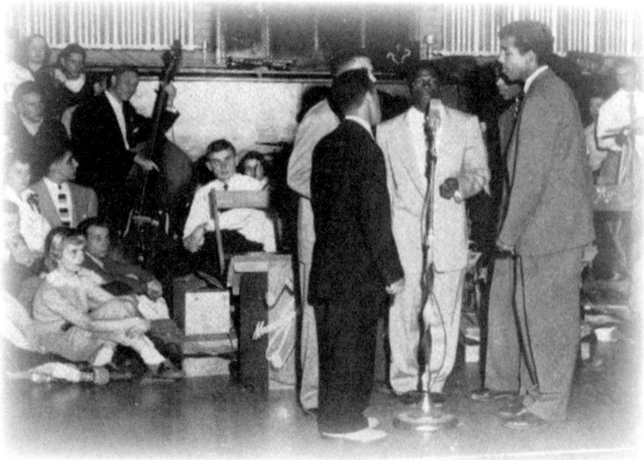

Otis and the Charms charm Withrow.

At 5-7, 150 pounds, Williams was referred to as a "scatback," which was the term used then for every quick, undersized halfback, and Williams was practically its prototype. For those following Withrow football in 1952 and 1953, electrifying runs by Williams were commonplace. He was a rare two-time All-City player whose breakaway running made him a target for opposing teams. His name, he learned, was plastered around the locker rooms of opposing teams.

He thought he could play football at the next level, and if not football, then baseball. But his other career got in the way of his career in athletics. In 1952, a Woodward group had one of its singers fall ill before a talent show and asked Williams to fill in. He sang with them and the group won the contest. "I don't even remember what we called ourselves," he said, "but that was the beginning." An agent for King Records heard them and soon Otis and the others were spending time after school polishing their act.

As graduation approached, Williams still saw himself primarily as a football player. He was headed to Ohio State on a football scholarship, but King record owner Syd Nathan talked him out of it. The group was known by this time as Otis Williams and the Charms, and the money, such as it was, made both college and sports seem superfluous.

What followed were recordings such as "Hearts of Stone," which reached Number 1 on the rhythm and blues charts and sold a million copies. He wrote "Two Hearts," recorded by Pat Boone, Frank Sinatra, and Red Foley, and in 1955, the Charms were *Downbeat* magazine's R&B group of the year. They played the Apollo Theater, toured with The Clovers and Big Joe Turner, and made *Billboard's* Top 20 seven different times. Otis arranged the original version of the "Twist," as well as helping arrange Little Willie John's classic, "Fever."

He found time to play a little football, too. He played for the Cincinnati Hawks, a semi-pro team where the players got $25 a game and played odd venues, one of them being the Ohio State Penitentiary. The prisoners weren't particularly good but they were mean. They were older than the Hawks, who were primarily kids just out of high school. So it was speed and guile vs. age and the nasty temperament. In Otis' winding-down athletic career, this meant that there was a brief moment of perfect symmetry between, well, the pros and the cons.

Otis managed to survive both his careers. In the 1970s, he even produced a country music album—*Otis Williams and the Midnight Cowboys*, which he did with an all-black country band. He survived that, too. It was, wrote one critic, "a passionately subversive union of two disparate but parallel modes." And: "His tenor doesn't equal Charley Pride's penetrating baritone, but Charley would never deliver the 'Come here boy' in 'Muleskinner Blues' with such sarcastic relish."

And, so it seemed, Williams was always something of a natural. There was music when he ran, and he brought a vocal athleticism to his singing. For a time, he'd been a city legend on the football field, then he found himself part of another bigger, more enduring legend—when rhythm & blues came out of the closet and into the living room. He wasn't even out of high school when he recorded what became one of the best-known doo-wop songs of all time.

His old audience is dying off, but people *still* listen to him. Otis and the Charms were on the soundtrack of *Goodfellas*, for instance, background witnesses singing—while Henry's mailman was being threatened—"Hearts of Stone." In a mob movie, what else? You can find Otis—still singing—all over ***YouTube***. It's been, you might say, a Charmed existence.

When **Freddie Jacobs** was piling up the yardage for Wyoming in the mid-1970s, *Enquirer* prep writer Denny Dressman referred to him as probably the most prolific ground gainer in Cincinnati history. Typically running wide while teammate **Steve Fletcher** took care of the dirty work between the tackles, Jacobs tallied 24 touchdowns and led the state in rushing in 1975. The Cowboys lost a close game to Cleveland Holy Name in the state finals, but their breakaway artist was named Ohio's AA Back of the Year. He went on to have a nice career at Pitt . . . **Mike Gayles** was very good at wrestling: district champion at 154 pounds as a sophomore. He was very good at track: district champion in the hurdles for three years, and in the 100-yard dash as a senior in 1973. And he was *really* good at football: Ohio Player of the Year in 1972. He stood out on the Princeton team that made history by beating Massillon in the first playoff game for both schools. Gayles played college ball at Tennessee, where in 1974 he was MVP of the Liberty Bowl . . . Prior to the 1979 season, Gerry Faust met with **Eric Ellington** and Ellington's mother in the Moeller cafeteria and expressed displeasure over his star halfback's work habits. He referred to Ellington as a con artist, at which point the player's mom pounded her fist on the table and said, "Eric, you've been a con artist at home, too!" The result was that Ellington was not permitted to be a Crusader captain. He did, however, work hard enough to score 16 touchdowns and become Moeller's all-time leading rusher up to that point. For his effort, Ellington was named Ohio Player of the Year. And at LSU, he played wide receiver . . . In the 1960s, there weren't many black players in the GCL. And there weren't many players like Elder's **Larry Parker**, conference Player of the Year for 1968. Parker, whose father, Jim, had played at Western Hills, left the Price Hill school with most of its rushing records, then took his game to Notre Dame . . . They tell **Harry Andreadis** that he once held a record at the University of Cincinnati, something about the most rushing yards in his first game. He was more distinguished, however, at Withrow, where, at mid-century, the yearbook referred to him as "the Gallopin' Greek" . . . Harry's son, **Jake Andreadis**, starred at Anderson High School, where his father, having graduated from coaching (Hughes, Withrow, Courter Tech), was athletic director. Jake was a state champion pole vaulter who went to Youngstown State on a track-and-field scholarship. But the Penguins' coach, Jim Tressel, was a fairly sharp fellow, and he persuaded Andreadis to carry the ball for the football team. As a fullback—one writer named him as the fullback on YSU's all-time team—he proceeded to run for 2,620 yards at six a pop. Andreadis was a vital part of Youngstown's I-AA national championship team of 1997. They called him the *Rumbling* Greek . . . Harry Andreadis' running mate at Withrow was a versatile athlete named **Dick Ernst**, who might have received more playing time at Ohio State had he not been stacked behind first Vic Janowicz and then Hopalong Cassady, both of them Heisman Trophy winners. Ernst's other distinction was captaining the Buckeye baseball team . . . **Jeff Hill** started out as a quarterback at Mt. Healthy High School, then dominated as a running back, which was what Purdue recruited him as. In 1989, he and Middletown's **Jeff Cothran** were considered the best in the area, which apparently didn't affect Hill's demeanor. He was so quiet that, at Purdue, they called him "Chill." As a sophomore and junior for the Boilermakers, Chill Hill produced six 100-yard games. In school history, he still stands second to Leroy Keyes in yards-per-carry. But he was switched to receiver as a senior, and that's the position he played with the Bengals for a few years. Actually, he did more kick returning than anything. These days, he coaches track and helps with football at the College of Mount St. Joseph . . . **Darius Ashley** began to build his legend two games into his sophomore season of 2005. While a dominant runner throughout grade school and middle school—he had practically memorized his Barry Sanders highlight tapes—the 5-9 tailback would have to wait his turn on the St. Xavier varsity. The starter was **Chris Cionni**,

Ellington and the wrath of Faust.

an All-City player, and Ashley's job was to learn from the senior. But all that changed when Cionni was injured. Ashley almost instantly became a sensation, amassing more than 1,600 rushing yards and leading the Bombers into the state championship game against Massillon. He was a bellwether on that big day, as well, until ten minutes remained and St. X, leading by two touchdowns, was inside the Massillon 20-yard line, on the verge of clinching the first Ohio title in its long grid history. But then the sophomore fumbled and one of the Tigers carried it all the way back for a touchdown. There were tears in Ashley's eyes when he took the field again. But he was up to the challenge, ripping off enough first downs in the final minutes to secure a 24-17 triumph. His star stayed high in the sky until his senior season, when this time the injury was his. Ashley missed the Bombers' early games as Danny Milligan pulled the St. X offense unbeaten through one of the nation's roughest schedules. Then the University of Louisville recruit was back doing his thing, which involved staying on his feet after it no longer seemed possible. Coach Steve Specht described him as "like a weeble-wobble." Behind Ashley, the Bombers again advanced to the state title game, this time against Mentor. And this time, there were no glitches in the super senior's final high school performance. While the St. X defense shut out Mentor and its Mr. Football, Bart Tanski, Ashley's 271 rushing yards broke the championship-game record that Colerain's Dominick Goodman had set in 2004, breaking the record that Elder's Bradley Glatthaar had set the season before that . . . And then there was St. Xavier's **Walter Gruber**. Dismissed in 1943 from the St. X freshman football team because of his size, he was allowed to continue practicing. In an intersquad scrimmage, Gruber caught the eye of Coach John Dromo, got himself promoted to varsity and became a two-year starter at halfback. He went to the University of Detroit on a track and football scholarship, lettered four years at halfback and safety, averaged 6.6 yards a carry, and set a school record for the longest run from scrimmage. He also lettered four years in track and made the finals of the U.S. Olympic Trials in 1948, then pulled a hamstring before his event, the 220-meter dash. At St. X, he held the GCL 200-yard dash record from 1946-1970, a phenomenal amount of time to go unchallenged . . . Goshen halfback **Craig English** scored four of his six TDs in overtime as Goshen beat Norwood, 65-64, in a 1993 score that resembled a basketball game. (Wags in Goshen called it "putting English on the ball.") Considered one of the most offensively uproarious games in Cincinnati history, the game was tied 30-30 at the end of regulation, then the teams traded TDs in all but the fifth overtime. It was one overtime short of the longest overtime game in Ohio history—the *National High School Sports Record Book* said that Clyde and Milan Edison played a seven-overtime game in 1990 (the national record was a *nine*-OT game in 1977 between Detroit Northeastern and Detroit Southeastern). The major oddity of the evening wasn't the number of overtimes; that belonged to the fact of both teams entering the game rated among Cincinnati's top defenses . . . At Ross High School, **Nick Wilson's** coach, Dick Ballard, liked to say that he could put ten tacklers in a row, have Wilson run at them in a straight line, and Wilson could make all of them miss. It was just his elusive way of moving, a sleight-of-foot that made tacklers lose him. As a 5-11, 190-pound junior in 1995, Wilson ran farther than any Cincinnati area player before him; he gained 2,267 yards in the regular season, breaking the 1991 record of 2,074 set by Marc Edwards. In the season's finale against Kings, Wilson had 350 yards, including touchdown runs of 70, 83, and 84 yards—in the first half. He finished the game with 388 yards and Ross finished undefeated. Adding 20 pounds for his senior year, Wilson's production tapered and he stopped just short of a second 2,000 yard season. His 5,795 career yards put him in the Number 3 spot among Cincinnati area rushers, and he was named Ohio's Davison II Offensive Player of the Year. He's still in the record books as the Number 6 all-time rusher in Cincinnati area football.

Walter Gruber

Here's the Cincinnati area rushing records, as of 2009 (the second number is the statewide rank):

1 (2)—8,216, Jason Bainum, Williamsburg, 1998-2001
2 (3)—7,761, Carlos Snow, Cape, 1983-1986
3 (5)—7,386, Richard Hall, Wyoming, 1995-1998
4 (10)—6,353, Donald Johnson, NCH, 1998-2001
5 (16)—6,001, Marc Edwards, Norwood, 1990-1993
6 (19)—5, 795, Nick Wilson, Ross, 1992-1995

. . .The fellows from Clermont County called him "the greatest player who never." He was an athlete who never played football, but no one has any doubt about what would have happened if he *had* played. They're just grateful they never had to face **Donald "The Tree" Ogletree** on a football field, which is because they saw what he did on the track and the basketball court in the mid-1960s. "That he did not play football was a big 'Thank you, Jesus' for the rest of us," said Phil Redrow, ex-Williamsburg quarterback. "He was unstoppable in a Jordan-esque way and he did things nobody in our county had ever seen. I played against the Tree as a sophomore, and he did one of those spectacular rebounds where he soared above everyone and as he landed I wondered what had just wafted over me in flight, and then he turned at the peak with the ball outstretched in his right hand and landed and dribbled at the same moment in time so that I swore he was dribbling in the air. As he broke toward me, I thought of Pamplona and the running of bulls and stuck out my arm, futilely, then merely watched as he took off from the foul line and floated to the hoop, gently laying the ball in the basket. My coach looked at me in disgust and I thought, 'Oh, you wanted *me* to stop *him*?' All we knew was that something unholy had descended upon us. Our slow-footed whiteness had been called to task and no one answered the bell. All we could do was be grateful that Batavia High did not have football. If The Tree had played football, we would have seen nothing but his numbers, fading into the distance . . . ."

Here's Jim Bolger, powerhouse Purcell's bad boy halfback of 1949 and 1950 . . .

Roger Bacon's Wayne Gallagher (34) gets a block to thwart Purcell's Mike Cameron (yep, THAT Mike Cameron, the onetime Moeller baseball coach). Gallagher scored the winning TD on a one-yard run in the third quarter as Bacon won 8-0. It ended the 1961 season 9-1 and Number 3 in the state UPI poll, behind Massillon, who had beaten the Spartans 12-0.

FB

Fullbacks

JIM "BOXCAR" BAILEY—*Hamilton/ Class of 1949*

MARC EDWARDS—*Norwood/Class of 1993*

RAY NOLTING—*Hughes/Class of 1931*

JOE NUXHALL—*Hamilton/Class of 1947*

DAVE PARKER—*Courter Tech/Class of 1970*

CLEM TURNER—*Woodward/Class of 1964*

Bench Strength—Ray "Sheik" Aug, Elder; Brandon Miree, Winton Woods; Kyle Koester, Elder; Mark Brooks and Chris Smith, Moeller & LaSalle; John Crowley, St. Xavier; Mister Simpson, Colerain; Jeff Cothran, Middletown; Bill Asbury, Princeton.

Jack Beyersdorfer, the Walnut Hills fullback in 1942 and that year's team MVP.

Boxcar Bailey

Hamilton fullback class of 19 *49*

49

Even the name itself was legendary—Boxcar. As a Hamilton High 10th grader, Jim "Boxcar" Bailey was already faster than a sophomore romance. By the time he was an imposing senior, he was both big *and* fast, the kind of runner who made an entire defense religious. By this time, *Boxcar* wasn't a name, it was an admonition.

Against Hughes in 1948, he was a long evening's nightmare. He carried four times and scored three TDs, on runs of 61, 84, and 78 yards. When the Big Blue beat up Canton Timken that year, Boxcar scored on runs of 39, 55, 60, and 58 yards. The local papers called that Hamilton High team, rated Number 2 in Ohio (behind Canton McKinley) "the best Big Blue team ever." It finished 9-1, its only loss a 27-20 upset by a powerful Mansfield eleven.

Hamilton scored 30 points or more in eight of its ten games, which included a 61-12 pasting of Springfield. And Bailey was its creative impulse. Unlike lightning, he might strike twice in the same place. He was a perpetual dark cloud on any team's schedule; he didn't just rain on their parade, he was a monsoon in cleats.

No less an authority than Terry Malone, the longtime Badin coach, said Boxcar might have been the best back he ever saw. He remembered Boxcar on defense, too, driving ball carriers off the field and over Hamilton's little wire fence. He thought the name was apparent. "When he turned uphill on you," Malone said, "he looked like a big ole boxcar . . . ."

Playing in the North-South All-Star Game in Massillon—that cradle of prep uncivilization— after his senior year, he scored twice, gained 167 yards, and gained another 96 yards on two kick returns. Glenn Sample, a West Side kid who made the All-Star team that year, remembered that "he was a stud compared to the rest of us. He was the closest thing to Jim Brown," if Jim Brown had been invented then.

Woody Hayes recruited Boxcar to Miami, and he was an immediate force there, too. Upstate sports fans remember the 1950 Thanksgiving weekend blizzard bowl as the one between Michigan and OSU, when Buckeye fans braved near-zero temperatures and 40 mph winds to watch Michigan beat OSU 9-3 in what was possibly the dullest football game ever played: the two teams punted 45 times, and Michigan went off to the Rose Bowl after gaining 27 yards and no first downs. To downstate fans, however, the Blizzard Bowl was played in Cincinnati between UC and Miami, with a foot of snow in Nippert Stadium and Boxcar and his teammates 13-point underdogs to a UC team already headed to the Sun Bowl.

Here's where the story gets interesting: Both UC and Miami were said to have been Sun Bowl contenders, but three days before their game, a bowl representative told one of the sportswriters that "Miami could not be considered because the Redskins have a colored player, Jim Bailey." They didn't object to having a "colored player" in the game, they said, but they weren't prepared "for the housing and entertainment of a colored boy" in El Paso.

Miami, to its credit, declined all invitations that did not include Bailey, then walloped UC 28-0 behind Boxcar's 7.5 yards per carry, as neat a piece of gridiron serendipity as ever witnessed. (It was also the first shutout ever handed to UC's gifted offensive football mind, Sid Gillman.) Bailey amazed the sportswriters, one of whom wrote, "He seemed to be wearing snowshoes on his size 15 feet. He seemed to stride on top of the snow, running for nearly 200 yards and two touchdowns . . . ."

Boxcar started Miami in spectacular fashion, although he didn't finish. He did send his coach to Columbus, though. Here, Boxcar (seated) shakes hands with Harry Phillips, Sr.

Said one of his Hamilton fans, "Everybody seemed to know it was snowing but Boxcar...."

Miami then headed off to the Salad Bowl in Phoenix where, presumably, Western Civilization maintained itself even while housing and entertaining "a colored boy," who helped Woody and his teammates dismantle Arizona State, 34-21. (Bailey scored twice, one of them a 50-yarder.)

And here's the kicker: The Blizzard Bowl in Columbus cost Wes Fesler his job, and the Blizzard Bowl in Cincinnati gave it to Hayes, who headed off to Columbus but without the big fullback he'd recruited away from OSU. In a small footnote little remembered, Boxcar had given his old boss the job of a lifetime.

Hayes remembered, though. Years later, after Archie Griffin had won his second Heisman, Hayes reminisced about his great backs. He allowed as how Griffin was likely the best; but until he came along, the distinction was probably Boxcar's.

Bailey played another season, was moved to defensive end by Ara Parseghian, then flunked out of school. After Woody, his greatest moments came on the track, where Miami won its fourth consecutive Mid-American Conference track championship with Boxcar setting the conference 100-yard record of 9.8 in a qualifying heat, then running a 9.7, and tying the 220 record of 21.6 seconds. He ran a 9.7 in the Drake Relays, in the face of a strong wind.

"Boxcar and I used to sprint against each other," said Erbil Barkley, a state champion in the 220 at Central High School. "Oh my goodness, he was fast. And he was 230 pounds, all muscle. Boxcar was something special. I only beat him one time. The last meet we competed against each other was a district meet. It rained hard that day and the track was full of water, and I could hear him behind me. He said he couldn't get through the water."

Boxcar is still third on Miami's all-time list for average yards per carry—7.9 in 1950—and his 90-yard run against Ohio University that same year is the fourth longest in school history. After Miami, Bailey played on a championship service team, then briefly with the Los Angeles Rams. He had injured a foot in the army, however, and he never again performed with his old brio. That, however, would be recalled by anyone who ever saw him play as they struggled for vocabulary, trying to describe the indescribable.

Present at the Creation

He was the first great Cincinnati football player and likely Ohio's first true All-American. While few today even recall the name, **Frank Butterworth** was a near-household word in his time—even during the first half century of American football.

He played fullback on the famous 1892 Yale team that shut out thirteen opponents. Then in 1893, Butterworth's junior year, the Yalies gave up only 12 points. He was a Walter Camp All-American that year and again as a senior.

While born in Maineville, the son of a United States Representative, there was not much football being played in the area in the late 1880s, and Butterworth prepped at Harrisburg Academy in Pennsylvania before heading for Yale.

In addition to his own accomplishments there, he was also a track man, an Eli pitcher, and he was voted "the most handsome man" in his senior class. The staid *New York Times*, not overly given to hyperbole, said before the Princeton game of 1893 that the Tigers "should watch that man Butterworth and keep track of the part he takes in the contest. This youth is tall and slim and runs like a deer and goes at the opposing line like a battering ram. He scored the single touchdown against Harvard and throughout the contest was the closure of all eyes. . ."

The Harvard game of Butterworth's senior year was one of

FRANK BUTTERWORTH.
The Cincinnati boy, who won the game for Yale.

the sport's more notorious moments, so famously violent that the series was suspended for two years. That game featured the unveiling of "the flying wedge," a spectacular formation designed essentially for human concussion. In it, Harvard suddenly divided its players into two groups of five men, each group on an opposite sideline. Just before the ball was put in play, the two groups, upon their captain's signal, sprinted toward the middle of the field. They came together at midfield, forming an arrow-shaped wedge that attacked Yale's front at fearsome speed.

"Sensation runs through the stands at the novel play," wrote historian Parke Davis, " which is the most organized and beautiful one ever seen upon a football field." The surprised Yalies threw themselves under it, but it was Butterworth, finally, who stopped the runner from scoring.

It was the most spectacular formation yet seen on the gridiron and quickly became every team's opener even though it was difficult and demanding, involving a precise coordination among eleven men. It was also extremely dangerous and after two seasons when several players died because of injuries as a direct result, the wedge was outlawed.

Butterworth was the star of the game called by the *Boston Post* "the most atrociously brutal game throughout," even though Harvard tacklers piled on Butterworth and he was helped off the field. Observers said Harvard players tried to kick Butterworth in the eye but Butterworth, sportsman that he was, said he thought the loose feet were unintentional. Yale won the slugfest, 12-4, and at the Princeton-Yale game the following week, 250 policemen came out to keep order.

After graduation, Butterworth coached briefly at the University of California at Berkeley, spent another two years coaching his alma mater, then became a well-known financier and a Connecticut state senator. When he died in August of 1950 at the age of 77, Maineville had long forgotten him but in New Haven they still remembered "the human pile driver," as the papers had once called the 158-pound fullback, and *The New York Times* gave him nearly a column of space. The Harvard-Yale game might have received more, but not much more.

Marc Edwards

Norwood fullback/linebacker class of 19 **93**

93

THE FASHION, AT THE TIME, WOULD HAVE BEEN FOR A PLAYER LIKE MARC EDWARDS TO GO TO A SCHOOL LIKE MOELLER. WITH A NEAR-A AVERAGE, he certainly had the brains for it. But not the fashion sense. You could tell by the crewcut.

And you could tell by the style with which he ran the football. There was nothing flitty or fetching in Edwards' footwork; just a hearty, humble rumble. In an age of Walter Payton, he was Bronko Nagurski.

He was Norwood.

No other kind of superstar could come out of a blue-collar, save-your-dollar enclave like the industrial outpost in Cincinnati's center. It was 1987 when the last Camaros and Firebirds rolled out of the General Motors plant that had defined the surrounded city for sixty-four years. By 1990, Norwood needed a hero.

It was then that a bruising sophomore led all of Cincinnati in rushing yards. Edwards did it twice more—the first ever to three-peat. And he did it with a bare minimum of sidesteps. One opposing coach noted that he hadn't detected a whole lot of blocking, either—just a willful, skillful smashmouther, shouldering his way through the waves of defense.

He also had his way at linebacker, commonly racking up more than 20 tackles a game. So complete a player was Edwards that he once recovered his own onside kick.

Behind him, Norwood prospered. When he was a junior, the Indians, a Division II team, scored what coach Jim Barre referred to as a "plaque victory"—one substantial enough to be engraved on the plaque that hung on the wall of his office. It came against undefeated Anderson, a Division I opponent. Edwards rushed for 202 yards and rang up four touchdowns. And made his customary 20 tackles.

On it went. In a victory over Winton Woods that year, he ran for an astounding 343 yards—111 in the fourth quarter alone. That performance came a week after Edwards had set his school's career rushing record.

As a 6-1, 210-pound senior, he led the state in rushing yards, with 2,074, was declared Ohio's Mr. Football, and saw his jersey hung in a local sports café. His final two yards put him over 6,000 for his extraordinary high school career, which was noted by colleges from coast to coast.

Southern Cal was the first school to send Edwards a recruiting letter. He was all set to visit when John Robinson, who had just taken over as Trojan coach, cancelled the trip. Edwards opted for Notre Dame. Three years later, he was hoisted onto his teammates' shoulders after scoring three touchdowns, passing for a 2-point conversion and running for another in a rout of USC.

None of it, of course, was particularly pretty. "He wears a crewcut," observed Irish coach Lou Holtz. "He's a throwback to the old-fashioned days when you played without a facemask."

After 27 collegiate touchdowns, Edwards' senior season at Notre Dame was cut short by a knee injury. He was nevertheless selected in the second round of the 1997 draft by the San Francisco 49ers.

He stayed in the league for nine years, by which time Norwood was back on its feet—as tough to topple as the rugged fullback who, unlike the auto plant, couldn't be shut down.

In more ways than one, Edwards was Norwood.

AN EDWARDS CHRONOLOGY

1981—**Marc Edwards**, age 6, has traumatic experience with football, getting hit and leaving the field in tears. He switches to soccer, then tries football again as a more mature 8-year-old.

In his first game, he has 80-yard run from scrimmage and never looks back. He is no longer trauma's recipient but instead its agent.

1984—"How do I become a professional football player?" Edwards, fourth-grader, asks his Aunt Cheryl.

"Buddy," she says, "you have to get out of high school first."

Nine years later, the All-American fullback graduates from Norwood High as a member of the National Honor Society, 13th in his class of 222.

1992—Norwood is tied with Western Brown, 20-20, twenty seconds left on the clock and the ball on Norwood's 20-yard line when Edwards, the big Norwood fullback, catches a screen pass in the flat. Cutting back against the grain, he breaks a tackle on the 50, fakes out three other defenders, bulls over two would-be tacklers at the 20 and scores standing up. There was no time left on the clock and he had run at least a hundred yards to win the game.

"I was mad," he said.

Edwards, a preseason *Street and Smith* All-American, is rated as the country's second-best senior running back.

1992— Edwards plays his most sensational game, oddly a 21-19 loss to Harrison. Down 21-0 at the half, he proceeds to run for three scores, kicks an extra point, kicks an on-side kick, recovers it, and attempts a 42-yard field goal, which is wide by a foot.

1993—"Here comes Marc!"—crowd at Willie DeLuca's Sorrento Pizza and Restaurant in Norwood watching freshman fullback Marc Edwards enter the Notre Dame lineup.

Ray Nolting

Hughes fullback class of 19**31**

31

UNDERSTAND THAT FOOTBALL WAS FAR FROM A SCIENCE IN 1936, WHEN THE NFL HELD ITS FIRST COLLEGE DRAFT. ON THE ONE HAND, A SHREWD coach and owner like George Halas of the Chicago Bears could identify a running back like Ray Nolting, a rough and romping All-American from the University of Cincinnati; and on the other he could choose lineman Danny Fortmann because he liked the sound of his name. Naturally, Fortmann became a Hall of Famer.

And Nolting was not exactly knackwurst. He was, in fact, a vital member of what was called the Backfield of the Century, along with the likes of Sid Luckman, George McAfee, Bill Osmanski and of course the legendary Bronko Nagurski. (Apparently, Nolting had to choose between the Bears and New York Giants, and yielded to the advice of Red Krueck, his old coach back at Hughes High School, who pointed out, "If I were you, I think I'd rather play *with* Bronko Nagurski than against him.")

Amid such company, Nolting—much appreciated in Chicago for his tackling and blocking, among other gritty talents—was three times the Bears' MVP. In 1940, the year the Bears made an historic shambles of the championship game by humiliating the Redskins, 73-0 —for which each winning player received a cut of $873 —it was Nolting who led the famous team in total yards and also interceptions. He was never the type, however, to be lavishly feted for his efforts—not with Luckman and Nagurski around.

There was, for instance, the day when Nolting forgot a play, and for his punishment was handed the ball eight times in a row. Not minding much, he advanced it to the 2-yard line, where his real punishment kicked in. The next handoff went to Nagurski, who of course barreled across for the glory and touchdown.

"There was always something workmanlike about Nolting," it was written in the *Chicago Sun-Times*. "Like a flannel shirt, like a bowl of oatmeal. Damned essential, but thoroughly lacking in glamour. An essence of a tragic inattention."

The fans called him Jolting Nolting. Luckman called him "my favorite launderer—he kept my uniform clean."

At any rate, it wasn't just the surpassing personnel that made Chicago the Monsters of the Midway. The Bears were also winningly innovative, owing largely to the designs of Clark Shaughnessy, who shared with Halas his snappy version of the T-formation. It featured far more passing than the prevailing alignments—hence Luckman—and also a wide-spread offensive line that permitted bold and mobile ball-carriers to plunge through without the use of interference.

"You run that back through there without a blocking back in front of him, you'll get him killed," argued Curley Lambeau of the Packers. But it made

THE FALLBACK TO FULLBACK

It's much like in basketball, where the big guys always want to be guards. **B.J. Askew**, a first-rate fullback, always wanted to be a halfback. At Colerain, operating out of the triple-option offense, it didn't really matter much because he got the ball. And he got the yardage—1,526 in his senior season of 1998, when he was All-State.

It was pretty much the same at Michigan. At 6-3, Askew was a 225-pound fullback until, at Chris Perry's expense, he switched to tailback as a junior in 2001. He led the Wolverines in rushing that year and returned to fullback as a senior and altogether scored 23 touchdowns in a terrific Big Ten career that ended with a team MVP selection.

A third-round draft choice of the New York Jets in 2003, Askew soon established a reputation as a dynamic tackler on special teams. He signed with Tampa Bay in 2007 and soon became a starter at the position he had been trying to wriggle out of, blocking and catching so proficiently that the Bucs promptly signed him to a sizable four-year contract. That, no doubt, made him appreciate fullback a lot more.

79
65

Nolting none the worse for wear. On the contrary, it made him thrice an All-Pro.

His was a distinguished eight-year career, effectively ended by a crushing knee injury in the preseason of 1944. The headline declared: *Nolting Injury Imperils Bears Title Chances.*

He had performed proudly, nobly, as UC's first representative in the NFL (simultaneously with Bearcat teammate Bill Feldhaus, a lineman also from Hughes who ended up with the Detroit Lions). It had been quite a jump for a young fellow who, to get to his university campus, had only to cross the street from his high school.

Nolting was a 1931 graduate of Hughes, where he played whatever was playable. Track was among his pursuits, enabling the Avondale native to exercise the speed that often pitted him against schoolmate Sam Stoller, a sprinter at the 1936 Olympics. In their 100-yard dashes, official or otherwise, Nolting would typically lead the Olympian for the first 50 yards and sometimes—though not every time—succumb in the latter stages.

He was only 16 when he graduated, but man enough, soon enough, to play both ways for Cincinnati, captain the Bearcats, and carry them to a 20-6-7 record while he was there. In a particularly valiant but losing effort against the University of Kentucky, he ran for more than 200 yards and piled up 20 tackles in his spare time. A rushing leader and three-sport threat, Nolting was one of the original inductees into the UC Hall of Fame, and thought so much of the football program that he returned to coach it in 1945. His charge was to rebuild the team after two dormant years during World War II. After a 4-4 restart, Socko Wiethe's good friend oversaw the memorable opening game of 1946, when UC traveled to Indiana to upset the defending Big Ten champions, 15-6.

Nolting starred at UC first as a player, and after an All-Pro career, starred again as its coach (far left).

At the other end of that stellar season, the Bearcats knocked off Virginia Tech in the Sun Bowl, their first-ever postseason classic. Later, Nolting helped coach the New York Bulldogs—which became the New York Yanks, which became the Dallas Texans, which became the Baltimore Colts, which became the Indianapolis Colts—and Green Bay Packers, who by that time had been persuaded by the advantages of the T-formation.

He later returned to his hometown, earned a living in business, and died in 1995, leaving Mary, his wife of fifty-eight years. "Football was the love of his life," said Mrs. Nolting, a reflection that qualified as poignant but perhaps excessively self-effacing, seeing as how her husband's career, wonderful as it was, lasted not nearly as long as his marriage.

Joe Nuxhall

Hamilton fullback/linebacker class of 19**47**

47

BECAUSE OF A MOMENT THAT HAD MORE TO DO WITH TIMING THAN TALENT, HE BECAME A LEGEND JUST AS HE FINISHED THE NINTH GRADE. JOE Nuxhall was all of 15 when he pitched for the Cincinnati Reds, and while he was schooled that afternoon by none other than Stan Musial, the National League batting champion, it meant that he would be a baseball man all his life. It was the moment that gave him fame, it fixed an appositive forever to his name—the youngest player in major league baseball (although the distinction wasn't so clear as all that)—and it obscured how good he was at other sports. And he was *very* good.

First, though, he had to get back to high school. Had anyone ever debuted in the major leagues of *any* sport, then gotten so homesick he wanted to return to high school? If not, it was likely because few lads at the age of 16 had been sent off to spend the summer doing penance in the boot camp industrial towns of Class D baseball. August in Lima made Hamilton seem like Miami Beach.

So the Hamilton principal (perhaps envisioning Joe the football player and Joe the basketball player) asked the Ohio High School Athletic Association if Joe could return. The association said yes, if he stopped playing professionally for a year. No pro baseball, and no high school ball, either.

Nuxhall thus began an impatient countdown to what would be one of the greatest years by any athlete in Ohio high school history. In the fall of 1945, he played sandlot football where, in the patented Nuxhall manner, he found himself in an imbroglio with Snip Huey, who was wearing lumberjack boots with long spikes on the soles. He spent the winter in the hardrock Shop League where the war veterans were fond of pick-and-rolling the youngsters, such as Joe, into the parking lot, and in the spring he pitched—brilliantly, of course— for the Moose Lodge.

In the autumn of 1946, Joe Nuxhall returned to Hamilton High, a battle-scarred veteran of boardinghouses, endless Midwestern bus trips, cold showers, and Shop League elbows. He'd played football in the back alleys, and his boyhood hero, Paul Sarringhaus, the OSU All-American, had taught him how to run pass routes, but he'd never before had on a real uniform.

When the coach walked in, Joe was wearing the shoulder pads like a chest protector. He was a quick study, though. He played fullback and linebacker, eventually the captain of a team he'd never played on before, and they went 6-2-1. Before Hamilton played Springfield at midseason, Coach Chuck Mather told the Springfield paper that Joe was "the finest back I have ever seen in high school circles."

There are still folks around who watched him play, remembering his presence—both his size *and* his temperament—for he towered over his linemen and he hated to lose. His boyhood friend, Joe Arminio, knew to avoid Joe when his head began to bob from side to side. That meant he was angry, and that something was about to happen. "He was big and fast," said Arminio, "and he was *mean*. His dad, Ox, rode him and rode him, and made him where he hated to lose. I remember after a game Hamilton lost and the guys came over to shake hands, and Joe slapped their hands away. There was a fight over at Springfield and six guys couldn't hold Joe...."

Joe's memorable moments included scoring 68 points, averaging nearly 40 yards a punt, and beating Middletown even after being knocked into the tuba section of the Middie band. He was All-Ohio, too, the third fullback on the team, and he played in the 1947 Ohio All-Star Game.

That winter, the former Shop League MVP became

Joe's HHS teammates; for him they considered making the Big Blue the Big Black and Blue. He's just right of the ball. The player at far left, first row, is thought to be Boxcar Bailey.

A song for Dwayne

At North College Hill, **Dwayne Crutchfield** had to follow the legend that was his cousin, Leon Murray. He did it with a vengeance. As a 220-pound running back and rebounder, he was called by the *Cincinnati Enquirer* "the undisputed heavyweight champ of the gridiron and hardwood." That description had to do with such items as Crutchfield sprinting off the floor during a basketball game to help out his brother with a little tussle in the stands.

Asked once about his notoriously physical manner, the big fellow replied, "I just don't like to be pushed around." He didn't do an excessive amount of *pencil*-pushing however, and the Ohio High School Player of the Year, only the second one from Hamilton, the first in basketball (the other was Joe's old idol, Sarringhaus). There were more than 15,000 boys playing basketball in Ohio and Joe was Number 1. But he still wasn't finished; there was baseball. He was thought to be the only player to have gone from the major leagues back to high school, something that certainly would not happen again, for after that 1944 season, a rule was passed that no high school player could be signed to a pro contract until he or his original freshman class had graduated, or he had dropped out of school and been out a full calendar year. Everybody said it was the Nuxhall case that brought the rule about.

In his first game, he tossed a no-hitter against Monroe. He pitched his final high school game in May at Crosley Field against Withrow in the regional semifinal, back to where he'd started three years before. And even though he wasn't facing Stan Musial this time, he lost both his temper and the game.

Wrote his biographer, Greg Hoard, "In football, Joe's anger made him a determined running back and ferocious tackler. In basketball, it sent him after each rebound with more intensity. As a pitcher, his anger was a thief. It jimmied the doors of his concentration and stole his composure...."

Perhaps, mused Hoard, he was more suited for football. His coach, Mather, thought so. Indiana, Purdue, Xavier, Miami, all offered him football scholarships. Even Joe, himself, thought he was better at football and basketball, and he knew his temper aided him in those sports. But he'd made his choice. Baseball was where he would stay.

And yet, with little background in football, he'd become one of Ohio's finest triple-threat backs. Years later, he'd reminisce about those long ago summer

after a prolific high school career found himself at two different junior colleges. Then came Iowa State, where as a junior he ran for 1,312 yards and as a senior in 1981, while scoring 17 touchdowns, he led the entire Big Eight in rushing.

For the Missouri game, Crutchfield was listed as questionable because of a badly sprained ankle. But he played, and kept playing, even after conking out when he landed on his head scoring a touchdown. He had three of them that day. Such was his local renown that when Barry Manilow played Ames that year and ripped open his shirt to sing "Copacabana," he was—to the great delight of the audience—wearing a Dwayne Crutchfield jersey underneath.

The burly fullback remains a key member of Iowa State's all-time team. He also spent some quality time with the New York Jets, whose star running back, Freeman McNeil, later identified Crutchfield—who by then weighed 240—as the best blocking back he ever ran behind. "If I'd had him blocking for me throughout my career, I could've had 2,000 yards rushing yards a season," McNeil said. What prevented that was a tragic death in Crutchfield's family that shook him deeply. He was out of the game a year later.

afternoons when he had watched the tall, lean Sarringhaus, bathed in sweat, running sprints on the Hamilton playground. And then Joe—who as a schoolboy was bigger and stronger than Sarringhaus—had *become* Sarringhaus.

Dying young always helps preserve the legend, and that's what Joe did when he left football. He wasn't thinking that way, of course, because it wasn't how his mind worked, but those other legends of his—football, basketball—died in high school. Still, he was so good so quickly—a big, powerful, instinctive runner—that those who had seen him play forever wondered what he *might* have been, should he have chosen otherwise.

Dave Parker

Courter Tech fullback class of 1970

HARRY ANDREADIS KNEW RUNNING BACKS. AT WITHROW, WHERE THEY CALLED HIM "THE GALLOPIN' GREEK," HE HAD PLAYED WITH DICK ERNST, who played with Vic Janowicz and Hopalong Cassady at Ohio State. Andreadis had run against, and often tackled, the celebrated Jim Bolger of Purcell. And though not especially large or swift, he knew running well enough that he had gone on to carry the ball with some distinction for the University of Cincinnati.

Andreadis, then, knew of what he spoke when he made this remark on a 6-5, 225-pound package of speed and power whom he coached at Courter Tech: "Dave Parker," he said, "was one of the best athletes Cincinnati ever had for baseball and football. David was probably one of the finest running backs we've had. He would have made a helluva college player, and I think a pro football player.

"Had he been on a team like Purcell or Elder, there's no telling what he would have done. He was just that outstanding. David in my opinion is probably as fine an athlete as there has been in this town. No question in my mind."

That assessment was based mostly on Parker's junior year at Courter Tech, which would have been the fall of 1968, when he rushed for more than 1,300 yards and fielded recruiting letters from Notre Dame, Ohio State and Southern Cal, among a pile of about 150. It wasn't common for so many colleges to come calling at a vocational school; but Parker wasn't common, either.

His physical assets made him the most freakish athlete the metropolitan area had produced since Hamilton's Boxcar Bailey. In baseball, those abilities translated to tools—and two National League batting titles, three Gold Gloves, a frightening arm, an MVP award, a World Series ring and the biggest contract in the game. In football, they led to a knee injury.

It wasn't career-threatening; but it was career-reconsidering. In the first game of his senior season, some cartilage was torn as Parker was tackled at Middletown. He came back and played a few more games, then had surgery and missed the rest. The recruiting slowed down considerably.

So did the interest of major-league baseball teams. Parker was a catcher then, and catchers with knee issues were not hot properties. The Pittsburgh Pirates found him still available in the 14th round of the 1970 draft, and Parker accepted their offer of $6,500 and a new glove.

It wasn't mad money, but it was fully within Parker's nature to believe that there would be a whole lot more where that came from. And it's not difficult, in retrospect, to understand his inclination toward baseball.

He had grown up on Poplar Street, a block from Crosley Field, and hawked peanuts or ice cream when Frank Robinson or Vada Pinson was not at the plate. The two Cincinnati stars drove matching white Thunderbirds, and from the trunk of Robinson's had come the gift of a glove. His heroes had nice things. They got them from baseball.

Less than a decade later, the Cobra, as he was called, was earning seven figures a season, the first black player to do so. He was also envied and despised in Pittsburgh, where fans blew up his mailbox and threw various hard things at him, including a bag of nuts and bolts, a bat on bat day, and a 9-volt radio battery (lending new meaning to assault and you know what).

The issues were many. There was the money, of course. And his pigmentation, of course. And his chains and diamond earring. And his braggadocio. The big outfielder spoke like Muhammad Ali in stirrup socks,

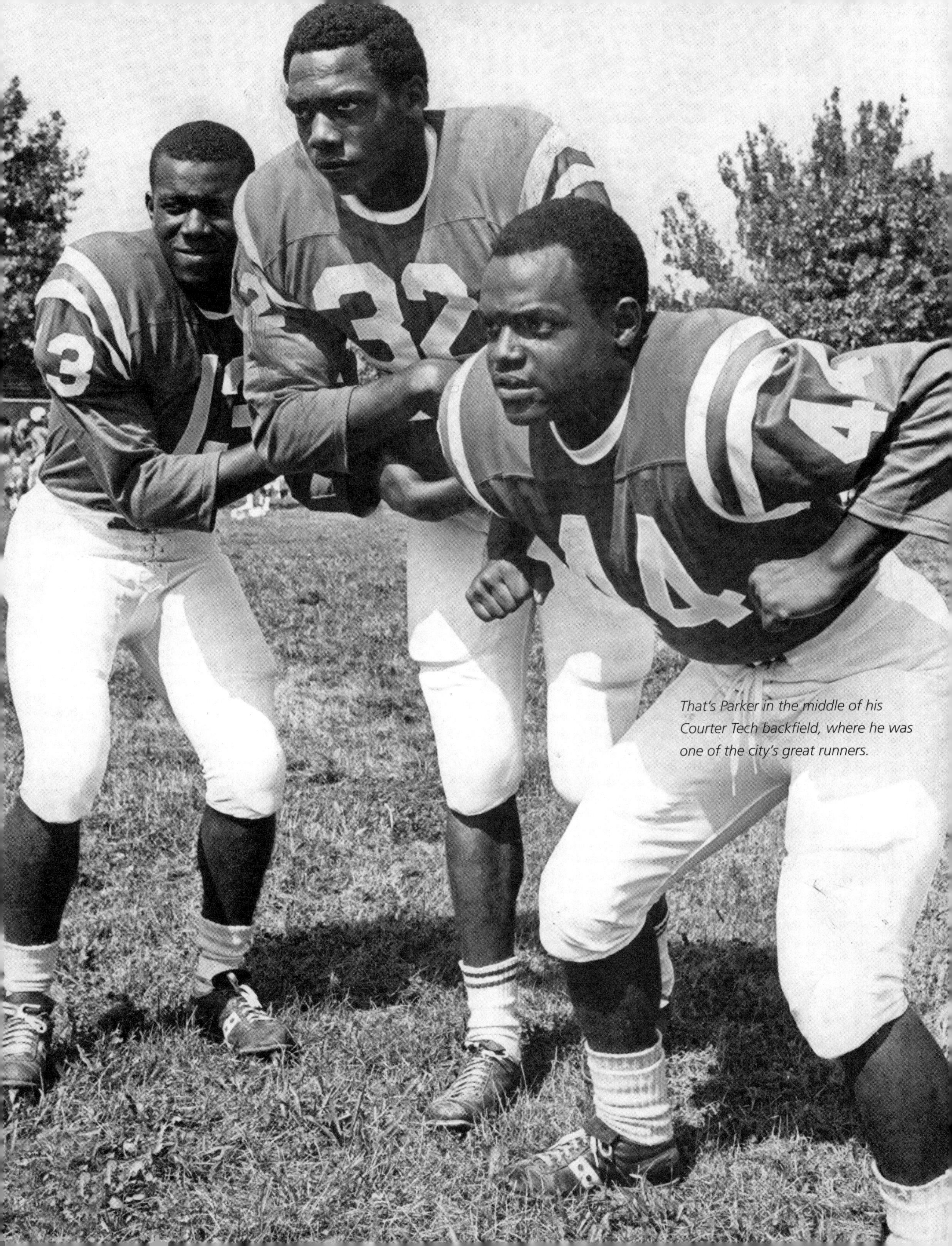

That's Parker in the middle of his Courter Tech backfield, where he was one of the city's great runners.

declaring such things as:

"When the leaves turn brown, I'll have the Triple Crown."

"I'm wall-to-wall and tree-top tall."

"There's only one thing bigger than me, and that's my ego."

And, regarding the Star of David he wore around his neck, "I'm David, and I'm a star."

It all got to him, eventually. There were some injuries and some down years and the thing that probably keeps him out of the Hall of Fame, the infamous Pittsburgh Drug Trial of 1985. In it, Parker admitted to using cocaine, and was heavily fined by the commissioner.

By then, though, he was playing in Cincinnati—he arrived as a free agent in 1984—and prospering. In '85, managed by Pete Rose, Parker actually drove in more runs—125—than ever before.

He chose his hometown in retirement, as well, and Popeye's Chicken for his franchise. Meanwhile, Courter Tech was long gone, of course, its Central Parkway campus occupied by Cincinnati State College.

The main parking lot was the former football field, and Andreadis, for one, can't drive past it without thinking back on the friendly fullback with all the size, speed, and confidence. What he remembers most is not an overmatching ground gain, but one poignant exchange that revealed quite a bit about the working pride of his future superstar.

"I had been brought up always saying, 'Boys, let's do this or that,'" the old coach recalled. "One day, David stopped me and said, 'Mr. Andreadis, do I look like I'm a boy?' I said, 'No, David, you don't.' And he said, 'Well, would you mind calling us men?'

"That was the day I went to the word 'men.' "

The Big Easy: NOT

There was nothing easy about **Easy Ed Shuttlesworth**, even in his formative years at Woodward High in the 1960s. The rare game photos from the period depict what must have been a familiar sight throughout the public school league: The Big Easy, all 220 pounds of him, head down, shoulders wide as surfboards, scattering defenders like tenpins. He was a large object amok, bringing to mind aerial photographs of a natural disaster overwhelming a village.

In October of 1969, for instance, he rushed for 170 yards and scored six TDs and two extra points for a school record 40 points as Woodward beat Western Hills, 60-6.

At the University of Michigan, early in the 1972 season, Big Easy ran for 151 yards against Tulane, scored on runs of 21, three, and four yards, and reached the 1,000-yard mark quicker than any previous Michigan player. "The human bulldozer from Cincinnati," the papers called him. "What I'd like," Ed said, "is to carry the ball more."

"What opponents would like," said the *Associated Press*, "is for Shuttlesworth to get lost."

For two of his Michigan years, he was teammates with another human appliance from Ohio—Clint Spearman, the "fabulously ferocious high school defensive end" from Hamilton Garfield, who made his transition into college ball as captain of the Michigan freshman team (and its top frosh player). In 1971, Spearman was a vital presence in UM's defense, ranked first nationally, and did a wrecking job in UM's 10-7 win over Ohio State that earned the Wolverines a trip to the Rose Bowl.

In 1972, the Wolverines rolled into Columbus on Thanksgiving Day unbeaten, ranked Number 3, and heavily favored to go to the Rose Bowl again. The game was one of Ohio's legendary games. Shuttlesworth scored UM's only TD, on a goal line fourth-and-one, but OSU, unfortunately for the Wolverines, held on two other goal line stands (the quarterback ran one of them). OSU won 14-11 and sent Michigan back to Michigan and itself to the Rose

Clem Turner

Woodward fullback class of 19 ***64***

64

THE LIKES OF CLEM TURNER—IF THERE IS SUCH A THING—MIGHT BE BETTER LEFT TO THE MYTH.

For starters, there's the story about the time Turner went to see Dick Kerin, the head coach at the new Aiken High School. Nearly every veteran coach in the city tells a version of it, with varying degrees of veracity; but the fundamentals are pretty much the same. In 1963, Aiken was set to entertain its first senior class, and one of its prospective members was Turner, already a rough and renowned running back from his underclassman years at Woodward. Knowing this, according to the tale, Turner sauntered into Kerin's office one day in the late summer, his hat turned sideways, pulled up a chair, and propped his feet on the desk.

"I hear you're the coach of this new team," Turner is alleged to have said. "I might be interested in playing for you." Then he proceeded to tell Kerin how it was going to be, the conditions including such items as how many times a game he would have to carry the ball, that blocking would not be part of the deal, and that his equipment would have to be thus and so.

When he stopped for a moment, Kerin, a Marine veteran, paused and said, "Are you done yet? Because now I'm gonna tell *you* how it's gonna be. First, you're gonna take your hat off when you're in my office.

"Second, you're gonna get your damn feet off my desk. And third, you're gonna get

Bowl. (This, after Michigan led in first downs, 21-10, and 334 total yards to 192. Statistics, obviously, didn't get you to Pasadena.)

It was some consolation that Spearman and Shuttlesworth were both All-Big Ten (Shuttlesworth got the nod over OSU's fullback, Champ Henson, who led the nation in scoring). Shuttlesworth was All-Big Ten again in 1973 and closed out a lunch pail career as Michigan's all-time leading rusher. He had run more plays—534—than any other player in Michigan history, as well as playing in only two losing games.

Easy Ed in action—top, rambling over the opposition, and at right, with his queen as WHS's homecoming king.

Turner (44) was a sensation, but there was a price to pay.

the hell out of here before I do something I regret."

The corollary is that, when Woodward and Aiken squared off in the fall, the latter devoted all of its defensive resources to shutting down (and up) Turner—who had returned to the Bulldogs—and succeeded in that respect, only to see the *other* Woodward running back, his path clear, rush for about 200 yards.

In terms of harder truth, we *do* know that, behind Turner, Woodward went undefeated that year, and that the 6-1, 230-pound bruiser led the city in scoring with 144 points (24 touchdowns worth) and made All-State. And that he had been every bit as good as a junior, when he ran for three touchdowns—one covering 87 yards—in a victory over St. Xavier and battled famously with Carl Ward in the league showdown game against Taft. Ward rattled the big fellow's molars a few times, and Taft won a close one, and afterwards the two stars walked off the field arm-in-arm.

We also know that Turner was a powerhouse beyond his years and company. "Nobody was stronger than Clem in high school," said his coach, Jack Campbell. And he wasn't the only one. After Turner dominated the North-South All-Star game with 198 yards on 22 carries—outrushing the entire North *team*—the *Cincinnati Enquirer* observed that the Woodward man-child "had the strength of a bulldozer and the grace of a ballet dancer."

It's safe to speculate that his athletic graces were more advanced than his social ones, but the particulars are murky. Turner did make it to the University of Cincinnati, and make it big. As a sophomore in 1966, he led the Bearcats in rushing, including a school-record (at the time) 267 yards in a victory at Kansas State. His 5.5-yard average was sixth in the nation.

And then he disappeared.

Turner played only two seasons at UC, and three years later was drafted in the fourth round by the Bengals. In between, he surfaced in the upstart Continental Football League, running the ball as a "rookie sensation" for the Toronto Rifles in 1967. He did not acquire the same description with the Bengals, however, carrying the ball just 23 times, and found himself in Denver for the next three seasons; then out of the league. The next time we heard from him, he was playing for the Hawaiians and Portland Storm of the WFL. The next time, he was wrestling in the WWA, cavorting about with the likes of Dick the Bruiser, Moose Cholak, and Cowboy Bob Ellis. That was a comparatively enduring gig.

After that, it's just a few police reports and repeated appearances in the Hamilton County court system, the trappings of a fellow down on his luck. In late 2007, he was interviewed for a story in the *Tampa Tribune* about the struggles of former players dependent on pain pills.

"It's hell, man," said Turner, whose medication was taken to allay the effects of nineteen surgeries. "I need it to exist. Honest to God, if I had known I was going to suffer like this for a moment of running up and down the field—oh, hell no!"

Reality, it turned out, hit even harder than the old fullback. Most times, the myth is better.

Where There's a Willet...

Reading High School, not coincidentally, reeled off a 17-game winning streak when **Dick Willet**, class of '36, was there and doing everything. His eighteen letters overall (three in basketball, three in track, four in golf, baseball and football) is thought to still be a local record. But the guy, like his younger brothers, was a football player at heart.

An All-State fullback, etc., as a senior, Willet missed just one game in four years. He was not so fortunate at the University of Kentucky, however, breaking his forearm as a sophomore and foregoing the rest of his career on the doctor's advice.

By that time, brother Irvin Willet was a Reading marvel, as well, playing the same five sports Dick did and winning league championships in every one. His favorite, of course, was football, in which he, too, made All-State. Offers arrived from the likes of Kentucky, UC, Miami and Tulane, but economic realities compelled Irvin to work during the day and attend evening school. His future would include five battle stars from World War II, two Cincinnati Senior Amateur golf championships, and a long stretch of officiating.

Irvin was off defending his country when brother Donald Willet was a Reading freshman. He was immediately designated for varsity duty but severely injured his knee in a bicycle accident and missed the entire year of athletics. In 1944 he was sufficiently recovered to start at fullback for another undefeated Blue Devil squad, only to reinjure his knee.

When he was ready to return, coach Ken Powers was reluctant to put his fearless star back in the backfield. Instead, Donald finished the season as a two-way tackle.

It was only temporary, however: Willet's prep career was then interrupted by a war stint with the Marines. When he arrived back home in 1946, he found himself at quarterback. That, naturally, qualified him to play defensive end at UC, for coach Ray Nolting.

Willet started his first two college games and hurt his knee again, ending his football career but hastening his entry into aerospace engineering, in which his famous brothers had *not* preceded him.

BENCH STRENGTH

The Sheik

When **Ray "Sheik" Aug**, Elder's junior fullback, scored five TDs against Batavia in 1923, he may have set the longest standing school record in Cincinnati. It was fifty-four years before it was tied. Ray was captain the next year, Elder's first, followed by his brother, George, who was captain in 1929. Another brother, Whitey (class of 1932), a four-year fullback, was Elder's first 100-point career scorer, thereby establishing a panoply of dazzling brother acts that would persist at Elder throughout the century. In 1966, Tom Aug, son of George, was co-captain (as well as the GCL's most outstanding back), demonstrating that Elder not only had brother acts, but family acts . . . Winton Woods had never been to the playoffs before **Brandon Miree** arrived. And Cincinnati had never seen a running back (with the exception of Wyoming's Richard Hall, that same year) rush for as many as 2,455 yards (302 against Harrison alone) in the the season. Not to mention 30 touchdowns. Somehow, he slipped to second-team All-State; but the recruiters were not deceived—especially after he won his third conference title in the 100-yard dash. Miree accepted a scholarship to Alabama, where he would team with former Boone County (Kentucky) star Shaun Alexander. The great Warrior played in every game as a freshman but left Alabama early in his sophomore year and transferred to Pittsburgh. In 2002, the punishing 230-pounder became a Big East sensation, beginning with 161 yards against Virginia Tech's top-rated run defense. He followed that with

118 yards against Miami, 121 against West Virginia and 113 against Oregon State in the Insight Bowl. A stress fracture in his leg undermined Miree's senior season, but he still managed to dazzle the media, entertaining a Pittsburgh columnist with references to the likes of the Allegory of the Cave from Plato's *Republic*. He also made some headway in his public-service career. When President Bush came to town, Miree volunteered to drive a van in the motorcade. He ended up transporting controversial advisor Karl Rove, and struck up a lively conversation about Alabama restaurants. Later, Miree enrolled in Pitt's prestigious Graduate School of Public and International Affairs, which came in handy when his NFL career was aborted after one season with the Green Bay Packers . . . It wasn't just any school's career rushing record that **Kyle Koester** broke. It was Elder's. And he had topped Larry Parker's hallowed total by the end of his junior year. That was the year in which, against Boone County (Kentucky), Koester scored five touchdowns in the first half. He weighed 240 pounds then. For his senior year, he filled out with another 10 and broke Parker's single-game school rushing record with 304 yards against Bishop Chatard (Indiana). By then, he had already smashed the touchdown record. But he was just getting loose. Against LaSalle, Koester carried the ball 35 times. In the playoffs against Fairfield, he hauled it 37 times. Needless to say, he was All-State and the Panthers' MVP. When there were no more Elder records to break, Koester accepted a scholarship to Indiana, and finished his college career at the University of Cincinnati . . . **Mark Brooks** and **Chris Smith** were GCL rivals at Moeller and LaSalle, respectively—that is, if any team could be considered a rival of Moeller back in the Crusaders' days of state and national eminence. But on the personal level, Brooks and Smith were both large, bruising runners with credentials that made them *Parade* All-Americans after the 1980 season. Brooks was the headliner, lugging the ball 33 times in Big Moe's thunderous state-title victory over Massillon in coach Gerry Faust's final high school game. But Smith had some numbers going for him, too, rushing for more than 1,300 yards as a senior against staunch competition. The two joined forces at fullback for Notre Dame, splitting time for most of their four years in South Bend. Mainly, the rugged roommates blocked for Allen Pinkett and Greg Bell. Smith did have a shining moment in the 1983 Liberty Bowl, running for 104 yards and earning MVP honors. He also played some NFL replacement ball with the Kansas City Chiefs during the strike of 1987 . . . Superlatives were thrown around more freely then, but it was said in a newspaper, a couple decades after **John Crowley** graduated from St. Xavier in 1924, that "Mr. Crowley was rated the greatest prep school football player in the country a good many years ago. He was a back, and they say he could really carry the mail. He

Koester (and looming at right, Colerain's Mister Simpson)

was lighting fast. He crashed into an enemy line with the power of a hopped-up bull." Exaggeration is suspected, because, although Crowley—they called him "Botts"—was twice an All-City fullback, he didn't actually play football his senior year at St. X. Nor did he play long at Notre Dame, where his services were eagerly anticipated. A broken shoulder during his freshman year ended Crowley's collegiate career, leaving Irish fans mourning that another Thorpe or Nevers had been denied. Ultimately, his sporting renown was perpetuated by his widely known work selling the equipment manufactured by the MacGregor company, whose president, Joe Kelly, had immediately preceded Crowley as a St. X football legend . . . **Mister Simpson** had the name and the game. At Colerain, he was already All-State as a junior. As a senior, he was the headliner on the Cardinals' undefeated state championship team. A coveted recruit, Simpson was the school's all-time record holder in rushing yards (3,167) and touchdowns (45), the Number 4-rated fullback in the country. His only deficiency, it seemed, was the occasional failure to hit somebody. "We sometimes call him 'Mrs.' if he misses a block," said Colerain coach Kerry Coombs. It didn't prevent Simpson from signing with Michigan, where, like most Big Ten freshmen, Mister didn't pass muster; didn't play much. Then he encountered some academic difficulties and transferred to the University of Cincinnati, where old friends—Colerain teammates Terrill Byrd, Andre Revels, and Dominick Goodman—awaited. But he wasn't quite as eligible as they were . . . A high school kid was no match for **Jeff Cothran**. As a 240-pound ball-carrier at Middletown in 1989, he led the area with 9.5 yards per carry, and all those 9.5's totaled up to 1,465. He expected to run the ball at Ohio State, too, but John Cooper had other ideas. By then, Cothran weighed 250, and the Buckeyes wanted him to block. So block he did, and the Bengals were impressed. They drafted him in the third round, 1994. He didn't carry the ball much for them, either. Instead, he got suspended a game in 1996 for conduct detrimental to the team. What happened was he got arrested for driving while intoxicated after his Chevy Blazer hit a construction divider in the vicinity of Monroe. Before the next season, he was cut . . . In 1960, **Bill Asbury** was MVP of Princeton's first varsity football team. He was a bookish athlete, and sufficiently talented to win All-State honorable mention. Kent State was interested in him, and spent the scholarship wisely. Asbury twice led the Golden Flashes in rushing, and in 1965, ringing up nearly 1,000 yards on the ground, he was an honorable mention All-American and the MAC Offensive Player of the Year. In 1967, working at fullback for the Pittsburgh Steelers (and known as Willie Asbury), the Original Viking pulled off a 73-yard run that was the NFL's longest of the season. After three years in the league, Asbury embarked upon an academic career that resulted in a vice-presidency at Penn State. . . . If **Howard Reis** failed to make the *Guinness Book of Sports and Games*, it was only because the *Guinness* wasn't up and running yet. Peanut Howard was the fullback for Walnut Hills in the 1923 season at a Lilliputian 111 pounds—believed to be the smallest regular of any Class A school, Ohio's biggest division then. In truth, he was likely the smallest mortal *ever* to play the position, which was known for its refrigerator-sized stalwarts, even in the Roaring Twenties. Here's the description of his play in the Hughes-Walnut Hills game (won by Hughes 19-14): "The little fellow who appeared a child in stature compared with the big and heavy Hughes backs, was a bundle of energy, brains and speed. His flying trips for huge gains around Hughes' ends put his team in a position to score its two touchdowns. Hughes feared the little rascal more than the rest of the Hills team, for his small stature makes him hard to catch or hold, once he is caught. His kicking game is as deadly as his running. He kicked two goals after touchdowns for his team, and has kicked 13 straight goals this season. Had the balance of the Hills team been able to perform as well as Reis, the Hughes team would have been swept off the field." So while he was a wee fellow in a burly world, he surely gets our More Sizzle than Size Award, given annually to the feistiest lowercase fellow amongst us.

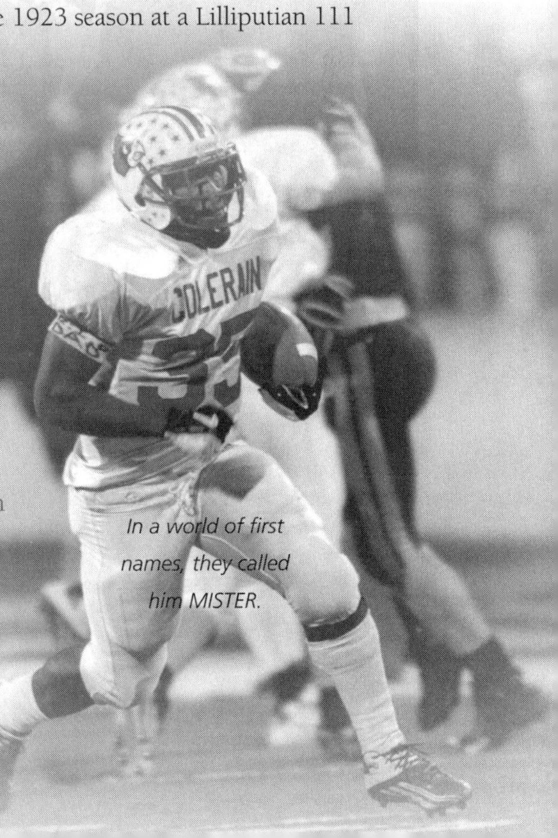

In a world of first names, they called him MISTER.

Cincinnati's ALL-TIME HIGH SCHOOL TEAM

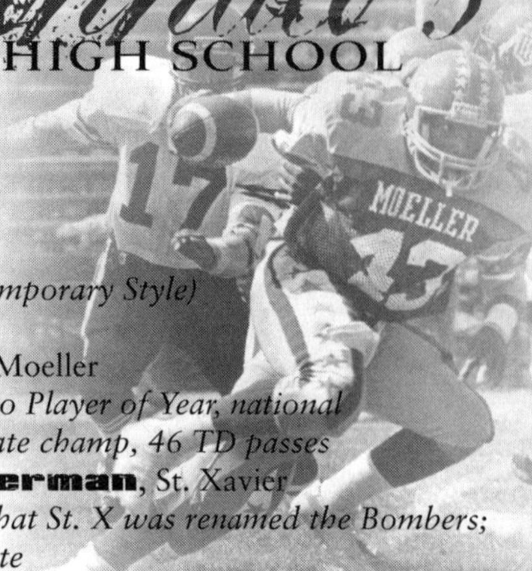

OFFENSE

Quarterback (*Contemporary Style*)

Tim Koegel, Moeller
All-American, Ohio Player of Year, national champion, 2-time state champ, 46 TD passes
George Ratterman, St. Xavier
Passer so prolific that St. X was renamed the Bombers; GCL champ, All-State
Greg Frey, St. Xavier
All-American, National Scholar-Athlete, Ohio Back of Year, OSU recruit

Arguable: Steve Tensi, Elder; Michael Taylor, Princeton; Tim Clifford, Colerain; John Shaffer, Moeller; Leon Murray, North College Hill; Roger Staubach, Purcell; Dick Selcer, Elder; Bryan Cupito, McNicholas; Skylar Jones, Middletown; Roger Franz, Purcell; Mark Kamphaus, Moeller; Brad Maurer, Kings; Ahmed Plummer, Wyoming; Mike Healey, St. Xavier; Chuck Hauck, Williamsburg; Mike Heizman, Colerain; Phil Redrow, Williamsburg; Rob Florian, Elder

(Running Style)

Bob Hoernschemeyer, Elder
Westside legend; versatile triple-threat star led Panthers to undefeated season as sophomore
Freddie Ratterman, Withrow
According to Enquirer, 1920s icon was "greatest high school player in the last twenty years"
Mike Daniels, Princeton
Ohio Offensive Player of Year; averaged nearly 370 yards total offense over last two seasons

Arguable: Bob Timberlake, Franklin; Mike Sensibaugh, Lockland; Bob Goodridge, Wyoming; Dominick Goodman, Colerain; Jason Bainum, Williamsburg; Tad Jones, Middletown; Don Zimmer, Western Hills

Running back

Carlos Snow, CAPE
Finished in top 3 in U.S. history in yards and TDs; Cincinnati Post *Offensive Player of Century*
Paul Sarringhaus, Hamilton
Butler County's greatest back never lost a game he played in full; Ohio State recruit
D'Juan Francisco, Moeller
Two-time All-American, two-time Cincinnati Player of Year; broke brother's school records
Jim Bolger, Purcell
All-Stater led Hackberry Assassins to perfect season, 14 yards a carry, then signed with Reds

Arguable: Richard Hall, Wyoming; Hiawatha Francisco, Moeller; Mike Harkrader, Middletown Fenwick; DeShawn Wynn, Reading; Carl Ward, Taft; Kelton Lindsay, Lebanon; Erbil Barkley, Central; Eric Ellington, Moeller; Napoleon McCallum, Milford; Larry Parker, Elder; Jim Herbstreit, Reading; Bradley Glatthaar, Elder; Ken Roundtree, Princeton; Freddie Jacobs, Wyoming; Nick Wilson, Ross; Mike Gayles, Princeton; Paul Jordan, Sycamore; Darius Ashley, St. Xavier; Claude Chaney, Hamilton Catholic; Paul Kelly, Elder; Ty Douthard, LaSalle; Jerry Harkrader, Middletown; Terry Killens, Purcell; Mike Harkrader, Middletown Fenwick; Jeff Hill, Mount Healthy; Harold Stapleton, Hamilton.

Fullback

Walt Roeckers, Roger Bacon
Rugged runner called by many (including Bron Bacevich) best prep player they ever saw
Marc Edwards, Norwood
Bruiser led state in rushing, led city 3 years straight; Mr. Football; Notre Dame recruit
Boxcar Bailey, Hamilton
"A stud compared to the rest of us . . . the closest thing to Jim Brown."

Arguable: Mark Brooks, Moeller; Clem Turner, Woodward; Eddie Shuttlesworth, Woodward; Tom Fouchey, Reading; Emerson Wendt, Middletown; Jeff Cothran, Middletown; Dwayne Crutchfield, North College Hill; Dave Parker, Courter Tech; Ray Nolting, Hughes; Shiek Aug, Elder; Mister Simpson, Colerain; Whitey Aug, Elder; Dick Willet, Reading; George Aug, Elder; Walter Johnson, Taft; Kyle Koester, Elder; B.J. Askew, Colerain

Wide receiver

Cris Carter, Middletown
Cocky, sensational athlete was All-State at both receiver and safety – and better at basketball
Jim Kelly, Moeller
Record-setting All-American changed Crusaders' style; Ohio Lineman of Year
Thad Jemison, Princeton
Parade All-American, Ohio Lineman of Year, local Player of the Year, OSU recruit
Tom Waddle, Moeller
Too small, too slow, and All-American
Devier Posey, LaSalle
Parade All-American signed with Ohio State as one of nation's top receiver recruits

Arguable: Darren Barnett, Princeton; Charley Wolf,

St. Xavier; Will Stargel, Woodward; Willie Townsend, Hamilton Garfield; Steve Junker, Elder; Bill Poland, Elder; Johnny Long, Princeton; Fritz Apking, Reading; Milt Stegall, Roger Bacon; Jim O'Brien, Aiken; Michael Larkin, St. Xavier; Danny Milligan, St. Xavier

Tight end

Arnold Franklin, Princeton
National high school Player of the Year; Enquirer *All-Century player; led GMC in rebounding*
Don Hasselbeck, LaSalle
Tall, talented, Parade All-American; considered Lancers' best-ever athlete
Merle Wendt, Middletown
Old-school Middie was captain, class president and big catch for Ohio State

Arguable: Tony Hunter, Moeller; Kyle Rudolph, Elder; Eric Kattus, Colerain; Ron Beagle, Purcell; Rocko Joslin, Middletown; Alex Higdon, Princeton; Brent Celek, LaSalle

Offensive Line—tackle

Dave Foley, Roger Bacon
Parade All-American; state-record shotputter; charter class of LaRosa Hall of Fame
Jefferson Kelley, Colerain
Gatorade Player of Year in Ohio; top-rated lineman in country; injured at Ohio State
Michael Munoz, Moeller
3 times All-State; Ohio Player of Year; highest-rated lineman in country
Connor Smith, Colerain
Anchored state-champion line; pummeled opponents; considered top tackle in Midwest

Arguable: John Anderson, Hughes; Steve Sylvester, Moeller; Dan Tehan, St. Xavier; Doug Williams, Moeller; Dave Metz, Harrison; John Peterson, Middletown; Rich Michael, Fairfield; Frank Clair, Hamilton; Dave Lafary, LaSalle; Joe Lukens, Moeller; Zach Strief, Milford; Joe Kelly, St. Xavier; Ryan Stanchek, LaSalle; Mike Biehle, Mason; Tim Foley, Roger Bacon; Steve Niehaus, Moeller; Alex Davis, Hamilton Garfield; Jim Brown, Moeller; Clyde Murrell, Hamilton; Tom Jones, Central; Joe Smith, Colerain.

Guard-Center

Raymond Pryor, Hamilton Garfield
Member of Enquirer's *All-Century team; caught Woody Hayes's eye*
Dan James, Elder
Huge and tough, prep All-American and West Side icon, Ohio State recruit
Bill Feldhaus, Hughes
Big Red captain; opened holes for Ray Nolting; represented city as early NFL player
Jim Mense, Hamilton Catholic
Rams stalwart was critical recruit for Notre Dame

Arguable: Tom Backhus, Moeller; John Kasselman, Roger Bacon; Glenn Sample, Western Hills; Bob Fry, Elder; Kyle Ralph, St.Xavier; Tom Luken, LaSalle; Rob Murphy, Moeller

DEFENSE

Defensive line—end

John Martinkovic, Hamilton Catholic
Hulking, All-State tough guy would hunt down ball-carriers; early pass-rusher, as well
Ron Beagle, Purcell
In Purcell system, played defense only as junior; All-State; rode bike to school from Covington
Tony Carvitti, Elder
Undersized overachiever was state's Tri-Defensive Player of Year; 18 sacks as senior

Arguable: Ed Bauer, Elder; Vic Koegel, Moeller; Clint Spearman, Hamilton Garfield; Mel Lunsford, Lockland; Kevin Bates, Wyoming

Tackle

Steve Niehaus, Moeller
Classic lineman was All-American, two-time All-State, prodigiously recruited
Terrill Byrd, Colerain
National Defensive Player of Year; spearheaded dominant Cardinal defense
Dan Tehan, St. Xavier
Early icon whom Cleveland Plain Dealer *called one of best tackles ever in Ohio*
Eddie Beamon, Withrow
Explosive All-American with 320 tackles and 80 sacks in career; recruiting coup for OSU

Arguable: Dana Stubblefield, Taylor; Eddy Herschede, Walnut Hills; John Kasselman, Roger Bacon; Brandon Mills, Colerain; Chris Norwell, Anderson; Bill Eilerman, Elder; Larry Faulk (Abdul Salaam), Woodward; Shane Curry, Princeton

Linebacker

Bob Crable, Moeller
Key figure in Crusaders' rise to top; Cincinnati Post *Defensive Player of Century*
Todd Bell, Middletown
Ohio Lineman of Year; surpassing athlete, smashing

hitter, speed to play DB at OSU

Steve Grote, Elder
Scholastic All-American; ultimate Panther; leader of defense that produced eight shutouts

Mike Larkin, Moeller
All-American vital to two state and national championships

Ben Martin, LaSalle
Tall, mobile All-American rated top overall player in Ohio

Arguable: Lee Wilschevick, Mariemont; Doug Becker, Hamilton Badin; Marc Edwards, Norwood; Glenn Sample, Western Hills; Mike Sensibaugh, Lockland; Steve Apke, Moeller; Hacksaw Reynolds, Western Hills; Shane Bullough, Moeller; Ike Reese, Aiken; Paul Maly, Elder; Steve Strinko, Monroe; Joe Schaffer, Elder; Dixon Edwards, Aiken; Brian Pillman, Norwood; Gordy Massa, Elder; Boxcar Bailey, Hamilton; Denny Dase, Central

Defensive back

Bob Goodridge, Wyoming
Played key spot in Cowboys' unscored-upon defense of '62; lost one game in prep career

Ahmed Plummer, Wyoming
Ohio D-IV Defensive Player of Year; 17 career interceptions; key recruit for Ohio State

Eugene Clifford, Colerain
All-American safety considered top player in Ohio; state Defensive Player of Year

Byron Larkin, Moeller
Crusader MVP, prep All-American who chose college basketball

Carlton Gray, Forest Park
Nation's top scholar-athlete became UCLA starter as freshman

Harlon Barnett, Princeton
Big-time safety set tone for state championship defense; Michigan State recruit

Arguable: Greg Stemrick, Lincoln Heights; Mike Townsend, Hamilton Garfield; Vinnie Clark, CAPE; Barry Larkin, Moeller; Dwayne Woodruff, New Richmond; Jim Herbstreit, Reading; Mike Middleton, Western Hills; Tony George, Winton Woods; E.J. Underwood, Hamilton; Rocky Boiman, St. Xavier; Vada Murray, Moeller; Bill Long, Moeller; Don Nuxhall, Hamilton; Troy Evans, Lakota; Paul Jordan, Sycamore

SPECIAL TEAMS

Placekicker

Kevin Kerr, St. Xavier
Post's *Offensive Player of Year in city; MVP of GCL; 56-yard field goal in state final*

Danny Milligan, St. Xavier
State record for field goals

Arguable: B.J. Sander, Roger Bacon; Jim O'Brien, Aiken; Harry Oliver, Moeller

Punter

Bernie Roeckers, Roger Bacon
Spartan marvel renowned for height of kicks as well as distance

B.J. Sander, Roger Bacon
Held state record for longest punt and *field goal*

Arguable: Jim Bolger, Purcell; Bob Hoernschemeyer, Elder; Kevin Huber, McNicholas; Mike Sensibaugh, Lockland

Kick returner

Erbil Barkley, Central
The reason teams couldn't stop him, he said matter-of-factly, was "they were too slow"

Carl Ward, Taft
Dangerous speedster would later lead Michigan in rushing

Arguable: Carlos Snow, CAPE; Milt Stegall, Roger Bacon; Steve Clay, Aiken

Punt returner

Bob Goodridge, Wyoming
Seven returns for touchdowns

Scott Sollmann, St. Xavier
Ohio Co-Player of Year racked up 2,512 all-purpose yards as senior

Arguable: Craig Thompson, Princeton; Steve Clay, Aiken; Danny Milligan, St. Xavier; Kirk Springs, Woodward

Danny Milligan

A pre-season practice moment from Aiken's new team, 1963.

Badin cheerleader Jenny Dubrucq, 1980.

WR

Ends & Receivers

STEVE CLAY—*Aiken/Class of 1992*
CRIS CARTER—*Middletown/Class of 1984*
RON BEAGLE—*Purcell/Class of 1951*
DON HASSELBECK—*LaSalle/Class of 1973*
ROBERT "ROCKO" JOSLIN—*Middletown/Class of 1950*
DANNY MILLIGAN—*St. Xavier/Class of 2008*
JIM O'BRIEN—*Aiken/Class of 1966*
KYLE RUDOLPH—*Elder/Class of 2008*
WILLARD STARGEL II—*Woodward/Class of 1940*
MILT STEGALL—*Roger Bacon/Class of 1988*
TOM WADDLE—*Moeller/Class of 1985*
MERLE WENDT—*Middletown/Class of 1933*

ALL IN A DAY'S WORK *(Fritz Apking)*
THE PRINCE OF PRINCETON *(Arnold Franklin)*
THE END THAT JUSTIFIED THE MEANS *(Tony Hunter)*
KATT-MAN-DO *(Eric Kattus)*
THE RECEIVING LINE *(The Kelly Family)*
A CATCH IN TIME *(Tom Smyth)*
THE LEGEND STARTS HERE *(Charley Wolf)*

Bench Strength—Darren Barnett, Princeton; Brent Celek, LaSalle; Thad Jemison, Princeton; Steve Junker, Elder; Alex Higdon, Princeton.

Jack Hoffman of Purcell mid-catch, 1947.

Steve Clay

Aiken | receiver/return artist | class of 1992

92

HE WAS THE ORIGINAL BIG LITTLE MAN OUT OF AIKEN HIGH, A FOUR-YEAR LETTERMAN AT EASTERN MICHIGAN WHO IN 1994 WON THE NCAA DIVISION I punt-return title by averaging nearly 20 yards a return. But lest one think Steve Clay was one-dimensional, read on: He *also* averaged 21.7 yards on 30 kickoff returns and caught 46 passes for 589 yards.

By the time he graduated in 1996, he'd been team captain, All-MAC, and on so many lists in the school football records, they must have considered devoting a pullout section to him. And more than a dozen years later, he was still there: Number 2 in kickoff return yards (1,772), Number 3 for his 14 career TDs, Number 4 in career receiving yardage (1,846) and career catches (133) *and* receiving yardage in one season (999).

Coming out of Aiken, Clay was the conference MVP and one of the best players in the city, but as soon as recruiters looked across the stat sheet and located him below eye level—there at 5-5, 145 pounds—they gave him the recruiting stink eye. "I expected that," he said. "I knew I had to put up big numbers..." Only two schools saw him as he saw himself: Kent and Eastern Michigan.

Soon, he was rewriting EMU's records, and other coaches were rewriting their early appraisals. "Little Man, Big Playmaker," read the headlines. And with the headlines came the jokes. "Certain folks may be able to eat peanuts off the top of the guy's head," wrote one, "but Steve Clay must be some kind of athlete."

Well, of course he was. First, he had to contend with being a Lilliputian among the gridiron redwoods. Then he had to contend with an unending tide of size jokes: "They'll see me and say, 'What you doin' out here? Ain't you supposed to be in high school or something?'"

Such repartee tended to come just before a reception (63 of them in 1995), or something like the 95-yard kick return against Pittsburgh. Nothing like a good retort to shut a guy up. Size wasn't everything, his actions said. If it were, Dana Stubblefield would be President.

Clay had a *loooow* center of gravity, and he was quick and smart, and he had good hands. He was quite likely the smallest serious offensive weapon in Division I, and pound-for-pound, he may have been the best offensive football player to ever come out of Cincinnati. He was a thoroughbred in a pony package, and wherever undersized athletes might need a role model to look up to, tell them about Steve Clay. He's the guy in the records book, and he's at their eye-level.

Cris Carter

Middletown | receiver | class of 1984

84

IT SEEMED AS IF CRIS CARTER WAS INTENT ON THE LEGENDARY EVEN WHILE IN HIGH SCHOOL. HIS ONLY DIFFICULTY WAS CHOOSING THE SPORT in which to *be* legendary.

There were four Carter boys (and two badly outnumbered sisters) living with their mother in an apartment in the Middletown projects—almost a basketball team, which seemed to be their sport, except that they were good at whatever they tried.

They jumped the barbed wire fence at Middletown High so they could get in the stadium and run the steps wearing weighted vests, beat each other one-on-one, and if competitiveness was not invented on the Middletown playing fields, then it reached its apotheosis there. Or as Cris himself said: "I was the worst loser in the history of sports." (His teammates recalled that once, because the other peewee team was winning, Cris clotheslined a kid and caused a boycott of the postgame handshake.)

Adversity, however, was defined by his buddies as having to face Carter on the basketball court. His teams were the customary five, plus Carter's pugnaciousness. As a 6-2 senior, he became a 1,000-point career scorer for the Middies, and Al Milton, Carter's high school quarterback, recalled a game in which his old receiver embarrassed

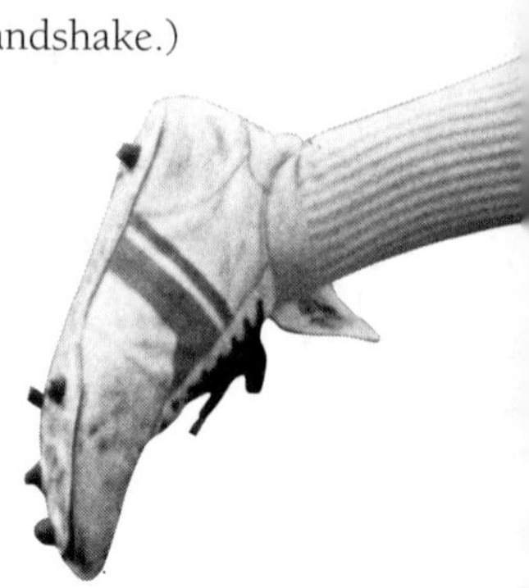

another major college recruit on the court.

"He talked about the guy's mother, then hit a jumper," said Milton. "He talked about the guy's father, then hit *another* jumper . . . ."

Jimmy Calhoun, the Middies' tailback, didn't play basketball but watched from the stands as the coach wiped his face with his hand. This meant Cris was off to dunk on someone, so Calhoun watched the hand and placed his bets. By the end of the game, he'd have $30 or so and take everyone out to eat.

Cris was deep into his professional football career before the home boys believed it. They laughed about him being slow. "He never ran routes in high school," said his old Middie quarterback. "I would be looking downfield for him, and he'd be over there, yelling for the ball. You had to throw him the Hail Mary because he couldn't get behind anybody. He was never open. But he caught it, anyway." Then Carter jived his way back to the huddle and announced to his teammates, "When in doubt, throw it to Carter!"

In 1990, the Vikings picked Carter off the waiver wire for $100. Eight years later, he was the highest-paid receiver in the NFL.

Even though he was the best player—maybe *ever*—on the Middletown football team, the family precedent was for basketball. It was the looming Carter problem: where do you put your legend? The other Carter boys turned basketball into their ticket out of a project apartment that didn't have a telephone. (A small privation that had college recruiters calling next door where their cousin lived, who would then come over and announce a phone call in a house that didn't have a phone.) Butch got out first, off to Indiana on a basketball scholarship, then seven years in the NBA, a demonstration—to the Carters still at home—of the larger world's concentric circles. And they got it, following Butch, at least as far as college.

So, okay, basketball it was.

That left Cris, who thought *he'd* be in the NBA, too. Then his Middie football coach explained to him how many 6-2 guards there were in the NBA. The coach, Bill Conley, said Cris was the most versatile athlete he ever coached. He pointed out that Cris made two different All-State teams, one as a receiver, the other as a safety. Conley said he could have been an All-State quarterback, too. But as a receiver, Conley said Cris could "snatch the ball with hands like a butterfly net." He told Cris if he played football, he'd be an All-American.

So he did and he was.

But wait a minute. This is the kid who only played football because it was the season for it. The kid whose heroes were Magic Johnson and Isiah Thomas. How did he leave basketball and find a home on the grass? Enter the Mama factor, a major instrument in any Carter family assessment. Mama was a Buckeye football fan, and she wanted her baby at OSU. She wondered at all those basketball recruiters sniffing about. Yes, basketball put three of her boys through college, but that last recruiter said that if Cris would sign with his school, he'd give her a horse. A *horse*. "I live in the projects," she snorted. "*Where* would I keep a horse?"

It was the horse, one might say, that Cris rode to Columbus. Proving Conley was dead-on about

Cris's versatility, the kid was a confirmed footballer before he even reached the OSU campus. When a Michigan recruiter told him a good receiver would regret playing for a running school, Cris said, "It's a running school because they don't have *me*. Once they see what I can do, they'll start throwing it."

So they did, and they did.

"Carter was the brash, talented kid who ultimately did more to help the Ohio State offense evolve than any quarterback who had ever played there, Art Schlichter included," said sportswriter Joe Menzer. "He routinely made one-handed grabs that left teammates agape in practice, then often followed them up with circus catches in games."

He cited a throwaway toss by quarterback Jim Karsatos in the 1985 Citrus Bowl with Carter making a spectacular one-handed catch that Karsatos even today calls the greatest catch he ever saw in football.

Carter was All-American that year, just as his old Middie coach said he'd be, but before his senior year, the legend fell; Carter was declared ineligible for taking money from an agent. The Bucks fell to 6-4-1, and then his coach, Earle Bruce, was gone, too. Even without his senior year, Carter left OSU with the school record for career receptions, 168, which—more than twenty years later—has been topped only once.

A 4th round pick in the 1987 supplemental draft, he went to Philadelphia where he suffered abuse from alcohol, drugs, and Buddy Ryan. In 1990, Minnesota claimed Carter off waivers for a bargain basement price, and the legend reclaimed itself. In 1994, he was his old self, setting out to rewrite the record book. By season's end, he'd caught 122 passes—a new NFL mark—for 1,256 yards. He then spent the remainder of the century drawing up a new definition of his position.

As his Middie quarterback had pointed out long before, Carter wasn't a burner. But Calhoun and Milton remembered their old teammate's favorite drill: he'd plant his toes just inbounds, stretching himself to catch sideline passes impossibly far outside, sometimes with only his fingertips. Now they could watch him do it on television, maneuvering himself into the secondary and using his tremendous vertical leap, tiptoeing the sidelines as if the chalk line—as well as the ball—belonged to him. Before long, receivers were all imitating him, or trying to. But in his time he owned the highlight reels featuring the one-handed catch, and few receivers had his soft hands. He was so good at what he did, he shamed the impossible; watching him, you could no longer tell how difficult it was.

When he retired in 2002, Carter was number two behind Jerry Rice in career receptions (1,101) and touchdowns (130). He had caught nearly eight miles of passes, gone to the Pro Bowl eight times, been named to the NFL 1990s All-Decade Team, and it was only a matter of time before he made the Hall of Fame.

And this odd thought: Mama had once been offered a horse to let her baby play basketball. She said she didn't know what she'd do with a horse in the Middletown projects, but the whole time she had a thoroughbred in her back yard.

Ron Beagle

Purcell end class of 1951

51

IT DIDN'T MATTER WHO YOU WERE. YOU WERE A JUNIOR, YOU PLAYED DEFENSE FOR JIM MCCARTHY. YOU WERE A SENIOR, YOU PLAYED OFFENSE. MCCARTHY HAD one way to play, and that was one-way. And so, as a Purcell junior, Ron Beagle made All-State at defensive

ALL IN A DAY'S WORK

A four-sport star at Reading in 1946, **Fritz Apking** became the only player from a Class B school to start in the North-South All-Star football game in Toledo. He went on to star at left end for the University of Washington, then turned down a pro career with the San Francisco 49ers to go to Hollywood where he was stunt double for Chuck Connors. (On the set of *The Rifleman*, Apking's hat never fell off, even when he tumbled off a horse, because it was fastened to his head by an iron wire around the hat's rim).

As a prepster, in one two-day stretch at the state track championships in Columbus, he won gold medals in the end. As a Purcell senior, he made All-State at *offensive* end.

And then, at Navy—which was obviously not as deep as Purcell—he played both, like everybody else. He played end, without stipulation or description. And made All-American, twice. In fact, he was Navy's first All-American. He was, in the estimation of those who handed out the cigarette case representing the Maxwell Trophy, the best player in the nation he was pledged to defend.

Beagle just *looked* Navy, with his blond crewcut and weather-treated, iron-sided jaw. Nor was it any surprise that he would travel so far for his post-secondary schooling. He traveled far to *high school*, commuting across the Ohio—starting at home in Covington and skirting Mount Adams to Hackberry Street—on his bicycle. Long before Gerry Faust came to enjoy his players from Northern Kentucky, Beagle's daily pedal naturally drew accusations of recruiting. But the family had lived in Bond Hill before moving where the grass was bluer, and the rule was that a kid could continue on at a school he was already attending. The estimable Purcell priest, Brother Larry Eveslage, attested to the whole thing, including the complicity of Beagle's bike.

Anyway, it says something—a lot, actually—

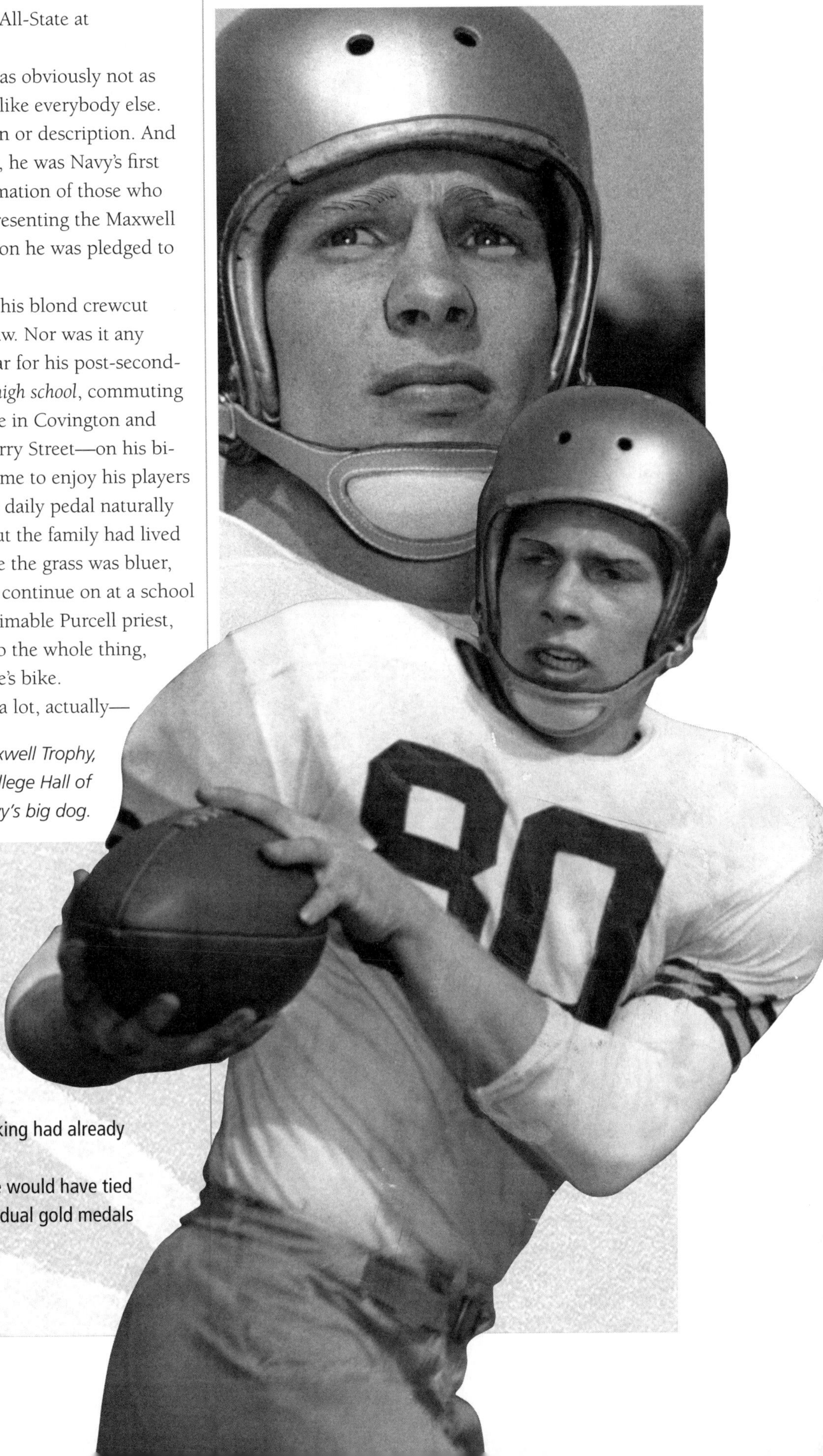

All-American, winner of the Maxwell Trophy, and ultimately, member of the College Hall of Fame. Beagle (at right) was Navy's big dog.

220 low hurdles and high jump, and in his spare time helped the Reading baseball team bring home another. His qualifying time in the 120 high hurdles, which was his best event, beat the winner's time in the final—but Apking had already left to play centerfield.

If he had run the 120 hurdles, he would have tied Jesse Owens' record of three individual gold medals at the state meet.

that Beagle followed Jim Bolger and Roger Franz by a year, and yet *his* was the first number (16) that Purcell retired. When the three of them were together in 1949, the Cavaliers were good enough to self-proclaim the state championship, which was all that any team south of Upper Sandusky *could* do in those days.

At Annapolis, Beagle also, inexplicably—swept up, apparently, in the newfound liberty to play both ways—made All-American in lacrosse. That, however, was not the sport that got him into *Time* as a junior in 1954. Twice.

The Notre Dame game: "On defense, Navy's Ron Beagle seemed like a fifth man in the Irish backfield; on offense he made Quarterback George Welsh look like the hottest passer around."

The Army-Navy game: "All-America End Ron Beagle was always a big stumbling block for the cadet attack. Time after time he pulled runners down from behind, smothered passes before they were thrown. Almost singlehandedly he broke the Army's heart."

Throughout the East, the former Hackberry Assassin was celebrated as the best lineman and possibly best player in the region. "This kid Beagle is wonderful, just wonderful," gushed Pitt coach Tom Hamilton. "He can do everything. He is the best college end I have seen in a long time."

Soon enough, Beagle's big-game performances attracted national attention; and after Navy beat LSU in the Sugar Bowl, the reward came in the form of the Maxwell Trophy. As a senior, when the Midshipmen took the Sugar Bowl again by shutting out Mississippi, he repeated as an All-American, in spite of a broken hand.

His service time was spent in the Marines, where the second lieutenant played fullback for the Sukiran Streaks in the Okinawa Interservice Football League. But in the process, Beagle banged up his knee badly enough that his doctor advised him to stay away from football.

Still, he tried. He tried out for the Oakland Raiders in 1960. By the end of the first workout, he knew it was fruitless. Less than a decade after leaving Jim McCarthy, he had become a no-way player.

And yet, his best day was still decades ahead. In 1986, while living in Sacramento—you didn't think he would stay *close*, did you?—Beagle was inducted into the College Football Hall of Fame. The ultimate end had reached his ultimate end.

Don Hasselbeck

LaSalle | tight end | class of 19**73**

73

IN DON HASSELBECK'S ARTWORK, THERE WAS A COMMENTARY THAT EXTENDED BEYOND THE WORK ITSELF. WHEN HE LEFT LASALLE HIGH SCHOOL, one of his metal sculptures—an abstract, futuristic invention he called "Tree"—remained on display. It spoke of two things.

1) That Hasselbeck, at a purposeful 6-7, was not just a big lug but a cerebral, sensitive student with skills to match; and

2) That the Lancers' great tight end, while blessed with size and no shortage of sporting aptitude—while roundly regarded as the best athlete the school has ever produced—was very much a product of Cincinnati punch-clock, machine-shop culture.

His father, John, played football for Elder before he became a plant manager for a metal fabrication compa-

An End That Justified the Means

One of Gerry Faust's strengths as a football coach was the capacity to conform his team to his fluid and ferocious talent. And in **Tony Hunter** he had the player he called "probably the best athlete I've ever seen."

Hunter was an uncommon high schooler—215 pounds on a 6-5 frame suited for multiple duties in a variety of sports. He was GCL Player of the Year in both basketball and football and captain of the track team besides. And to Faust, he was a compelling reason to feature the tight end.

With Hunter returning kicks and catching passes from three different quarterbacks (Tim Koegel, Mark Schweitzer and Larry Gates) in his celebrated career, Moeller ran a diversified offense that often involved the tall guy going deep from his scrimmage position next to All-American tackle Joe Lukens. He averaged 18.6 yards per catch over the years, an absurd figure for a tight end. He also scored 110 points, made All-American as a senior in 1978 and

Hasselbeck was a student of the arts, and with his great latitude, they ranged from the Fine Arts to football's dark arts.

ny. Don hung out there, toiling summers as a boilermaker. It was how he started messing around with metal.

There was poetry in that. Hasselbeck could not only work with his hands but *catch* with them, too. He was rugged enough to play defensive tackle for LaSalle and talented enough, as a junior, to set a school record with 32 pass receptions. Lining up next to 6-7, 270-pound tackle Dave Lafary (who was another kind of Boilermaker, heading off to Purdue before the New Orleans Saints), the two of them pretty much eliminated one side of the defensive front.

Hasselbeck was a LaSalle starter for four seasons, among other athletic and academic distinctions. As a sophomore, he actually won the GCL high jump championship. As a junior and senior, he was All-City in both football and basketball. In the former, he was a *Parade* All-American with aspirations of playing at Notre Dame. Except that, inexplicably, Notre Dame wasn't interested.

"I'll never forget Notre Dame," he told a wire-service writer when he was at Colorado, on his way to becoming a first-team All-American. "When a kid grows up in the Cincinnati area, the goal of his life is to play at Notre Dame."

In the Rocky Mountains, majoring in Fine Arts and

was decorated as Ohio's Lineman of the Year.

That was otherwise a bittersweet season for the Holy Steamrollers. It came on the heels of three consecutive state championships and two straight national titles. But in the second game of the schedule, Princeton, by virtue of a late field goal and 13-12 final score, snapped Moeller's 53-game regular-season winning streak and proceeded on to break the Crusaders' string of crowns. It was the only defeat Hunter ever suffered in high school.

Along the way, his reputation swelled to national proportions—and perhaps more important, took on extra luster at Stewart Park in Madisonville. By the time Hunter was setting records at Moeller, Joey Jackson was winding down an NFL career as a defensive lineman and making wise decisions on his old home turf. "I was never beaten in one-on-one at Stewart Park," he said, "but it was because I knew who to play. I never played Tony Hunter. Tony Hunter

was a young guy that everybody feared. We feared he would take over the park."

Instead, he took over the Crusader offense and then moved along to Notre Dame, where his immense talent made him the Buffalo Bills' top draft choice in 1983. After two adequate but unspectacular years there, his third season found him in Los Angeles, where offensive coordinator Ernie Zampese determined that Hunter should be a major component of the Rams' game plan. The result was 50 catches.

But in the end—which arrived surprisingly soon—L.A. was not Moeller and Zampese was not Faust and Hunter was not the force of nature he had been back home. When Hunter was in high school, the end had lined up tight and arrived often, from every conceivable direction.

making almost straight A's, Hasselbeck became a starter as a freshman. And a husband to his school sweetheart, Betsy Rueve. And, as a junior, a father to a future Super Bowl starting quarterback (Matt, Seattle Seahawks).

It happened that Betsy had seven brothers who played football, and six of them were quarterbacks. So are two of her sons, the other being Tim, who has played for several NFL teams. The third Hasselbeck son, Nathaniel, was a wide receiver at Boston College, where the other two preceded him. Matt and Tim needed somebody to throw to, after all.

At the outset, though—before Don had the time to coach the boys' youth teams for nine years —their football duties were not quite so exciting. After being drafted in the second round by New England in 1977, Hasselbeck played most of his professional career there (best year, 1981: 46 catches, 808 yards, 6 touchdowns), and raised his family outside Boston. Applying the old machine-shop work ethic, he bought a Jugs throwing machine—at the recommendation of Raymond Berry, the Hall of Famer and Patriots receivers coach—and dedicated himself to catching 500 balls a day from it.

So the Hasselbecks set up an assembly line. After pulling in the pass, Don would flip the ball to Matt (the oldest), who would flip it to Tim (next oldest), who would flip it to Nate (youngest), who would load it into the machine, where Betsy and only Betsy was allowed to shoot it to the 245-pound tight end.

The deal was that Dad would catch 500 balls. The other deal was that, if he missed any of the last 100, he'd

The Prince of Princeton

In 1981, Tom Lemming was a Chicago postal worker with a heightened interest in the high school football scene around Cincinnati. The Queen City had been regularly producing some of the nation's best teams and players, which made it surpassingly pertinent to the arcane publication he had undertaken, *Midwest Prep Football Report*.

To stay abreast of what was going on in Southwest Ohio, Lemming kept in touch with Enos Pennington, the prep writer for the *Cincinnati Post*. Pennington had much to say about the 6-3, 228-pound man-child named **Arnold Franklin** that Princeton was using as a linebacker and tight end. Finally, Lemming had to drive down to a Vikings practice to see for himself.

To *see* Franklin—especially with his shirt off—was to be impressed, and Lemming duly was. When he got home, he penciled in the Princeton star at the top of his player list, which by that time embraced not only the Midwest but the entire nation. Other entities took note, and just like that Arnold Franklin had become the Number 1 high school player in America.

The leading authorities of Ohio were certainly in agreement, celebrating Franklin as the state's Player of the Year, a designation that probably had more to do with stature than statistics. While the sculpted Viking was a first-rate pass-catcher, it was his physical presence on the field that set him apart. He was, of course, a *Parade* All-American. And then came the *recruiting* parade.

After the football season ended, Franklin was a bit distracted with leading the Greater Miami Conference in rebounding. But he found time to make his half-dozen recruiting trips, which took him from coast to coast. At Notre Dame, he was heartily greeted by the old Moeller coach, Gerry Faust. At UCLA, he watched beach volleyball. At Ohio State, he visited with his former teammate, Thad Jemison. And at North Carolina, he was persuaded.

He would become the Tar Heels' all-time leading receiver among tight ends (78 catches), and an 11th-round draft choice of the Miami Dolphins. Franklin didn't make the Dolphins, however, and appeared in the NFL for only a portion of the 1987 season, as a strike replacement player. He then failed a physical with the Green Bay Packers, which is hard to imagine.

But football can take its toll on even a young man who appears indestructible. Returning to the scene of his eminence, Franklin accepted a position running his alma mater's Intervention Center, and coaching football and basketball on the side. Princeton, it seemed, was his Paris—he would always have it.

Before Franklin (right) left Princeton, he had been called the top high school football player in the country.

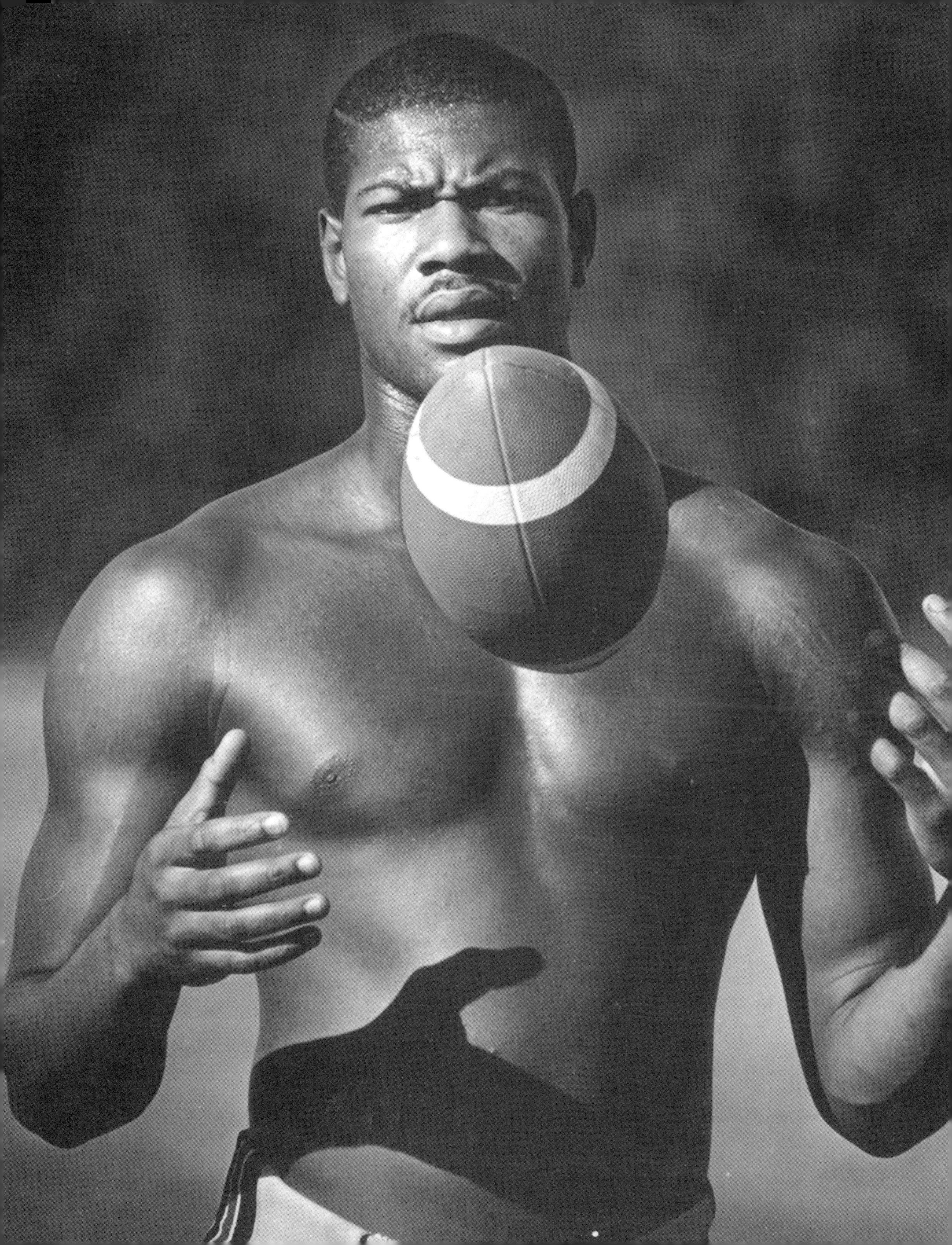

have to go back to 400. This went on every day.

For the Hasselbecks, football was such a family routine that the boys never made a fuss about it. As far as Matt recalls, the only time his father's physical prowess ever came up was on a camping trip with friends. The youngsters heard an unfamiliar noise and one of them—not a Hasselbeck—started to go get his father.

"No, get mine," said Matt. "He's bigger."

When the kids were a bit older, after Don had been traded to the Los Angeles Raiders and blocked an extra-point attempt in Super Bowl XVIII, which the Raiders won, the Hasselbeck show moved to Minnesota, where the old Westsider was a teammate of Archie Manning. Manning's three sons (Peyton, Eli, and Cooper) were about the same age as Hasselbeck's, and they played epic games of three-on-three in the Vikings' parking lot. The families remained close. When Peyton Manning led the Indianapolis Colts into New England for a conference championship game in 2004, the Mannings watched with the Hasselbecks from the Reebok luxury box that Don was able to arrange as a senior director of the company.

"If the Mannings are the first family of the NFL," wrote *The New York Times*, "the Hasselbecks are the second."

"If not the first family of New England football," added the *Boston Globe*, "then the Hasselbecks are one of its dynastic clans." Maybe so. But their roots, don't forget, are embedded in a Cincinnati machine shop.

Rocko Joslin

Middletown end class of 1950

50

SO IT WAS A STEAMY AUGUST JUST AFTER THE WAR, AND TIGER ELLISON WAS IN THE LOCKER ROOM BEFORE THE START OF HIS THIRD SEASON AT Middletown High when he heard someone beating on the door. It was no casual knock but rather an impatient resounding banging, the knock of a midnight bill collector, an angry husband, a man with a warrant.

When Ellison opened the door, he found before him a redheaded, freckle-faced Irish kid who was, to use the felicitous phrasing of Tiger's daughter, who related the story, "no bigger than a bed slat."

What Tiger immediately saw, however, was the size of what coaches like to call "the intangibles." The kid, for instance, had a spirit large enough to stop a native

Katt-Man-Do

Eric Kattus has found himself at the center of at least three remarkable movements in local football.

Over an extended stretch of time, there has been the somewhat inexplicable migration of Cincinnati-area stars to the University of Michigan, where Kattus matriculated after a distinguished career at Colerain and in fact led Bo Schembechler's team in receptions as a senior. Before him, Southwest Ohio Wolverines included the likes of Bob Timberlake (Franklin), Carl Ward (Taft), Clint Spearman (Hamilton Garfield) and Ed Shuttlesworth (Woodward). After him came Dave Metz (Harrison), Michael Taylor (Princeton) and Mister Simpson (Colerain).

Next, bracketed closer around Kattus's prep career, was an extraordinary succession of Cincinnati tight ends. It started in 1978 with Tony Hunter (Moeller), followed in 1980 by Kattus, in 1981 by Arnold Franklin (Princeton) and in 1983 by Alex Higdon (also Princeton). That's four All-Americans in six years *at the same position*.

And in 1980 specifically—actually, the announcement was made in and technically applied to 1981—there was an astonishing and record total of six Cincinnati players named to the *Parade* All-American team: Kattus, offensive lineman Doug Williams (Moeller), fullback Mark Brooks (Moeller), linebacker Mike Larkin (Moeller), running back Brian Mercer (Forest Park) and running back Chris Smith (LaSalle).

Seven years later, Kattus was the only one of the bunch still in the NFL. He had been drafted by the Bengals in the fourth round of 1986, and lasted six years in Cincinnati, plus one more with the New York Jets. As a pro, Kattus was not a game-breaker—Rodney Holman was the Bengals' starter at tight end for all of those seasons—but he had his moments. In 1990, the year controversy broke out in the Bengals' uprising or, perhaps, to launch one. He radiated enough energy to embarrass a race horse.

He was Robert Joslin from down by the tracks where he was called "Rocco" by an Italian buddy, although Robert, having small familiarity with Italian, spelled it "Rocko." It meant, he said, that he was tough as a rock, which, in fact, he was. He liked a good brawl, something he inherited from his dad, a machine shop tool grinder.

Here's Tiger's account of his initial meeting with Rocko Joslin:

"This skinny kid, who might have been 150 pounds soaking wet, said to me, 'Tiger Ellison, the coach? Rocko Joslin, the player. Give me a uniform because I came to play football!' I told him he was early, and to wait an hour, then go down to the sophomore locker room. 'Why the sophomore locker room? You've let other sophomores start on the varsity, and that's where I want to start. See this red hair? Now, you know, football is a fighting game, and this red hair means I'm a fighter, so why don't you just start me on varsity?' I knew no such thing about red hair, but I admired this little guy's spirit. I said, 'If you're such a fighter, you start with the sophomores and fight your way up to the varsity.'

"We had two-a-day practices in August, and after the morning session I was in the shower when Coach Harold Mason came in and said, 'Tiger, come out of that shower because I have a story that will put hair on that old balding head of yours. This kid Joslin says to me, "Coach Mason, I understand you are a fine coach, but I won't be with you long because I'm fighting my way up

Robert (right) spelled his name "Rocko," and since he was a tough kid, who was going to correct him?

locker room over the admission of female reporters, Kattus scored two touchdowns in a game against the Houston Oilers, both on a play somewhat embarrassingly known as "Buck Naked." (Understand that Sam Wyche was a creative head coach.) It involved Boomer Esiason faking a handoff and rolling without blockers in front of him until he found the tight end for a TD.

When he thought back on it, Kattus concluded that his professional success probably redounded, in large part, to that which he'd had as a Colerain Cardinal. "When you start getting recognition on the national level," he said, "you start thinking, 'Maybe I *am* good.' It raised my expectations."

There's no similar explanation, however, for the good fortune that Kattus carved out when he bought Feldhaus Sporting Goods in 1993 and renamed it Kattus Pro-Team Sports. Before long, he had moved the store to a larger location and was profiled in *Inside Sports* magazine for his entrepreneurial achievements.

According to the story, Kattus, as a product of the NFL's Career Internship Program, was part of a movement along those lines.

Yet another one.

to the varsity." So I told the kid to throw a block on Big John Burney, who's six feet seven and goes 280 and is solid as a redwood. Like lightning he rammed Burney to the ground flat on his back, jumped on his chest, buried his face in the dirt and wouldn't turn him loose! I was standing there like a stupefied jackass, it happened so fast. We finally got him pulled off, but Tiger, I'm telling you, the kid is like hot squirming wire, tough as nails and slippery as a snake!'

"'I said to him, "What in the hell do you think you're doing? I'll kick you off this squad if you pull another stunt like that." He said, "Why don't you just kick me up to the varsity before I hurt any more of these little sophomores?"' Coach Mason thought I might want to take Joslin off his hands.

"So before the afternoon practice, I called his junior high principal, and asked him if he knew this Joslin kid. 'Know him? All too well, Tiger. The kid is always in a fight, always in my office, and he hates school. He flunked seventh grade and nearly flunked eighth. When I asked him why he fights, he says, "Oh, just for the hell of it." See, that's the problem, Tiger, he fights without a cause. He's from a rough neighborhood and I understand there's fighting going on all the time at home, and he seems to have the idea that the good Lord put men on this earth just to fight. You give that boy something to fight *for*, and you'll have yourself a good man.'

"That afternoon, I told Joslin to get over and practice with the varsity. At the suggestion of my line coach Stan Lewis, I started him at right end after watching him block in the drills. He was much too small for the end position, and not particularly fast, but he could catch the football, and he had all the instincts and intensity and muscular reactions of a mountain cougar. And once he had been tapped as starting right end for the varsity, he refused to let anybody else take it away from him for three years straight..."

And that was part of the Rocko Joslin story, but not all of it. He went to Ohio State on a football scholarship and he lettered three years and was captain his senior year, in 1953. A half century later, his play would still be among the top ten performances among all the university's ends—720 yards, 54 catches, and five TDs. And the best part: the grade school flunkee from Middletown graduated with honors. He'd finally learned what his old coach, Tiger, had taught him: "You don't punch 'em in the family jewels. You hit 'em where it hurts the most, on the *scoreboard*, baby..."

Danny Milligan

St. Xavier receiver class of 20**08**

08

FOR A LONG WHILE THERE, EVEN AS HE WAS LEADING ST. XAVIER TO AN UNDEFEATED SEASON AND 2007 STATE CHAMPIONSHIP, IT APPEARED THAT Danny Milligan, the Bombers' inspiration and all-around everything, would not be offered a scholarship to play at the Division I college level. What hogwash.

Milligan's problem was the dastardly measurables. Speed: Not quite. Size: Not close.

The opponent's problem was everything else. Seldom, if ever, has a single player done so much for a team so good. If, when a game started, St. X had the ball first, Milligan was the first Bomber to touch it, on the kick return. If the other team won the toss, Milligan was the first one to touch it, on the kickoff. Invariably—in the biggest games especially—he was also the first player to touch the ball in the end zone.

In the nationally televised triumph over third-ranked DeMatha, it was Milligan who got the Bombers on the board with a 23-yard pass reception. The next week, against Cleveland Glenville, it was Milligan who put St. Xavier in motion by scoring on a 10-yard reverse. When the Tarblooders later stiffened, he dropped a punt on their 1-yard line. Later, he caught the clinching touchdown pass from John Hurley and, for good measure, added a field goal.

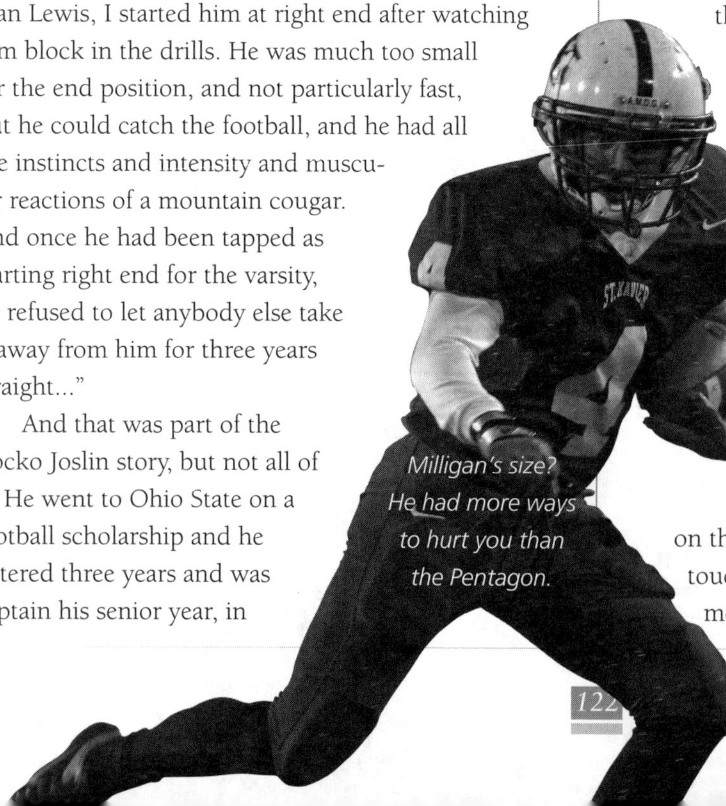

Milligan's size? He had more ways to hurt you than the Pentagon.

The Receiving Line

The football history of **the Kelly family** bears more than a faint resemblance to Cincinnati's. It starts, of course, on the West Side, with brothers Jim and Paul, who were not discernible descendants of *Joe* Kelly, the undersized and locally heralded lineman from St. Xavier, circa 1923 (and later Xavier University).

Jim was a pass-catcher with advanced technique. "He was one of the first I'd ever seen catch a ball with his *hands*," recalled Glenn Sample. That, as we now know, is the way to do it; but in 1946 the aerial game was still in a juvenile stage of refinement.

Anyway, Kelly was the captain and leading touchdown-maker on Elder's 1945 team, and his skill played well at the University of Cincinnati. Suiting up for Ray Nolting and then—good news for him!—Sid Gillman, the former Panther was the school's leading receiver by the time he graduated.

His brother followed him at Elder by nine years, and played for a better team. Paul Kelly shared the backfield with Mike Honold and Dick Selcer, and ran behind the great Dan James, the effect being an undefeated season that may well have been the school's best ever. But Cincinnati was still primarily a baseball town at that time, and Paul considered himself primarily a baseball *player*.

So he signed and tried and got hurt and became the UC ticket manager, and then the Bengals'. Presently, his son, Tim Kelly, holds that job.

Meanwhile, Jim took a coaching job in Deer Park, which moved his family across town, which worked out well for his son, Jim II. Moeller was cranked up by then—but not entirely to the young Kelly's satisfaction. He, too, was a deluxe pass receiver, and had become smitten by watching Greg Cook throw the ball around for UC.

So, during the summer before their senior season of 1971, he and the Crusader quarterback, Dan Hauser, went to Gerry Faust with the idea of doing as the Bearcats did. Faust had been using a run-based offense, but he appreciated the respective skills of his players and, happy to abet their scholarship opportunities, consented to study some UC film.

He found it interesting, and in the opener against Princeton, Kelly caught eight of Hauser's passes. He burned Roger Bacon for 14 catches and 214 yards. All told, Jim II set most of Big Moe's receiving records, made All-American — along with defensive lineman Steve Niehaus—and was chosen by one wire service (the other named Niehaus) as Ohio's Lineman of the Year.

The whole thing worked for Kelly, who signed with UC and began to challenge his father's records. He got close, and led the Bearcats in catches for three years running, but fell a few short of the Elder Kelly—who by then was coaching the UC freshmen.

Jim II, too, maintained his ties with the university, putting in a long term as the team's color commentator for radio broadcasts. He was still doing it when yet another non-related Kelly—Brian—introduced the Bearcats to a contemporary passing game.

Concerning that, color the commentator well-pleased.

Jim Kelly, the elder, at Elder, where he was one of Coach Babe Bartlett's favorites, and with good reason.

The next week, against Louisville Trinity—the top-ranked team in Kentucky—he again carried a Hurley hurl into the end zone for the Bombers' kick-start, and finished off the game with 22 points. And on it went. During the early portion of St. X's perfect season, when star running back Darius Ashley was sidelined with an injury, Milligan personally lugged the Bombers through the toughest schedule in the country.

In the shutout of Elder, he got his team rolling with a 64-yard touchdown catch. In the narrow victory over St. Ignatius, he didn't start the scoring, for a change, but ended it with a game-winning field goal in triple overtime. The next week against Moeller, he was back to old habits, chalking up St. Xavier's first points with a 26-yard touchdown catch.

We're not finished. Against Centerville in the second round of the playoffs, Milligan again put St. X on its way by catching a tipped pass in the end zone. Against Colerain in the regional final, he produced a touchdown, a field goal, and a 43-yard reception. In the state semifinal against Dublin Coffman, it was Milligan who scored all 10 of the Bombers' points—an 8-yard touchdown on a reverse, the extra point, and a 37-yard field goal. And in the state championship game against Mentor—facing off against quarterback Bart Tanski, with whom he shared Ohio Offensive Player of the Year honors—it was Milligan, of course, who got the rout underway by turning a screen pass into a touchdown.

Did we mention that, for his career, Milligan set an Ohio high school record with 40 field goals?

Needless to say, Mr. Everything was named Most Valuable Player on his celebrated team, in spite of the presence of several classmates who were more heavily recruited. Ashley, receiver Stephon Ball, and defensive end Greg Scruggs would all sign with Louisville. Linebacker Fred Craig, the state's Defensive Player of the Year, landed at Stanford.

And Milligan waited. A few Division I schools talked to him about walking-on as a kicker, and possibly getting a chance to return punts. But there were no scholarship offers. It frustrated not only Milligan but St. X coach Steve Specht, who told the *Cincinnati Enquirer*, "I watched him dismantle guys that have already committed to Division I schools. I've coached since 1990, and I know enough to know if a kid can play; and Danny can play."

One party that agreed was the U.S. Army, which, recognizing the countless facets of Milligan's game, chose him for its national Army Iron Man award. Meanwhile, if the cat had the tongue of the college coaches, his praises were sung by anyone who paid attention to results rather than tape measures and stopwatches.

Ultimately, the University of Cincinnati joined the chorus. The Bearcats' coach, Brian Kelly, seeing the light and signing him as a receiver, recognized Milligan's heart and competitive spirit and versatility and innate ability to do good things.

He also recognized the ancillary value of bringing on a popular local hero from one of the most fertile programs in the nation. Over the recent years, UC had not done well with St. X recruits. By spending a scholarship on Milligan, Kelly set about to change that.

As always, the little guy was just the one to get things going.

Jim O'Brien

Aiken | receiver/kicker | class of 19**66**

66

COMING FROM THE CITY'S NEWEST HIGH SCHOOL, AIKEN'S JIM O'BRIEN WAS THIRD IN THE CITY IN BASKETBALL SCORING, WAS FAIR AT TENNIS (HE AND his doubles partner were 5th among Ohio schoolboy players), a sprinter on the track team, and good enough at football to be named All-City. But when he entered the Air Force Academy where he hoped to play basketball, it seemed as if he might become another of those Cincinnati athletes who go off to school and are never heard from again.

His career in the Air Force ended before it could really get started. O'Brien developed a bad case of ulcers and the Academy gave him two choices: leave with a medical discharge or take half his stomach out and enter regular service. He left, went home, and enrolled midterm at the University of Cincinnati with a partial scholarship for basketball. Hanging around Tay Baker's Bearcats, however, convinced him that at six feet, he was too short for that game; if he had a future in UC sports, it was going to be on the gridiron.

There seemed to be a precedent for athletes of another stripe arriving at UC disguised as basketball players. Tony Trabert came to play basketball but made his name on the tennis court. Then there was Sandy Koufax, thought to be primarily a basketball player before he became one of history's greatest pitchers.

So in the fall of 1967, the latest in this distinguished line of athletic changelings walked onto the football team. At first, he was a kicker, but when coach Homer Rice needed a receiver, O'Brien was pressed into duty. Soon the newspapers were calling him "the Bearcat Wonderboy."

Against Louisville, for instance, he recovered a fumble, made a 27-yard diving catch in the mud for one TD, then made a 17-yard catch on the 1-yard line, setting up the 13-7 win. (He also kicked the point after.)

By his junior year in 1968—when he was the only hometown boy on the team—O'Brien headlined Greg Cook's aerial circus. His 142 points led the nation in scoring—12 TDs, 13 field goals, 31 PATs—and he averaged an incredible 25.2 yards per reception. (He also barely missed being elected student body president.) He and Cook were called two of the best football players to ever wear a Cincinnati uniform.

Together, the two of them produced one of UC's most memorable all-time games—the 1968 classic with arch-rival Miami. It is still regarded as one of the most amazing games the two teams ever played.

UC was a middling 4-4-1 that year but with a great offense; Miami came in 7-2, with the nation's stingiest defense.

They thought he was everything except what he naturally was: a really good receiver.

Down two touchdowns in the fourth quarter, Cook finally found himself—and O'Brien as well—throwing for 263 yards and three TDs—in the quarter alone. O'Brien caught a 53-yard TD pass with 4:35 left, then at 1:09 the Bearcats got a last chance. O'Brien kept the drive going by catching a 23-yard pass on fourth and nine.

With three seconds left and the ball on the 30, O'Brien was rubbing dirt out of his eye and trying to change into his kicking shoe. Then: Miami unexpectedly called timeout.

O'Brien got his shoe on and settled down. He was 47 yards from the goal, and there was a stiff crosswind. Cook held. He remembered the ball was six or eight feet wide of the post when it was halfway there, "but with the wind and the natural hook in his kick, it went in by a foot and a half or two feet . . . ."

In Cook's words: "Phenomenal."

In O'Brien's words: "It was an act of God—or I planned it awfully well."

Fans swarmed onto the field and lifted O'Brien into the air.

The next year Cook was gone (the game solidified his position as the Bengals' first draft pick) but O'Brien continued his knack for catching the deep pass: in 1969, he averaged 21.04 yards per reception on throws from Middletown quarterback Jim Ousley.

He clinched the NCAA career record for average yards on receptions—22.2 (missing several games with a shoulder separation). He was an honorable mention *UPI* All-American, his team's MVP, and he left with 17 school records.

Two years later, in Super Bowl V, he was faced with another Miami situation, this one in the Orange Bowl. "Jim O'Brien, 23 years old and nicknamed Lassie because of his long hair, warmed up his kicking leg," wrote *Sports Illustrated*. "With nine seconds left . . . O'Brien came on."

The resulting 32-yarder gave Baltimore a 16-13 win over the Cowboys in a game called "the Blunder Bowl" because of its record 11 turnovers. O'Brien, called "an instant hero in an otherwise heroless game," said it was an extremely hard-nosed game. "It wasn't just guys dropping the ball. They fumbled because they got the snot knocked out of them."

Years later, when he looked back on his career, he said that while the Super Bowl kick made him famous, the one he liked best was the kick that won the Miami-UC game. There was just as much pressure, too.

"You don't know anyone in the stands in professional football," he said. "At Cincinnati, there weren't that many people in the stands and I probably knew half of them...."

Kyle Rudolph

Elder | tight end | class of 20**08**

08

HE WAS A CROSS BETWEEN EDDIE HASKELL AND MIKE DITKA, HYBRID IN BOTH ATHLETICISM AND PERSONALITY, WHICH IS TO SAY THAT ONE MOMENT he might be helping an old lady across the street and the next moment running her over. (Memo to senior citizens on the West Side: don't wear grandson's old football jersey near Elder practice field.)

Kyle Rudolph, by all West Side accounts, is the nicest guy to ever deliver a pancake block. In other words, if you've gotta get yourself pancaked, Kyle's your man.

He's also Elder's finest two-sport star in thirty-five years, going back to when Steve Grote set the two-sport standard. Grote was an All-American linebacker and captained Elder's 1973 state championship basketball team before going on to a stellar career at Michigan. Rudolph was All-American, too, and during his senior year he set the national standard for tight ends. Then, at 6-7, 240 pounds, he had basketball scouts salivating—he set Elder's rebound record, became only the second Panther to score more than 1,000 points (Chad Kamstra had 1,404 from 1993 to 1996), and was three times the GCL Player of the Year.

Even at his size, he ran a 4.6 40-yard dash, and, noted one writer, "he has hands the size of tennis rackets, which enable him to dominate video game play because he can reach all the buttons on a controller with one set of fingers."

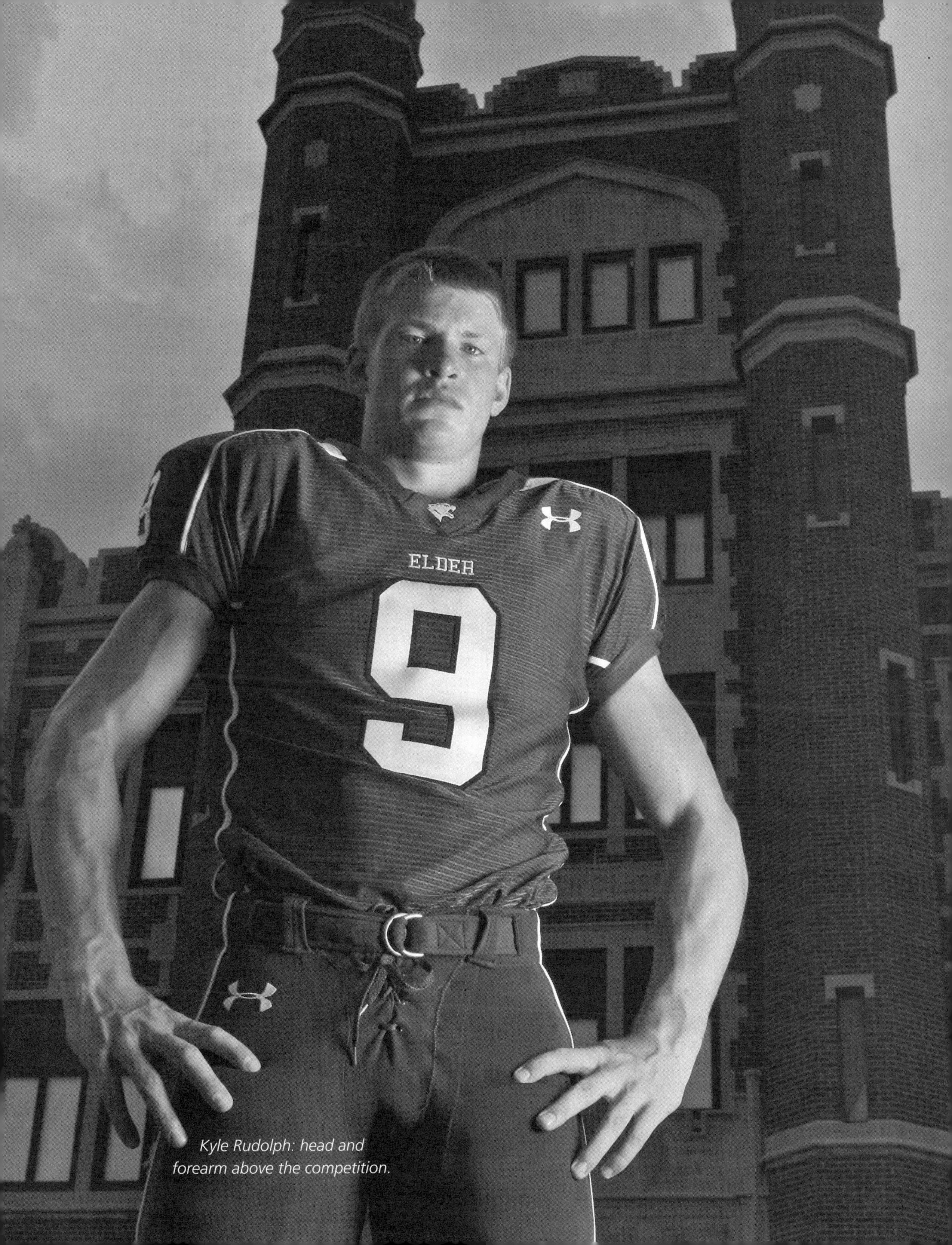

Kyle Rudolph: head and forearm above the competition.

Early on, his coaches thought that he might be able to do anything. Then Rudolph set about making geniuses of them. The summer before he was a junior, Elder scrimmaged Fairfield and in the Panthers' first set of ten plays, Rudolph had ten pancake blocks. Then, on a pass play in which the ball was thrown behind him, Rudolph reached backward and caught the ball with one hand.

It was the kind of performance one wasn't sure was really happening. And it became a harbinger for his special plays. His junior year, playing Oak Hills, he boomed a 68-yard punt. His senior year, when Charlotte Independence came to town with a 109-game winning streak (and a Number 3 *USA Today* national ranking), Rudolph went over the top of three defenders on a crucial 4th-and-20 play to keep the drive alive, and the Panthers upset Independence in OT, 41-34.

"He did it with the attitude that he, personally, was not going to let his team lose," said Craig James, the defensive coordinator. "Against Lakota West, he's back to punt and notices that Lakota sent only one guy out to cover. When he saw that side of the field was open, he took off and got the first down. He had the presence of mind and was secure enough to go and do it. That was two wins he got for us almost by himself."

He could do it on the basketball court, as well. Against Dayton Carroll, Rudolph grabbed an offensive rebound and went up for the putback. When Carroll's Kevin Vest got his hand on the ball, Rudolph's powerful upward movement took Vest with him, dislocating Vest's shoulder.

In the interval since his senior season in 2007, Rudolph has gotten even bigger and stronger. Working with a nutritionist, his weight went to 248 while his body fat dropped from 9.7 to 7.4 percent. (The regimen: seven meals a day, four of them shakes with 21 grams of protein in each.)

A prized Notre Dame recruit, Rudolph was being looked upon as the player to restore the Cincinnati/Catholic schoolboy pipeline into South Bend, which in its heyday—read the Moeller years of the 1970s and 1980s—transported eighteen Crusaders to Notre Dame. The last Cincinnatian on the roster was Kallen Wade, a big junior linebacker from Withrow, the first Irish scholarship player from the city in almost a decade. (Wade hardly counts, though; he's an *Episcopalian*.)

So tradition fell on the kid from Elder and his coaches said: Not to worry. Elder being nothing if not tradition, Rudolph was well-schooled in the whole package.

"You don't have to coach him," said James. "He's an anomaly, a freak athlete. And as good as he is as an athlete, he's even better as a person. He's what you want your kids to be . . . ."

At the end of Rudolph's first Notre Dame season, the kid whom Irish coach Charlie Weis called "All-Everything" surely seemed to be: he started all 12 games (the first freshman TE to start the season opener), set freshman TE records with his 25 receptions and 262 yards, and was named All-Freshman by *Sporting News*, *CollegeFootballNews.com*, *Rivals.com*, and Phil Steele.

No surprise to Cincinnati's West Side. Almost anybody there could have told you.

A Catch in Time

McNicholas High graduate **Tom Smyth**, a Marshall University freshman, missed the fateful DC-9 crash in 1970 that wiped out the university football team because he was an ineligible underclassman. The following year, a new squad of 89 traveled to Morehead State, 72 of them freshmen (the school had been given special permission to play them). Smyth, a tight end, caught a 10-yard pass that would be Marshall's first post-tragedy score, the only points in a 29-6 loss.

"I caught a little screen from our quarterback, and I remember carrying the ball and seeing a group of Morehead guys on the goal line. They weren't going to stop me. I just went airborne."

He was both prideful and self-conscious about that first TD. "My buddies died playing for that program," he said. "They're the ones that deserve the accolades."

The other Cincinnati connection came the following week when Marshall upset Xavier 15-13 on the last play of the game. *Collegefootballnews.com* named it one of the greatest games of all time. Calling it "an outstanding game between two teams without a lot of talent," it was named for its circumstances and emotions, and later made more famous by the movie, *We are Marshall.*

Willard Stargel

Woodward | tight end/coach | class of 1940

40

There were no listed weights in those days, and it's difficult to say, exactly, how skinny Willard Stargel was. But the Woodward yearbook provides us a hint, at least, identifying him as "Wee Willie," which obviously didn't refer to his height, seeing as how he was the tallest fellow on the Bulldog basketball team. His son, Willard III, estimates Willard Junior's high school dimensions at about 6-2, 155 pounds.

These days, of course, they don't make defensive ends that size. *Those* days, on the other hand, they seldom called them defensive ends. Most of them were just ends. They went both ways, and the job called for an athlete rangier than today's wide receivers and faster than modern pass rushers. It's a skill set that doesn't really exist anymore.

That's one reason to celebrate Willard Stargel II. But there's a better one.

His life.

Stargel was the offspring and namesake of a Cincinnati cop. The original Willard Stargel and another black officer patrolled the city's West End with motorcycles and billy clubs. The father was somewhat ahead of the civil rights curve; and so, in turn, was his son.

In 1941, Willard II, refusing to be handicapped by either his race or his slenderness, became the University of Cincinnati's first black football player. The next year, an African American student organization, capitalizing on Stargel's impressive manner and relative celebrity —he was known also as a UC basketball player and record-setting hurdler on the track team—placed him on the ballot for student council. He lost the election but won admiration.

Shortly thereafter, his collegiate experience was interrupted by a couple of years in Italy and Germany with an all-black artillery unit, during which time he played wartime basketball with the Buffalo Big A's of the 92nd division. Basketball is also what Stargel played first upon his return to UC in 1945. In the fall of 1946, he once again distinguished himself at right end for the footballers. At 9-2, it was the Bearcats' best team since the 1897 version lost only to the Carlisle Indians. They were even better when Stargel was on the field.

The '46 season was the one that began with the memorable upset of Indiana. Less renowned was the second game, against Kentucky. The Wildcats refused to take the field in the company of a "colored" player—and one, they surely noted, who happened to be the best man on the squad. In Stargel's absence, Cincinnati lost. The same thing happened when the Bearcats played at Tulsa.

It was consequently an issue of considerable controversy when UC was extended an invitation to play Virginia Tech in the Sun Bowl. But the bid was only valid if Stargel would forego the trip. At his urging, the UC players voted unanimously to accept it.

"Dad was humble in that regard," said Willard III. "He didn't want his teammates to miss the opportunity to play in the bowl game."

However, the university president, Raymond Walters, was not so quick to indulge the others. He asked the Board of Trustees to reject the bid for "ethical and patriotic reasons." The issue escalated into a civic debate and power struggle. In the end, the Bearcats made the journey to El Paso—without Stargel—and won, 18-6.

There was a casualty, however. Electing not to reprise the ordeal in basketball season, Stargel instead put a premature end to his athletic career. As a player, that is.

On another front, he was just starting. After earning a master's degree at Ohio State, he spent thirty years teaching and coaching at Taft—he was the football coach when the Senators had four future NFL players in their backfield—Walnut Hills and Newport, Kentucky. Around the Public High School League, Stargel's accommodating manner was as renowned as his results.

"Dad's coaching style was innovative," said Willard III, better known as Will. "In football, his idea was spreading his players out and using speed and passing. In terms of how he dealt with young people, he loved talking to them. His way was that he always allowed them to talk and express themselves but never allowed them to be disrespectful.

"I remember one time, when he was older and his

knees were bad, he was at Walnut Hills during the summer and there were some kids who didn't know he was there and they were throwing rocks at the windows. He yelled at them to stop, and when he did that the kids threw rocks at *Dad*. And he started *running* at them, old as he was. He wouldn't permit any disrespect. And you could tell how the kids he coached respected him. When he was at Taft, my brother and I were going to Walnut Hills and every morning he'd drop us off at the corner where Gilbert, Hewitt, and Woodburn all come together. At the same time he dropped us off, there would be some guys from his track team waiting there so they could put their clothes in his car. Then they'd run all the way to Taft. You have to command some respect to get kids to do something like that—especially in the '70s."

At Walnut Hills, Will Stargel was a quarterback and conference Player of the Year. He had an offer to play at Michigan and was about to accept it until he received a better one—an academic scholarship to Harvard. His father's younger brother, Bob, an end locally known for the way in which he would smother passes in his chest, had played football at Harvard (one of four players from the 1946 Walnut Hills team to move on to the Ivy League); and Will would. too, also starring as a receiver.

Meanwhile, his brother, Scott, went to UC and broke his father's hurdles records. A much younger brother, Jason, later became a Bearcat and one of the program's most productive pass-catchers ever, averaging more than 20 yards a reception over a period of three seasons.

Stargel II retired in 1986, at which point the Taft stadium was named for him. In 2004, it was handsomely renovated to accommodate five Cincinnati public schools—Taft, Hughes, Jacobs, Shroder, and Woodward—and in some cases revitalize them.

And so, while the exemplary player, coach, and role model died in 1990, his name is still going strong. In fact, it carries more weight than his slender frame ever could.

Milt Stegall

Roger Bacon wide receiver class of 19**88**

88

IT WAS SEPTEMBER, 1995, WHEN MILT STEGALL, HIS GIG UP IN THE NFL, REPORTED TO WINNIPEG—WINDY-PEG, THEY CALL IT—TO PLAY FOR THE BLUE Bombers of the Canadian Football League. He stepped off the plane in shorts and a T-shirt. It was the last time he would be uncomfortable up there.

The Green Bay Packers had just cut him because, well, he was that type. Stegall had been an All-State player at Roger Bacon—in fact, he had set a school record by averaging 26.5 yards per pass reception—but he was not a Big Ten prospect. He went to Miami, was the Redhawks' offensive MVP as a sophomore, honorable mention all-conference as a junior and captain as a senior, but was not drafted by the NFL. So he caught on with the Bengals, returned kickoffs for three years (led the team as a rookie), signed with Green Bay, was released by Green Bay, showed up in Manitoba without the appropriate apparel, not quite ready to consider himself finished as a football player, and became, of course—isn't it obvious?—a Canadian legend.

One way to measure a football player's celebrity is by the nature and number of his nicknames. The more famous a guy is, the more of them he accumulates. The one most often attached to Stegall is The Turtle Man,

Chocolate Milt learned that if appreciation did not come in one league, perhaps it would arrive in another.

for reasons that only a few must know. After all, he is not *slow*, by any stretch. At Miami, in fact, he holds the third-best time, ever, at 100 meters; fifth-best at 200. He is not *homely*, by any stretch. In fact, Stegall was voted the best-looking man in the CFL. And he is hardly the type of fellow to draw himself into a shell. In fact, his best-known of numerous familiar quotes goes like this:

"There's only six guarantees in this world. Death, taxes, trouble, Milt Stegall being on time, Milt Stegall being pretty, and Milt Stegall being in top-top shape. Only six guarantees."

Well, maybe seven. There's Milt Stegall catching a touchdown pass.

In 2002, when he was named the CFL's Most Outstanding Player, he caught 23 TDs, a league record. In 2007, he caught the 137th of his career, also a league record. That would account for another of his nicknames: Milt Stegall, the Touchdown Beagle.

Now, the fact that Canadians are not particularly good at nicknames—Chocolate Milt is another—should not diminish Stegall's accomplishments up there. In September, 2008, Stegall added to his considerable legacy with a spectacular catch-and-run of 92 yards, becoming the CFL's all-time leader in reception yardage. That would pretty much make him the greatest pass-catcher that our northern neighbor has ever seen.

His eminence is such that the clean-living Cincinnatian—no smoking, drinking, red meat, or staying up late—is known, also, by his number.

In French.

Quatre-Vingt-Cinq.

And that's all for the nicknames. There seems to be no end, however, to Stegall's accomplishments as a slotback, a position that wasn't really available to him in the NFL. Nor, consequently, was superstardom.

That status never seemed to be much of a prospect for Stegall back in the days when his father was running a convenience store—Stegall's Freezer Fresh—in South Avondale. Garland Stegall died when Milt was a senior at Roger Bacon, where, by then, the glory years of Bron Bacevich and the Roeckers boys were long gone.

In spite of the Spartans' relative lack of visibility—they've never made the state playoffs—Stegall did not go unappreciated as a high school star. In addition to Miami's interest, the University of Cincinnati had a recruiter on the case. His name was Dave Ritchie, he was a graduate of Withrow High School, and in 1999 he became the head coach of the Winnipeg Blue Bombers.

Not unnaturally, Ritchie and his star receiver developed a lively in-house rivalry over the annual games between UC and Miami. The winner would get to choose what the loser had to do. One year, Stegall had his coach working all day in a dress.

At that, Ritchie was more properly outfitted than Stegall when he first showed up in Winnipeg.

Tom Waddle

Moeller | wide receiver | class of 19**85**

85

HOW COULD HE HAVE SEEN THAT FAR INTO THE FUTURE, WHEN A WHITE WIDE RECEIVER WITH A PRIVATE SCHOOL PEDIGREE—NAMELY HIMSELF—WOULD NEED AFFIRMATIVE ACTION TO LAND A JOB IN THE NFL?

Well, he couldn't, and therein lies a story. It was a story that took a Cincinnati kid to the pinnacle of American football, and if it happened to be more short story than novel, it still had best-seller written all over it. It had, after all, improbable action, an engaging hometown hero up against overwhelming odds, and finally a triumph of the spirit.

> "Tommy Waddle—you or me in shoulder pads.
> —Jay Mariotti.

It started at home, which was Moeller, with Tommy Waddle and his All-American season, one he topped off with a three-touchdown performance in early November of 1984 as Moeller beat Toledo Central Catholic 50-27. That gave him 12 TDs for the season and the school's single-season record.

From there, he went on to Boston College and became one of BC's all-time leading receivers, *still* tops in the Eagles' record book—nearly a quarter of a century later—for his 13 receptions against TCU in 1988, as well as his 70 receptions that year. He was number four

"The great white wideout has gone the way of the spotted owl," wrote one football mag. In 1981, Cris Collinsworth's 67 catches put him 7th among the top three NFL receivers—3rd among white guys. In 1991, Tom Waddle's 44 put him 30th in the league—and 2nd among the white guys.

among all the nation's receivers in 1988, and when he graduated, his one-handed grab against Penn State in 1986 was talked about in the same exalted company as Gerard Phelan's 1984 Hail Mary grab from Doug Flutie in the Miracle in Miami.

"There have been other receivers before him at Boston College who have distinguished themselves, but only a select few have been immortalized by an unforgettable catch," said that august publication, the *Boston Globe*.

"If getting hit is a God-given talent, I guess I have it."—Tom Waddle, former Moeller wide receiver.

He was off to Chicago in 1989 as an undrafted free agent—the last man signed—where the young wideout with the most ironic name in all of receiverdom made similar remarkable catches over a six-year career with Da Bears, even as he was setting a record for most times cut or released.

His Chicago resume looked like a rap sheet: he was cut on September 4, 1989. On September 5, he was signed to the Bears' developmental squad. On September 22, he was waived. And on September 25, the Bears re-signed him. In February of 1990, he was left unprotected in free agency, released on September 3, brought back to the active roster on September 4, then...well, you get the picture.

Now here's what *else* happened in those six years. He played his heart—and cartilage—out, caught two thousand of the hardest won passing yards in the industry, earned the affection of Mike Ditka himself (a man who dispensed affection with a teaspoon), and become a near-cult figure in the Windy City.

He had hung tenaciously on through 1989 and 1990, and seen some spot playing time; then in the 1991 Bears' opener—a few days after being cut and brought back—Waddle went in, courtesy of an injury to the regular starter. Here's the report from the Chicago papers on Waddle's second quarter catch from Jim Harbaugh: "Harbaugh lofted the ball long and right on the money, 50 yards in the air, and wee Tommy Waddle proceeded to earn his keep. He dove in classic belly-flop form, caught the ball in mid-air and fell into the end zone in a play you've already seen fifty or sixty times on the highlights."

And, as the sportswriters put it, a legend was born.

For the rest of the year, Waddle was the go-to receiver. "He can catch a football with handcuffs on," said one of the Chicago scribes. Against the Jets he caught eight passes for 102 yards, and then the defining moment: his performance against Dallas in the Bears' playoff loss. His nine catches and 104 yards under duress had even the hardened Ditka watching his receiver rather than the scoreboard. Many of the plays were "spectacularly acrobatic," with Waddle being steamrolled by the Dallas linebackers. The Soldier Field crowd was chanting his name: "Wad-dle, Wad-dle, Wad-dle." Four of his receptions were for first downs, and he ended the day with a TD, a team record for most catches in a playoff game, a bruised sternum, a possible concussion, and a night in the hospital.

He was on the All-Madden Team that year, made up of the toughest, smartest players in the NFL, or as Madden himself said, "It's about a guy who's got a dirty uniform, mud on his face, and grass in the ear hole of his helmet."

"A lot of people wonder why Tom Waddle is playing in the NFL," said Ditka. "He plays the game with his heart, that's why."

He started for the Bears in 1992, won the opener by catching a TD with one second left, burned the NFL's fastest man, Deion Sanders, for a TD against Atlanta, and caught a 70-yard bomb at Cleveland. He led the team in receptions and yards in 1993, but the old Bear, Ditka, wasn't around anymore and it was just a matter of time before the conventional wisdom caught up with Waddle. The new coach, Dave Wannstedt, wanted blazing speed (even though Waddle's 20-yard shuttle time—the test that measured quickness—was a team best).

Waddle had an offer from his hometown Bengals but then he reconsidered; even at 28 he felt like a middle-aged prizefighter. He'd had three surgeries and so many various injuries the family vehicle should have been an emergency transport. And so in 1995 he retired.

He had been given membership in the Caucasian Wide Receivers Association of America, that organization of underprivileged white boys from the wrong side of the gridiron track who were called "gritty" and said to have "deceptive speed." Or as one such receiver said, nailing precisely what was *really* being said about himself and receivers like him: "Them slow-ass, Bass Pro Shop sticker-havin' cracker zombies."

"Waddle was big-time," said Jim Lippincott, a Bengals personnel official and one-time Moeller athletic director. "He was fierce; he played with a chip on his shoulder. He was too small and too slow all the way through those good years he had with the Bears."

Maybe so.

But Waddle was one of those rare players whose old-fashioned ethic had swept up his audience who recognized you didn't need blue blood to be an aristocrat. The Moeller kid rose by nerve, wit and intensity, and they gave him the key to the city. Yes, he was a black hightop in an Adidas world but if ever a white boy had game, Tommy Waddle had it.

Merle Wendt

Middletown | end | class of 1933

33

Merle Wendt might have been just one more in an illustrious line of Middletown schoolboy heroes, but he wasn't. For one thing, few of them played virtually every down of every football game for four years, and even fewer captained both the football and the basketball teams his senior year (he was a four-year letterman there, too). Throw in the presidency of both his junior and senior class, and you've got a fellow to reckon with.

But Wendt wasn't finished. He headed off to Ohio State, which—by hiring Francis Schmidt—was intent on alleviating what it could of the Great Depression plaguing the rest of the country. Schmidt was an anti-Depression kind of coach. Joyously offensive-minded in the face of adversity, his belief was simple (even if his offense was not): To win, he said, all you had to do was score more points.

And he did.

And who helped him mightily?

The iron man from Middletown, Merle Wendt. And if they didn't exactly lift the economic doldrums that had shut out the country, they *did* make Columbus—and Ohio—feel better.

In 1934, Wendt scored on a 66-yard pass play on OSU's way to a 34-0 win over Michigan (and a 7-1 season), and the Ohio Stadium crowd pulled down the goal posts for the first time.

In 1935, in an important league game at Chicago, Wendt's 30-yard touchdown helped cut into an OSU deficit—one of Chicago's scores was by Jay Berwanger, who, at the end of the season, won the first Heisman Trophy. The eventual win secured the Bucks a Big Ten co-championship (the last title had been 1920, meaning that the OSU drought had lasted longer than the Depression), and the Bucks finished the year by shutting out Michigan again, 38-0, a game historically notable for beginning the now famous season-ending rivalry. (There was one more historical note: Michigan had an All-American center that year, a man named Gerald Ford, who later became President. Ohioans, having long gridiron memories, claim that Ford's Ohio loss in his 1976 presidential race dated back to his days as a Wolverine.)

In 1936, with Wendt the team captain, OSU trashed Michigan a third time: 21-0. This meant the kid from

Merle Wendt: raising the bar on being illustrious.

Middletown had helped blank Michigan three straight times, all told by a 93-0 margin. He was also named All-American all three years (in 2008, he was still one of only seven Buckeyes who had).

He was drafted in the sixth round by Green Bay and his wife, Jane, had modeling and acting jobs to pursue on the West Coast. Instead, they chose not to be separated, which meant that he chose not to play professional football. By their own accounts, which came late in the twentieth century, neither of them ever regretted it.

BENCH STRENGTH

In 1942, **Charley Wolf's** favorite priest left Newport Catholic High School, which didn't have an athletic program, and the sporty lad—who would later coach the Cincinnati Royals, among other distinctions—decided to take the streetcar every day to St. Xavier. In football, he played end for the Conquerors, which put him in cahoots with star quarterback George Ratterman, who was possessed of an uncommonly potent arm. After Wolf and Ratterman blew up Highlands with their long-range aerial assault, the local papers took to calling them St. X's bombers. By Wolf's senior year, the school nickname was officially changed . . . **Jack Hoffman** liked Ed Kluska so much as a coach that he followed him from Purcell (where Hoffman was his All-State end) to Xavier University (where he was a sophomore starter on Kluska's 1950 Salad Bowl team). Hoffman was a big man in a smaller era, 6-5, 234 pounds, a two-way player teamed up with John Martinkovic to give XU one of the best defensive end tandems in all of college football. During Hoffman's three varsity years, Xavier lost only two games and both Martinkovic and Hoffman went on to excellent pro careers. Hoffman went to Chicago in 1952's fifth round, started as a rookie, missed the 1953-'54 seasons serving in the army, reclaimed his spot, and stayed there until breaking his arm in 1958 . . . **Clint Haslerig** was a St. Xavier wideout, class of 1970, who played on two of the best St. X teams of the era—one was unbeaten (and ranked fifth in Ohio), and the other (Haslerig's senior year) went 8-2 and outscored the opposition 320-42. The team captain, Haslerig was receiver, halfback, and kick returner. Needless to say, a good part of the offense belonged to him. Going off to Michigan, he repeated himself, becoming the leading receiver on the frosh team, then losing only two games in his three varsity years. On 1973's unbeaten Number 6-ranked team (the only blemish was a tie with old nemesis Ohio State, Haslerig made All-Big Ten, along with teammate Ed Shuttlesworth, another Cincinnati kid. Both of them made the All-American Blocking Team, too (as Dave Foley did before them and Steve Sylvester afterwards), which meant they probably could. Haslerig went to San Francisco in the 4th round of the '74 draft and spent three years in the pros . . . In 2001, **Darren Barnett** set a Cincinnati-area receiving record—81 catches in the regular season, followed by 10 more in Princeton's only playoff game—that lasted just a year. Thanks to the brilliance of quarterback Mike Daniels, the record was reset the following season by another member of the "Sticky Bandits," Johnny Long, with 85. But not even Long could top the game Barnett had his senior year against Moeller—17 catches for 260 yards. Nephew of former Princeton defensive back Harlon Barnett, Darren followed his kin to Michigan State, where the All-State receiver was converted to the position at which his uncle had been an All-American. The younger Barnett, however, was not. He played a bit for the Spartans, then transferred to Southwest Missouri State, then, after the New York Giants won the Super Bowl, got a crack at making their roster . . . When **Brent Celek** was a University of Cincinnati senior, it was generally agreed that he was the best player on the Bearcats' roster. Not many people saw *that* one coming. Celek had been the MVP at LaSalle in 2002, but was considered, tops, the *second*-best tight end in school history, behind Don Hasselbeck. Nevertheless, he had the brains and the hands to make it big, and, at 6-4, 250, the brawn as well. Celek showed it all on a winning November night in 2006 when, as a UC senior playing against Rutgers in perhaps the most important game of his collegiate career, he made a tough catch near the sideline, broke a tackle, swerved by a couple of others, and managed to stay inbounds and keep his balance at the same time for an 83-yard touchdown that made the momentous evening complete. Celek had hoped to be drafted by the hometown team for which his family had ten seasons tickets, but the Philadelphia Eagles intervened in the fifth round. He immediately solidified his professional status with a strong rookie season. To conclude his second season, Celek broke out with ten catches and two touchdowns in the NFC championship game against Arizona. One way or another, his future was secure . . . Pat Mancuso was considered a fairly close-to-the-vest head coach—but not when he had **Thad Jemison** at his disposal. In 1980, Princeton didn't hesitate to throw the ball Jemison's way, the result being that just about every school receiving record was broken that season. Jemison was a *Parade* All-American and the Ohio Lineman of the Year, the sum of which got him a scholarship to Ohio State. For most of four years, he did comparatively little for the Buckeyes, but made amends for all of that in his final game, the Fiesta Bowl, when he caught eight passes for 131 yards, including the game-winner with less than forty seconds to play. OSU trailed Pittsburgh 23-21 when Jemison grabbed the 39-yard spiral from Mike Tomczak, ensuring his selection as MVP of the game . . . **Steve Junker** came along at Elder a little too early. Dick Selcer—who two years later would lead the Panthers to an undefeated season—was a sophomore quarterback when the 6-3, 217-pound end was a senior in 1952, and the Panthers were running a split-T offense that didn't feature much passing. Junker was recognized as only an honorable mention All-City player, which made it somewhat surprising when he signed up at Xavier University and twice led the Musketeers in receptions. It was even more surprising what came next: Junker was a starting end in the East-West Shrine Game, then went to the Detroit Lions (back when the Lions were Lions) in the fourth round. There, "the big redhead," as the papers liked to call him, became a hero in Detroit's drive to the 1957 NFL championship. He caught eight passes for 92 yards (five of them for first downs) and a TD in the Western Division playoff win at San Francisco, and his TD catch from Tobin Rote on a fake field goal attempt broke open a close title game with the Cleveland Browns. Junker added another TD catch as the Lions buried the Browns 59-14. Junker was called "the best first-year end" in the league, but suffered a knee injury the following year . . . **Alex Higdon**, who starred at Princeton, could have starred at the *other* Princeton, the one that plays Harvard and Dartmouth. This is a guy who made Academic All-Big Ten three years in a row; a guy with a master's degree from Vanderbilt and a Ph.D from Ohio State, where he also played some tight end. As one of those, he was good enough to be a high school All-American and Ohio Lineman of the Year after helping Princeton to the 1983 state championship; good enough to be drafted in the third round by the Atlanta Falcons in 1988. On the football field, Higdon was not reluctant to rest his brain and throw around his 6-5, 245-pound body. Half an hour after reporting to the Falcons, he was fighting with another rookie, linebacker Marcus Cotton. "It didn't look like he wanted to be held," Higdon explained to the press. Beyond that, he had a good start, catching two touchdown passes in his first three games. But an injury limited him to just that. After a single season, Higdon had to give up the sport for a safer career in corporate psychology . . . At Ball State University, **Dante Love** was such a devastating receiver—as a junior, he caught 100 passes for nearly 1,400 yards—that, before his senior season, the Cardinals' coaches spent a portion of the spring devising a new offense that would make greater use of the 5-10 dynamo. It was a conspicuous success. Heading into the fourth week of the 2008 season, Ball State was unbeaten and the crowd-pleasing Withrow graduate was leading the nation in receiving yards. But after a clash of helmets with an Indiana player, Love left that game strapped to a stretcher. It was a fracture of the cervical spine. After five hours of surgery, he recovered well enough to resume a normal life, but a career in the NFL—once a near certainty—was out of the question. In addition to his spectacular pass-catching talents, Love was also a gifted kick returner, and left Muncie, Indiana, as Ball State's all-time record holder in that category. His remarkable career with the Cardinals followed a memorable senior season at Withrow, in which, as an All-City quarterback, he led the Tigers to their first-ever berth in the Ohio playoffs. In January, 2009, Love became the first Withrow player to have his jersey retired . . .

Junker

The men of LaSalle, circa 1960s, participate in the time-honored ritual of receiving their equipment.

the linemen

JOHN ANDERSON—*Hughes/Class of 1925*

MIKE BIEHLE—*Mason/Class of 1970*

TERRILL BYRD—*Colerain/Class of 2005*

SHANE CURRY—*Princeton/Class of 1986*

DAVE FOLEY—*Roger Bacon/Class of 1964*

JOHN JACKSON—*Woodward/Class of 1983*

THE JAMES GANG—*Elder/Classes of 1955-plus*

JEFFERSON KELLEY—*Colerain/Class of 1995*

JOHN MARTINKOVIC—*Hamilton Catholic/Class of 1947*

MICHAEL MUNOZ—*Moeller/Class of 2000*

STEVE NIEHAUS—*Moeller/Class of 1972*

THE SMITHS—*Colerain/Classes of 1978, 2006, 2007*

DANA STUBBLEFIELD—*Taylor/Class of 1988*

DAN TEHAN—*St. Xavier/Class of 1924*

JOHN "SOCKO" WIETHE—*Roger Bacon/Class of 1930*

AN IMPROBABLE TACKLE *(Eddie Beamon)*

THE MURPHY FAMILY ACT *(Bob, Rudy, Rob, et al.)*

MOE-MENTUM *(The Moeller years)*

LANGENBECK & FRIENDS *(Dick Langenbeck, et. al)*

LAKOTA'S MAN MOUNTAIN *(Steve Rehring)*

SUPER-SIZED *(Steve Sylvester)*

BRINGING HIMSELF UP *(Butch Wilburn)*

Bench strength, offensive line—Bill Feldhaus, Hughes; Dave Lafary, LaSalle; Ryan Stanchek, LaSalle; Tom Luken, LaSalle; Bob Fry, Elder; Eric Wood, Elder; Joe Kelly, St. Xavier; Paul "Chip" Cain, St. Xavier; Zach Strief, Milford; Eddy Herschede, Walnut Hills. Defensive line—Melvin Lunsford, Lockland; Ben Martin, LaSalle; Bill Eilerman & Ed Bauer, Elder; Vaughn Booker, Taft; John Kasselman, Roger Bacon; Chris Norwell, Anderson; Richard Langenbeck, Western Hills; John Peterson, Middletown.

The Pit, Elder High, 1947–

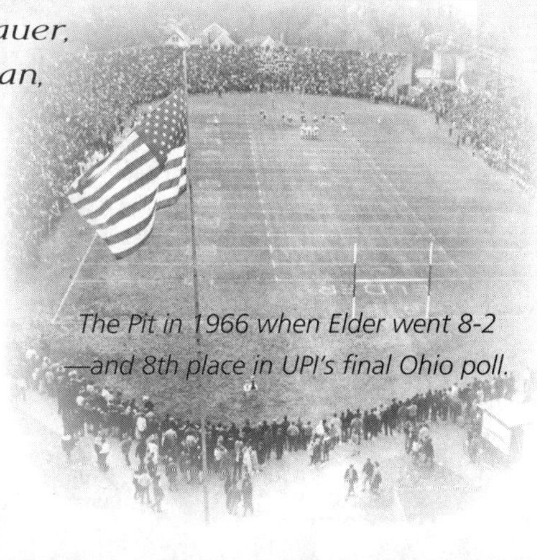

The Pit in 1966 when Elder went 8-2—and 8th place in UPI's final Ohio poll.

John Anderson

Hughes lineman class of 19*25*

25

AS FAR AS FOOTBALL GOES, JOHN ANDERSON'S LEGEND IS LEFT MOSTLY TO THE IMAGINATION. BUT IT DOESN'T TAKE MUCH.

We know that he became an All-American at Cornell. We know that at 6-3 and nearly 220 pounds he was bigger than most of the boys he played against in 1924 and the seasons just preceding. We know that, given the Olympic record he would set in the discus in 1932—by *seven feet*—he was no doubt immensely stronger.

Anderson also competed at the 1928 Olympics, placing fifth in the discus, but it was at the '32 Games in Los Angeles that he became a national star and local celebrity, declared on John Anderson Day as "Cincinnati's greatest athletic hero."

The gold medal, of course, made him, in retrospect, a far better football player. "He is the same John Anderson," according to the *Cincinnati Post*, "who illumined the pages of Hughes High School football with his gridiron triumphs." This assessment was seconded in his 1948 obituary, which observed that, "The handsome blond giant capped four years of legendary football exploits under the late Charles (Red) Krueck . . ."

We know, as well, that Anderson was "the ideal Hughes man," because it says so in the 1925 yearbook. A state champion in track—he carried Hughes to the team title—and the son of a Procter & Gamble executive, to his schoolmates he was "just unassuming Johnnie," the fellow whose friendship was solicited by all and enjoyed by most.

Anderson's niceness, in fact, may have extended a bit far for football purposes. Apparently, Krueck would sometimes take him to task for the big guy's manner of gently picking up his ball-carrying opponents rather than slamming them to the surface. Nonetheless, the manchild led his school to a 7-1 record his senior season.

He was a scholar, too, which took him to Cornell, which prepared him for the world stage, which made him attractive to Hollywood's. The studios had begun to seek out such compelling athletes as Buster Crabbe, Johnny Weissmuller and Eleanor Holm—all swimmers—but Anderson was the first track star to be signed. A model American born, literally, on the Fourth of July, he was "judged a perfect specimen of male beauty on the basis of physique, stance, virility and general appearance."

Anderson's movie career didn't amount to much, however; not as much as his military career. He was a lieutenant commander in the navy, and in World War II served as a navigator in the Pacific Ocean. He found the big water to his liking, and after the war signed on as a navigator for a salmon fishing company in Alaska.

There, at the age of 41, unassuming Johnnie died from a brain clot. It hardly seemed possible.

Ah, Johnny, we hardly knew ye....(and with team, in circle.)

Mike Biehle

Mason | offensive tackle | class of 19***70***

70

BEFORE THE FARMLANDS AROUND MASON TURNED TO CONDOS, NO ONE IN DRIVE-PAST COUNTRY HAD EVER SEEN A FOOTBALL PLAYER LIKE MIKE BIEHLE.

At 6-4, 250 pounds, he combined size with quickness and agility in a way that was rarely seen outside the city. There was an occasional heavyweight, but the big farm kids tended to be slow and heavy-footed. And none of them had the athleticism Biehle did, attested to by fifth-place finishes in the shot and discus at the state track meet, in addition to his presence on the Comet basketball team. A decade later the basketball style of Curt Stevens (another Mason offensive lineman who went on to play at Ball State) was described by a Dayton journalist as being like "a thug standing under a streetlamp," a description that also applied to Biehle taking care of his lane.

No one could compete with him when he played in the Fort Ancient Valley Conference, even though—as with most offensive linemen—Biehle wasn't the star on his own team; he helped *make* the star. Since grade school, Roger Koepfle had been the luminary on whatever Mason football team he played for. When he and Biehle reached high school, they helped the Comet football team continue its domination in the early days of the FAVC, rampaging through the league and winning four of the first six championships. Koepfle was fast and ran with power, a quietly competitive player who inspired his teammates by a good hit. In pre-game warmups, Koepfle didn't stand out, but Biehle did; the Mason coaches could see their opponents looking sideways at Biehle, as if they were thinking, "I've got to play against *that*?"

And behind the power of Biehle, Koepfle ran for over 1,100 yards his junior year and scored 140 points. Injuries hampered his offensive production the next year, but his three years at linebacker got him to Ohio University. Biehle, meanwhile, elevated his game at Miami University where he continued to dominate his position. A three-year starter, he was twice All-MAC (first team) and played in two bowl games, proving that good players didn't need a big-school pedigree to play big-time football. When *The Enquirer* named its pantheon of all-time great Redhawks, Mike Biehle was at offensive tackle.

His old teammate, Koepfle, a little undersized at 5-10, 200, was also a three-year starter for OU and second-team All-MAC. So finally there was parity: *Biehle* was the star, at least among his peers—and the MAC defensive linemen who had to deal with him every Saturday. And because he and Koepfle were now playing across from each other, there was even a wider audience, in the form of the student body that followed the teams, made up of all the local kids, relatives, and ex-teammates at OU and Miami who had known Biehle and Koepfle, and all their friends, and their friends' friends.

The OU-Miami games, and even the ones with Bowling Green, promoted what the kids called "migration weekends," when they migrated to one stadium or another for the ostensible purpose of watching Biehle and Koepfle. For many of these fans, the battle of Biehle vs. Koepfle was more important

Biehle was from a smaller school but at Miami he played big time.

than the score. Each of Miami's offensive plays was scrutinized and rehashed to evaluate which of the two got the best of the other. The record shows that Miami won each of the games.

The record also shows that by the third quarter there was such a beery haze over the stadium that birds flying through it became disoriented and began nesting in the tubas belonging to the marching band. On one other such afternoon, when Bowling Green upset Miami in Oxford, the *BG* students tore down the *Miami* goalposts and carried them through town, where they were deposited in front of one of the local watering holes.

Undersized Koepfle

When OU and Miami played, only the most ardent—and sober—among them saw much of either Biehle *or* Koepfle after halftime, and as time passed, the matchups and individual victors receded into legend.

"I kicked his ass," Koepfle would say much later. And then he added, circumspectly: "But I'm sure *he* would say the same thing..."

Terrill Byrd

Colerain defensive tackle class of 2005

05

HIS OWN COACH ADMITTED THAT, IF TERRILL BYRD HAD NOT PLAYED ON AN UNDEFEATED, STATE-CHAMPION, NATIONALLY RANKED HIGH SCHOOL team, he might never have seen a scholarship. On the other hand, Byrd didn't just *play* for the Colerain Cardinals in 2004; he *defined* them in a way, perhaps, that no other defensive lineman had ever defined a local team so accomplished and spectacular. (In fairness, Moeller's Steve Niehaus might have made a run at it if the playoffs had started a couple years earlier.)

That's not to understate the talent across the board at Colerain that fabulous year, because it was immense. Dominick Goodman, upon switching from halfback to quarterback, came through with a smashing season and lit up the state championship game—a 50-10 thrashing of Canton McKinley—with a record 259 rushing yards. There was also the prolific and unforgettable running back, Mister Simpson, who went on to Michigan before transferring to UC, where his Colerain classmates had already collected. In addition to Byrd and Goodman, linebacker Andre Revels was there. The same Colerain team also sent the coach's son, safety Brayden Coombs, to Miami, and Byrd's twin brother, Tirrdell, to Tennessee-Martin.

While Goodman and Simpson—by virtue of a relentless option offense that frequently fumbled but was never humbled—put up gaudy numbers for Colerain's state title team, the Cardinals were built around defense, and that was built around their 6-0, 290-pound nose tackle. Byrd—my word. The kid had 21 sacks as a senior, and that, frankly, wasn't his forte. If an opponent ran it, he was granite.

Colerain gave up an average of just 76 yards a game that season, competing against one of the toughest schedules in the country. "He's the best defensive player I've ever coached," said Coombs, "and one of the best I've ever *seen*."

An Improbable Tackle

In a family of twelve kids, **Eddie Beamon** *had* to be tough. It worked out nicely that when he lined up at defensive tackle for Withrow High School and peered across the line of scrimmage, there were eleven of them to deal with—the same number he saw at home.

At about 250 pounds, Beamon was as close to unblockable as the Public High League had ever entertained. By the time his senior season concluded in 1973, the big fellow, renowned for the force and frequency of his hitting, had 320 career tackles, and fully a quarter of them had come at the expense of

Coombs was hardly alone in that assessment. Byrd was not only the Defensive Player of the Year in Ohio, but also in the *nation*, according to the prep mavens who dared to identify such a thing. Tell you, though, who *didn't* make that call—the college coaches.

UC's Mark Dantonio recruited Byrd with the appropriate enthusiasm, owing in part to the need to sign more of the best players from a bountiful hometown for high school football, and in another part to the importance of building the local fan base. As it so curiously happened, Dantonio pretty much had the great tackle to himself. There was not a single other offer from a BCS program.

"I think the biggest fallacy in recruiting," remarked Coombs, who came to UC as an assistant when Brian Kelly took over as head coach at the end of the 2006 season, "is people looking too much at the raw statistical data—the height, weight, and speed—and too little at how many plays a kid makes on the field. Terrill Byrd was a kid I believe was a national recruit, and the coaches at UC were loyal to Cincinnati; they took some kids off that team and also off Elder's state championship team.

"But I think that if Terrill Byrd wasn't at a school that had some success and notoriety, nobody might have recruited him. The Louisvilles and West Virginias, they wouldn't offer him. The Michigans and Ohio States, they wouldn't offer him. And now, I guarantee you, every single one of those teams would love to have that kid."

The problem, they all said, was that Byrd was too *short*. Well, he must have hit a growth spurt right after high school, because by his first game as a college

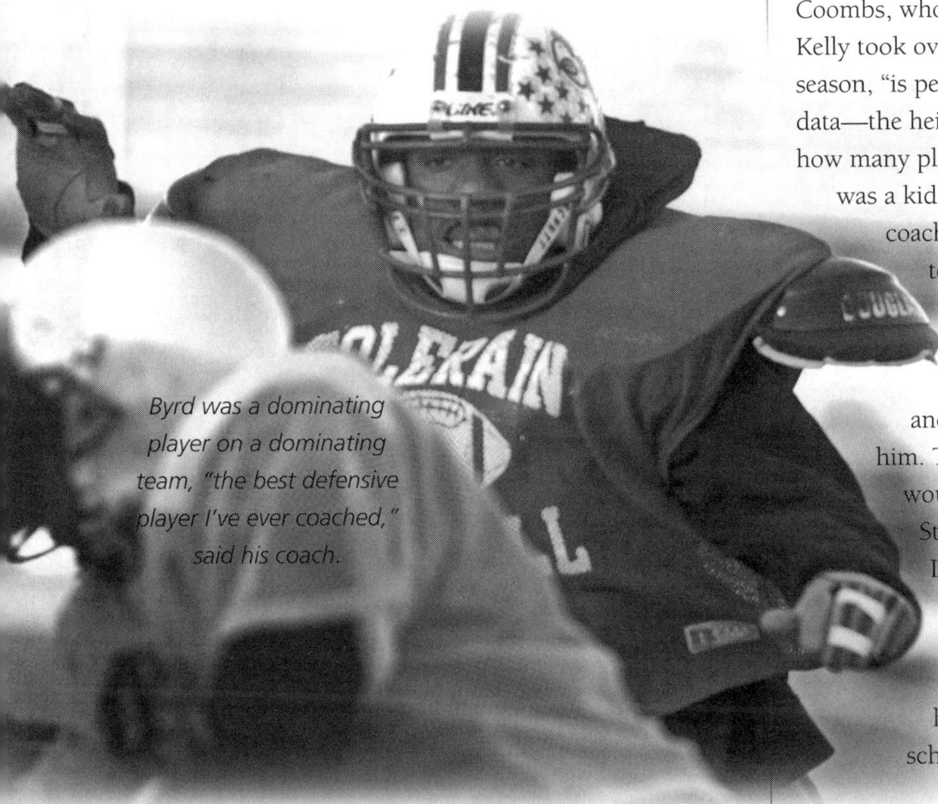

Byrd was a dominating player on a dominating team, "the best defensive player I've ever coached," said his coach.

the opposing quarterback. Eighty seems like a highly improbable number of sacks—but then, Beamon was a highly improbable tackle.

Woody Hayes certainly thought so, an assessment that put him in agreement with most of the college coaches in America. The explosive Tigers star, a *Parade* All-American, was considered the equal of any defensive lineman in his class and recruited with the appropriate relish. His signing with Ohio State was a happy day for the Buckeyes.

As a sophomore, Beamon lined up next to Nick Buonamici at tackle as OSU rolled to the Number 1 ranking and a Rose Bowl date with UCLA. Before the game, Bruins coach Dick Vermeil observed that Ohio State's two interior defenders were the equal of any pair in the country. Beamon then proceeded to sack his quarterback three times, albeit in defeat. The next year brought an Orange Bowl championship, but as a senior, Beamon sustained a severe ankle injury that prematurely ended a striking career.

Twenty years later, he was inducted into the LaRosa's Hall of Fame alongside Carlos Snow and Ken Griffey Jr. Snow, no doubt, was the most accomplished runner of the group; but there could be considerable debate as to which of the three was the best ***hitter***.

freshman, the Colerain star was starting at tackle. By his second year, he was All-Big East. By his third year, he was All-American.

His collegiate career was not without its minor setbacks, however. Twice, he was held out of the season's first game for disciplinary purposes. And also twice—in the *same game*—he was reprimanded for bad dancing. Against Miami in 2007, after his first sack of the season, Byrd marked the occasion with a little step he called the Murk Out. That time, the official—firm but amused—merely warned him. Then came his second sack of the season, and a spontaneous impersonation of rapper 50 Cent's "I Get Money," which was assessed a 15-yard penalty.

Kelly took the indiscretion in stride, however. In a backhanded way, he blamed the other players, then enacted a remedy. "We have the Terrill Byrd rule in effect," he said. "When Byrd does anything good, we're going to celebrate with him, because if you celebrate as a team, you're okay."

Thereafter, there was quite a lot of collective celebrating.

Shane Curry

Princeton defensive lineman class of 1986

86

IT WAS FOOTBALL THAT BROUGHT SHANE CURRY TO CINCINNATI IN THE FIRST PLACE. BROUGHT HIS DAD, THAT IS.

Back in Altoona, Pennsylvania, Jim Curry fancied himself a pretty good quarterback; good enough for college scholarships. He accepted the University of Cincinnati's, largely because he was impressed by the way Oscar Robertson had succeeded there as a conspicuous minority. As a black quarterback in an age when there weren't many, Curry would need that assurance.

What he didn't need was the coaching change, George Blackburn to Chuck Studley. When Studley arrived in 1961, Curry became a disenchanted receiver. A good one, though. In 1962 and '63, he led the Bearcats in catches, including 10 one day at Indiana. He was drafted in the third round by the Cowboys. But his heart was in *throwing* passes, and he didn't stick in Dallas. He stuck around Cincinnati, though.

And he raised a fine son.

After the divorce, Jim and Shane's mother, Sandra, a probation officer, brought up their big kid together and separately. Dad was a contractor specializing in restoration and, later, matters of the spirit. Shane—named, just as it sounded, for the noble hero of the old cowboy movie—lived with Mom in Bond Hill, in the Woodward district.

But he wanted to go to Princeton to play football. He had a friend, Maurice Calhoun, who lived in Lincoln Heights. To make it happen, Maurice's mother agreed to become Shane's legal guardian.

There were a lot of winners in that arrangement, including the Vikings, who brought home a state championship in 1983, Curry's sophomore season. He played on the same defense as Harlon Barnett, a defensive back who later started for the Brown, Patriots, and *Minnesota* Vikings. It was the Princeton defense that saved the monumental victory that year over Moeller, Barnett forcing D'Juan Francisco to fumble late in the game. The Crusaders had prevailed, 28-21, the week before, when the two giants played in the final regular season game, and the public school turned it around the next week in the playoffs, by the very same score.

Curry was a tackle on that accomplished club, the kind of player who didn't often come Princeton's way. Pat Mancuso's teams were known to take advantage of their considerable speed, but generally found themselves at a size disadvantage when lined up against the likes of Moeller. At 6-5 and about 240 pounds—on his way to 270—Curry evened the odds a bit.

"When he moved in and came out for the team, we made a position change with him, and he was reluctant about it at first," Mancuso recalled. "He was used to being a defensive end, but we wanted to move him inside because of his quickness and

He was good at Princeton, better at Miami, and on his way as an Indianapolis pro when his life ended, "senselessly snuffed out," wrote GQ magazine, calling him "a kid with all the promise in the world." (At left, a scene from his funeral.)

toughness. Then he accepted it and came out to be a great kid and really, really good football player. He was recruited heavily because of his size and quickness."

Curry loved his visit to Miami (Florida), but found it too gorgeous and tempting. He was a sensitive young man who wrote poetry, drew religious designs, and tried to make his parents proud. He thought Georgia Tech would be more to his liking, but that didn't work out so well. Then he transferred to Miami, after all, and that worked out well enough that Curry started at defensive end—what he wanted all along—and the Hurricanes won a national championship and the tall pass rusher they called China (for his light skin and Oriental look) was drafted in the second round by the Indianapolis Colts.

He had a promising rookie year, and the word was that he would become a starter the second time around. Curry was working hard at bulking up, and was pleased with the results and feeling good about life in general when he decided to drive home one weekend during a break in spring camp. He called his dad that Friday. Jim Curry suggested that Shane come to the Upper Room, the no-alcohol, Christian-based club featuring a gospel-jazz mix that he had opened as a safe haven for Cincinnati's young people. The son said he might drop by later. He had made arrangements to meet Maurice and some other friends at Brandy's, a club in Roselawn that did *not* feature a gospel-jazz mix.

Shortly after 12:30 a.m., Curry and Calhoun walked out of Brandy's, only to find a black Volvo blocking the red and white Blazer that the player had bought with his signing bonus, along with another car for his mother. The two friends chatted about rap music as they sat, waiting, in the Blazer. Then Curry cracked his door, stood up, and asked if anybody was going to move the car. There may have been some more-contentious conversation; that much isn't clear. What happened next, though, is tragically clear.

The Volvo was the ride for a 15-year-old named Artise Anderson, who had been brought to Brandy's by his uncle and uncle's friend. Anderson had only recently moved to Cincinnati. Back in Washington, D.C., his mother had lost her job and her apartment in the suburbs, and couldn't stomach the notion of her son growing up in the capital city, as she had. So she sent him to live with her mother and stepfather in Cincinnati. That was a few months before the May night when he saw a large, unfamiliar man arguing with his uncle in the parking lot. The man had then sat back down in his fancy Blazer, and Anderson wasn't sure why; but, from his decade and a half of life experience, he figured a gun might be involved. It turned out, a gun *was* involved. His. He shot through the windshield, and Shane Curry, less than a month after his 24th birthday, slumped over toward his high school buddy, his head awash in blood. An hour later, Curry died at the hospital.

Four years after that, his mother, who had spent her career trying to save kids, died, too, her heart never mended. She had started a foundation in the memory of her thoughtful son. His father started another.

They wished for the memory to be not grievous but encouraging, in the fuller view; a memory of a big, gentle man who respected his father, pampered his mother, praised his deity, and offered free haircuts to his friends and teammates. A memory of a champion.

Dave Foley

Roger Bacon offensive tackle class of 19 **64**

64

DAVE FOLEY WANTED NO PART OF OHIO STATE UNTIL HE SAW THE MARCHING BAND. IT FIGURED. HE WENT TO HIGH SCHOOL AT ROGER BACON, where tradition holds tackles and trumpeters in similar esteem. Foley was the former, and the best around.

As a junior, he bulldozed defensive linemen for the undefeated 1963 team that would have been state champion if the wire-service polls had demonstrated any credibility. His senior season, the 6-4, 238-pound scholar was a *Parade* All-American, and so unassailably respected that, eleven years later, he was one of five football players inducted with the charter class of the Greater Cincinnati Sports Hall of Fame.

He was a no-slouch shotputter as well, setting a state record (61'-8.75"); and in fact, a fine athlete whose chief weakness was golf. "He hits the ball a mile," said his father, Tom, a postal clerk. "The trouble is, he hits the putts a mile, too."

But that didn't matter to the countless recruiters who phoned the Foley house in 1964. Woody Hayes, facing an early deficit, made a persuasive appearance, and let the greatest band in the land do the rest.

Hayes, of course, had a soft spot for big blockers who could make big spaces for his big running backs. Foley was a three-year starter, and, according to his irascible coach, "one of the best linemen I've ever seen."

Having played on Bron Bacevich's best team—and that's saying something—Foley then became a leading member of Woody's. That would have been the 1968 Buckeyes, who clobbered Michigan to take over the top ranking in the country, just ahead of Southern California. The Rose Bowl paired 1 vs. 2 for the first time in twenty-two years.

It was a grave matchup that found Hayes at his grimmest. "The coach told us he was taking us to a secluded hotel and we weren't in Pasadena for a good time," Foley, a co-captain and first-team All-American, remarked to *Sports Illustrated*. "When I saw the folks in the lobby playing dominoes, I knew we were in the right place."

Indeed they were. After falling behind 10-0 on an 80-yard touchdown run by O.J. Simpson, Ohio State peeled off the next 27 points, with Foley and Rufus Mayes blocking fiercely for Rex Kern and Jim Otis. Afterwards, Simpson slipped into the OSU locker room to say, "You're the best team in the country, and don't let anybody tell you you aren't."

Five years later, Foley—a former first-round draft choice of the New York Jets—would be moving large opponents out of Simpson's way as the great running back became the first NFL player to rush for 2,000 yards in a season. They called Buffalo's offensive line The Electric Company, because it turned on The Juice. The left tackle was All-Pro that year.

He played in the league for nine seasons, the best of them in upstate New York. When Foley retired in 1977, his bigger brother, Tim, was manning a tackle for Notre Dame's national championship team.

In all, there were four Foleys at Roger Bacon, and all four—including Jerry and Peggy—were subsequently elected to the school's Hall of Fame.

But not for band, if you're wondering.

Foley looms large, receiving his official high school All-American plaque from the National Football Foundation. Jack Farcasin and Dolly Cohen present for the foundation as Coach Bacevich looks on.

John Jackson

Woodward | offensive tackle | class of 19**83**

83

At the conclusion of his junior year at Woodward High School, John Jackson had yet to put on a shoulder pad. "I'd had a bad experience in junior high," he said. "The coach was just yelling too much, and I was like, 'I'm not going to be doing this.' "

So he didn't. He wrestled and threw the shot put and discus and did all of that with distinction, and he also took driver's education, for which the teacher was Tom Sharp, the varsity football coach. Jackson stood 6-5 and weighed about 230 pounds and he was always in shape from wrestling, so you can imagine what Sharp talked about before the seat belts were snapped shut.

Jackson was tempted. He had a notion, even then, that football might he something he could do after high school. So he reported for practice in the late summer before his senior year, and the line coach took one look and told him to get some proper shoes. When he came back with the shoes, it was on. "I'd been itching to do it," Jackson said.

It happened that one of the starting tackles took off for vacation about that time, and when the poor sucker got back, he was second-string. Woodward was not a particularly distinguished team—the Bulldogs might have beaten Elder at The Pit if a touchdown hadn't been called back—and Jackson was not a particularly decorated player in his only year of high school football, but he was big enough and fast enough to get the attention of forty-three Division I (Kentucky, Tennessee . . .) or I-AA schools. He preferred the latter, understanding that he was still only months removed from getting the right shoes.

He chose Eastern Kentucky, which worked out well for the run-blocking portion of the job. The Colonels had two 1,000-yard rushers, owing, at least in part, to the paths cleared by Jackson's gaping shoulders. But when the Steelers drafted him in the 10th round (1988) and he arrived at training camp as a 6-6, 287-pound project, he admittedly had not a clue about pass-blocking. His first exhibition game, he found himself lined up against Lawrence Taylor. Afterwards, he expected to be cut.

What he didn't expect was that the starting left tackle, Buddy Aydelette, would mess up his knee, and Chuck Noll would put the young North Avondale native in the starting lineup. And that he would stay there for ten years, make All-Pro twice and then agree to a free-agent contract with the San Diego Chargers. And it wasn't just any free-agent contract. It was the biggest one that an offensive lineman had ever signed.

When he caught on with Cincinnati two years later, Jackson became the 171st NFL player to participate in 200 games, a longevity mark that he attributed, somewhat, to his balky beginning. "I kind of like the way it worked out," he said in retrospect. "I wasn't burned out like a lot of kids were. At Eastern, a lot of the guys were happy when they were seniors and their careers were over. Mine was just beginning."

He played his last game with the Bengals in 2001, but didn't retire with them. Instead, he struck a deal with Pittsburgh, signing a one-day contract so his career could end as a Steeler. When it did, the procrastinating tackle had been in the league for fourteen seasons, third-longest (behind Cris Carter and Hacksaw Reynolds) of any player from Greater Cincinnati, and longest of any lineman.

There's something to be said, it would seem, for starting fresh.

The James gang

Elder (and X) offensive linemen class of 19 **55+**

55

In the three generations since Dan James set the West Side standard for offensive linemen, the family has produced so many of them that surely the old homeplace on Saffer Street has been tested for substances that altered the James DNA to produce large infants who teethed on chinstraps and went straight from the bassinet to a three-point stance. The Jameses are not a family; they're a franchise.

There was Dan's undefeated 1954 Elder team, of course, then little brother Bob was center on an 8-2 team in 1959. Two of Dan's boys, Dave and Tim, were All-State guards while Bob produced two more offensive linemen and—God forbid—a nose tackle. No one seems to know how that happened, but the nose man, Craig James, redeemed himself somewhat by making the All-City team as a junior and helping Elder to a 10-0 regular season in 1991.

For those who remember Dan, it all made sense. He was a 250-pound center/linebacker in high school when colleges didn't have *tackles* that big, and he ran windsprints with the backs. The closest score all season was Elder's 25-13 win over Culver Military Academy when the Panthers had three TDs called back. St. X's Hall of Fame coach, Tom Ballaban, said it was the greatest high school team he'd ever seen in the city.

Late in the Roger Bacon game, played on a partly cloudy mid-November afternoon and Elder driving, Dan shoved three defenders ten yards into the end zone as quarterback Dick Selcer waltzed in behind him to score. As he did, the late afternoon sunlight broke through the clouds and a shaft of light fell over Dan and the vanquished linemen. It was as though his performance had been so spectacular that even the Almighty had decided to take notice of a high school game (a suspicion forever habored by the Elder faithful).

On the sidelines, Coach Virgil Scardina smiled. "Would you look at that," he said. "Divine intervention."

Dan was known as the nicest guy on the West Side, as long as you weren't across from him on the field. "Teddy bear off the field," they said. "Grizzly bear on." Xavier's unceremonious Mick Connelly came to recruit him, his mouth watering at such a prospect in his own backyard. When he learned that Dan was headed to Ohio State, he snapped, "They'll make dogmeat of you over there," stalked out of the James's living room, and slammed the front door.

Instead of dogmeat, Dan was top dog. On the freshman scout team, he knocked down Jim Parker (the next year Parker was All-American and won the Outland Trophy). Woody Hayes screamed at Dan for his audacity. But Parker had been punching Dan.

"Okay," said Hayes, walking away. "I guess I'da hit him, too."

Little brother Bob was watching when OSU played Northwestern and Dan hit the ball carrier on a kick return, the collision so loud the entire stadium inhaled collectively.

"Danny got up slowly," Bob remembered, "but the ball carrier didn't get up at all..."

Dan was a three-year moving van for hauling running backs into the end zone, sometimes played both ways (on defense he was a

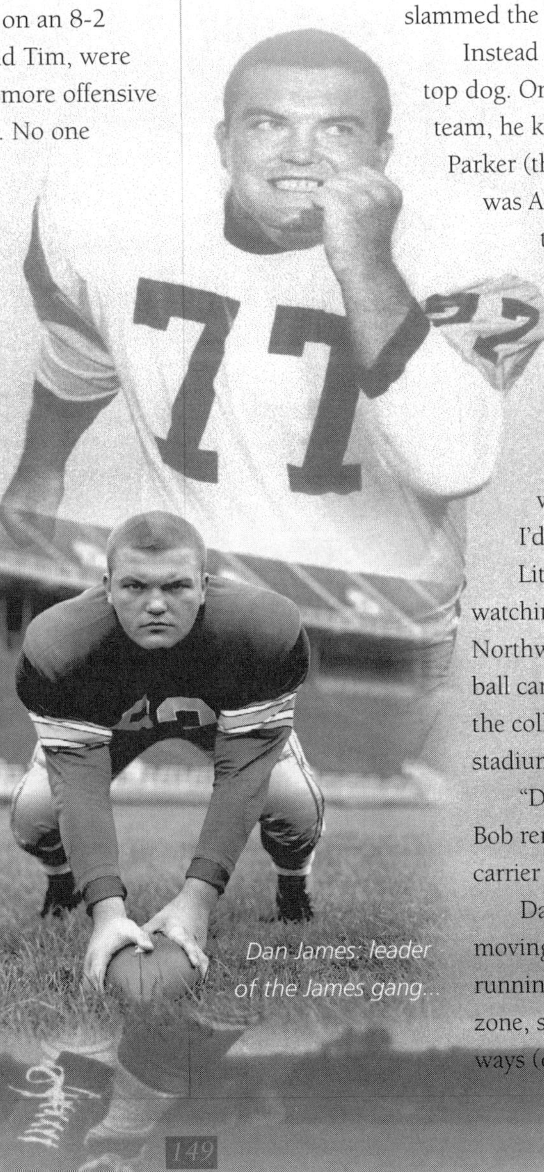

Dan James: leader of the James gang...

Below is Dan James's little brother, Bob, a one-time Elder center and the school's long-time equipment guy. Dan's son, Dave, who played at Tennessee, is in smaller photo below.

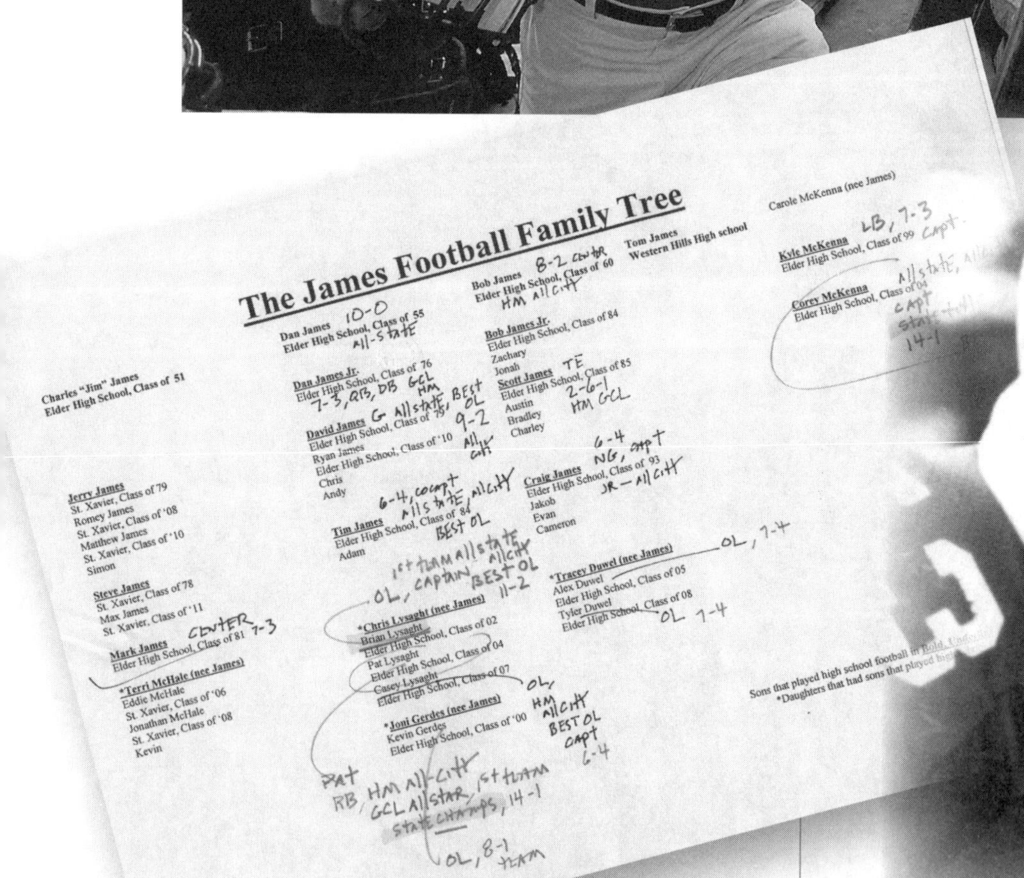

The James Football Family Tree

Charles "Jim" James
Elder High School, Class of 51

Dan James
Elder High School, Class of 55

Dan James Jr.
Elder High School, Class of 76

David James
Elder High School, Class of 79
Ryan James
Elder High School, Class of '10
Chris
Andy

Tim James
Elder High School, Class of 84
Adam

*Chris Lysaght (nee James)
Brian Lysaght
Elder High School, Class of 02
Pat Lysaght
Elder High School, Class of 04
Casey Lysaght
Elder High School, Class of 07

*Joni Gerdes (nee James)
Kevin Gerdes
Elder High School, Class of '00

Jerry James
St. Xavier, Class of 79
Romey James
St. Xavier, Class of '08
Matthew James
St. Xavier, Class of '10
Simon

Steve James
St. Xavier, Class of 78
Max James
St. Xavier, Class of '11

Mark James
Elder High School, Class of 81

*Terri McHale (nee James)
Eddie McHale
St. Xavier, Class of '06
Jonathan McHale
St. Xavier, Class of '08
Kevin

Bob James
Elder High School, Class of 60

Bob James Jr.
Elder High School, Class of 84
Zachary
Jonah

Scott James
Elder High School, Class of 85
Austin
Bradley
Charley

Craig James
Elder High School, Class of 93
Jakob
Evan
Cameron

*Tracey Duwel (nee James)
Alex Duwel
Elder High School, Class of 05
Tyler Duwel
Elder High School, Class of 08

Tom James
Western Hills High school

Carole McKenna (nee James)

Kyle McKenna
Elder High School, Class of 99

Corey McKenna
Elder High School, Class of 04

Sons that played high school football in Bold, Underlined
*Daughters that had sons that played high school football

linebacker), captain of the College All-Star Game, and the first pick of the 49ers in the 1959 draft.

The West Coast seemed light years from the West Side, though, and his wife, Carol, was having trouble with her pregnancy. "I can't play in California and have my family in Ohio," he said. The 49ers traded him to the Steelers, a better fit, for Pittsburgh was a West Side kind of place. He earned his position during an exhibition game his rookie year. Quarterback Bobby Layne had been sacked twice, and he was furious. Coming to the hash mark, he pointed out his underachieving tackle to Coach Buddy Parker and yelled, "Get him out of here!" Dan came in and didn't leave for eight years.

He shared his hard-earned education with Bob, coaching up his little brother when Elder faced a strong Alliance team in 1959. The Stark County team blitzed Cincinnati with fliers about their remarkable upstate cred: "Stark County teams have never been beaten by any team from the south!"

Said Bob, "I was a center without Danny's height or weight and I was facing this All-American so I says to Danny, 'You got any suggestions?' He says, 'Hook your arm around his knee and go that way with him, but don't let the ref see you.' He told me that when I pass blocked, get my hands under his shoulder pads and push like hell. This guy normally got about 80 percent of his team's tackles and that night he got about two..."

Small wonder. He was playing two of the James boys when normally you didn't want to play *one* of them. (Elder beat the highly touted Alliance team, 14-8; it was the Panthers' fifth straight win.)

With the Steelers, Dan knew every position on the line. He even learned how to contain troglodytes such as Bill Glass, the Browns' defensive end who liked to poke his fingers in Dan's eyes. Dan was a stalwart at left tackle—the position that protected the great, free-spirited quarterback Bobby Layne.

After football, Dan returned to the West Side where there was even more football. Dan helped anyone undrstand the game, whether it was Elder players or a kid in a neighborhood backyard. He'd talk technique but not much about his own playing days. If it were left up to Dan, said his son Dave, no one would have known Dan ever played. Then at the age of 49, he was gone, dead of a heart attack, and the West Side had lost one of its greatest football players. More tragically, it had lost one of its nicest people.

The Jameses weren't finished, though. Dan's sons, Dave (1979) and Tim (1984), were offensive linemen who not only looked like him; they played like him. Dave was the superlative technician while Tim had "an aggressive, defensive temperament that was always looking for someone to hit." Tim followed his father to OSU and Dave went to Tennessee. (Tim might have been most like his dad; even rival coach Tom Grippa at LaSalle said he was the best offensive lineman he'd ever seen. "You should have seen him leading backs on the edge," said his cousin, Craig. "Out in space, rolling up backs and safeties...")

Dave was Elder's captain the same year Jerry James—the son of Dan's older brother, Jim—was St. X's captain. The two cousins met at midfield for the coin

Formidable Tim James at work, just another James All-Stater

toss, a small moment of familial recognition passing between them before the rivalry struck. Elder won 7-0, in spite of two fumbles and an interception.

Brother Bob's namesake, Bob—another guard—played in 1983 with Dan's son, Tim. And Dan's baby sister, Carole, had a son, Corey McKenna, who played on Elder's back-to-back state championship teams of 2003 and 2004. He was—what else?—Elder's best offensive linemen, as well as team captain and All-State. (His college career was at Wofford where as a 280-pound center he was a Sports Network second-team All-American.)

Dan's daughter, Chris Lysaght, carried on the family tradition by producing more players, notable among them Brian and Pat Lysaght. Brian (2002) was an undersized offensive lineman who was an Elder captain and first-team All-State. Younger brother Pat (2004) was a fullback on Elder's back-to-back title teams and went on to play fullback for Brown University.

On the maverick St. X side of the family inhabited by Dan's nephew, Jerry, the third generation of Jameses has installed itself: Matthew James, class of 2010, a 6-7, 285-pound behemoth, a sometimes-starter as a sophomore on St. Xavier's state title team of 2007. He was a member of St. X's FOOLS—the Fraternity of Offensive Linemen Society—and already one of the top prospects in the country. (In 2009, he was rated as the nation's Number 15 offensive tackle.)

As his Cousin Craig pointed out, "A freak show. Just wearing the wrong color." Craig, Elder's assistant athletic director, had been hearing about that for some time. How many times had the Elder coach, Doug Ramsey, asked him why a James, of all people, was over *there*?

The world was sometimes a peculiar place, filled with mystery. What was important, though, was that the kid, Matthew, had become an offensive lineman. Surely the ghost of Uncle Dan rested easy. The family lineage—even if it persevered in foreign climates—seemed secure.

The ghost of Dan presided over Dave James's Rose Bowl chili, too. Every New Year's—no matter who is playing—the extended family gathers at Dave's house to watch the game and eat halftime chili. It started back in Dan's day—his old school, after all, used to be in Pasadena almost every year—and now, each New Year's, it's almost like the big guy is still in the house. As traditions go, it's got to be one of the West Side's best.

Jefferson Kelley

Colerain offensive tackle class of 19**95**

95

HE CAME OUT OF COLERAIN IN 1995, GRADUATING EGREGIA CUM LAUDE FROM A PREP CAREER THAT HAD MANY SAVVY ONLOOKERS SAYING HE WAS THE BEST high school offensive lineman in the country. Interesting fact, since Jefferson Kelley didn't seem entirely certain football *was* his game.

Word was, he wanted to be an *actor*. He was tentative at first but intelligent and articulate, and soon there was no place to hide him. One of Colerain's former players watched him hold a block from the middle of the field all the way to the sidelines. "The kid on defense looked like he was wearing roller skates," he said.

Kelley was a varsity starter two games into the 10th grade, and of his thirty-five starts, Colerain won thirty-three of them. As a senior, he'd have certainly anchored a state championship team had not Colerain unwittingly played an ineligible player, resulting in the forfeit of 13 mostly one-sided wins.

The Murphys' Family Act

He always said it started with the Sycamore Spartans. The Spartans were, pardon the oxymoron, the city's peewee titans. And **Rob Murphy**—of the *football* Murphys—was 12 before his Spartans lost a game (they were unbeaten when he was 10 and 11). They lost that game only because Murphy was blocked from behind, an early goad toward personal excellence, as though the clip had been *his* fault.

Those who knew the family merely assumed it was the family inheritance. Rob's paternal grandfather, Bob, was a 250-pound Notre Dame lineman, Rob's dad was a Miami fullback who played briefly with the San Diego Chargers, 6-7 Uncle Rudy was a 300-pound lineman at Slippery Rock, and his mother was a high jumper. Family legend has it that Grandfather Bob,

At 6-6 and 300 pounds, Kelley appeared Bunyanesque in the hallways, which belied his stature as a polite and serious student, 16th out of the 430 students in his class. That not insignificant little statistic was hidden behind a barrage of gridiron honors: he was the only Cincinnatian to play in the Big 33 Classic in which Ohio all-stars played the Pennsylvania ones, Gatorade's Circle of Champions player of the year in Ohio (named ahead of Ohio's Mr. Football, Andy Katzenmoyer),

Kelley made so many All-Star teams, it seemed as if they were inventing some, just for him.

after a stint at Notre Dame, moved on to at least three other colleges—thought to be Syracuse, St. Lawrence, and Columbia—a not uncommon practice of the day. So what did anyone expect from a kid with such a pedigree?

If nothing else, it proved that size, given his relatives, *was* relative. Between the time he was a Moeller freshman and his junior year at OSU when he became a consensus first-team All-American, he'd gained a hundred pounds. (It was all presaged by his shoe size before he was a teenager, the two of them reaching 12 at the same time.)

His appetite at OSU was feared, whether it was for defensive linemen across from him or the twenty-four tacos he'd once eaten at Taco Bell. Or that vanished three-foot sub sandwich.

At OSU, he was also known for staring down defenses before the game began. In the Sugar Bowl in 1998, during a TV timeout, Murphy stood over the ball and yelled at the Florida State defense, huddled 10 yards away.

He said he'd thought of professional wrestling as a career in which he'd become "The Foreman," a wrestler who arrived in the ring wearing coveralls and a tool belt.

"It's *me*," he said. "The blue-collar man. I just hope nobody steals the idea...."

Instead of wrestling, though, Murphy had stints with four NFL clubs and a season as starting guard for the Frankfurt Galaxy in Europe, before finding a home in Canada. In 2006 he helped the B.C. Lions win the 2006 Grey Cup, being named the CFL's Most Outstanding Offensive Lineman in both 2006 and 2007 and considered one of the league's most dominant left tackles.

Moe-mentum

Up front, it seemed in their glory days, the Moeller Crusaders were producing assembly linemen. Year after after, massive All-Americans would roll out of the Montgomery school for distribution to campuses like Ohio State and Notre Dame.

It started with **Tom Backhus**, who in 1964 became Big Moe's first MVP—he is one of only three players to win the honor twice, the others being Steve Niehaus and Tim Koegel—and as a senior in 1965 became the Crusaders' first prep All-American. As an OSU junior in 1968, Backhus started at left guard on the Buckeyes' national championship team. He later coached at several universities, including Notre Dame, where Gerry Faust fired him and later, in his book, lamented the mistake. After he'd had enough, Backhus moved to Vail and opened up a popular dude ranch.

The year after Backhus graduated, tackle **Jack Harpring** represented the Crusaders' offensive line on the All-American lists. For two years at Michigan, Harpring manned one tackle and Hall of Famer Dan Dierdorf took the other. Harpring's son, Matt, plays in the NBA for the Utah Jazz.

The year after Harpring graduated, yet another offensive lineman, **Dan Novakov**, was feted as an All-American. Novakov was recruited to Notre Dame, where he became a standout center and team MVP in 1971, earning an appearance in the East-West Shrine Game. A generation later, his son, also Dan, who grew up in Dallas, would make the Irish as a walk-on quarterback.

After Novakov, there followed an unimaginable season without an All-American. **Vic Koegel** got the Crusaders back on track in 1969. Koegel was a defensive

A near historic moment: Elder beats Moeller, 7-0 in 1972 after a Moe fumble—the Crusaders' last GCL loss until 1988.

The Moeller years

Offense—The offense ran thirty-five plays from twelve formations; the offensive line could block five ways for each play. Gerry Faust's offense was imaginative, entertaining, and aggressive. He liked traps, dives, draws, and the power sweep. He disdained rollouts, screens, and the quarterback option. He liked to throw 12 to 15 times a game—from the pocket—and could count on roughly 150 yards passing whenever Moeller threw that often. He could count on scoring, too. In the 193 varsity games he coached at Moeller, his quarterbacks threw 216 touchdown passes.

Defense—The four-four defense was developed and perfected at Moeller in the late 1960s, and when the assistant coach who conceived it left Moeller, he extracted from Gerry Faust a promise to never share the fine points of the defense with anyone. Its effectivenes was well documented. In almost 6,000 rushing attempts, Moeller opponents gained barely more than two yards per carry. They averaged less than 10 points per game and scored three touchdowns or more only six times in 193 games.

—Denny Dressman, *Gerry Faust, Notre Dame's Man in Motion, From Moeller High to Notre Dame* end at Moeller but played linebacker at Ohio State. In fact, in 1973 he played with Randy Gradishar and Rick Middleton on what is considered by some to be the Buckeyes' greatest-ever linebacking corps. Ohio State led the nation in scoring defense that year, allowing just 4.3 points per game, a modern-day school record. Koegel was drafted by the Atlanta Falcons and played a few games for the Bengals in 1974. At Moeller, meanwhile, he was succeeded by Moeller's most decorated linemen to date, in turn **Steve Sylvester** (All-American in 1970) and **Steve Niehaus** (All-American in 1971).

Then, in 1973, Gerry Faust's team produced a remarkable mother lode of three linemen who made various All-American teams: **Harry Woebkenberg**, **Mark Lang**, and **Greg Storer**. They repaired, respectively, to Notre Dame, Ohio State and Ohio State. At Notre Dame, Weobkenberg was at first stuck behind Sylvester at tackle, making his way into the starting lineup as a junior. With the Buckeyes, Lang started at both center and guard, Storer at tight end. The latter, however, has become better known around Cincinnati for his professional artwork

In 1974, Moeller's designated All-American lineman was defensive tackle **Jay Case**, who took his game to Notre Dame and won some fame by returning a blocked punt 30 yards for a touchdown against Southern Cal. As a junior, Case moved to defensive end and earned a starting position.

In 1976, the man was the big offensive tackle **Jim Brown**, who later played at Penn State.

Two years after Brown it was **Joe Lukens**, who became a stalwart at Ohio State, lettering four years and making All-Big Ten at right tackle. After graduating, Lukens actually established an endowment there for the right tackle, naming it after his line coach, Bill Myles.

Lukens was followed by **Joe Apke**, an All-American center at Moeller who started his collegiate career at Ohio State and then transferred to the University of Cincinnati. In Apke's year, 1979, the Holy Steamrollers sent an almost unimaginable nineteen players to Division I colleges (including I-AA) on football scholarships.

Apke was succeeded by All-American tackle **Doug Williams**, who by most accounts was the equal of any offensive lineman the Crusaders ever had—as a high schooler. Williams accepted a scholarship to Kentucky, then transferred to Texas A&M and in 1986 was drafted in the second round by the New York Jets. But he stayed away from training camp in a contract dispute. Shortly after he finally arrived he was rudely released—the highest draft pick the Jets had ever cut. Williams ultimately played with the Houston Oilers for a couple years, and in the World Football League.

We'll conclude this crazy countdown with 1981, which can't be topped. After that, under Steve Klonne, the balance of power seemed to shift toward the skill players, what with the various Franciscos and Larkins and all. The 1981 season was the only one coached by Ted Bacigalupo, who took over after Gerry Faust left for Notre Dame. Its All-Americans, true to the tradition, were a couple offensive linemen, **John Askin** and **Tim Odom**. That made sixteen All-American linemen in seventeen seasons. It was almost automatic.

Askin, like so many Crusaders before him, went on to Notre Dame. (He was later involved in the controversy surrounding the book, *The Tarnished Dome*, in which he was quoted making remarks critical of Irish coach Lou Holtz. Askin subsequently denounced the book as "outright fraud.") Odom, sticking to the pattern, played at Ohio State. But on the same high school line, there was also Cliff Brooks, who received a scholarship to North Carolina; Mark Gowetski, who got one to Boston University; and Dusty Stoy, who opted for Austin Peay. And let's not forget Scott Parkinson heading off to Harvard, which doesn't offer athletic scholarships but recognizes scholarship.

There was *that*, too, at Moeller.

and a *Parade* magazine All-American. After everything else, making All-State seemed like a demotion.

At Ohio State, the school that won the Kelley recruiting wars, he was regarded as the Great Wide Hope, the school's next All-American offensive lineman, in the manner of Orlando Pace and ex-Moeller standout Rob Murphy, the Buckeyes who waited in the trenches ahead of him.

At first, OSU wasn't high on his list. His sister had attended OSU, and all Kelley really knew about the school was that it was one miserable car ride from Cincinnati. Then he attended the OSU-Notre Dame game in 1995. It was the game with the largest Ohio Stadium crowd ever, OSU trailing through the first half, then coming back to win 45-26.

He'd never heard 95,000 pairs of lungs being exercised all at once. He'd never imagined a sound so all-encompassing. "He thought for a moment what it would be like to play in front of so many people," wrote one of the sportswriters following the Kelley recruiting story, "and that sound crashing around him, and he turned to his mom and smiled."

His freshman class—featuring himself, David Boston, Andy Katzenmoyer, and Michael Wiley—was rated the nation's best.

Then the shoulder injury. At first, he played with it, which is what football players do. When the doctors took a closer look, they found that his shoulder resembled a bad freeway accident.

If Kelley wanted to be certain his right arm would work, the doctors said, he shouldn't play football.

And being a student, as well as a football player, he forfeited one life for another.

Sportswriter Paul Daugherty, who followed his career, admired the decision. "The urge to play comes and goes," Daugherty wrote. "He could be sitting in his room studying and he'll hear the sounds of metal crashing in the weight room. He'll remember the running. He'll remember what it was like to sweat, to share, to win. And then maybe he'll touch his shoulder, to recall the finality. Life goes on, changed. No worse, really. Just different."

Those who'd watched Cincinnati football through that time, though, would always remember the big Colerain kid. College career or not, he was the best they'd ever seen, they said, and they had the votes.

John Martinkovic

Hamilton Catholic defensive end class of 19**47**

47

JOHN MARTINKOVIC WAS, SAID HAMILTON CATHOLIC PLAYER AND COACH TERRY MALONE, "THE MEANEST BOY I EVER SAW." HE LUMBERED UP out of Second Ward, a 6-4, 240-pound behemoth that terrified the Hamilton sandlots for several years, then suited up as a freshman and terrified the high school landscape. He played both ways, sometimes at tackle, sometimes at end, and on defense no one had seen anything like him. Even his own teammates remembered him as mean and cantankerous. The fact that he was silent—and the size of a Buick—only heightened his sense of menace.

He played on some of Xavier University's best teams; his junior and senior years, the Musketeers dropped only two games, one to a highly-rated Kentucky team, which, as Martinkovic remembers it, was lost on a fumbled punt. He hit Kentucky quarterback Babe Parilli so hard that when Parilli's thoughts unscrambled he called Martinkovic "a dirty son-of-a-bitch."

Martinkovic's bride-to-be, Clare, whom he met in grade school, was across town at the University of Cincinnati where John was known by reputation.

"Isn't he that guy who knocks people down and then sits on them?" one of her classmates asked, puzzled that such a nice girl was betrothed to a hooligan.

Martinkovic was drafted by Washington in the 6th round, believed to have been the first XU player to turn pro. Washington, however, didn't understand that little Xavier could produce players (even though seven of them went to the NFL from the teams of 1950 and '51), and soon traded Martinkovic to Green Bay.

"Where the hell *is that*?" he asked Clare. She didn't know either. They had to consult a map. All Clare knew was that while she was making $1,700 a year as a medical lab technician, John would be making $5,000. She thought she was marrying a millionaire.

So in the fall of 1951, Martinkovic showed up in the great north, "the ass-end of the world," as he put it. The pro game looked nothing like the modern pro game. There were 33 guys on a team, only four coaches, everybody made about the same money, and all of them needed an off-season job.

At Green Bay, Martinkovic continued his malevolent ways. Even in the pros, in a XX era, he was an XXX specimen. He was so large he even scared the neighborhood kids who showed up at the house. He scared the opposing players by chewing Beech-Nut and spitting on their hands. In two years, Martinkovic was in the Pro Bowl, the first of three times.

Green Bay began to grow on him, as he and his teammates helped bridge the gap between Curly Lambeau (who founded the Packers) and Vince Lombardi (who won the first two Super Bowls in 1967 and '68). He got to meet Babe Parilli again, too, when the Babe turned up in the Packers camp.

"I suspect you don't remember me," Martinkovic said.

"Oh, I remember *you*, all right," Parilli said, giving Martinkovic a steely eye.

He liked the train travel in those days, when the Packers took two days riding out to the West Coast after Thanksgiving to play Los Angeles and San Francisco, the last two games of the season. He liked it when the Pack came home, too. Sometimes the wives would meet them at the station, sometimes it would be what seemed to be the entire town.

He even tried to recruit his old XU roommate, Steve O'Dea, when O'Dea came out of service but O'Dea decided to go get a real job when Martinkovic told him what the pay was, and that he had to bring his own shoes. Then after six years, Martinkovic was traded to the New York Giants. He missed Green Bay's new stadium by one season, personally christening it by helping New York win. True to temperament, he said that beating his old teammates "didn't bother me a bit."

And after a season in New York, he said the hell with football. Clare and their three babies were back in Green Bay and he missed them. So he returned to Green Bay and never left. The ass-end of the world had made another convert.

Martinkovic was so menacing the neighborhood kids in Green Bay thought his house was haunted.

Michael Muñoz

Moeller offensive tackle class of 20**00**

In the matter of Michael Muñoz, a career in the NFL was a foregone conclusion. The kid was born in 1981, the year his dad, Anthony, anchored the Bengals in their first Super Bowl. By the time he was a sophomore at Moeller, he was 6-6 and, with a size-15 cleat, literally filled his father's shoes. A year later, he was introducing his old man for the great tackle's Hall of Fame ceremony.

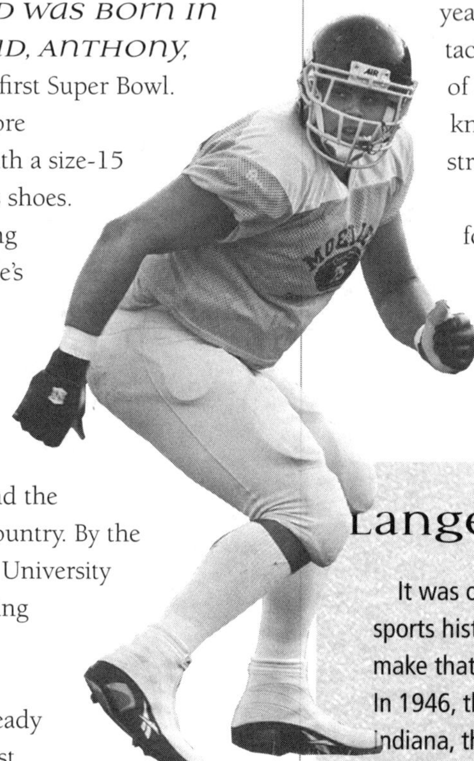

By the time he was a senior at Moeller, the younger Muñoz was three times an All-State selection, the Ohio Player of the Year, and the highest-rated blocker in the country. By the time he was a freshman at the University of Tennessee, he was dominating practice and starting on the offensive line. By the time he was a junior at UT, he was already the Volunteers' captain, the first non-senior to hold that position since World War II. He held it again as a senior, when he was first-team All-American and winner of the Draddy Trophy as the nation's top scholar-athlete.

And then, a funny thing happened. Nobody drafted him.

It was an astonishing development from the outside, but fully explicable from within. During his four years in the Southeastern Conference, Muñoz had missed a season with knee surgery and part of another—his last one—with a shoulder injury. Rather than risking a draft choice, NFL teams preferred to sign the tall Vol as a free agent and check him out on their own terms. The Bengals offered, among others.

But on the day after the draft, before he could sleep twice on his professional prospects, Muñoz up and retired from the game. "Football isn't who I am," he told a Knoxville radio station. "It's time to make a clean break."

The Draddy Trophy gave him $25,000 in scholarship money, and Muñoz, with a bachelor's degree in political science, used it to earn a master's in public administration. Before he could finish, he was already in office.

In November, 2005, at the age of 24 and less than a year out of shoulder pads, the freshly retired tackle was voted in as a 290-pound trustee of Hamilton Township, Warren County. He knocked out a fellow on a six-term winning streak.

And that was *not*, by any means, a foregone conclusion.

"He does things a person that big shouldn't be able to do," the Warren Harding coach said about Muñoz.

Langenbeck and Friends

It was one of the greatest upsets in Cincinnati sports history, and a couple of Queen City schoolboys—make that *former* schoolboys—helped make it happen: In 1946, the University of Cincinnati Bearcats toppled Indiana, the defending Big Ten Champions, and the university saw its sports program in Jesus-Returns headlines for the first time in, well, maybe ever.

The Bearcats didn't even have a team in 1943 and 1944, and 1945 was a trial season. Indiana, on the other hand, had eight starters returning and a 12-game unbeaten streak. UC had nothing much to recommend it but a platoon of hardened veterans just back from playing fields upon which terms such as "the blitz" carried an entirely different meaning.

Tackle **Bill Smythe** was from Roger Bacon and **Dick Langenbeck** was from Western Hills; Smythe had survived the Battle of Iwo Jima and Langenbeck, the other tackle, had been on a mine sweeper (his senior class motto was "shoulders that could hold the sky").

Some of them had been at UC when Pearl Harbor was

Steve Niehaus

Moeller lineman class of 19*72*

72

WHEN STEVE NIEHAUS FLATTENED HIS FINAL RUNNING BACK FOR MOELLER HIGH SCHOOL, THE CRUSADERS WERE STILL FIVE YEARS AWAY FROM A national championship. And yet, he did his part.

It's around guys like him that programs like Moeller's are built. Gerry Faust recognized that so intuitively that, in September of 1968, he made Niehaus, *as a 13-year-old freshman*, the youngest starter in school history.

He was too young, at that point, even to lift weights, for which he would have needed a ride to assistant coach Bill Clark's house, where they kept the sewer lids and soup cans filled with concrete.

But size was never a problem for the big defensive tackle. Strength was not an issue.

At that stage of their famous development, the Crusaders had won but two GCL championships. Roger Bacon was still the league's dominant entity, but Elder, St. Xavier, and Moeller had made occasional claims. And by the time Niehaus was a two-way sophomore—and linemate Steve Sylvester a junior—the Crusaders would be dominated no Moe.

They won the conference title that season, and two years later in 1971, when Niehaus, now at 6-5, 260, was named All-State for the second straight occasion; and All-American to boot. A tradition of excellence in the trenches had been forcibly established.

It was also widely noted. Niehaus was recruited, shall we say, heavily—over so many steaks, in fact, that he put on twenty pounds, which was sufficient to make him a starter the next year at Notre Dame. This time, though, it was just defense.

attacked and the athletic director, Chic Mileham, said, "Sit tight, boys, it's all going to blow over." So they wrote cards from one battlefront to another, advising each other: "Sit tight. It'll all blow over."

For these guys, and others on the team like them, playing Indiana was an outing in the country. Langenbeck recovered an Indiana fumble on the Indiana 26 and UC's **Don McMillan** (three years in the navy) came in with Coach Ray Nolting's plays on his taped wrists and two passes later, UC was in the end zone.

Elbie (Elbows) Nickel, who was also at Iwo Jima, scored the winning TD, blocked a punt, kicked a field goal, and UC won 16-6. The vets concluded a 9-2 season with a Sun Bowl victory over Virginia Tech. Indiana, the first—and most notable—casualty of the season, was lucky its whole team didn't end up in a POW camp.

Langenbeck: Mr. Broad Shoulders, just back from The Really Big Game.

Moeller's Steve Neihaus shreds his way through the St. Xavier line to loom as every running back's worst nightmare.

He would keep his position for four consecutive years and, in spite of a couple of knee surgeries, twice make All-American. Over that stellar stretch, Niehaus racked up 11 tackles per game, set a senior record in that department and actually finished 12th in the Heisman Trophy balloting. In the spring of 1976, the expansion Seattle Seahawks, with the second pick of the NFL draft, made him their first choice ever.

"He reminds me of Merlin Olsen," said Seattle coach Jack Patera. "But he's stronger."

Niehaus thus became the first of three Moeller players tapped as first-round draft choices, preceding Bob Crable by six years and Tony Hunter by seven. And once again, he had been identified as a young man to build around.

It seemed that the Seahawks had selected wisely when, with 9.5 sacks, Niehaus was voted NFC Defensive Rookie of the Year. Unfortunately, that would be his *best* year. A shoulder injury undermined his second season, and the few that followed, as well. In 1979, the big fellow was traded to Minnesota for an eighth-round draft choice, played in three games for the Vikings, and called it quits.

For the record, that was the year Moeller, prospering madly from the precedents, pulled off its fourth state championship, with three more to follow shortly. By the time the seventh had been won, Niehaus was driving a soft-drink truck in Seattle.

"I'm embarrassed sometimes when people ask how come I drive a truck," he told the *Seattle Post-Intelligencer*. "I hate that. I hate that.

"It's very strange working for a living, because pro football is a joyride. You eat at the finest places, go freewheeling around—you really got it made. And then you get six months off. Six months. Right now I'd kill for six months off."

In the context of Moeller, it seemed that Niehaus had come to the game prematurely. In the context of the NFL, he left it the same way.

REFEREE: "COACH, YOU NEED TO GET THAT NUMBER 77 OUT OF THERE BEFORE HE KILLS SOMEBODY."

COACH COOMBS: "WHAT?"

The Smith boys

John, Joe, Connor & Spencer

Colerain mostly linemen classes of 1978, '06, '07

78, 06, 07

THE FAMILY'S ORIGINAL ATHLETE, JOHN SMITH, COULD NOT POSSIBLY HAVE KNOWN HOW MUCH DAMAGE HIS PROGENY—CHILDREN, GRANDCHILDREN—would inflict upon various defenses yet unborn. *He*, after all, was a basketball player, circa the era of Jerry Lucas, against whom he tested himself while attending Hughes High. A man of the hardwood, Mr. Smith had little knowledge of the foul instincts of football's genuine O-lineman, which—unknown to the elder Smith—festered even then in the tiny breast of his mewling offspring.

It was some time, however, before young Joseph's talents were realized. He grew so large that he was too big for peewee football. This put him on the soccer field in the autumn, a fortuitous circumstance that would, ironically, improve his footwork and flexibility so that he was even more dangerous on the football field when he was finally allowed on it.

As a sophomore, he played on what was one of the first really good Colerain teams (9-1). It occurred early in a winning decade (the 1970s) that was the beginning of Colerain's present football prosperity. One of his teammates was a fiery kid named Kerry Coombs.

By the time Joseph was a senior—playing both ways at tackle—everybody in Division I, it seemed, came calling. Ohio State, though, had a first-rate veterinarian program and it was *The Ohio State*, coached by *The Woody Hayes*.

"If you were an Ohio kid," Joseph said, "and you could play for Woody, you *did*..."

He was captain of the South team at the North-South All-Star Game, along with an arm named Art Schlichter, whose coach, Fred Zechman, was their All-Star coach. Joseph kept Schlichter safe through the

Connor Smith, front, braced by a couple of his Colerain mainstays, Terrence Sherrer and Cobrani Mixon.

game (which they won), Zechman moved to Ohio State with his quarterback, then lobbied Joseph off the D-line (where he had been originally recruited) to keep up the good work.

Suffice it to say, veterinary school, O-line, and Joseph Smith was a marriage made in heaven, and as a senior he was an academic All-American. Flash-forward some twenty years, and keep in mind that Joseph had been present at the Colerain creation, in a manner of speaking. He was now building his vet practice during the day, except for two afternoon hours at Colerain where he was helping his old teammate Coombs with *his* large animal practice.

The circle, in a sense, had closed, both men back at Colerain, and *they* had sons. The offspring learned their early skills as Joe, himself, had done—on the soccer field. Neither coach would say it publicly but privately they thought kids who began football down in the grades were often burned out by the time they reached high school. And few of them had the footwork soccer gave them.

So Joe's boys, Connor and Spencer, played soccer, basketball, and baseball, and they took ballet and tap dancing (sometimes the only boys in their recitals), and by the time they were in middle school, he could see how athletic they were, and he knew they could *play*.

And they did.

The two one-time Colerain waterboys, especially Spencer, could play most anywhere; in Joe's decade of coaching there, he was the only kid to ever start both ways, at offensive tackle and inside linebacker. Connor, a year older, settled in as an offensive lineman.

By the end of Connor's sophomore year, Joe was already seeing himself. He was seeing even *more* of himself. There was the heartbreaking loss to Elder in the regional final, but it seemed as if Connor won *his* game. Elder fans stopped him after the game and tried to recruit him.

"What's the chances of you coming to school at Elder?" one Elderite asked him.

"With all due respect, sir," Connor said, "my mother doesn't even let my little *sister* wear purple."

Implying, of course, that respect *wasn't* due.

By the time he was a junior, Connor, and Spencer, and Coombs' son, Brayden, among others, led Colerain to its first state title—the apogee of Colerain prosperity first sniffed back in Joe's time. Their 2004 championship win, 50-10 over traditional Ohio power Canton McKinley, was the most one-sided title victory in state history.

Connor's reputation had grown. He was considered the most dominating lineman in the Midwest, a quick, inordinately disciplined player who approached offense with the fierceness of a good defensive player. Most linemen held their blocks two seconds; Connor—taught by Joe—went for five seconds.

In the second half of the championship game, one of the referees approached Coombs with the oddest request he'd ever heard.

"Coach," he said, "you need to get that Number 77 out of there before he kills somebody."

"What?" asked Coombs.

He couldn't believe he'd heard the man correctly.

"You need to get Number 77 out of there."

"Maybe we can substitute now," Coombs said to Joe.

Odd fact, but the biggest, nastiest lineman on the field was the nicest off it.

"The best lineman," Joe said, explaining the position

Lakota's Man Mountain

He was always spectacularly big. Even in junior high, mothers would call the Rehring household and say, "Tell your son not to hit my kid in practice." It was as if they were calling into another, more outsized zip code. "They would tell the coaches," Eileen Rehring said, "'Don't let that **Steve Rehring** knock my son down.' They were always so worried because he was so big."

After his freshman year at Lakota West, his coach, Larry Cox, asked him what his goals were. He said he wanted to play for Ohio State, then for the Rams. He seemed a little embarrassed by his declaration, as if he had suddenly blurted out that he was going to marry Jessica Simpson. Cox told him he was 90 percent there; he had the size, now he had to make sure that the skill set followed.

he himself had played so well, "plays as intensely as he can. He can be nasty, but he must stay within the rules." It was a duality taught first at the Smith dinner table, then transferred by way of his sons' athleticism onto the field. There, for instance, Connor drove defensive linemen downfield twenty yards, flattened safeties, then helped them up.

His coach once received an e-mail from a girl in the Oak Hills band, impressed at how Number 77 kept picking the Oak Hills guys up after he had knocked them down. His senior year, he had an average of 15 pancake blocks a game.

Teams that played Colerain knew going in that casualties would be high; the bruises and grass stains were marks of honor, a kind of modern day Heidelberg dueling scar that said the D-lineman had survived an evening with Connor Smith.

"He finishes his blocks as well as anyone I've seen," said OSU coach Jim Tressel, who had seen a few blockers in his time.

In Joe's span of coaching, Colerain had a decade that included seven undefeated regular seasons, and the coaches' boys—Connor, Spencer, and Brayden—had played in only one regular-season loss. Connor had been the captain of his football team, the basketball team, *and* the baseball team. He was the GMC Player of the Year—the first time ever for an offensive linemen—twice All-City, twice All-State, a *Parade* All-American, and the first Cincinnati player to be named to the Army All-American team.

Spencer, a year younger, wasn't too far behind. He was the captain of both his football and baseball teams, All-City, and an East-West All-Star—between them, they won fourteen letters.

For the next year or two, it looked as if both might be on the Ohio Stadium field at the same time—Connor on the O-line and Spencer at fullback. There would be more trips up the interstate for Joe, and John, too, where the one-time Hughes basketball player could sit beside his son and watch his grandsons and wonder at the mysterious processes of DNA and how the pick became a pancake—such a distance, and in only one generation.

As a junior in 2002, Rehring practiced against senior defensive tackle Brandon Maupin (a 6-6, 280-pounder rated among Ohio's top ten prospects), but during his senior year there was no one on the team to really bang heads with him. No hat sizes large enough. To challenge him, the coaches placed quicker kids on him, giving him a difficult target to block. Perhaps that's why he developed a nasty temperament.

His twelve personal fouls during his senior season for blocking after the whistle are an unofficial Lakota West record. When pressed, however, Rehring admitted it's a record he's a little proud of.

He amazed a University of Tennessee recruiter by working to exhaustion, throwing up, then continuing to work out. He was an All-State player, consistently ranked among the country's top 100. When Ohio State offered Rehring a scholarship the summer before his senior year, he accepted. At OSU he was reunited with Ryan Hamby. The two lived across the street from each other and had developed a friendship, as well as a driveway basketball rivalry. Hamby was a 6-5 tight end, a few years older, and reached the Buckeyes via Moeller. "I want to play with Ryan, hopefully play next to him," Rehring said.

He left high school early and enrolled at Ohio State for the winter quarter, participating in Ohio State's off-season workouts. Soon, he was 6-8, 345, a mainstay on the Buckeye offensive line beginning in 2006. On the fourth play of the 2008 national championship game with LSU, he blocked down on the NFL's 5th draft pick, Glenn Dorsey, locking him up long enough for Beanie Wells to cut back behind the block and dash 65 yards for the score. If the game didn't end on the same high note upon which it began, Rehring had another year to rectify it. Mothers around the Big Ten would probably be calling Jim Tressel.

Dana Stubblefield

Taylor defensive tackle class of 19 **88**

88

It had to have been a momentous occasion when Dana Stubblefield arrived at Taylor High from inner Cincinnati, because of his sheer physical presence, if nothing else. He weighed 300 pounds as a teenager, and finding such a fearsome specimen as Stubblefield across the line—at the Division V level—was something like the villagers of the island community of Amity being menaced by the big fish ("We've got a problem on our hands..."). Saying that Stubblefield was dominant in high school is like saying Katrina was dominant in New Orleans.

> *"I was* BIG *when I was* LITTLE.*"—Dana Stubbblefield.*

Before he was a high school junior, his mother moved back to Cincinnati; but Dana liked living in the country. He ended up on an Addyston farm belonging to one of his teachers, where he learned survival skills, i.e. milking a cow. Picture the heavyweight African-American kid on a farm with a pair of white country guardians. But by all accounts, they'd become a family, no matter how unlikely. Not that it was all Norman Rockwell. As one writer said, "Black-kid-lives-on-farm-with-family-of-white-strangers is not a story that's going to make everyone instantly comfortable." Or as Dana himself said, "Strange, going to their family reunions."

But when the big heavyweight arrived at the University of Kansas he immediately showed he belonged by winning a hay bale-throwing contest at the county fair. And when his Ohio guardians, the Heaths, came out to watch him play, he introduced them as his parents. "This is my mom and my dad," he'd say. "It's just a long story."

He played on one of the best defensive lines in Kansas history, an All-American who left with 19 quarterback sacks. As team captain in 1992, he led Kansas to the Aloha Bowl where he was named MVP after sacking Brigham Young's quarterback three times, pressuring him into incompletions and an interception as Kansas beat BYU 23-20. Said the quarterback, Tom Young, "All I remembered was big guys coming at me."

Said one of the reporters, "It was just *one* big guy. Stubblefield."

After that game, Stubblefield was regarded as the Number 1 defensive tackle/nose tackle coming out of college and he was a first-round pick of the San Francisco 49ers. He led the 49ers with 64 tackles and ten and a half sacks and was named the *Associated Press* 1993 Defensive Rookie of the Year. He was in the Pro Bowl in 1994 and 1995, and had—by his standards—a mediocre 1996. But in 1997 he reinvented himself as the former Dana Stubblefield, recording 15 sacks and being named NFL Defensive Player of the Year (even if there were those who thought his DT teammate Bryant Young, doubled-teamed all year, deserved the award).

He was All-Pro again (his fourth time) and had played in three NFC championship games and a Super Bowl. He had established himself as one of the NFL's best at what many considered football's toughest position. "Despite having his face punched, his knees chopped and his

Super-Sized

Among the things that **Steve Sylvester** loved about the Moeller Crusaders was this: They let him *play*. That was no small thing for a kid who was no small thing. In fact, for numerous years before he finally arrived at Moeller as a freshman, Sylvester was too large for youth football.

When he was in the fourth grade, he signed up for the fifth-grade Milford team sponsored by Lehr's Meats, barely getting under the 125-pound cutoff. It was the last time he made weight until high school, when Gerry Faust was pleased about every pound.

Even on the famously massive Moeller offensive line, Sylvester loomed large. "We didn't know kids grew that big," said Princeton coach Pat Mancuso. "Sylvester and those kids, they looked gigantic."

In his senior season of 1970, Sylvester was a prep All-American and the only Cincinnati player to make shoulders battered for most of the last five seasons," wrote the *Washington Post*, "he has still managed to terrify quarterbacks and destroy game plans."

When he became a free agent after the 1997 season, he signed with the Redskins. He played another six years, but the second half of his career could not match the near-legendary performances of his first half. One of his greatest hits, actually, came in 2000 when he accidentally knocked actor Ben Affleck unconscious while the two were making the movie, *Reindeer Games*. "He really took his concussion well," Stubblefield said afterward. It was a remark in keeping with a good lineman's general outlook.

"I've been to the top," he said of his time. "I've been to the big dance." And he had.

For a time, Stubblefield was in fact the NFL's very best defensive tackle. The accolades don't last long in the big time, but back home in the country west of Cincinnati where his ride had started, Stubblefield was still known as Taylor High's foremost football player. *That* title might be around for a while.

Stubblefield wrestled in high school, too, as fearsome on the mat as he was on the playing field.

first-team All-State. (His brother, Mike, had been the state's Player of the Year the season before in basketball.) His stellar blocking got the attention of Notre Dame, and his work there—as an All-American—was of great interest to the Oakland Raiders, who drafted him, kept him around for nine years and played him at several positions on the same offensive line as Hall of Famers Art Shell and Gene Upshaw.

As a Raider, Sylvester earned three Super Bowl rings, the last of them coming in 1984, in his final game, against the Washington Redskins.

Years later, when Shell was in Cincinnati as vice-president of football operations for the NFL, he told local reporters, "I know about football in this area because I know about Moeller High from Steve Sylvester, an old teammate of mine who lives here in town. He used to talk about Moeller High more than he talked about Notre Dame."

Yeah, well, there was a good reason for that.

Sylvester's gridiron resume was gold—All-American at two levels and three Super Bowl rings.

Dan Tehan

St. Xavier tackle class of 19 *24*

24

Tehan: "One of the remarkable players..."

A dollar went a whole lot farther in Dan Tehan's day; and so, obviously, did a pound. Tehan had 210 of them spread effectively over his 6-4 frame.

These days, as far as football goes, that would buy him a shot at quarterback, maybe, or perhaps possession receiver. But it was 1924 when Tehan graduated from St. Xavier High School, All-State in both football and basketball. It was 1925 when the Cleveland *Plain Dealer* called him one of the best tackles ever to play in Ohio. And you read it right. He was a 210-pound tackle, and just right for the job.

In fact, it was 1927 when the *Associated Press* wrote of the illustrious Dan the Man, then dominating the trenches for Xavier University, "Tehan, measuring 6-foot-4 and carrying 210 pounds, is the ideal type of tackle. Tehan has been the bulwark of the Musketeer line this season, and has put terror and fear into the minds of opposing gridders . . . Tehan is not only heralded in the state but has been cited as one of the remarkable players in the country."

But that only brings us back to the generation gap. With credentials such as those, and the kind of size that pumped up the local prose, one would presume the NFL was the next step.

Except that in 1928 the league, still morphing annually, was in the less auspicious likes of Pottsville and Frankford, Pennsylvania, among Dayton and more enduring professional cities. All in all, Tehan figured there was a better living to be made, year-round, as a referee.

So it was that he entered the NFL in 1930, with a whistle, and didn't leave until he had officiated longer, and in more playoff games, than anyone else in the profession. He didn't stop until 1964, and even then he just scaled the steps up to the press box as an evaluator of officials, or an official evaluator.

It's not that he didn't have the stuff that playing the game required. Don't even *think* that. This is a man who, at Xavier, where he won six varsity letters (three of them in basketball), once played a game less than a week after breaking his jaw. To prevent the other team from realizing this inconvenience, he rubbed mud across his face. (No telling what he would have done if it hadn't rained.)

Tehan was a local high school ref before Trader Frank Lane, the one-time general manager of the Reds, recommended him for an NFL job that Trader himself was too busy to take. It wasn't long at all before The Man was working championships. His first was the league's first, 1933.

He made $30 and the winning players for the Bears took home $210 apiece. Tehan was also on hand for the 73-0 shellacking the Monsters of the Midway put on the Redskins in 1940, with his younger homeboy, Ray Nolting, among the Chicago perpetrators.

Six years later, Tehan was elected sheriff of Hamilton County, a development that might not have been so startling, considering the high esteem in which he was held, had he not run as a *Democrat*. For the next twenty-six years, still officiating most of the while, the ideal tackle remained in office as an immovable figure and political anomaly.

If party lines could not cow the trusty sheriff, neither could a professional or collegiate coach of whatever renown.

There was the occasion, for instance, when Paul Brown took issue with one of Tehan's decisions, to which the tall official quietly replied, "I'll be back in two weeks.

Let me know how it turns out on the film."

At the return meeting a fortnight later, Tehan was quick to ask PB how the play had looked in black and white.

"You know darn well how it looked," snarled Brown, "or you wouldn't have asked."

It was much the same in basketball. Back in 1933, Tehan was calling a rugged game between Kentucky and Tennessee in which Adolph Rupp's Wildcats were pursuing a physical approach to Tennessee's Dick Mehen. Mehen's firm reply, at one juncture, was to let go with an elbow, then grab the ball and score. In the hotel after the game, the Kentucky brass inquired of Tehan as to whether he had seen the elbow thrown, and Tehan answered, "No. And I didn't see the Kentucky man roughing him up before he threw it. They have to learn to take care of themselves."

Characteristically, and in all walks, he was a man whose dealings with trouble generally kept it to a minimum. At the county jail, for example, there was a thief named Sleepy Zellis who lapsed into deep slumber no matter the time of day or where he was. This was accompanied by a snoring so loud that the other prisoners couldn't sleep, work, or enjoy a moment of silence.

Tehan's solution was to release Sleepy to probation so everyone else could get some rest. On another occasion at lock-up, there were repeated disturbances that seemed inexplicable until Tehan's investigation revealed that the inmates in charge of baking bread had been rerouting the yeast toward the fruit juice for purposes of fermentation. His response was the one of yeast resistance. The sheriff simply cut off the leaven supply and began ordering the bread from a commercial bakery.

It can be safely surmised that Tehan, in turn, did not overindulge in the product. By running year-round on fields and floors—he also umpired minor-league baseball in the summer—he remained a trim and towering figure. Even as a classic tackle, Dan the Man had not been a respecter of bulk, and he apparently still felt that way in 1967, when, as an official observer, he was asked about the difference between the referees in the NFL and those in the rival AFL.

"There isn't any at all," he said, "except that the AFL lets its men get a little fat."

Socko Wiethe

Roger Bacon guard/tackle class of 19 ***30***

30

PERHAPS IT WAS MERELY THE TIMES, BEFORE TELEVISION, SATELLITE FEEDS, AND CELEBRITIES COME AND GONE BEFORE LUNCH. IT WAS, AFTER ALL, back in the day, when sports of all sorts—both stories *and* players—were relegated to their own pages in the back of the daily press, tucked safely away in a circumspect black and white.

Sports weren't quite a profession yet, more an *avocation*, and John Wiethe, growing up in cramped quarters over his family's grocery store in Clifton Heights, would pronounce his time the best of times, for the middle of the American century would be the last time genuine multi-sport athletes could flourish in its increasingly specialized culture. And Wiethe was one of the best practitioners of what would—even in *his* time—become a lost art. He may have been, in fact, the best all-around athlete Cincinnati ever produced.

It all started on the hillsides of Clifton Heights, and since the store was at the bottom of the hill and most of the customers at the top, little Wiethe made the deliveries. "I could carry four baskets full of groceries," he once said. "Sometimes I had a small package, just a pint of coffee, and I would run all the way down McMicken to Ravine Street, and then all the way up Ravine Hill. That's how I developed strong legs."

The name, like his school wear, was handed down from his older brother, Peter, a sandlot football player who hit so hard he was called "Socko." When Peter forfeited football for the seminary, he had to give up his nickname, too—priests weren't supposed to call one another "Socko," or even "Father Socko."

So the nickname went to Johnny, who was a household name around town even before he had a house. There was an early family story from that moment which exemplified young Johnny's competitive zeal. On the day the rector came to the Wiethe household to formally welcome Peter into religious studies, 9-year-old Johnny was there.

"Father," he asked, "do they have boxing in the seminary?

"Yes, John," said Wiethe's dad. "You get to box the devil real good."

The young Socko was not only good at whatever he tried, he excelled. He was a splendid lineman in high school and even better at Xavier University. (His father, the grocer, was unsure about his son attending university. "Maybe you should get a yob," he said, lapsing into his German accent. But his son was the school's first player to be named All-Ohio in two sports, football *and* basketball.)

Wiethe was famed for holding Notre Dame's All-American cage scoring sensation, Moose Krause, to one point. ("He stood on Moose's feet," said one of the oldtimers who saw the game.) He was the football team captain and star of XU's 6-0 upset of Indiana in 1933. He might have been an All-American, but he was from a small school. The All-Americans that year were Fred Crawford of Duke and Michigan's Whitey Wistert. Crawford spent a year with the Bears and Wistert was a cup-of-coffee guy with the Cincinnati Reds in 1934. Socko, however, was the whole pot.

First, he was offered a spot on Cincinnati's NFL team, the original Bengals, playing in 1938 as an independent. They upset the Bears 17-14, beat Pittsburgh 27-0, and finished at 7-2-2 (a record that would, ironically, shame half the history of the *new* Bengals, arriving in the 1960s with Wiethe leading one of the early franchise groups).

At the same time, Socko was teaching history at Roger Bacon and coaching. His 1938 team was unbeaten (7-0-1, outscoring its opposition 178-6) and claimed the state championship—which is what *all* undefeated teams in the state did before the playoff system. This claim was relegated to the same place as Socko's old Xavier bid for All-American—the circular file. The state title went to—you guessed it—Paul Brown's Massillon team.

Before the start of the 1939 season, the Detroit Lions had made Socko an offer he couldn't refuse. He may not have been an All-American, but now he was playing with them. In November, the Lions, having lost only at Green Bay, upset the unbeaten world champion New York Giants 18-14, breaking a 15-game winning streak and handing the Giants their only loss of the season. Later in the month, Wiethe was tossed out of the game with the Bears for unnecessary roughness, always to him an oxymoron, for he thought roughness was mandatory. How could a *prerequisite* be unnecessary?

In December, the *United Press* picked "aggressive lineman John Wiethe" as one of its best eleven, the only rookie lineman on the first team, an upstart next to such battled-scarred veterans as Mel Hein and Joe Stydahar. His teammate, Byron "Whizzer" White, who became a U.S. Supreme Court justice, would say Wiethe was "about as fearless and tireless a player as I've ever seen." And none other than the old Bear himself, George Halas, said that Wiethe was the first linebacker who blitzed.

Socko had come to the Lions without portfolio, and now he had one filled with press clippings, a rarity for any of those invisible *mensches* in the trenches. There were three Cincinnatians in the big leagues that autumn: Socko, Ray Nolting, and Bill Feldhaus. Butch Feldhaus was a 225-pound Hughes graduate, Socko's teammate in Detroit who played guard, and Feldhaus and Nolting were locally famous for being UC's first pro players. When they returned after the season, they were the toast of the Queen City, and their friends gave them a testimonial dinner and brought in Red Grange as the speaker. It was all heady stuff for the local boys, but Socko was just getting going.

To keep himself busy, he played basketball after football season (the seasons didn't overlap much in the old days) and he attended law school at night. The basketball team was the Cincinnati Redlegs, an independent pro team, and when the weather broke, he played a little semi-pro baseball, trading that in for umpiring in the Mountain States Baseball League. He worked his way up to the American Association, and umpired the Little World Series. He liked to call games with fellow ump Hal Weafer; they made a fine pair, able to spot and head off potential trouble—Socko was mellowing, thwarting trouble rather than promoting it. When games became heated, Weafer would sidle up to

As a player, Socko was fiery and hardnosed. As a coach, though, he was fiery and hardnosed. When his players won, they got steak. When they lost, it was hamburger.

bedlam's candidate and say, pointing over to Wiethe, "Remember now, you're no Joe Stydahar or Mel Hein and you know what *he* did to *those* fellows..."

When Socko retired from the Lions in 1942 he was first the assistant football coach at UC, then in 1946 took over the basketball program, which had languished for a decade, without a conference. Wiethe got UC into the Mid-American Conference, then his team proceeded to claim the league title, half their home games played in an arena jerry-rigged at Music Hall.

He was, as one might have expected from a guy who'd played football before the era of facemasks, hard-nosed and autocratic. Sometimes the 6-2, 230-pound Wiethe scrimmaged half-court with his players, even got into a fistfight with Joe Luchi, who'd been in the military and was older than his teammates. The remainder of the team was a bit frightened of both Luchi *and* their coach.

Once, he'd been driving a carload of players down to Music Hall for a game and stopped for a red light, where he kept discussing game strategy, not noticing that the light had changed. When the driver behind him leaned on his horn, Socko walked back to the other car, opened the door, grabbed the man's keys, and tossed them down the street. Then he drove away. The press called Socko "fiery," one of its grander understatements. Socko was, as someone said about Bobby Knight, "Krakatau with feet."

When the Bearcats won on the road, he bought them steak. When they lost, he gave each player fifty cents for a hamburger. But they won five straight MAC titles and in 1951 played for the first time in the NIT. He left in 1952 with a 106-47 record. He'd put the first Cincinnati team into Madison Square Garden, he'd coached a UC team into winning 20 games for the first time, and he'd taken the Bearcats off Clifton Avenue and given them a national address.

When he turned completely to his law practice and politics, nothing much changed. Wiethe stayed in shape by inventing something he called "jog golf." He'd run from shot to shot, wearing a sweat suit and carrying nothing but his 2-iron. He boasted that he could play the course in eighty minutes, "and I run four and a half to five miles every time I go out," he said. There was no word on how many bodies of slow golfers surfaced later in the area's various sand traps.

Socko also played in the winter, no matter the weather—his limit was three inches of snow—and he used a yellow ball with a red stripe on it, so he could find it. He'd become the chairman of the Democratic Party in Cincinnati, and the golf kept him in shape for recruiting voters on the upper floors of apartment houses. He particularly liked to sprint up the stairs in four-story buildings.

"They looked at me like I was from Mars," he said. "No one goes up that high."

Fitting epitaph. In Cincinnati, few ever did.

SIZING HIMSELF UP

George "Butch" Wilburn played one of the glamour positions at Lakota—fullback—but he wanted to play at the next level, where size was easier to acquire than great speed. Shifting to the line, he became the first Lakota player to begin intensive weight training. Blessed with athleticism passed down from his father, Hub, and Uncle Steve (Hub was an end on Mason's first football team and scored the Comets' first touchdown; Steve was an outstanding basketball player at Kings), he attended an Iowa football camp the summer before he was a senior. There, he learned he could compete with the country's top linemen. When Lakota's season began, he was no longer a good high school lineman, he was a dominating one. Wilburn was first team All-State at offensive guard in 1982—Lakota's first All-State player—and after a redshirt year at the University of Kentucky, he was a four-year starter on the offensive line.

The Hughes High School yearbook, 1931, shows us that **Bill Feldhaus** was not an ordinary fellow. In the photo of the football team, he stands, bigger than the other boys, in the front row, arms folded, the only gent on the squad wearing a bow tie. Below the picture is the summary of the 1930 season. He wrote it. As humble as he was well-dressed, Feldhaus neglected to mention himself, though as a lineman he was surely the class of the club and perhaps the city. We know this by virtue of the fact that he, along with teammate Ray Nolting, would go on to star at the University of Cincinnati—where, as a senior in 1936, he, not the better-known Nolting, was named the Bearcats' MVP. (He was also All-Ohio.) After that, Feldhaus and Nolting would become the first UC products in the NFL. Playing for the Detroit Lions, the former was also one of the first two players to wear a hinged knee guard, the invention of teammate Jack Johnson. Most extraordinarily, however, Feldhaus, at 226 pounds, was the ultimate ironman. In 1940, his final season, he played every down and minute up until the last five of the last game. Later, Feldhaus coached at Miami, Xavier and Indiana. His son, Dan, a Withrow grad, became a quarterback at Yale . . . Between **Dave Lafary** at tackle and Don Hasselbeck at tight end, LaSalle High School in 1972 lined up 13 feet 2 inches of professional football talent, evenly divided between the two of them. While Hasselbeck headed out west to begin his legacy, Lafary was well-suited for the Big Ten. After Purdue, he was a 5th-round draft choice of New Orleans, and stayed with the Saints for nine solid seasons. At least one critic has placed Lafary on the Saints' all-time team . . . Coming out of the same school in 2004, **Ryan Stanchek** was not the type of massive offensive lineman that fit the profile of most major-college football powers. But he had sufficiently distinguished himself against GCL competition to be named All-State, and to intrigue, among others, West Virginia University, where the wide-open offense required nimble big men to do the blocking. Stanchek fit *that* profile, starting at guard as a redshirt freshman on a dynamic team that won the Sugar Bowl. As a sophomore, he moved to tackle, and by then the WVU offense was well-established as one of the best in America. The same went for the offensive line. As a junior in 2007, Stanchek made most of the All-American teams as the Mountaineers rolled to a Big East championship and routed Oklahoma in the Fiesta Bowl, and he was an All-American once more as a senior—all of which was unabashedly celebrated at Abby's Pub & Grill on Harrison Avenue in Dent, where as a student at LaSalle, Stanchek waited tables and washed dishes for his mom, who owned the place. The restaurant had always featured a local sports décor, but when the dishwasher made it big as a Mountaineer (and getting bigger all the time, up to 300 pounds by the time his senior season commenced), an entire floor was devoted to West Virginia . . . Stanchek's prospects, at that point, were on pace to earn him a professional place in the tradition of Lafary and **Tom Luken**. A 1968 Lancer grad who made All-Big Ten at Purdue, Luken was drafted in the third round by the Philadelphia Eagles and put in six years with them . . . At Elder in 1948, **Bob Fry** was an All-GCL halfback. His brother Ted, meanwhile, was an All-City end. Here's where it gets mixed up. Bob went to the University of Kentucky as an *end*, then switched to offensive tackle his senior year, then started at that position for 10 years in the NFL, five each with the Rams and Cowboys. In both L.A. and Dallas, he is well-remembered for his ability to maintain a working grip on his opponent's jersey without the official taking notice . . . For that matter, **Eric Wood** was not a big-time lineman at Elder, either. As a junior, he played a backup role in the Panthers' 2002 state championship, stepping into the lineup at tackle for the 2003 encore season. He was an All-GCL player, but not a headline talent. The University of Louisville recognized, however, that Wood was a late bloomer, and after a redshirt season he stepped in as the Cardinals' starting center,

Large Fry

earning notice as a Freshman All-American. As a senior in 2008, Wood was named to the all-Big East team for the third consecutive season . . . In 1922, as an All-City tackle and center weighing but 162 pounds, **Joe Kelly** was considered the first sporting hero of St. Xavier High School. Regarded as one of the best all-around athletes in Ohio—he played just about everything—Kelly would take his talents to what was then called St. Xavier College, where he would pitch for the baseball team, captain the basketball team and carve out an even more memorable reputation as a fullback and linebacker. They called him "the Balkan Bonecrusher." Later, the Bonecrusher enjoyed a distinguished career as president of MacGregor Sporting Goods . . . When Kelly was a junior at XU, he was joined by former schoolmate—but not teammate—**Paul "Chip" Cain**, two years his junior. Cain lacked Kelly's reputation as a high school athlete, owing largely to the fact that, as a working boy, he wasn't able to play any sports until his senior year at St. X. The Conquerors, as they were called then, placed him at center that season. But by the time Kelly graduated from XU, Cain was the Musketeers' quarterback. In praise of him, the 1929 Xavier yearbook reads, "Every sport fan in Cincinnati realizes that in Paul Cain, Xavier has one of the greatest athletes of her history. Last fall as captain of the Musketeer eleven, 'Chip' performed almost perfectly. He is the real Musketeer ideal, an athlete, a student, a gentleman, and a good fellow" . . . In terms of football, Milford High School had no particular history. But then, **Zach Strief** didn't either. It was a good match. It was good, also, that Strief was 6-foot-7, on his way to 345 pounds; and good that he took his father's advice, which was to give the game a try. Zach had been too big to play on grade-school teams, instead wrestling his way to a state championship. When he got to Milford (from St. Elizabeth Seton) and was free to play football, he was surprised to find that he actually *liked* it; and football liked him. He was the first Eagles player to earn All-Greater Miami Conference honors for three consecutive seasons. At Northwestern, Strief started at tackle for three years and made All-American as a senior. He also made the New Orleans Saints, which was handy because his parents already owned a timeshare in the French Quarter . . . In the late 19th century, **Eddy Herschede** was the type of hale fellow that came to define early football. As captain at Walnut Hills, he essentially ran the practices and coached the team. He was also the leading halfback, but, in an inspiring show of leadership, moved himself to tackle when it was evident that experience was lacking on the line. According to the *Cincinnati Post*, Herschede "has played such star games all season that he has drawn commendation from all sides."

BENCH STRENGTH/Defensive Linemen

Lockland was little and **Melvin Lunsford** was big. In the late 1960s, he was so big, for a school so little, that people remember him at about 6-7, 275, even though, as a veteran of the NFL, he was listed at 6-3, 256. "He was a giant," recalled his coach, Ben Hubbard. In Hubbard's reflections, Lunsford is the two-way tackle who, in Lockland's annual rivalry game, swallowed up Reading's talented quarterback, Jerry Edwards, on an option play. And not only Edwards, but the guy he was intending to pitch to. They both went to the ground—one by Lunsford's right arm, the other by his left—and so did the ball. Lunsford played collegiately at Central State, was drafted by the Raiders in 1972 but spent all eight of his active NFL seasons with New England as a defensive end, mostly, but also a tackle and nose guard. As a pro, Lunsford's defining moment came in 1976, when the Patriots hadn't had a winning season in nine years. In the first quarter against the Buffalo Bills, he put a hit on O.J. Simpson that the Juice didn't appreciate. Simpson took a swing at Lunsford and was ejected from the game. The Patriots prevailed in that one and proceeded to end the season on a six-game winning streak, setting a then-franchise record with 11 victories . . . As a high school linebacker, **Ben Martin** was so good that everyone expected him to go to Ohio State, as was the fashion. But Martin was not the traditional football player. He didn't take up the game until he enrolled at LaSalle, and as a sophomore he was already confident with a reason. The way he tells it, one of St. Xavier's offensive linemen was giving him what-for, and Martin inquired of the gentleman if he was ready to rumble, more or less. He

Eilerman

Ed Bauer

then sacked the quarterback on the next two plays and quite enjoyed the reaction from the home crowd. From there, Martin became Ohio Player of the Year and the top-rated recruit in the state as a senior in 2006, projected as a collegiate defensive end. His choice of Tennessee was a jolt to Buckeye fans. But at least it wasn't Michigan . . . In 1970, defensive tackle **Bill Eilerman** was recognized as Elder's first *Parade* All-American. However, the guy in the next foxhole, **Ed Bauer**, was named Best Defensive Lineman in the GCL—proving, presumably, that the GCL is a tougher league than the United States. The two of them shared the honor as the Panthers' top defensive lineman, while Bauer, who also played tight end, was named team MVP. He went on to captain Notre Dame as an offensive lineman. "If I was forced to single out one all-time captain," wrote his coach, Dan Devine, in his memoir, *Simply Devine*, "it would probably be Ed Bauer" . . . When he was playing street ball around Ezzard Charles Drive, where he grew up, **Vaughn Booker** assumed the role of James Brooks, the Bengals' man with the moves. Booker, at 6-5, was a little tall for a scatback, but he was plenty thin and plenty lively. Upon graduating from Taft in 1986, he accepted a scholarship to the University of Cincinnati and, as a redshirt freshman linebacker, led the Bearcats in tackles. There then followed some legal charges that were ultimately dropped but caused UC to dismiss Booker from its program. He spent a couple years in the Army and returned as a rededicated and substantially bigger man, up from 216 pounds to 285. He had become a large defensive end. The other players called Grandpa. Two years in the Canadian Football League made Booker 26 when he caught on with the Kansas City Chiefs. He lasted nine seasons in the NFL, the final three on a $12-million contract with the team he so admired as a skinny kid . . . When viewed over the generations, high school stardom is a curious thing. While Booker, as a raw and rangy athlete at Taft, went generally unnoticed on the larger scale, in 1963 **John Kasselman**, at 5-foot-10, 207 pounds, was an All-American middle linebacker at Roger Bacon. At that, he was up nearly 20 pounds from his junior year, when he was an All-City offensive guard. Kasselman earned his honors. He was a workhorse of Bacon's illustrious Bron Bacevich era. In 1999, the *Cincinnati Post* listed him as a defensive starter on its All-Century team . . . The records that **Chris Norwell** holds at Anderson High School are mostly for basketball, in which he led the city's Division I schools in scoring for two straight seasons. He also, as a defensive lineman, led Cincinnati in tackles for loss, which got him a scholarship to the University of Illinois. His record there is for starting the most games as a defensive lineman. Norwell held down a tackle position for all four seasons. After a couple NFL tryouts, Norwell was diagnosed with cancer in the fall of 2008. As he underwent treatments his brother, Andrew, a highly regarded offensive tackle, was leading Anderson to a second straight Division II title game . . . In his Western Hills senior yearbook, **Richard Langenbeck** was a big fellow for 1941 when he went to the University of Cincinnati to play whatever sport he chose. He chose football; and then World War II chose *him*. Langenbeck was a mine sweeper in the Pacific, returning to UC in 1946 and co-captaining the team that beat Virginia Tech in the Sun Bowl. He was drafted by the Philadelphia Eagles, but in deference to a bad back, opted for law school. . . . **John Peterson** was an imposing 6-4, 274-pound Middletown High specimen who started 30 straight games for the Middies, along with setting the Ohio shot put record—held for the previous twenty-eight years by Middletown basketball legend Jerry Lucas. He was a prep All-American, Ohio's 1985 AAA Lineman of the Year, and captain of the South All-Star team. At Ohio State, he was a four-year letterman, then turned to coaching, with line coach tours at Akron and Miami, and in 2008 he was Ohio State's tight ends coach and recruiting coordinator.

The Pit, Elder High, 1947–

It's known across Ohio as the best place to watch a high school football game and—if you're the opposition—the worst place to play one. There is, after all, considerable information in the fact that Elder's front yard is that hundred-yard greensward where the elephants go to die: **The Pit**.

"The stadium," wrote Bill Koch in *The Pride of Price Hill*, "serves as the gathering place for the vast Elder community on Friday nights in autumn when fans stream into the old concrete structure, most parking their cars on the streets in the blue-collar neighborhood and making their way toward the stadium lights much as West Side fans have been doing since The Pit was completed in 1947."

That's from the viewpoint of the home team. The visitors have a different description of the place. To them, it's half an Edgar Allen Poe story narrated by Doug Ramsey. It's a crowd of villagers with lanterns and pitchforks, an imposing home-field record, the tradition of your usual Papal coronation, and the atmosphere—for the visiting team—of an Inquisition basement. It is, in other words, Mordor with a field judge.

There was nothing normal about it from its very inception. First, the stadium was designed by two Elder seniors, and the schoolboys themselves volunteered their lunch breaks to clean up debris on the site. "The students of Elder have a right to boast about the stands," said the school newspaper, the *Purple Quill*. "We are the only school in the country that is making its own stadium." Everybody helped—students, family, and friends of the school, which was most of the West Side. No one even seemed to mind too much when the stands were poured and concrete ran into the neighborhood backyards.

Construction stopped during the war years, then resumed with a flourish. The stadium was finished in 1947 and dedicated before the Turkey Day classic with Western Hills, which Elder won, 7-0. It had cost something in the neighborhood of $250,000, not a bad price for a budding institution. No bond issues. No skirmishes with county commissioners. And if any lawyers were involved, they were probably pouring concrete.

It wasn't the greatest field in those days, but it was on its way to greatness. It was, as Koch's book pointed out, "a dusty cow pasture on Cincinnati's West Side adorned with a manhole on the 30-yard line. It was the only known playing field in Ohio where a manhole was home-field advantage, and its sewer lid icon became a kind of trademark for the school's rough-and-ready working class play. From that inauspicious beginning was born one of the Midwest's most storied prep traditions: Elder High athletics."

The stadium wasn't even called The Pit in those days. Father Edwin Bertke, the athletic director then, thought The Pit sounded like an illegal chicken fight out in the country. That, of course, was exactly the atmosphere the students wanted. They set about becoming one of the most imposing cheering sections in the state, viewed by other schools "with a mixture of envy, disdain, and disbelief."

First, it was a politically-incorrect males-only bastion of leather-lunged excess. It was, wrote Koch, "a discriminating social unit that has one basic, unalterable rule: No girls allowed. Those girls who try to penetrate the forbidden zone of the cheering section used to be passed down from row to row until they were outside the zone. Now they are simply hooted out vocally."

Second, there are no duly appointed cheerleaders. No girls, no uniforms, just a handful of guys leading several hundred *other* guys on, until the sound approximates—from the visitor's point-of-ear—a prison riot. It would not be unthinkable that an opposing quarterback, in his first varsity season and finding himself in front of this purple mob, might look distractedly up from his own huddle and picture himself in an even more ancient place, a coliseum, say, in which the entire crowd was giving him the thumbs-down gesture.

A few years ago, the school's unorthodox approach to cheering almost got Elder's masters of hurrah disqualified from the state basketball tournament. The rules said school cheerleaders must have uniforms, or they would not be allowed on the floor.

As usual, the guys rose to the occasion: they dressed in black pants, tuxedo shirts, purple bow ties, and gym shoes. And the show went on.

In its sixty-plus years of football business, more than a million and a half fans have seen games at The Pit. The stadium itself has been designated by no less a source than that extraordinary listmaker, *USAToday*, as one of the top ten places in America to watch a high school football game. Its homefield record in all that time—270-79-5—keeps eternally alive the notion that while it is one of the best places to watch a football game, this is so largely for the West Side. On nearly three of every four occasions at The Pit, visitors do not agree.

It's a beautiful thing to run into an Elder grad in a dimly-lit San Francisco sushi bar and say, 'Dude, I went to Colerain and we hated you fuckers! Sake bomb!'

—Danny Cross, CityBeat, September 17, 2008

When Flyin' Brian Pillman was with the Bengals, Bruce Coslet said he'd hit anything. "Even if it was his own guy. He didn't care."

LB

Linebackers

Todd Bell—*Middletown/Class of 1977*

Rocky Boiman—*St. Xavier/Class of 1998*

Dustin Cohen—*Country Day/Class of 1996*

Bob Crable—*Moeller/Class of 1978*

Denny Dase—*Central/Class of 1959*

Steve Grote—*Elder/Class of 1973*

The Larkins (Mike, Barry & Byron)
—*Moeller/Classes of 1981, 1982, 1984*

Brian Pillman—*Norwood/Class of 1980*

Jack "Hacksaw" Reynolds—*Western Hills/Class of 1966*

Glenn Sample—*Western Hills/Class of 1949*

The Intangibles Gene *(Troy Evans)*

A Man for All Positions *(Terry Killens)*

Antman Grows Up *(Antwan Peek)*

Kamikazi Reese *(Ike Reese)*

Monroe's Mr. Big Ten *(Steve Strinko)*

The Champion of Glen Este *(Matt Maupin)*

Bench Strength—Shane Bullough, Moeller; Dixon Edwards, Aiken; Ike Reese, Aiken; Lemar Marshall, St. Xavier; Greg Jones, Mark Woehler, Steve Spatz, Rob Klocke, Steve Koehne, and Steve Apke, Moeller; Dixon Edwards, Aiken; and Dick Ullrich, St. Xavier.

All-Time College Team of Cincinnatians

Practice session at Elder before its title run in 2003.

Todd Bell

Middletown linebacker class of 1977

77

TODD BELL NEVER TOLD THE KIDS HE TAUGHT IN SUNDAY SCHOOL THAT HE HAD PLAYED FOR THE CHICAGO BEARS. HE NEGLECTED TO BRING UP THAT HE was an All-Pro defensive back, or to mention what he did to put Ohio State in the Rose Bowl, which was recover a fumble and carry it in for the touchdown that won the 1979 Michigan game, 18-15.

In the interest of humility, Brother Bell never alluded to that New Year's Day in Pasadena, with the national championship on the line, when he took away a Southern Cal touchdown by catching the Heisman Trophy winner, Charles White, from behind. He had been unable to save the game—the Buckeyes still lost by a point—but had since tackled a bigger job, with better success. He saved kids.

The kids, of course, knew about him in spite of his self-unimportance. One of them drew a picture of Bell bringing down White in the Rose Bowl, and Mr. Todd, as they called him, said he would keep it in his Bible. And he did.

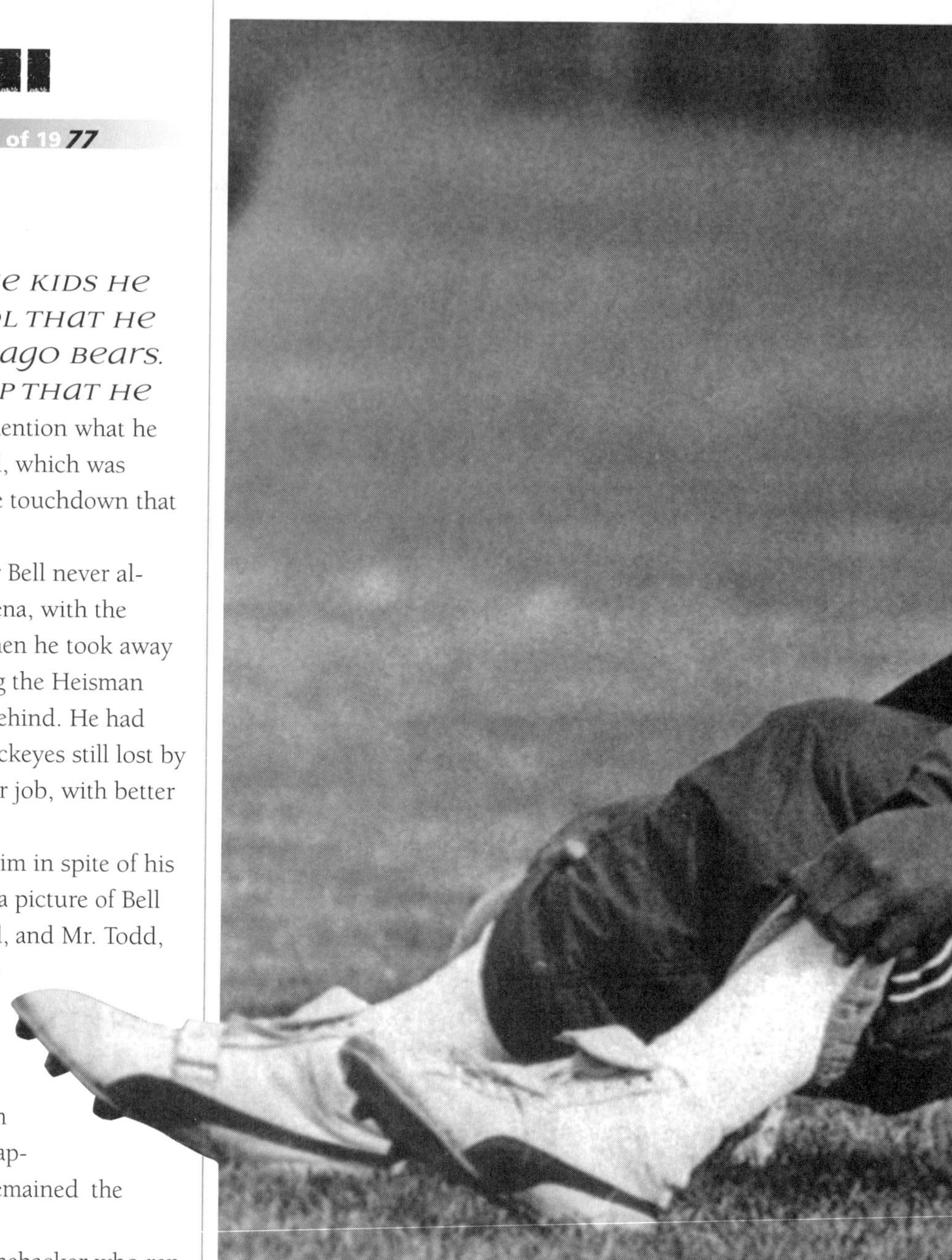

Bell's father was a minister, and a role model who raised a role model. Even at Middletown High School, in an age of loosening morals, with all the trappings of stardom at his disposal, Bell remained the straightest arrow in the quiver.

And the fastest, by far. He was a linebacker who ran the length of the field in 9.7 seconds. He also won the state championship in the long jump, three times. He broke the Ohio record for that event, by six inches. It had been held for forty-four years. By Jesse Owens.

And yet, he didn't play football on merely his physical gifts. Bell was filled with the unholy spirit of the game, famous for smashing ball-carriers as though his very soul depended on it. In 1976, he was named the Lineman of the Year in Ohio.

It was difficult, nevertheless, to imagine Bell a lineman. Woody Hayes couldn't. Hayes made him an immediate starter in the Buckeyes' defensive backfield.

In Chicago, it took him three years to acquire a similar status, then another to make the all-star squad. Next came 1985, when the Bears won the Super Bowl with a defense that refuses to be forgotten. Unfortunately for Bell, it didn't include him. He sat out the season in a contract dispute.

He was with the Eagles in 1989 when he broke his leg in a Monday Night game against the Bears, of all teams. It ended his career prematurely, but quickened the service he considered more essential.

Whether for spiritual purposes or general, Bell often advised his students and friends to live every day as though it would be their last. He must have known something. His last was a March day in 2005, when he suffered a heart attack while driving and his car crashed into a house in Reynoldsburg. He died at 47, in what those who knew him would assuredly call his prime.

In Middletown, the stretch of road running past Rosa Parks Elementary School—which was a middle school when Bell attended it—is now known as Todd Bell Memorial Way.

Rocky Boiman

St. Xavier linebacker class of 1998

98

AFTER ROCKY BOIMAN DEPARTED ST. XAVIER AND MOVED ON TO NOTRE DAME WHERE THE PRO SCOUTS WERE SOON APPLYING SUCH LANGUAGE to him as "fills the rush lane quickly" and "has relentless motor coming off the edge," other graduates of the GCL back in Cincinnati—notably running backs and receivers—rolled their eyes and instinctively rubbed the spot over their kidneys where he'd left his autograph.

He was that kind of impact player in high school. Even the studly GCL didn't have many 210-pound safeties who played like linebackers and ran down wide receivers. When he was a freshman, Boiman started lifting weights with the other freshmen, but soon he was working out with the varsity. Not enough action, not enough plates. He loved practice, too, which is like saying you love traffic accidents or muggings in which you are the principal.

"On the field, he's nasty," said his coach, Steve Rasso. "Off the field, he's soft-spoken, a booksy type of guy."

Perhaps a book such as *The Art of War*, wherein Sun Tzu says things like "Forestall your opponent by seizing what he holds dear," surely making it a tactical manual for a guy like Boiman.

He would say things such as, "After the game, I don't even want to be able to walk," although generally it was the opposition that limped away. When he was a senior, Boiman helped St. Xavier into the playoffs with a sterling game against Anderson in which he returned a kickoff 77 yards to set up one St. X score and forestalled an opposing score by literally ripping the ball out of the hands of an Anderson receiver.

He was the Bombers' captain and their MVP, All-City, All-State, the captain of the track team, and twice All-City as a shortstop and second baseman. He went to the Ohio North-South All-Star Classic, and the Ohio-Pennsylvania Big 33 All-Star Game, and he signed with

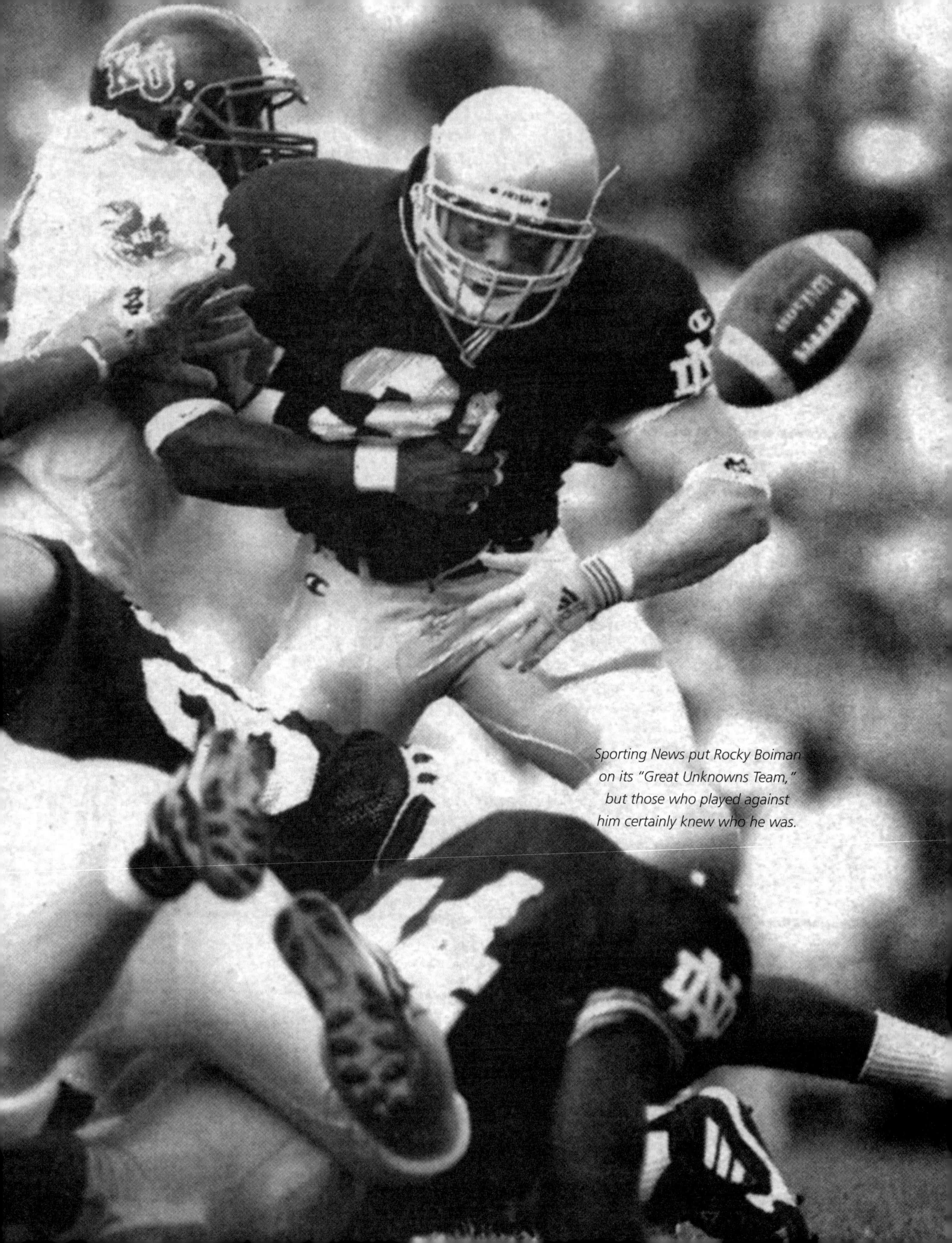

Sporting News put Rocky Boiman on its "Great Unknowns Team," but those who played against him certainly knew who he was.

Notre Dame over any number of other suitors. But he'd been going to Notre Dame ever since he could envision such a thing.

It didn't take him long to make his mark there, either, although he was playing linebacker, exactly what his St. X coach had prophesied. "The sight of linebacker Rocky Boiman sends shivers down opposing players' spines, with his devilish fire-red hair, glare that shoots bullets, and imposing physique," said one writer.

Before his junior year, he was selected to *The Sporting News'* "Great Unknowns" team, which meant that he wasn't. He'd kept his speed, added thirty pounds or so, and as a senior he was one of the Irish captains, a three-year starter. Tennessee picked him in the fourth round of the 2002 NFL draft, and he soon made a name for himself on special teams and at backup linebacker. He earned a Super Bowl ring with the Colts in 2007. He occupied one of the NFL's more difficult roles, that of the yeoman, and he brought to it that same fiery intensity he'd always carried with him. Some things really didn't change.

Dustin Cohen

Country Day linebacker class of 19**96**

96

DUSTIN COHEN WAS ANOTHER OF CINCINNATI'S SMALL SCHOOL EXPORTS WHO SPRINTED OUT INTO THE LARGER WORLD—IN HIS CASE, MIAMI OF Oxford—to prove it wasn't where you were from, it was where you were going. He'd always seemed to know, too. He was playing the game by the time he was 5 years old, and one day, he said to one of his coaches, "If you tie my shoe, Coach, I could run faster." He knew the game before he knew how to tie his shoes.

So he was from Summit Country Day, Division VI. In actuality, he was from a larger place called Enterprise, which is just down the road from an even larger place called Aspiration. In high school, he was a four-year starter: two years at receiver, one at quarterback, one at running back, and on defense—always a linebacker. His 45 TDs and 560 tackles were school records.

His father was worried about what was next. Would others see in Dustin what *he* saw? So his father sent out letters and videotapes. Every Division I school in the country got a letter, and of the sixty that answered, he sent out forty videotapes. When twenty of the videotapes came back, he sent them to twenty *other* schools. It was fun, he said, until the tapes ran out.

With his dad—and his game—doing the promoting, Dustin got eight offers. He chose Miami, where he was being recruited as an "athlete." Ostensibly, this meant he might play anywhere, but when he was put on the scout team as linebacker, no one could block him. Late in his freshman season, he was starting. And soon after that, he had bulked up from 198 pounds to 240, strong enough to give linemen fits, yet still quick enough to play safety.

Said his coach, Terry Hoeppner, "It's hard for an offensive player to affect a game single-handedly, but a defensive player can create havoc by himself. *That's* what Dustin does."

In his tenure at Miami, from 1996-1999, Cohen imprinted himself all over Miami's record book. He was All-MAC, third-team All-American, a finalist for the Butkus Award (given to the nation's best linebacker), and he held an NCAA record for most interceptions returned for TDs by a linebacker in his career (four). He's still in the top ten of at least six of Miami's statistical categories, including tackles for loss (Number 7, 51 tackles) and solo tackles (Number 8, 251 solo tackles). He had a cup of espresso as a special teams player with St. Louis, but his reputation was made at his previous stops, Country Day and Miami. There, the legend persists.

Three yards and a cloud of Dustin

Bob Crable

Moeller | linebacker | class of 19**78**

78

THE SOVEREIGNTY OF HIGH SCHOOL FOOTBALL IN THE STATE OF OHIO WAS HELD IN THE CLUTCHES OF THE NORTHEASTERLY INSTITUTIONS UNTIL the late fall of 1975, when it was knocked from the hands of a Lakewood St. Edward player and fell provocatively at the Moeller 12-yard line. There, it became the possession of a sophomore linebacker, and of his Catholic school from the Cincinnati suburb of Montgomery.

For the rest of his career at Moeller, Bob Crable would not lose a game or a state championship. Upon busting the myth of Cleveland-Canton-Massillon and thereabouts, the Crusaders embarked on a reign of preeminence that exceeded even Ohio's parameters. As a junior and senior, Crable personified the commanding defense—seven shutouts in 1977—of a team declared on both occasions as the nation's greatest.

Shortly after Gerry Faust became Moeller's first football coach in 1960, he resolved to develop a squad on which players would focus their efforts on either offense or defense, as opposed to both. The concept was to keep them fresh, train them specifically, and accommodate them in greater number.

When Steve Niehaus held sway as a two-way, All-American lineman from 1969-71, the Crusaders had not yet reached the critical mass of talent that would enable the likes of him to leave the field when the ball changed hands. But as the program prospered, it saw a guy like Niehaus beget a guy like Crable.

From the time the latter was a seventh-grader at St. Vincent, Faust had known that he could build a defense around the big kid who policed the field with slanting-eyed intensity. One of Faust's assistants, Phil Gigliotti, had scurried back from a St. Vincent game to tell Faust about the tackling prodigy who was just the kind of young fellow he was looking for.

As a growing boy, Crable fancied himself a baseball

player, as well, and planned to demonstrate it in college, if not beyond. But in the summer of 1977, he had a little chat with Bud Middaugh, the baseball coach at Miami University. Middaugh allowed that he'd gladly offer Crable a scholarship, provided that he cease playing football. That, the teenager decided on the spot, was something he simply couldn't do.

He was much too much the football player, in a classic, old-school sense. Ruthless and unrelenting, with a discipline that rounded out the perfect profile of a linebacker, Crable dominated his day to the degree that, in 1999, he was named by the *Cincinnati Post* as its high school Defensive Player of the Century. He was also named by the New York Jets as a first-round draft choice in 1982.

That followed an All-American career at Notre Dame, during which Crable twice captained the Irish and also broke their season record for tackles, whereupon—playing as a senior for Faust—he broke it again. He still holds the career mark.

He played for the Jets until his knees opted out of the deal six years in, then started a successful sportswear business in Cincinnati. Crable was somewhat less successful coaching the Crusaders from 2001 to 2007.

Working against him, in that capacity, was the rarified standard that Moeller had established a quarter century before, starting with a fumble recovered by a sophomore linebacker who wasn't about to lose—not that day or any other, as long as he wore the uniform of the Catholic high school in the heart of Montgomery.

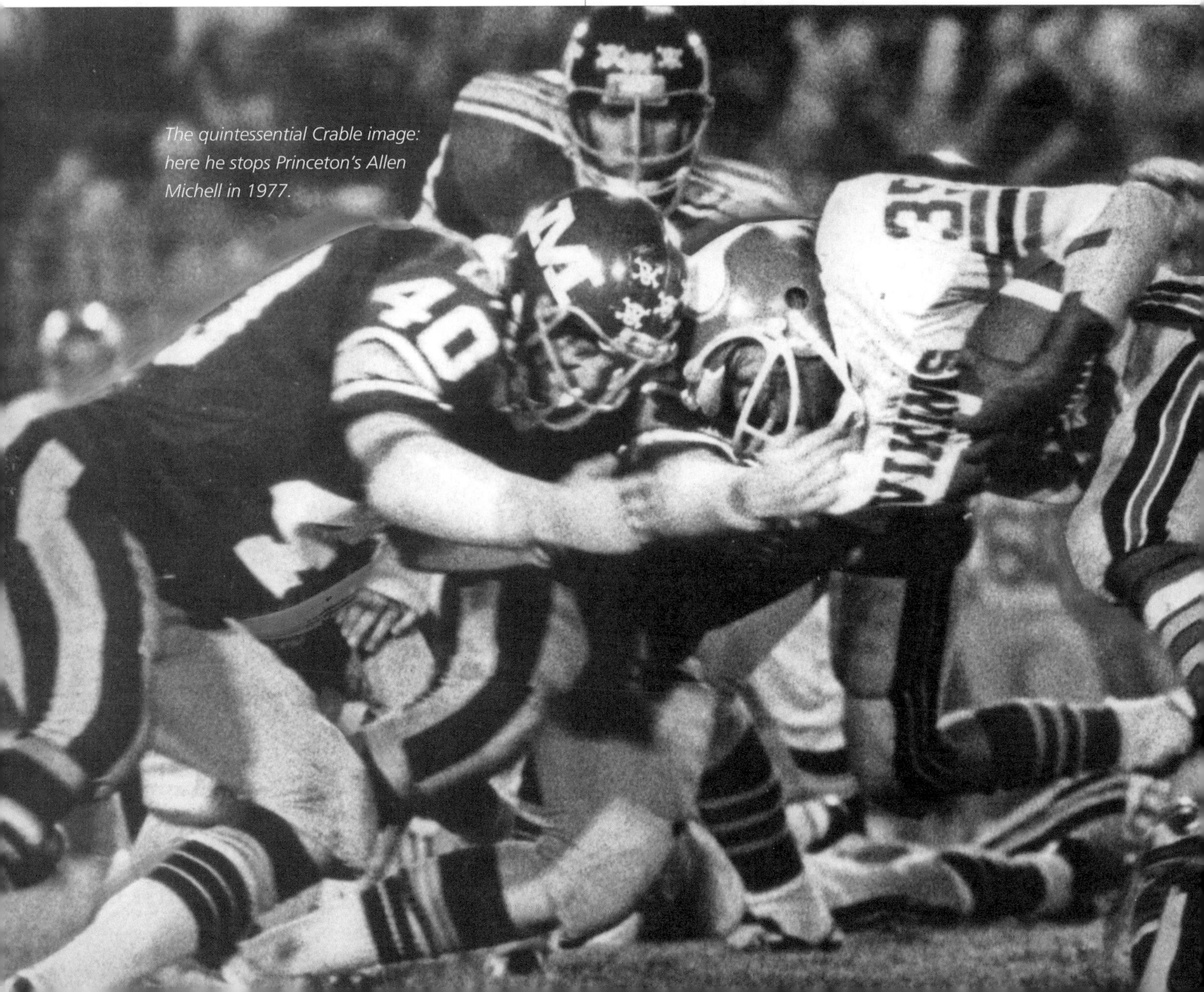

The quintessential Crable image: here he stops Princeton's Allen Michell in 1977.

Denny Dase

Central | linebacker | class of 19**59**

59

DENNY DASE WAS A BIG TOUGH CITY KID WHO EARNED HIS FOOTBALL REPUTATION BY KNOCKING PEOPLE DOWN. IN 1957, AS A JUNIOR, HE HELPED CENTRAL win its first ever PHSL title. The next year, on his way to earning first team All-City honors, the 5-11, 210-pound center and middle linebacker knocked down enough Cavaliers to help Central upset Purcell 18–8. It was the first time since 1941 that the Hackberry Assassins had lost as early as their second game.

Dase's reputation of knocking people down followed him after high school.

Dase knew how to throw his weight around, and in several venues.

He was known as a brawler and it was whispered that he was an enforcer for the teamsters. By the early '70's, following stints as a bouncer for some of the bars around town, he had his own place—Dase's.

By this time he had gained over a hundred pounds, his head was shaved, and the prominent scar that ran across it lent credibility to the rumors that followed him. In truth, the scar was from surgery he had for a brain tumor in 1960, which cut short what the newspapers called "a brilliantly forecast grid career" at the University of Arizona.

Somewhere along the way, Dase had developed a passion for arm-wrestling, and he occasionally appeared on television refereeing matches. His place on McMillan Street near the UC campus featured, of course, an arm-wrestling table, although the bar's main lure to the college kids was that he sold 25-cent beer.

The bar attracted few women and became a place for college boys to go when they had little money and fewer prospects. Each night after pouring a few for the early, serious drinking crowd, Denny settled into his seat near the door. He kept forever his old linebacker's persona, in which all the world was nothing more than an offense trying to get outside on him. His bulk didn't allow him to sit up straight so he was forced to lean back against the wall, surveying his patrons malevolently over the vast promontory of his waistline.

From there, he checked IDs and stared down any possible troublemakers. Trouble, however, was only hinted at in his place because (1) trouble was *his* province, and (2) no one wanted to be the last person knocked down by Denny Dase.

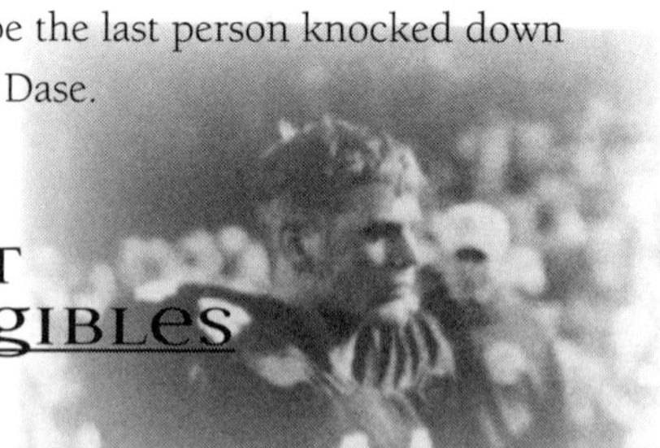

THAT INTANGIBLES gene

When Lakota coach Greg Bailie called a slant pass against Middletown, he wasn't entirely prepared for what was to come. His sophomore receiver, **Troy Evans**, ran the slant, and as the ball arrived, so did the Middletown defender. Evans did a complete 360-degree flip. "I don't even remember if he caught the ball," Bailie said, "but I do remember him on the sidelines a few minutes later and I heard him asking another player 'Did you see me flip? That was awesome.' I suspected then we had a special player."

By the time he was a senior in 1995—and co-captain on a playoff team—he was also playing cornerback, leading the city in interceptions. Either side of the field, he had an eye for the ball, which explains, perhaps, the fact that he was first-team All-Conference in basketball, as well, setting the school record for consecutive free throws—33.

But in spite of being a Division I All-State defensive back, the D-I guys came and went. Another real player done in by the paper on him. *Too small for linebacker*, they wrote. *Too big for corner*. What they missed was Evans' intangibles gene. No Division I offers? Go Division I-AA. So Evans went to Wofford College and played an AA season but with an A mindset.

Convinced of himself when no one else was, he returned to Cincinnati and walked on with the UC Bearcats. He played every game as a sophomore and the next spring was a starter at outside linebacker. He stayed there two years, led the team in tackles his senior year, and made second-team Conference USA.

Of course, the scouts didn't come around again. Evans signed with the Rams as a free agent and was cut. Same story. A little slow. Not quite big enough. His Lakota coach knew what most people would have done: Gone home and sat in a dark basement, a little sorry for ourselves, a little embarrassed. Not Evans. The day after he was cut, he showed up on the Lakota practice field.

Bailie offered his condolences. Evans would have none of it. "I'll get called back," he said. "My agent's working on something." Sure enough, he was. The Rams called him back. Released at the end of the season, he went through the same thing with Houston: signed, released, then re-signed, this time to begin a five-year run with the Texans.

Working primarily as a special teams player, Evans was soon heading into his seventh year as a pro, a special teams standout in an occupation where every year was a dog's year. Evans had installed a measure of belief wherever he'd gone, just a little extra chore, and his Lakota coach had been the first victim of Evans' irrepressible faith in himself.

"They won't run Troy Evans out of the league," Bailie said. "I really believe he'll find a way to play as long as he wants."

Steve Grote

Elder | linebacker | class of 19**73**

73

TOSS THE NAME OUT AND FOLKS WILL SAY "BASKETBALL." THIS WOULD MARK THEM AS LESS-THAN-HARDCORE ELDER FANS, THOUGH, FOR THE WEST SIDE knows that Steve Grote was one of the toughest linebackers ever, in a league known for the manufacture of tough linebackers. He was first-team All-GCL, All-City, and All-State at outside linebacker, as well as a *Scholastic* magazine All-American, the quintessential Elder kid and the heart of the purple-collar Elder defense on the 1972 team still considered one of the school's greatest.

The defense that year shut out its first eight opponents (read: victims) before giving up a single score against St. Xavier in a 6-6 tie, the only imperfect mark on an otherwise perfect season. Grote and fellow linebacker Paul Maly were both first-team All-State, as Elder finished second to Princeton in the newly instituted Harbin Ratings system that determined which teams made the state playoffs.

(Eight teams from each region go into the playoffs now; only one did then. The Panthers were done in partly by their Thanksgiving Day game with Western Hills, a win that wouldn't be factored into the ratings, and it was the beginning of the end for that notable West Side tradition. Princeton lost to Warren Western Reserve in the state final as the Elder boys looked helplessly on; they had scrimmaged Princeton in the preseason and beaten the Vikings easily.)

The game the West Side liked to recall from that year, however, was the win over Lancaster, one that featured a smash-mouth evening between Grote and Lancaster's Rob Carpenter, an All-American high school running back who went to the NFL through Miami of Ohio. Elder had lost a close game to Lancaster the season before, and Grote read a Lancaster newspaper article about Lancaster's staggering superiority in their earlier meeting.

Grote: A once-in-three-decades guy.

Grote was incensed, which seemed to be his standard gridiron mood—he was so fiery a competitor there was a joke about Grote's shoulder pads being ordered from an asbestos factory. At any rate, it was one press clipping Lancaster—and Carpenter—could have done without.

"I was yelling and screaming at Carpenter between plays," Grote said, "until the referee threatened me with a 15-yard penalty if I didn't shut up."

Elder beat Lancaster 26-0 and never let Carpenter get past his own 40-yard line. He rushed for 93 yards but it took him 26 painful carries, hit fiercely on every play. The last play of the game was a trap with Carpenter carrying. Grote shed the guard, hit Carpenter head on, drove him to the sidelines, and slammed him to the ground. Carpenter was so dazed he wandered into the Elder huddle. (The next week, Grote worked on another future NFLer, LaSalle's 6-7 tight end Don Hasselbeck,

A man for all positions

If **Terry Killens** wasn't a household name, but no matter: he could play anywhere in the house. He made All-State in 1992 as a Purcell Marian running back, became one of the Big Ten's dominant defensive players—as a Penn State senior, even he wasn't sure exactly what position he played—and he went to the Super Bowl with the Tennessee Titans as a linebacker.

Perhaps such versatility came to him in the old days, when the Kennedy Heights neighborhood kids formed the Tyne Avenue Tomahawks, and the teams were determined by which side of the street you lived on. They played basketball under street lights, stop signs for backboards.

When he reached high school, the Purcell Marian coaching staff was glad to have him anywhere. He was the team MVP as a *sophomore*. "He was scaringly good," said Tom Stickley, his defensive coordinator. In the first game of his senior season, Killens got into Colerain's backfield so fast that he intercepted the quarterback's pitch to his running back.

Purcell Marian won its first seven games, leading Ohio's Division III schools, and was headed for the playoffs when Killens broke his hand. He missed the last shivering him at the line and keeping him from catching a single pass.)

But if Grote couldn't get to the title game in one sport, then he would do it in another, and he finished a spectacular senior year by leading the basketball team to its first state title, beating Akron Central-Hower. It was the first basketball title by a team from Cincinnati proper, and Grote was the tournament MVP. He was also All-State for the second time in a year (third team), and he'd done it using his old gridiron manner. "Keeping 'em off balance," he'd say, or, "You might bump them accidentally once in awhile."

Grote was a tough, gristly kid, mentally as well as physically, with the focus of a Trappist monk, and it would be more than three decades before Elder would have another two-sport star of such magnitude—2008's Kyle Rudolph, a football All-American and a three-time GCL Player of the Year in basketball, bound for Notre Dame to play football.

Grote, as everyone in Cincinnati knows, went to Michigan and played basketball. And how. He helped Michigan to the national title game in 1976 and was a three-time academic All-American. He was one of their greatest guards, so much so that Michigan named the Steve Grote Hustle Award after him. It came from his old Elder temperament, and he just couldn't help himself.

three games and was still named the Southwest District back of the year. He finished with 1,079 rushing yards and was AP's co-back of the year in Ohio.

Ohio State, Michigan State, and Purdue recruited him as a running back and while Penn State got him, the Nittany Lions didn't need a running back; they needed him on defense. And they needed him quickly. He became one of only two freshmen to play at Penn State that year. He played in every game, mostly special teams. By the time he was a senior, he was a defensive stalwart, even if he didn't know where he might be playing. He could move to defensive end; more often he was at linebacker. In a 1995 game with Indiana, Killens forced a fumble, had four sacks, and scored after blocking a punt.

In the 1996 draft, the Houston Oilers picked him in the third round. He was a little undersized at 230 pounds, but his old running-back quickness served as compensation. Five years later, when the newly named Titans went into the Super Bowl against Jacksonville, Killens was their top special teams player and third-down linebacker. Before the ride was over, he'd had seven years in the NFL. He was a testament to flexibility and perseverance, and while his name might not have been found on America's billboards, it was still quite a distance from the Tyne Avenue Tomahawks.

Killens: "Scaringly good..."

Barry Larkin (above) was a great safety before he became a great shortstop. His brother, Byron, (at right) was a prep football All-American before opting for basketball.

The Larkins

Mike, Barry, Byron

Moeller linebackers, etc. classes of 1981, 1982, 19

81, 82, 84

AT THEIR HOME IN SILVERTON, WHERE THE GRASS WAS CHRONICALLY TRAMPLED AND THE BASEMENT LIGHT BULBS PERMANENTLY BROKEN, MIKE AND Byron Larkin would put capes on their backs and jump superhero-style to the bottom of the stairs. One day, brother Barry wanted in. He tied on the cape and proceeded to make the leap *headfirst*.

Yeah, they were football players. All of them. Mike, the oldest, is best known for it, because he was a captain and linebacker at Notre Dame. He was also the biggest of the bunch, and possibly the baddest. When the boys played "knee football" in the Larkin basement, it was Mike as ballcarrier—rumbling through on his knees, of course—while the other two attempted to knock him the rest of the way onto the unforgiving floor, or make him say he'd had enough.

But the fact is, Mike's the only one of the three who wasn't an MVP on the Moeller High School team. He and Byron were prep All-Americans. And Barry, well, "Barry would knock your teeth out," said Jim Lippincott, a Bengals personnel official who was Moeller's defensive coordinator at the time. "He was a complete safety."

Barry Larkin—before he became the best shortstop in Reds history—opted for baseball at Michigan, even though Bo Schembechler wanted him badly for football, too. "Bo would come out to the games and start yelling at me," Barry recalled years later.

"He'd yell, 'Larkin, you're a sissy! You're a big sissy! You're hitting a ball that can't hit back. Come on out and hit a *man* that can hit you back . . . Besides, I could strike you out anyway!' "

Plenty of people remember Barry as the best safety Moeller ever had, and others lean toward Byron Larkin. The only thing holding Byron back was basketball. Before he became Xavier's all-time leading scorer, he was a Moeller prodigy as a freshman, scoring 29 points in his first game and 44 in another after being promoted from the junior varsity for the postseason tournaments. Once he realized what he could do in basketball, football lost the premium he had placed on it.

There was, for instance, an occasion when Byron missed a day or two of football practice for an all-star basketball camp. The young defensive backfield coach responded by demoting him to the third team. When Larkin promptly soared into a nearby tree to snatch an interception, the coaches conferred and he found himself back in the first-team huddle.

Mike Larkin won state championships as a junior and senior (1979 and '80), and Barry was a sophomore in the first of those, a crushing victory over Parma Padua. Parma did make some progress, however, when one of its receivers caught a ball in Barry's area. The correction was mandated by Mike, who, as he later recalled, "kind of pointed at him and asked him kindly not to allow that to happen again." It didn't, and it didn't happen the next year, either, when the Crusaders crushed Massillon at Nippert Stadium.

When Byron was a junior two years later, Moeller again took the measure of Massillon, this time at Ohio Stadium. Lippincott remembers it well: "Chris Spielman was playing tailback for Massillon, and he was awesome that day. He had like 32

The Larkin ensemble, 1984: In back, Byron, Mr. Robert Larkin, Robin, and Barry. That's Stephen and Mrs. Larkin in front. (Mike was off at Notre Dame, playing linebacker.)

carries and double-digit tackles. But he came around in front of our bench with the ball, and Byron hit him, face to face, and knocked them both cuckoo. Spielman still talks about that."

The family's mean streak, however, was embedded in Mike. He's the one who would drown bees and then pick their wings off. He's the one who set the tone for the Moeller defense. And later, Notre Dame's.

Mike went to South Bend with Gerry Faust and piled up 110 tackles as a sophomore. But he broke his forearm the next spring, broke it again in preseason drills, and missed a full season. He also tore ligaments in a knee and ankle, and separated a shoulder. The NFL was not in his future. He played for a while with the Montreal Alouettes of the Canadian League, but when they went out of the football business, so did he.

Meanwhile, there was a talented fourth brother, Stephen, who was tracked by Faust from the outset. Faust once spent a Saturday morning watching the youngest Larkin play for the Deer Park Cobras.

At one point, Stephen peeked out of the huddle to see if Faust was paying attention, then broke off a long touchdown run, looking over his shoulder and grinning mischievously at the Moeller coach.

But when Stephen Larkin was at Moeller, the school refused to let him play without medical certification, which he couldn't attain due to an abnormally thick wall on his heart.

The Larkins sued, and a federal judge denied their appeal. He was permitted to play only baseball, and subsequently spent time in the minor leagues, some of it in the Reds' organization.

By that time, Barry was an all-star, Mike was handling his endorsements, Byron was announcing Xavier games, and the family was out of football altogether.

But yeah, they were players. All of them.

Brian Pillman

Norwood linebacker class of 19**80**

80

He was the answer to the trivia question: "Who do you want on the barstool next to you when the fight breaks out?" In any contest of Brian Pillman vs. buzzsaw, the saw got the long odds. On the football field, he frightened the guys on *his* team; they were afraid he'd forget who they were. He was a human demolition derby, and at the altar of linebacking excess—where *he* worshipped—his body was the original sacrificial ram.

Who knows where the fierceness came from. Maybe at Jewish Hospital, where he seemed to have spent much of his first few years undergoing more than two dozen operations to remove polyps on his throat. He was small, he had a raspy voice from all the surgeries, and perhaps he wished to reinvent himself. He did, too.

Antman grows up

Antwan Peek always knew he'd make the NFL. He just didn't know how.

He figured it would be as a receiver, of course, the same way Jerry Rice made it, and in the same style, only taller. He loved Jerry Rice; watched tapes of him over and over; imitated him; identified with him. The trouble was, Woodward High School couldn't put together enough players for a real passing game. The first day of practice Peek's senior year, which was 1997, only eight guys showed up. Two of the games were cancelled for lack of men.

Somehow, he found his way to UC at 6-2, 185 pounds. He got a little taller and a lot bigger. Too big for wide receiver, Rick Minter moved him to safety. Then to linebacker. Then—at 250 pounds, with less than 7 percent body fat—to defensive end.

As a junior in 2001, Peek set the Bearcat record for sacks with 12½. As a senior, he was All-Conference USA for the second time. He was drafted in the third round by the Houston Texans. They moved him back to linebacker. He lost a little weight. By his third season, he was a starter, racking up six sacks.

And he still hadn't caught a pass.

When he first showed up for football practice at Norwood, they thought he was a manager. The kid was 5-7, about 150 pounds. One day, the coach, Don Rahe, pointed at him to lead calisthenics and the kid started squeaking, *One, two, three...*

Jeez, thought Rahe, *what is this?*

He didn't know the kid had undergone thirty operations. There'd been a time when he'd written notes so people could understand him. (He wrote a note to one of his teammates once, and the teammate took the pad and wrote back the answer.) Some of the coaches thought perhaps Pillman was the answer to the deaf kid who called the defensive signals. Not hearing might have been a kind of aid: it improved one's concentration.

Concentration was not something Pillman lacked, however. He concentrated on lifting, and he concentrated on the game. Rahe had long since been won over. "You could cut off his fist with a sword and he'd jam what was left down your throat," Rahe said, in that pictorially vivid way some coaches have.

> "He was an overachieving, HIGH energy, upbeat guy. He would hit anything that moved. Even if it was his own guy. He didn't care."
>
> —Bruce Coslet, Bengal coach, on Pillman.

The point of convergence might have been at the end of Pillman's junior year. That was when Rahe nominated his kid for All-City. Smart guy that he was, he told the kid what had happened.

"Brian," he said, "I gotta tell you the truth. I put you up for All-City and they laughed."

The kid shrugged. "Okay, Coach," he said, then spent the winter in the weight room. When he came out, he weighed 190. Before he'd graduated off the Norwood field, the other coaches had stopped laughing. And he made All-City.

None of it came particularly easy to him, and in this he was a reflection of his neighborhood, Norwood, which was always having to reinvent itself, too. So the kid was about to remake himself again, even as no one wanted him as a college player.

The University of Cincinnati didn't want him, even as a walk-on. They weren't even impressed with Pillman's game film of the Colerain game, in which he leaped over several blockers and buried a punt. Finally, Miami agreed to let him try out. Their overture was so low key, he might have been auditioning for a position in the band.

If so, it was the percussion section, for Pillman took his old coach's words to heart. "If you go

Pillman was one of the Queen City's greatest schoolboy legends—even to the tragic fact of dying young.

up there," Rahe had said to him, "you've got to be an assassin, even in the half-speed drills. It can't ever be half-speed for you."

And it wasn't.

He was a first-team All-American at middle guard—by now he was 5-10, 225 pounds—and he was the Mid-American Conference's defensive player of the year in 1983. He set new MAC records for tackles-for-losses, both season and career (39 tackles for 142 yards of losses in 1983, 76 career tackles and losses of 337 yards).

When he finished his collegiate career, he found himself back where he had started: the undersized guy no one wanted. The NFL draft came and went, and finally the hometown Bengals invited him into camp. He played one season as a backup, his every move followed and discussed in Norwood where he was already an alehouse legend.

Then he played two more for the Canadian Football League's Calgary Stampeders where he was discovered by the World Wrestling Federation. It was here that Pillman's talent for reinventing himself found its full expression. Soon, he was "Flyin' Brian" Pillman, one of the most popular wrestlers in America.

Then, in a single-vehicle crash in 1996, he was thrown from his Humvee, shattering his ankle and breaking bones in his face. He was in a coma for a week. He returned to wrestle but the injury meant Air Pillman was down to earth again. He was fortunate to be anywhere, actually, but there was a price.

It was paid the next year when he was found dead in a Minneapolis hotel room. While he had a history of prescription drug abuse, the autopsy said he had previously undetected arteriosclerotic heart disease, a familial condition.

He was 35 years old, and in death he had become a kind of posthumous cyberspace celebrity. There were pictures and bios, discussions of his lost legend, and theories that, like Elvis, he wasn't really dead. As if death were an act from which he might—on any given Saturday night—return with one of his signature moves, such as the flying clothesline, mortality itself just more unpredictable behavior from the WWF.

The tough kid from Norwood, it seemed, had reinvented himself one final time.

Kamikaze Reese

In 2004, **Ike Reese**, a Philadelphia linebacker from Aiken High (class of 1993), made his first Pro Bowl, as a special teams player. From the ground (where the *real* game goes on), this is the Pulitzer position, the top prize for the NFL's most thankless job. It requires an odd kamikaze kind of fellow who will make himself into both pilot and plane, hurl himself fearlessly at the enemy, and imagine that he will walk away unscathed.

The kid from Westwood had been doing it for seven years, an eternity in a job with the life expectancy of a fruit fly. Since arriving in Philly, he had made 141 special teams tackles, making him the Number 1 kamikaze. His position coach in those years was John Harbaugh, an ex-UC assistant, who worked diligently to recruit Reese out of high school. (He lost him to Michigan State where Reese was considered one of the top linebackers in the country.)

While playing "at the tip of the spear," as the Eagles called it, is fraught with a particular peril, the fans in the stands don't know the half of it. But let Reese explain: "When we played the Patriots last year Brian Westbrook fumbled a punt, and we were all down there scrambling for it. Mike Vrabel (Patriots linebacker) had my testicles in his hand, and he was squeezing them. Where the football ends up depends on who has the strongest will—or the strongest hands. Guys reach inside the face mask to gouge your eyes. But the biggest thing is the grabbing of the testicles...."

And that, sports fans, makes for an entirely *different* ball game.

Hacksaw Reynolds

Western Hills linebacker class of 19*66*

66

JACK REYNOLDS WAS A WESTERN HILLS GUY WHO GRADUATED TO THE BIG TIME THROUGH TENNESSEE, WHERE A LOPSIDED UPSET PROVOKED HIM into the singular act that resulted in one of football's all-time big league nicknames—"Hacksaw."

It was an Archie Manning-led Ole Miss team

that whipped up on undefeated, Number 3-ranked Tennessee, 38-0, and the next day linebacker Reynolds released his frustration by sawing a Chevy in half. (Some said it was a Jeep, but Reynolds said not so. "I love Jeeps," he said. "It was a '53 Chevy.")

Then he described his work: "I cut through the entire frame and drive shaft, all the way through the car. I started on Sunday and finished Monday afternoon. It took me eight hours total time," he said. He used a cheap hacksaw and thirteen blades, and before he was finished he had broken all of them. Then he went to bed. The next day, when he brought more of his friends to see his artistry, the car was gone. Nothing was left but the hacksaw blades—and, of course, Reynolds' new nickname.

"To this day," he said, "I don't know what happened to the car."

His Fierceness was a first-round pick in 1970 by the Los Angeles Rams where he played for eleven years, leading the Rams in tackles for six of those years. In 1981 he went to San Francisco, played for three more years, and won two Super Bowls there.

When Hacksaw reported for duty, he was lugging his own projector for watching game film and an old suitcase full of notebooks and pencils. At the first curfew check of summer camp, the linebackers coach found Hacksaw in his room with his projector, running game film on the dorm walls.

In meetings, Hacksaw wrote down every utterance, and it was obvious that none of his old intensity had been lost in the intervening decade. 49er rookie Ronnie Lott walked into his first team meeting and heard Coach Bill Walsh tell the players to take notes. So Lott looked over and saw Hacksaw, who had what seemed to be at least four dozen finely sharpened pencils. Lott thought, *He's got 100 pencils there and I don't have one. Maybe he'll loan me a pencil.*

Hacksaw said no.

"You mean you've got a hundred pencils and you won't give me *one*?'" Lott said.

And Hacksaw replied, "No, and I bet you won't come to another meeting without a pencil, will you?"

"What it told me," said Lott afterward (when he had recovered and thought about it), "was the definition of trying to be great. Greatness comes from how you prepare every day. Every day." And, if you'll pardon the obvious pun, to get the lead out.

The coaches gave Hacksaw his own key to the facilities where he would often be the first man in, making coffee for the defense. He was usually the last man out, too, carrying home another armload of film.

On game days, he turned up for the team breakfast with his pads on—even his eye black—and drove himself to the stadium in an old smoke-spewing Lincoln Continental while wearing his full uniform.

He explained that it helped him focus on the task at hand (or fist), which was, of course, the game. Both Lott and his coach, Bill Walsh, said Hacksaw taught the 49ers how to win. Something that Hacksaw seemed to have been born with. A West Side Cincinnati gene, one might say.

Inset is Reynolds at Western Hills while drawing is from his days as a Los Angeles (battering) Ram.

Glenn Sample

Western Hills | linebacker | class of 19**49**

49

AS THE LONGTIME OFFICIAL SCORER FOR THE CINCINNATI REDS, GLENN SAMPLE DEVELOPED AN AMPLE APPRECIATION FOR NUMBERS. AND YET, he was never quite certain of the pertinent number involved with that game in 1948 against Purcell Marian, when he was a Western Hills linebacker and the estimable Jim Bolger was carrying the ball for the Hackberry Assassins.

It was either 27 or 29. Tackles. Either way, it was a prodigious figure against a great team, and a performance, even in defeat, that attracted the attention of college recruiters and people who picked the all-star teams.

Funny thing about those all-star teams, incidentally. "When I made the All-City team, I was listed at about 5-7, 175 pounds, or something like that," Sample recalled, "and somehow you get a little bigger as you go along to the next all-star team. When I made All-State, I was about 5-10, 190."

At any rate, it was small for a linebacker, and even smaller for an offensive center. When the Mustangs had the ball, Sample snapped it to Don Zimmer, who was smaller yet.

The two of them were teammates in baseball, as well, and members of the 1947 Bentley Post team that won the national American Legion championship, their trophies handed to them by Babe Ruth himself. The national tournament was played in Los Angeles, and it made the fellows late for football practice.

But that would be the year Western Hills stopped Purcell's winning streak that spanned five seasons, 14-13, and established a legacy that later earned Sample the distinction as the greatest defensive player in the school's first half-century. He was also known as the guy who did magic tricks and sang in the barbershop quartet and never ran short on enthusiasm or good humor and never forgot a face or name—"everybody's buddy," they called him in the yearbook—and never, ever, missed a day of school, or a day of playing ball, it seemed.

As a senior, Sample was voted the top defensive player at the Ohio All-Star game. Scholarship offers ensued, as did a trip with Zimmer to Kentucky, at the invitation of UK coach Bear Bryant. Woody Hayes also made a pitch for Miami.

Zimmer accepted an offer from the Dodgers instead, and Sample—whose friends referred to him as "future All-American"—decided to stay home so his parents could maybe watch him play on Saturdays. They had never been able to do that on Friday nights because they were obligated to mind the family grocery store at Findlay and John. Another advantage for the University of

Glenn Sample was a Bearcat forever, and never a day off.

Glenn Sample's Western Hills team in 1948; that's Sample up front, Number 30, and Don Zimmer left, Number 11.

Cincinnati was having Sid Gillman in charge of the program. Sample so admired Gillman that, like the famous coach, he strolled the campus in bow ties.

Those were UC's best football days, including the 1950 Sun Bowl team. Sample played offensive line and excelled at linebacker and, his senior year, was captain, MVP, and an SAE All-American. Yeah, that's a fraternity, and there's an explanation. At UC in those days, only women could live on campus, except for Greeks and football players who holed-up under the stadium in double bunk beds. So Sample joined SAE, which in the day carried enough cachet to name its own All-American team.

He also played third base for the Bearcat baseball team, and afterwards fielded offers in both sports. The one that prevailed came from Uncle Sam, who had a big game going in Korea. When Sample got back, it was between seasons, and he was trying to sort out his sporting future when Gillman offered him a job as backfield coach. And you know how he felt about Gillman.

So he stayed at UC for thirty-seven years, a few of them as the wrestling coach and twenty-one as the baseball coach. In all that time, Sample never missed a day of work. And when Varsity Village was built in the heart of the campus, one of its pedestrian thoroughfares was appropriately named for him.

It was either that, or Bow Tie Boulevard.

Monroe's Mr. Big Ten

Strinko centering the ball as Bo looks on.

Out at Monroe High, linebacker **Steve Strinko**—who had first put on pads at age 6—was such an irresistible force that nearly forty years after his graduation no one has broken his records for either most solo tackles in a game (18) or a season (90). He was All-State and the MVP of the North-South All-Star Game, then went off to Michigan where he was the freshman team's defensive MVP. Three years of experience later, he was a 6-3, 235-pound All-Big Ten middle linebacker on UM's 1974 10-1 team (AP's Number 3) and—what else?—the team MVP. He was a second-team All-American (UPI), and he led a defense that was Number 1 in the nation. (For a moment, it seemed like Cincinnati was taking on the Big Ten: Strinko, Ed Shuttlesworth, Clint Haslerig, and Harrison guard Dave Metz all played on the same team.) Strinko's senior year in 1974, before the notable archrival game with Ohio State, he was famously quoted as saying, "If you gave me an elbow pad before the Ohio State game I'd be ready to eat it." The game, wrote *Sports Illustrated*, "would be an athletic Armageddon, a holy war waged in behalf of God, country and well-groomed men everywhere." And so it was, but it turned on the foot of another Cincinnati kid, kicker Tom Klaban, a walk-on Czech refugee from Princeton High who took kicking tips from his younger sister and booted four field goals. He kicked Strinko out of the Rose Bowl, one of only two games Strinko lost in his varsity career, a small scar on one of the greatest linebacking careers ever at Michigan, where his 297 career tackles still rank among the top 15 in UM history.

Shane Bullough's father, Hank, had starred as a guard on Michigan State's 1952 Rose Bowl champions, and by the time he arrived in Cincinnati as the Bengals' defensive coordinator he had earned the reputation as "the Doctor of Defense." His kid picked up the vibes and carried them to Moeller, where, as an All-American on the Crusaders' 1982 state and national championship team, he headlined the most decorated linebacker corps in the school's history, a unit deep enough to rout Massillon in the title game in spite of the fact that Bullough had to miss it with a broken leg. Unfortunately for Moeller, the Doctor took a head coaching position with the Buffalo Bills in 1985, which prevented Shane's brother, Chuck, from completing his schooling in Montgomery. Chuck ultimately followed Shane to Michigan State, and when he arrived, big brother stood second in school history for tackles in a season. Chuck passed him twice . . . It seemed that Shane (whose son Max, at this writing, is a highly coveted linebacker recruit out of East Lansing, home of MSU) somehow started a stream of Cincinnati defensive stars to Michigan State. A year after Bullough left Moeller, he was followed north by safety Harlon Barnett of suburban rival Princeton. Two years after Barnett came **Dixon Edwards**, who had been a tight end and defensive tackle at Aiken but found a home at linebacker in East Lansing. His father, Dixon Edwards Jr., who had played football at Marshall, wished only that Dixon III had found a closer home. Director of vocational education at Aiken, the elder Edwards put countless miles on his pickup truck driving around the Big Ten. After his son made honorable mention All-American—he had 16 tackles in a delicious upset of Number One-ranked Michigan—Dad negotiated his young tackler's second-round contract with the Dallas Cowboys in 1991. Edwards won three Super Bowl rings with the Cowboys, and that might not have been the best of it. After five years in Dallas he signed the largest contract the Minnesota Vikings had ever awarded a free agent from another team. Three years later, his total of NFL starts at 108—18 of them in the playoffs—Dixon left the game due to an irregular heartbeat . . . Dixon was also remembered for a 1996 radio interview in which he set an unofficial record for use of "you know" in a single sound bite. "Umm," he told WTCK, in answer to a question that nobody remembers, "you know everybody in the back of their mind, they hope, you know what I'm sayin'? You know, um, you know, you always hope, but you know, it, you know, the first day, that Friday, you know they had an opportunity and they just didn't take advantage, you know, you know, and, you know, a lot of those guys, you know, I'm quite sure, I'm not speaking for everybody else, but I'm speaking for myself; but if, umm, you know, a lot of guys would, you know, I guess would take a lot less, you know, just to be in a comfortable position, and you know, you know, and, you know what I'm sayin'? And be, you know what I'm sayin'? But uh, you know, it gets to a point, you know? So, you know." . . . Following Edwards out of Aiken, though not closely, was **Ike Reese**, a four-year starting linebacker at Michigan State beginning in 1994. His senior year, Reese was his team's Most Valuable Player and passed Chuck Bullough on MSU's career tackles chart, settling into third position. As a Philadelphia Eagle, he enjoyed the rare distinction of making All-Pro (2004) as a special-teams tackler. The former Aiken Falcon completed his nine-year NFL career as an *Atlanta* Falcon . . . And then, just a year later, there came **Lemar Marshall** to East Lansing. St. Xavier's Marshall, whose younger brother Mike was a basketball star at Butler, was a linebacker in the NFL but not at Michigan State or in high school. Actually, *Mike* was a linebacker at St. X. The Southwest District Defensive Player of the Year in 1994, Lemar was a cornerback, and that's how he started at MSU. Then he moved to safety, an indication that he had gotten a bit bigger and more formidable. In spite of making honorable mention All-American, Marshall was not drafted. Nevertheless, he spent five strong seasons with the Washington Redskins, the last three as a starting linebacker, the last two as starting *middle* linebacker, described by the *Washington Post* as "the most productive member of the Redskins' defense." The Bengals signed him as a free agent in 2007, and Marshall immediately became a starter. Just as immediately, he tore his Achilles tendon . . . The year Marshall joined the Bengals, Moeller grad **Greg Jones** was named a freshman All-American by *The Sporting News*, having moved swiftly into the starting lineup at, you guessed it, Michigan State, where head coach Mark Dantonio had just arrived from the University of Cincinnati. As a Crusader, Jones once recorded five sacks in a game against Elder. As a rookie collegian, he was just as inspired against Ohio State, racking up 14 tackles. The 220-pound linebacker led Big Ten freshmen in tackles and, in conference games, led the Spartans as well . . . Now, back for a moment to Shane Bullough. We mentioned the remarkably deep set of linebackers that he headed up at Moeller in 1982. That year, Bullough actually shared the award as the school's Best Linebacker with **Mark Woehler**, who went on to captain Vanderbilt and lead the team in tackles. Moeller's backers were so good that year that the *second-stringers* played college ball: **Steve Spatz** at Dayton, **Rob Klocke** at St. Joseph and **Steve Koehne** at Carson-Newman. The missing starter, meanwhile, is **Steve Apke**, who acquitted himself well enough to make All-GCL; but Moeller had six All-State players that year and Apke wasn't one of them. The Crusaders had ten All-City players and Apke wasn't one of them. Yet, he became one of the leading linebackers the University of Pittsburgh has ever produced, the Panthers' Number 3 tackler all-time. He was captain of Pitt's 1986 team, and even played briefly for the Steelers in 1987. Of course, the Steelers weren't *Moeller*. . . . Then there was **Dick Ullrich**, St. X class of 1956 and captain of the traveling squad. Well, we made that up, but consider that Ullrich rode a Trailways bus from Indiana to St. X for three years, played guard and linebacker, made All-City twice, and his feats at linebacker earned him the sobriquet "Killer." Or perhaps his nastiness at the position was due to bus lag. Whatever it was, he was called at the time "the best linebacker in the history of the league." He went off to Purdue where he played with Alliance High's Len Dawson. . . .

THE CHAMPION OF GLEN ESTE

In 2004, a solemn crowd of about 500 gathered at the Glen Este High School football field to pray for **Matt Maupin**, a private first class in the Army's 724th Transportation Company who a week before had turned up missing in action outside Baghdad, Iraq. A 2001 graduate of Glen Este, Maupin, who also wrestled and rowed, had not been a gifted football player for the Trojans, but a dedicated reserve who inspired his teammates with his work ethic, selflessness and hard hitting. On one occasion, he had put a particularly effective lick on an opposing player, prompting his coach, Gary Denton, to tell him, "Matt, you just crushed that guy."

"I know," Maupin answered with customary humility.

Two months after the vigil, Al-Jazeera, the Arab television network, would air a videotape that purported to show an American soldier being executed. But the tape was unclear and inconclusive, and for four excruciating years the Maupins and Clermont County community held out hope that the 20-year-old hero would be found alive and sent home.

But in March, 2008, Maupin's death became official. His remains had been located in Iraq. His spirit, meanwhile, can still be found east of Cincinnati, where his name is closely associated with the concept of courage.

Princeton's cheerleaders, 1961: Clockwise, Ginny Duermit, Sally Kingsley, Dianne Williams, Hilda Brockmeyer, Ginny Tucker, and Connie Kingsley.

Cincinnati's
ALL-TIME COLLEGE TEAM

OFFENSE

Quarterback

Roger Staubach, Purcell/Navy
Heisman Trophy winner
Bob Timberlake, Franklin/Michigan
First-Team All-American, Big Ten MVP
Tad Jones, Middletown/Yale
All-American, three national championships

Arguable: Roger Franz, Purcell/Fordham; Tim Clifford, Colerain/Indiana; Steve Tensi, Western Hills/Florida State; Greg Frey, St. Xavier/Ohio State; Mike Healey, St. Xavier/Vanderbilt; Dominic Randolph, St. Xavier/Holy Cross; Bryan Cupito, McNicholas/Minnesota; Bob Hoernschemeyer, Elder/Indiana

Running back

Napoleon McCallum, Milford/Navy
Two-time All-American, record for all-purpose yards
Paul Sarringhaus, Hamiliton/Ohio State
All-American, OSU's first national title
Bob Hoernschemeyer, Elder/Indiana
All-American led nation in total offense
Marc Edwards, Norwood/Notre Dame
27 TDs, second-round draft choice

Arguable: Eddie Shuttlesworth, Woodward/Michigan; Ray Nolting, Hughes/Cincinnati; Mike Harkrader, Middletown Fenwick/Indiana; Markus Thomas, Princeton/Eastern Kentucky; Dick Gordon, Walnut Hills/Michigan State; Carlos Snow, CAPE/Ohio State; Dwayne Crutchfield, North College Hill/Iowa State; Brandon Miree, Winton Woods/Pittsburgh; Al Nelson, Taft/ Cincinnati; B.J. Askew, Colerain/Michigan; DeShawn Wynn, Reading/Florida; Bill Asbury, Princeton/Kent State

Wide receiver

Bob Goodridge, Wyoming/Vanderbilt
SEC Player of the Year
Cris Carter, Middletown/Ohio State
All-American, then-OSU record for receptions
Dominick Goodman, Colerain/Cincinnati
Prep QB set UC records for receptions, TDs, yardage
Michael Larkin, St. Xavier/Miami
Miami career record for receptions and TDs
Dante Love, Withrow/Ball State
Led nation in yardage before career-ending injury

Arguable: Jim O'Brien, Aiken/Cincinnati; Tom Waddle, Moeller/Boston College; Jay Hall, Walnut Hills/Miami; Willie Townsend, Hamilton Garfield/Notre Dame; Tom Waddle, Moeller/Boston; Clint Haslerig, St. X/Michigan; Jim Kelly (father), Elder/Cincinnati; Jim Kelly (son), Moeller/Cincinnati; Willard Stargel, Woodward/Cincinnati; Steve Junker, Elder/Xavier

Tight end

Ron Beagle, Purcell/Navy *
National Player of Year, two-time All-American
Merle Wendt, Middletown/Ohio State *
3-time All-American, OSU all-century team
Don Hasselbeck, LaSalle/Colorado
All-American

Arguable: Rocko Joslin, Middletown/Ohio State; Tony Hunter, Moeller/Notre Dame; Eric Kattus, Colerain/Michigan; Brent Celek, LaSalle/Cincinnati; Arnold Franklin, Princeton/North Carolina

Offensive line

T: **Dave Foley**, Roger Bacon/Ohio State
All-American, captain, first-round draft choice
T: **Michael Munoz**, Moeller/Tennessee
All-American, nation's top scholar-athlete
T: **Zach Strief**, Milford/Northwestern
First-team All-American
G: **Socko Wiethe**, Roger Bacon/Xavier
Captain, All-Ohio
G: **Rob Murphy**, Moeller/Ohio State
First-team All-American
G: **Bill Feldhaus**, Hughes/Cincinnati
First UC player in NFL (along with Nolting)
C: **Dan James**, Elder/Ohio State
Three-year starter; captain of College All-Star game; first-round draft choice
C: **Raymond Pryor**, Hamilton Garfield/OSU
Highest praise from Woody Hayes

Arguable: Jim Mense, Hamilton Catholic/Notre Dame; Ryan Stanchek, LaSalle/West Virginia; Mike Biehle, Mason/Miami; Steve Sylvester, Moeller/Notre Dame; Dave Lafary, LaSalle/Purdue; Joe Lukens, Moeller/Ohio

State; Jim Brown, Moeller/Penn State; Eric Wood, Elder/Louisville; Dan Novakov, Moeller/Notre Dame; Kyle Ralph, St. X/UNC; Tom Backhus, Moeller/Ohio State; Butch Wilburn, Lakota/Kentucky

** Until and beyond the mid-20th century, players who caught passes and didn't play in the backfield were called ends, with no qualifiers. Teams employed two ends on offense, and typically they were lined up close to the tackles. Given this, and given that those types usually played on the defensive line as well, we're calling Beagle and Wendt tight ends.*

DEFENSE

Defensive line

E: **Ron Beagle**, Purcell/Navy
Maxwell Trophy winner, two-time All-American
E: **John Martinkovic**, Hamilton Badin/Xavier
Big and agile, Navy veteran starred on Salad Bowl championship team
T: **Steve Niehaus**, Moeller/Notre Dame
All-American, first player drafted by Seahawks
T: **Dana Stubblefield**, Taylor/Kansas
First-team All-American, first-round draft choice
T: **Dan Tehan**, St. Xavier/Xavier
Future sheriff described as "one of the remarkable players in the country"

Arguable: John Anderson, Hughes/Cornell; Richard Langenbeck, Western Hills/Cincinnati; Terrill Byrd, Colerain/Cincinnati; Antwan Peek, Woodward/Cincinnati; Mel Lunsford, Lockland/Central State; Shane Curry, Princeton/Miami (Florida); William Reese, Princeton/Michigan State; Alex Davis, Hamilton Garfield/Purdue; Ed Bauer, Elder/Notre Dame; Clint Spearman, Hamilton Garfield/Michigan; Joe Schaffer, Elder/Tennessee; Chris Norwell, Anderson/Illinois

Linebacker

Bob Crable, Moeller/Notre Dame
Two-time All-American, set Irish records for tackles
Hacksaw Reynolds, Western Hills, Tennessee
All-American best remembered for parting a Chevrolet
Dixon Edwards, Aiken/Michigan State
All-American played in four bowl games
Brian Pillman, Norwood/Miami
All-American, MAC Defensive Player of Year

Arguable: Mike Larkin, Moeller/Notre Dame; Rocky Boiman, St. Xavier/Notre Dame; Glenn Sample, Western Hills/Cincinnati; Steve Strinko, Monroe/Michigan; Vic Koegel, Moeller/Ohio State; Paul Maly, Elder/Northwestern; Ike Reese, Aiken/Michigan State; Doug Becker, Hamilton Badin/Notre Dame; Dustin Cohen, Summit Country Day/Miami; Steve Apke, Moeller/Pittsburgh; Terry Killens, Purcell/Penn State; Kevin Bates, Wyoming/Stanford; Greg Jones, Moeller/Michigan State; Art Reynolds, Western Hills/Tennessee

Defensive back

Mike Sensibaugh, Lockland/Ohio State
All-American, two-time national champ, OSU interceptions record and all-century team
Mike Townsend, Hamilton/Notre Dame
All-American led nation in interceptions
Jim Herbstreit, Reading/Ohio State
Woody Hayes called him best DB in nation
Carlton Gray, Forest Park/UCLA
All-American and Academic All-American; second in nation in interceptions
Harlon Barnett, Princeton/Michigan State
All-American for defense ranked first in Big Ten
Ahmed Plummer, Wyoming/Ohio State
Buckeye MVP; first-round draft choice

Arguable: Ron Carpenter, Princeton/Miami; Tony George, Winton Woods/Florida; Vinnie Clark, CAPE/Ohio State; Maury Bibent, Western Hills/Florida State;Mike Middleton, Western Hills/Indiana; Mike Heizman, Colerain/Indiana

SPECIAL TEAMS

PK: **Harry Oliver**, Moeller/Notre Dame
Irish record for field goals in season
P: **Kevin Huber**, McNicholas/Cincinnati
Two-time All-American, led nation in punting average

Arguable (PK-P): B.J. Sander, Roger Bacon/Ohio State; Bernie Roeckers, Roger Bacon/Xavier; Jim O'Brien, Aiken/Cincinnati; Kevin Kerr, St. Xavier/Ohio U.

KR: **Milt Stegall**, Roger Bacon/Miami
Second in MU history
KR: **Dante Love**, Withrow/Ball State
School records despite missing most of senior season
PR: **Steve Clay**, Aiken/Eastern Michigan
Led nation as sophomore

Arguable (KR-PR): Carlos Snow, CAPE/Ohio State; Al Moore, Central/Miami; Rodney Heath, Western Hills/Minnesota; Napoleon McCallum, Milford/Navy; Craig Thompson, Princeton/Eastern Michigan

It was a singular distinction for Wyoming's Bob Goodridge; in 1962, no one scored on his secondary. No one at all.

Defensive backs

VINNIE CLARK—*CAPE/CLASS OF 1987*

TONY GEORGE—*WINTON WOODS/CLASS OF 1995*

BOB GOODRIDGE—*WYOMING/CLASS OF 1964*

DICK GORDON—*WALNUT HILLS/ CLASS OF 1961*

CARLTON GRAY—*FOREST PARK/CLASS OF 1989*

JIM HERBSTREIT—*READING/CLASS OF 1957*

AHMED PLUMMER—*WYOMING/CLASS OF 1995*

MIKE SENSIBAUGH—*LOCKLAND/CLASS OF 1967*

THE TOWNSENDS, MIKE & WILLIE—*HAMILTON GARFIELD/CLASSES OF 1970, 1969/CLASS OF 1967*

GREG STEMRICK—*LINCOLN HEIGHTS/CLASS OF 1970*

DWAYNE WOODRUFF—*NEW RICHMOND/CLASS OF 1975*

THE MASTER CARPENTER *(RON CARPENTER)*

MAURYS, AD INFINITUM *(MAURY BIBENT IV & V)*

MUSIC IN HIS TIME *(WAYNE DAVIS)*

BENCH STRENGTH— HARLON BARNETT, PRINCETON; VADA MURRAY, MOELLER; DAVID POOL, CAPE; NEAL CRAIG, TAFT; EUGENE CLIFFORD, COLERAIN; AND RODNEY HEATH, WESTERN HILLS.

CINCINNATI'S ALL-TIME PROFESSIONAL ALL-STARS

Carlton Gray and Dante Ware at Forest Park

The Master Carpenter

Count the ways that **Ron Carpenter** loved football. Start with Princeton, where in 1987 he helped the Vikings—perhaps more than anybody else—win their last state championship. Carpenter's affinity for the game no doubt started *before* that, given the relish with which he played for Pat Mancuso. Anyway, that was Carpenter's first significant title, and possibly his dearest.

At Miami University, he was the first defensive back in more than a decade to earn All-MAC honors for three straight years, and as a senior was nominated for the Jim Thorpe Award as the nation's finest DB. In 1990, he tied the school record for interceptions (7). In 1991, he tied it *again*, which not surprisingly added up to the *career* record.

Then, as a pro, that's where the real love showed up. Because Carpenter could never find a team that embraced him as long and hard as he embraced the game; and yet the passion never stopped pouring out of him.

In 1999, after appearing in the Arena Football League title game, the hard-playing Princetonian earned a Super Bowl ring as a role player with the St. Louis Rams. The next year he was in the short-lived XFL with the Las Vegas Outlaws and Los Angeles Xtreme, the latter's league championship representing his third at three different levels.

Carpenter also had two tours with the World Football League, a couple seasons with the New York Jets—leading the NFL in average kick-return yardage in 1995—one with the Minnesota Vikings, and then, in 2005, was keeping himself in touch with the game as a coach with the Cincinnati Marshals of the National Indoor Football League. He was 35 at the time, with every reason to be burned out. Not the least of those reasons was the dysfunction of the Marshals.

See, the scoundrel owner, H.P. Patterson, had slithered out of town without paying the players, and the coach, Reading product Ed Biles, had quit because, well, nobody was getting paid or anything, and the players, not making much money anyway, had decided to go ahead and keep playing and maybe coach *themselves* for a while if they had to. Carpenter had been helping Biles, and when the ranks of defensive backs grew thin, the players noticed him backpedaling in his street clothes and generally acting mysterious. (*He's not really thinking about . . . ?*)

Shortly after he decided to play again, his wife, Sherri, died, at which point Carpenter needed football more than ever. His new teammates, sensing that, rallied around him in moral support. So when the Marshals somehow won a couple playoff games (including 70-69 against Fayetteville) and found themselves in line to host Rome in the conference finals but with no money to do so, Carpenter rallied around *them*.

What he did, specifically, was fork over $20,000 of his own money so that the club could bring the Renegades to U.S. Bank Arena.

"Ron's just giving back to his teammates," said the replacement coach, Tom Wells. "It's to give them a home game and see the smile on their face and the pep in their step. That's what Ron's all about."

By the second quarter, Cincinnati, super-charged, led Rome 31-13. By the end of the fourth, the Marshals had lost 51-41. There was no fourth championship for their middle-aged safety; but his shoulder was appreciatively squeezed and his hand sincerely shaken, nevertheless. He won the *moment*, if not the title. He had spread the love.

Vinnie Clark

CAPE defensive back class of 1987

87

MOSTLY, IT WAS VINNIE CLARK'S GOOD FORTUNE TO BE A TEAMMATE AND FAST FRIEND OF CARLOS SNOW. IT WAS, AFTER ALL, SNOW'S RECORD-SETTING RUNNING ABILITY THAT THE Cincinnati Academy of Physical Education rode to two state championships. Snow also provided Clark with a warm and familiar face when they both moved on to Ohio State.

In the historical context, however, it may have been Clark's *mis*fortune to shine his brilliant light on a playing field that was already glistening with Snow. While the latter is still remembered with reverence, the fact is, a person would be hard-pressed to identify the better athlete.

To wit, whereas Snow claimed a state sprint championship at 100 meters, Clark still holds the district record at 200. In the distant trumpeting of

Maurys, ad Infinitum

Maury Bibent's father—same name, different Roman numeral—ran three things of similar significance on the west side of Cincinnati. There was his gas station, which provided his stake, and there was his Maury's Tiny Cove restaurant, known for its steak. Opened in 1949, the Tiny Cove was a Cheviot institution with its Naugahyde booths and entrees named for the local high school mascots.

And then there was the Sunday football team that played behind the Cheviot fieldhouse in the so-called semipro league that Pete Rose's father made famous. Bibent's outfit generally consisted, in part, of tough Western Hills kids who couldn't play school ball because they had to work or maybe just *didn't* because they liked to drink beer and smoke cigarettes at halftime.

Maury IV—that's the dad we're talking about—was both the rugged type, holding his own himself in those Sunday tussles, and the magnanimous type, his generosity showing in the time he provided Andy Williams' family with gas-ration stamps for their trip to California, so the kid could start crooning. At any rate, this was the environment from which Maury V became one of West High's most distinguished football players.

In 1958, the young Bibent was a sophomore in the same backfield as Pete Rose on the team that beat Elder on Thanksgiving morning. It would be the last time that happened until the final installment of the pre-turkey tradition in 1978.

Two years after Rose scurried out of Western Hills to play professional baseball, Bibent went deep, landing at Florida State as a two-way back. (Somehow, Bibent IV still managed to make all the games.) By his junior season, Maury V was pretty much excused from his ball-carrying responsibilities and dedicated to the secondary. To him, however, football was *not* secondary.

He later coached the game, including a stretch as defensive backs coach at Kent State, where one of his protégés was future Miami Dolphins head coach Nick Saban. One of Maury V's twin grandsons, in fact, was named Saban Bibent. No Roman numeral.

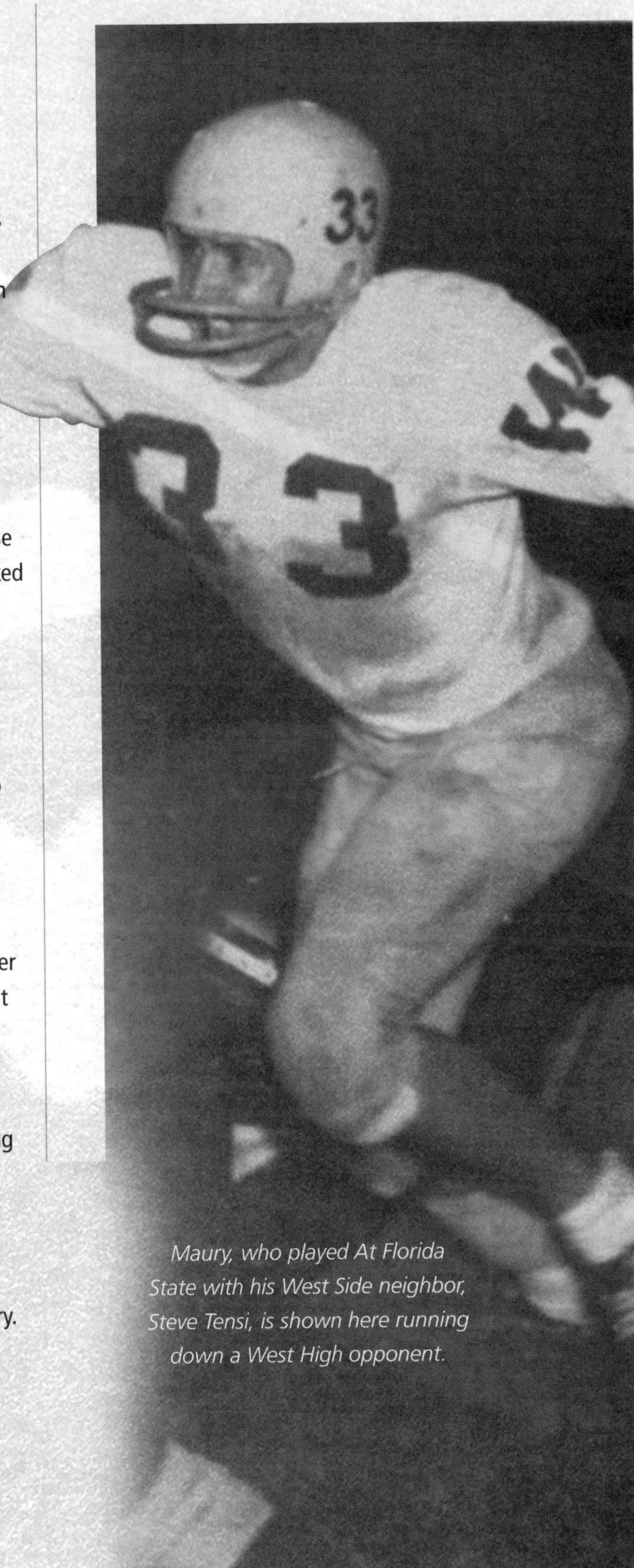

Maury, who played At Florida State with his West Side neighbor, Steve Tensi, is shown here running down a West High opponent.

CAPE's football feats, it's forgotten that, behind its pair of superstars, the short-lived school also won a couple Ohio titles in track and field.

But the two of them were footballers first. In the undefeated autumns of 1985 and 1986, Clark was to the Crusader defense what Snow was to the fearsome ground attack. And if Vinnie's Friday night triumphs were not widely celebrated, they were at least shared with the congregation at New Jerusalem Baptist Church. Every Sunday morning, the young conqueror would stand during the service to apprise the folks in the pews of how the last game had gone.

Among those who appreciated his efforts was OSU coach Earle Bruce, who successfully recruited both of CAPE's speedsters before handing them over a year later to John Cooper. Clark was a three-year starter for the Buckeyes, all the while remaining uncommonly close to his high school buddy.

In fact, it was out of concern for Snow that he ran into a bit of legal trouble the summer of his junior year. Snow was involved in a minor traffic accident near their dormitory, and Clark caught wind of it and ran out of the dorm to see if his friend was okay. Police had gathered, and in his haste Clark pushed his way through them. He was charged with disorderly conduct and obstruction of official business, and fined $50.

Naturally, the Green Bay Packers made certain to check out the particulars before they drafted him in the first round, 1991. Clark soon became a starter, but not a distinguished one. The *Milwaukee Sentinel* once referred to him as "a washout."

Back home, however—especially at New Jerusalem—sentiments were considerably different. Following his rookie season, Clark walked unceremoniously into his lifelong church and presented pastor Damon Lynch Jr. with a contribution of $50,000. "This is something I've always wanted to do," he said.

When he came back to Cincinnati four years later, this time representing the Jacksonville Jaguars, Clark was feeling a little less magnanimous. He was, in fact, ejected from the game for punching Bengals receiver Darnay Scott. The recollection of that event may not have served his interests early in the 1996 season, when the Jaguars released him after four games. The Bengals immediately took a look at the hometown kid but neglected to sign him, in deference, ostensibly, to a neck condition he had acquired.

Shortly thereafter, Clark embarked on an itinerant career of coaching Arena football. In between, he was at a traffic light in 2001 when Cincinnati policemen, searching for somebody else, allegedly pointed guns at him and friend Terry Horton, then destroyed the videotape of the incident. Clark joined a racial-profiling lawsuit that eventually resulted in a $4.5 million settlement. It was hailed as a landmark agreement for police reform in the city.

Once again, his misfortune and good fortune had proved to be one and the same.

MUSIC IN HIS TIME

There is some dispute about when and where rap music was started; but in the Indiana State locker room, the originator was positively **Wayne Davis**. "Wayne was a rapper before anybody knew what rapping was," said Tom James of the *Terre Haute Tribune-Star*, who was around the Sycamores as a sports information official when Davis was with them in the mid-1980s.

Davis' talents, though, far exceeded music. He had been a two-way star at Mount Healthy High School (class of '81), but Indiana State needed him most desperately on defense. As a cornerback at ISU, he was a three-year starter, the Missouri Valley Conference Player of the Year in 1984, an All-American, and the highest draft choice (second round, San Diego Chargers) that the school has ever produced. He lasted six years in the NFL, splitting time with the Chargers, Bills and Redskins.

It was a lot to accomplish in a short time; and a short time, it turned out, was all that Davis had. In 2007, he died from Lou Gehrig's Disease at the age of 44.

Tony George

Winton Woods defensive back class of 19**95**

95

HE WAS ONE OF THE MOST UNUSUAL FOOTBALL PLAYERS TO COME OUT OF CINCINNATI. A SKINNY RECEIVER AND DEFENSIVE BACK, TONY GEORGE exited Winton Woods in 1995 with a triple-double (187 tackles, 17 interceptions, and 17 touchdowns), a spot on *Parade* magazine's All-American team, and the captaincy of Ohio's All-Disability Squad.

Okay, so there's no such thing as the Ohio All-Disability Squad. And, no, type 2 diabetes is not always considered a disability but *you* try watching your diet so stringently, measuring your blood sugar constantly, and giving yourself two insulin shots a day so that you don't lapse into a coma. Defensive backs don't go into comas; defensive backs *induce* comas.

And here's the good part—*before* Tony George became a four-time letter winner at Florida, the leader of the Gator secondary, and All-SEC, he learned how to handle *his* illness from his little sister, Tari. At age 2, she was diagnosed with cerebral palsy, walked with a limp, and her left arm hung loosely at her side.

When Tony learned of his diabetes as a high school sophomore, Tari came to see him in the hospital. She was 9. He was imagining his young life as finished.

"Don't be silly," Tari said. "You're going to be okay."

And he was. He thought about what it took for her to tie her shoes with one hand, and he watched his diet, learned to give himself two shots a day, and had a stellar career at Florida. He said it was for Tari. There was, for instance, the big game against Tennessee when he was a junior and intercepted Peyton Manning, running it back 89 yards to score.

It was the longest runback at Florida in over forty years and it finished off Tennessee. When Tony reached the end zone, he raised his hand to the sky, and Tari—in the players' family section—knew it was for her.

"Everything I do is for her," he said. "I started thinking about her as soon as I reached the sideline and turned up." Said the *Sports Illustrated* headline: *Sparked by a jarring defense and the inspiration of a little sister, Florida again pushed around Peyton Manning and Tennessee.*

George had this other thing he did when he made a play. He pumped his arms, gave himself a swagger-step, and swayed from side to side. Tari called it the Big Man Walk. His teammates regarded it as something to fire them up. But Tari knew it was for her. When she saw him do it, her smile stretched all the way to Otter Creek. The Big Man Walk said that she and Tony were big, they were bad, tougher than their illnesses, and none of it was going to take.

Anyway, if there'd been justice in the world, Tari would've lettered at Florida that year. As it was, she and Tony were an unbeatable combination. Who could've known? The Gators' twelfth man was a kid sister.

Bob Goodridge

Wyoming defensive back/RB class of 19**64**

64

FOR NEARLY A DECADE, MR. PITIFUL'S, THE BAR WITH THE BEST NAME IN TOWN, HAS SURVIVED ON MAIN STREET, PROVING ITSELF IMMUNE TO THE VICISSITUDES OF YUPPIES ON THE thoroughfare, rioting, a sour economy, and enough sad stories to make the priest at St. Mary's throttle himself with his own rosary. It has, in other words, fulfilled its charter nobly, maintaining a safe harbor for the regulars who ally themselves sporadically along the bar, or at Mr. Pitiful's tables, under clocks that are set perpetually at a quarter-til-three, an homage to the Johnny Mercer song, "One for the Road," which is a favorite of the bartender, Bob Kramer.

It is, first and foremost, a neighborhood bar, and as such may not be considered a sports bar. Although, like most neighborhood bars, the sporting life is a conversational staple here, perhaps because of Kramer's own associations. Kramer was a Wyoming man of sports, and if he, himself, was not quite legendary, his best friend, another Bob—Bob Goodridge—was.

The two Bobs played on one of Cincinnati's legendary teams—the 1962 Wyoming team that scored 446 points in ten games and, even more impressive, went unscored upon. None. Nada. Zip. Zilch. Zero. The first Bob—Kramer—was on that team but his efforts, he is quick to point out, played no part in its success. He says, perhaps tongue in cheek, that the coach, Bob Lewis, gave him number 138.

This is when he thought that perhaps he was better suited for the hardwood. He played on Wyoming's District Championship team in 1964 when Wyoming fell two points short of playing the great Dayton Belmont team of Bill Hosket and Donnie May. Belmont then won the state title by almost 30 points—and the first Bob was thus deprived of measuring himself against the very best, even if in doing so, he might have died.

The second Bob—Goodridge—*did* have much to do with the undefeated, unscored upon Wyoming football team of 1962. In four years, Goodridge played in only

one losing football game (there were also three ties, a dark blot upon his prep career). He was a back—both offensive and defensive—during the 1962 season, then became quarterback the next. That year, the offensive production dropped to a mere 345 points while the defense gave up 30. Goodrich scored 84 points (near the top of the city scoring list), and Wyoming finished with its second undefeated year. (In his last two seasons, he also scored seven touchdowns on punt returns and one on a kickoff return).

At 6-2, 170 pounds, he was not heavily recruited by the local schools. He thinks that most recruiters believed he was going somewhere to play basketball. One exception was the Miami coach, who had just finished his first season in Oxford, but Bob hadn't heard much about Bo Schembechler so off he went to Vanderbilt.

As he did at Wyoming, Goodridge broke into the starting lineup on defense. Playing strong safety at 180 pounds in the Southeastern Conference was, however, taking a toll on him. When his senior season arrived, the

At Wyoming in 1962, Bob Goodridge was a two-way back on one of the most flawless teams in Cincinnati history.

In four years at Wyoming, Goodridge played in only one losing game.

revolving door of assistant coaches at Vanderbilt brought in a new one, and this one wanted to open up the offense. Between the "stingers" he had suffered playing defense and the quarterbacks lobbying for him to come over to the glamour side of the field, he made a choice few starters would have made: He switched positions.

The Commodores continued to struggle in the SEC, but Goodridge thrived. While he did not possess the blazing speed usually associated with a wideout, Goodridge had uncommon moves and hands, and ran precise patterns. His two years on defense schooled him on what defensive backs were doing, and he used this knowledge to create the seams and angles he needed to get open. In 1967, he got open enough times to lead the nation in receptions with 79. His 1,114 yards gained—aided by a 201-yard game against Navy and a 177-yard game against William & Mary—made him the first SEC player to top the 1,000-yard mark.

After being drafted in the sixth round by the Minnesota Vikings, Goodridge reported to Bud Grant's training camp in the summer of 1967, where Grant called for a one-on-one blocking drill between wide receivers and the linebackers. Uncertain as to whether Grant was trying to toughen his receivers or frighten them away, Goodridge stepped into the drill wearing a single bar facemask. When the drill was over, he had a bloody face and a reputation for purposefulness.

It was going to take more than toughness for a 6-2, 180-pound receiver from Wyoming, Ohio, to make the club, however. One of the rookie competitors was a sprinter type from Montana, but one day the player just disappeared from camp and was never seen again. Goodridge moved one step closer to the NFL. Grant, seeing his talent dwindling, then brought in a player he had known from his coaching days in the CFL, and Goodridge found himself competing for a spot on the taxi squad. Fate, in one of its stranger manifestations, intervened: The CFL player came down with a terminal case of hemorrhoids. Unable to even sit the bench, he, too, disappeared, and Goodridge won Grant's battle of attrition. He was awarded a year in the NFL courtesy of homesickness, hemorrhoids—and his own handiwork.

After a year in the pros, Goodridge finished his degree and kicked around as a coach and teacher in Florida and Tennessee before returning to Vanderbilt as an assistant. During a coaching change, he returned to his office to find it occupied by the newly hired Bill Parcells, who promptly tossed him out. Eventually, he returned to Cincinnati where he taught and coached, his deeds and accomplishments secured in Vanderbilt's all-time records, the Cincinnati Sports Hall of Fame, and, of course, at Mr. Pitiful's, where his old teammate keeps the embers of legend glowing.

Dick Gordon

Walnut Hills | defensive back | class of 19***61***

61

YOU SAW THAT RIGHT. AT WALNUT HILLS, THEY HAD DICK GORDON PLAYING DEFENSIVE BACK. THAT'S A GALLANT AND VITAL POSITION AND ALL, BUT come on. This was a team that went 1-7-2 in the fall of 1960. A team that was *shut out five times.*

And there are supposed to be *smart people* at that school.

Now, we know the *students* at Walnut Hills are of the highly intelligent variety, which only makes this puzzlement all the more inscrutable. When they voted for the most athletic male of the class of '61, it wasn't our Dick Gordon. It was a guy named Henry Neloms, who no doubt was a fine and fit specimen of a teenager. But he didn't make All-Big Ten at Michigan State. He didn't make All-Pro with the Chicago Bears.

In fairness, Gordon's parents, understanding what Walnut Hills is all about, didn't allow young Richard to play football until his junior year, and even then he could stay with it only if his grades didn't suffer. On such a foundation was built an Academic All-American at Michigan State. It didn't, however, get Gordon into the offensive huddle in high school.

Somehow, Duffy Daugherty saw enough to let Gordon play some defense for him up in East Lansing; and eventually he saw enough—enough *speed* (he also ran on the track team)—to give the kid the ball. That was a concept.

He was an MSU senior by then, and when he set a Spartan record by slicing up Wisconsin with 199 yards on only 13 carries—including touchdown sprints of 75 and 57 yards—*United Press International* observed that "before Saturday, Gordon was the proverbial unknown quantity everywhere perhaps but in Spartanville."

The fact is, until then, Gordon was pretty much unknown even back in Madisonville. Willard Stargel III was four years his junior, and like most of the sporty kids in the neighborhood he played ball—all kinds—at Stewart Park. If Gordon had been something special, he would have known. And then, about the time Stargel was starring at quarterback for Walnut Hills, there was Gordon exploding all over the Big Ten. For the 1964 season, he averaged seven yards a carry and was Michigan State's MVP. Back home, nobody could figure it out.

"I couldn't ever understand how Dick Gordon couldn't make the starting backfield, or receiver, at Walnut Hills," said Stargel, still perplexed nearly half a century later. "Dickie was lightning fast. When he was out of Michigan State, the kids in Madisonville would come out to the park and everybody wanted to prove they could play with Dick Gordon. But nobody could run with him. Nobody was faster than him. That has always baffled me, how he couldn't make the starting backfield at Walnut Hills."

If it's any solace, the undervalued Eagle couldn't make the starting backfield of the Chicago Bears, either. See, in 1965, when the Bears drafted him in the seventh round, they also drafted Dick Butkus, who has no particular relevance to this subject, and Gale Sayers, who does. Mr. Sayers would be the one carrying the ball, thank you very much. Now, Gordon, if you're interested in catching it . . .

He was interested. And he was good, which is no small thing for a Chicago Bear. The passing game is a bit delicate for the Bears' mud-splattered sensibilities. Gordon made All-Pro in 1970—leading the NFL in receptions with 71, racking up 1,026 yards and 13 touchdowns—and after he made the Pro Bowl again in 1971, no Chicago receiver would get there for more than thirty years.

He was, in more ways than that, a dashing departure from the Chicago fashion. The *Sun-Times* called him "the Beau Brummell of receivers." Gordon, according to columnist Chet Coppock, "led the league in fur coats at least six different years. He still holds the Bears' record for dress-code violations."

Ultimately—in fact, immediately after his second Pro Bowl season—the stylistic differences became too great for Gordon to stay in George Halas's town. Although he was there for the *Brian's Song* times—in the movie, Brian Piccolo is standing at his locker between Sayers and Gordon and says, "I feel like an Oreo cookie"—he didn't feel the love so much. Actually, he wound up calling Halas a racist. Something about the old man refusing to help him with his tax problem.

At any rate, between the antipathy and the money thing, Gordon decided that free agency was the way to go. That wasn't such a common alternative in those days, and the Bears started making noise about a whole bunch of compensation and Gordon started making noise about an antitrust suit and the commissioner, Pete Rozelle, had to step in. His ruling was that whichever team signed the former Walnut Hills defensive back would have to give Chicago its first-round draft choice. It was a few more years before the draft-pick compensation package was refined a bit and became a basic principle of free agency; but its roots were in a fast fellow from Madisonville.

When the commissioner had finally sorted it

all out, the Bengals took a look at Gordon. But Paul Brown wasn't buying. "The Rozelle Rule was not a consideration," Brown said in a story circulated by *UPI*. "Gordon wanted too much money." The asking price was $85,000.

It was the Rams that signed him. The next season, it was the Packers. The next season—Gordon's last—it was the Chargers.

It was a ten-year professional career. And it was an eventful one.

That is, for a guy who couldn't carry the ball for his terrible high school team.

Carlton Gray

Forest Park | defensive back | class of 1989

89

IN THE SUMMERS, WHEN HE WAS YOUNG, CARLTON GRAY WOULD TRAVEL WITH HIS GRANDFATHER TO VARIOUS MEETINGS AND OCCASIONS AROUND the country. He remembers being in their hotel room one night when the knock on the door belonged to Ted Kennedy. A little later, Stevie Wonder wandered in.

It was then that he realized that his pinochle partner, Dr. Benjamin Hooks, was no ordinary grandpa. He was a judge and minister and, for sixteen years starting in 1977, the formidable executive director of the NAACP. He was the man with whom Martin Luther King had a home-cooked dinner when he was in Memphis. They were together, at Hooks' house, the night before King was assassinated in 1968.

That's one thing Gray, out of respect and sensitivity, never asked his grandfather about. It remains a poignant part of a family legacy by which Hooks himself had a remarkable grandparent. His father's mother, Julia Hooks, was a native Kentuckian who studied classical music at Berea College and, with her head in controversy's mouth, taught piano to white students.

After moving to Memphis, she founded the Hooks School of Music and tutored W.C. Handy, among others. She also, in 1881, paid a $5 fine after being escorted from a theater for refusing to move from the

At Forest Park, he was the nation's top scholar-athlete.

white section to the colored. Julia Hooks was a charter member of the NAACP chapter that would foster an executive director of her direct descent.

Gray, in turn, was appropriately inspired by all of this. In his own way. When still in grade school, he decided on *his* contribution to the family resume—to become the best football player possible.

He demonstrated that at Forest Park (now Winton Woods) High School, at the same time not neglecting basketball or track. In the former, he was good. In the latter, he led Forest Park to two straight state championships, anchoring the winning 4x100 relay team. Along with Gray's academic diligence, the sum of it all resulted in Dr. Hooks' grandson being honored with the 1988 Dial Award, given to the nation's top scholar-athlete.

Not one to limit his scope, Gray accepted a football scholarship to UCLA, and became the first freshman to start full-time there in a decade. As a junior, he finished second in the country with 10 interceptions. As a senior, he was an All-American. Twice, he was an *Academic* All-American. In 1993, Seattle drafted him with the first pick of the second round, and he lasted eight years in the league, four of them as a starter. Gray signed with the Bengals in 2001, but was cut in training camp. That was it.

Already, though, he had committed himself to education in various forms. He started a foundation at Winton Woods that offers tutorial services and scholarships to the University of Cincinnati. Later, he took a position at Lakota West as the learning lab coordinator and an assistant coach in football, track and girls' basketball.

The basketball job represented an area of emphasis. Since his daughter, Amber, had been young, tall and talented, Gray had applied his skills to schooling her game. Their private sessions numbered at least two a week. As a Lakota West senior in 2008, Amber Gray—who often played before more than a dozen kin, spanning multiple generations from both sides of the family—was named Ms. Basketball in Ohio.

Her college choice was Tennessee, where the Lady Volunteers had a long-standing relationship with the national championship. But there was also a deeper, ancestral connection to that part of the country—a number of Hooks, you could say.

Jim Herbstreit

Reading halfback/db class of 19**57**

57

JIM HERBSTREIT LEARNED TO LOVE FOOTBALL ON THANKSGIVING DAY. RATHER, MORNING. THE GAMES WERE ALWAYS AT 10 A.M. ON THOSE full-plated autumn holidays, the West Side might have been goo-goo over Elder and Western Hills, but up in the Mill Creek Valley, where life was arranged by changes of shift and sport season, the big event was Lockland-Reading.

Through that apple-pie rivalry, Herbstreit developed his deeply held sense of how the game ought to be. He was a Reading guy. And he loved his coach, Ken Powers. And he loved the *Lockland* coach, Herald Roettger.

"The rivalry had been going since Ken came to Reading in the late '20s," recalled Herbstreit, whose first Thanksgiving game came as a 115-pound freshman in 1953. "Herald Roettger had been at Lockland a couple years longer, and Roettger was a special guy. The whole thing was a reflection of the camaraderie of those two men, and it was just a beautiful thing to see. It was a brutal rivalry, and they were like brothers. And that was the way it was. When the game was over, everybody would walk home, over the bridge, in their uniforms.

"That rivalry, in my life, is very similar to Ohio State and Michigan. A lot of people miss what it's all about, in my opinion, because the great part of rivals is, you don't want to hate them. I don't hate Michigan. I love them. I root for them every game except the one when I want to beat the hell out of them. When I was at Ohio State and people from Reading would come up to visit and see me play, there were just as many people from Lockland who came up to see me and visit."

The neighboring boys all played baseball together, and pee-wee football if they were big enough. For an unusually long time, Herbstreit wasn't. You had to weigh 95 pounds to qualify. Little Jimmy weighed 75. So he loaded his helmet with twenty pounds of lead and embarked upon a career that ended in the LaRosa's Hall of Fame.

His first Lockland-Reading game was Roettger's last. That morning, the old coach announced his retirement. Then Lockland went out and whipped up on the Blue Devils, 42-7.

"I always thought that was a tribute to him," said Herbstreit. "No way were they better than us that year."

Or maybe it was the strategy. Roettger's team ran from a single-wing formation in which the ball-carrier was led by both guards and a fullback. Most of the time, Lockland aimed that critical mass straight at the wispy freshman.

"One play," he remembered, "they drove me over to the sideline and I got hit so hard—they knocked me so far out of bounds—that when I got up my head was stuck in the water bucket."

But it got better. Herbstreit fattened up to about 155, with speed to match anybody in the state. He proved that in track, and later at OSU, from which he would return every summer to work in the shipping department at Procter & Gamble. The plant hired college kids and coaches for the season, and the undersized Buckeye found himself side-by-side with Roettger's successor at Lockland, Chick Payne.

"You know what I told my kids?" the old rival confided once. "I told them, 'Make that little bastard throw the football, because we don't want him running.'"

In Powers' offense, Herbstreit floated between quarterback and halfback. Reading and Lockland split the four games that he played in, with Herbstreit's team taking the finale in 1956. That year, Powers was the coach retiring. The Blue Devils—who had spoiled Wyoming's perfect season, on the strength of Herbstreit's three touchdowns—might have been a bit better than their Thanksgiving partners, but not better enough to pound in 56 points, which they did, in deference to their beloved coach.

Powers was still around for track season, though, and he prevailed upon his fleet halfback to run in the major meets. Otherwise, Herbstreit was committed to baseball. The compromise worked sufficiently well that the Reading baseball team—behind ace pitcher Claude Osteen—made it to Columbus for the state finals and Herbstreit qualified simultaneously for the state track meet in the 100 and 220-yard dashes. Trouble was, they were the same weekend.

At the time, the OSU baseball field was located where the dormitory towers now stand, which meant that Herbie could run the 100 prelims before Friday's semifinal game, hustle over to the diamond to rap out a couple hits against Barberton, then excuse himself in the seventh inning and race back across campus to the stadium, where he stripped off his baseball uniform and qualified for the finals in the 220. But he wanted no part of that routine on Saturday, when the baseball team would play Lorain for the championship. He would have eschewed the track meet altogether had not Powers been so adamant, and had Herbstreit not regarded the veteran coach with such esteem—like a second father, he said—that he couldn't deny him.

What he didn't know was that Powers had been plotting behind the scenes. Not only had he worked out accommodations from state track officials to make the schedule work and arranged a golf cart for Saturday's dash across campus; he had also supplied Woody Hayes with game tapes of Herbstreit and persuaded the Buckeye boss to come watch the little guy run.

In the morning, the kid placed fifth in the 100. Then he helped Reading build a big lead against Lorain—on the way to breaking up what was otherwise five straight state titles by Elder—before checking out in the 7th inning and carting back to the stadium to finish second in the 220, behind Olympic silver medalist Paul Drayton, with his best time ever.

"Powers was an old Ohio Stater," reflected Herbstreit, "and he never had anybody who played at Ohio State. At my size, I had told John Pont that I would come to Miami with one exception, and that was if I got the opportunity to go to Ohio State. Well, at the state track meet, Woody came with several assistants who were standing around the finish line, and after the race he invited me to come up the next week for a visit. We were up in the faculty club, and when he offered me a scholarship I waited about fifteen seconds before I accepted it."

Woody admired both the speed and the sporting ethic of his young halfback, and wasted no time in putting Herbstreit on the field as a freshman. Though the fans clamored to see more of his flashing feet on offense, the Reading grad was more essential to Hayes on defense. When Herbstreit was a senior and unanimously elected captain, the crusty coach called him the best defensive back in the country.

He showed it in the prestigious East-West Shrine Game, in which he was named Most Valuable Player. As reported from San Francisco by the *Associated Press*, "While a capacity crowd of 60,000 sat in Kezar Stadium, pint-sized Jim Herbstreit of the Buckeyes intercepted a pass by UCLA's Bill Kilmer during the third quarter and raced it back 55 yards to set up the day's only score."

After the game, Reading honored Herbstreit with a special night at the high school, and the Baltimore Colts and Dallas Texans expressed serious interest in his services. But he had sustained four concussions as a senior, and Hayes had a better idea. He offered Herbstreit a position on his staff. Discretion prevailed, and Herbstreit joined Bo Schembechler among the Ohio State assistants. After three years, he became Schembechler's defensive coordinator at Miami.

His next move was into the real estate appraisal business in Dayton. Herbstreit stayed in communion with football by acquainting his boy, Kirk, with the best features and purest spirit of the sport.

In turn, the son once said, "I used to go to bed at night when I was in high school—this was in the middle of the Cold War, and nuclear bombs were a serious threat—and I would pray to hold off on the nuclear bombs until I got a chance to play in the Ohio State-Michigan game."

He did, as the starting quarterback and, like his father, Buckeye captain. Afterwards, he became known as perhaps the top television commentator for college football, and a producer of high school extravaganzas played across Ohio.

On the set and even off it, Kirk Herbstreit's love for the game was out there for all to see. But its origins were tucked far below the surface, visible only to those who understood. It came from his dad, who got it from Reading.

Here, 160-pound Herbstreit hitches a ride with his OSU linemen, Ernie Wright (250) of Toledo and Granville's Jim Tyrer (255).

Ahmed Plummer

Wyoming quarterback/db class of 19***95***

95

WHEN HE FIRST SHOWED UP FOR FOOTBALL AT WYOMING HIGH SCHOOL, AHMED PLUMMER WAS JUST A BIT BEHIND ON THE LEARNING CURVE. "He had his thigh pads in the opposite direction," recalled his coach, Bernie Barre.

But there's a pattern here. This is a kid who repeated second grade and then graduated (in 1995) from a demanding high school with a 3.6 GPA; a kid who was *twice* an Academic All-American at Ohio State.

And so it was with the football, as well. Not long after he got his pads turned around, Plummer was starting at quarterback for the Cowboys as a quick-study sophomore. "My high school coach really was the first one to break down the game for me so I could start to understand it," he told the *Contra Costa Times* years later, when he was well-established with the San Francisco 49ers. "There were some positions I didn't know—like what's a guard, what's a tackle?"

The rest of the positions, he seemed to play himself. As a quarterback, Plummer ran and passed with equal aplomb, and on the other side of scrimmage he led his team in tackles and interceptions, setting various school records and distinguishing himself as 1) Ohio Division IV Defensive Player of the Year, and 2) the humblest kid in his small community. There was the time, for instance, when he led the Cowboys to their first victory ever over CAPE, and in the triumphant afterglow a young fan thought it not the best time to approach his hero for an autograph. Later that evening, a friend phoned Plummer at home to inform him of the boy's fervent wishes, at which point the weary star got in his car, drove to the kid's house, and signed on the spot.

The adoration was perfect preparation for what would be ahead at Ohio State, which recruited Plummer as a cornerback and put him on the field immediately. What most impressed the Buckeyes—well, in addition to his penchant for getting to the ball—was the former quarterback's appetite for learning.

"The Plum Man's going to know how to get it done," remarked his secondary coach, John Tenuta. "If I tell the Plum Man one time that his guy is going to work inside and to play it that way, *boom*, it's automatic. He's a very intelligent young man on and off the field."

The dedication to study was merely a work-habit thing that Plummer learned from his mother, Babette, who raised him and his brother alone while pursuing her doctorate in clinical psychology. The prolific pass-picker also took a cue from her scholastic acumen, keeping his grades up in spite of football and a girl named Tiffany, whom he met in church and proposed to at an ice cream parlor. They were married a couple months after the 49ers chose him in the first round of the 2000 draft.

Plummer left Ohio State as its MVP and Most Inspirational Player. He was All-Big Ten, in addition, and by most accounts would have been All-NFL had not injuries intervened and cut his career short in 2005. After breaking into the starting lineup as a rookie, the Plum Man pulled down seven interceptions in his second pro season.

"He's our best corner," declared San Francisco coach Dennis Erickson. "He's a real talented guy, really smart."

Never mind second grade.

Mike Sensibaugh

Lockland quarterback/db class of 19***67***

67

IN 1967, WOODY HAYES WAS AT THE TOP OF HIS GAME AS A RECRUITER. THAT YEAR, HE FOUND JOHN BROCKINGTON IN BROOKLYN; JACK TATUM IN NEW Jersey; Jim Stillwagon—the last man recruited—in a military school in Virginia, though he grew up in Mount Vernon, Ohio; Rex Kern, the quarterback and closely cropped son of the town barber, in Lancaster, Ohio; and, mining the Mill Creek Valley, he came away with the intelligent and talented minister's boy, Mike Sensibaugh.

Sensibaugh was a quarterback at Lockland, and Hayes actually studied him as such. "Woody was aware of Mike as a sophomore, for some reason," recalled

Ben Hubbard, Sensibaugh's high school coach. "He came down often. We had a nice little coach's office, and one day he came by and we were talking about passing—Woody and I aren't guys who throw the ball all over the place —and I'm showing a movie of Mike on the white wall of the office, and all of a sudden he said, 'Do you have anything we can hang on the wall to stick something in?'

"I had no idea what he was up to, but the phys ed teacher says, yeah, we got something, and he gets a sheet and puts it over the chalkboard so we can watch the movie on that. Then Woody wanted a couple darts. And as we're watching the film, he'd say, '*This* is when Mike should throw the ball,' and he'd fire a dart at the picture. You could tell he was serious about it."

Sensibaugh, though, wasn't all that serious about the passing part of his game. He was good enough at it—he was good at *everything*, the city's best basketball player and maybe best baseball player as well—but consider his influences. As a peewee player for Lichty's Golden Eagles, his first coach had been Ray Nolting, who did the dirty work in the Monsters of the Midway backfield that included Bronko Nagurski. And Sensibaugh knew Woody.

Soon enough after Sensibaugh arrived at Ohio State, Hayes had the Panther star at safety, which he had played a bit of at Lockland. "He played," said Hubbard, "wherever I needed him. Middle linebacker. He was a linebacker with quarterback skills, and he might have been one of the most aggressive football players I ever coached. And he was the kind of kid who said nothing and did whatever you asked. Mike was a unique individual who had a competitive spirit like no one I've ever seen. He was a straight-A student, and he had some ridiculously high score on the ACT. He kind of lived in his own world.

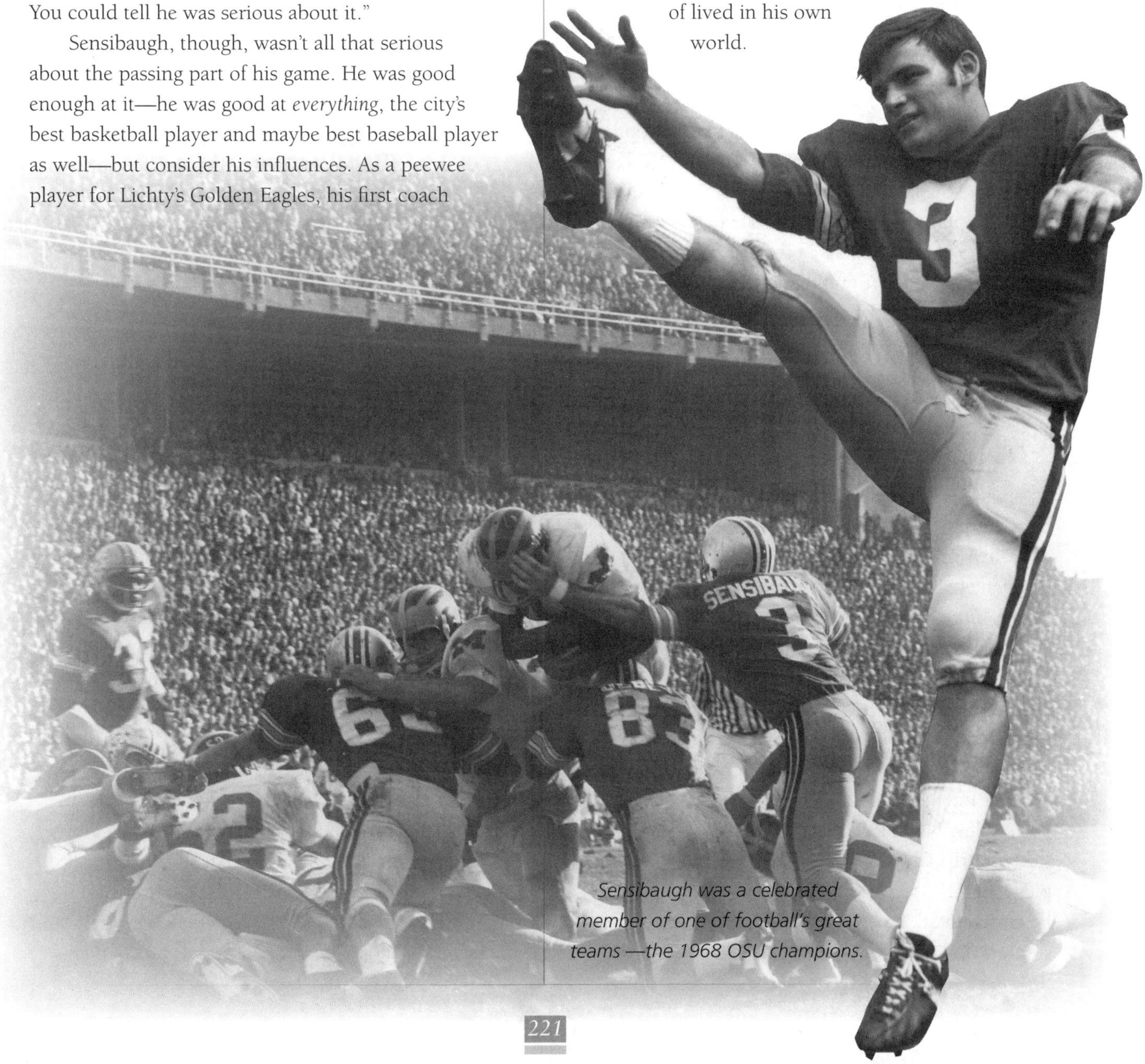

Sensibaugh was a celebrated member of one of football's great teams—the 1968 OSU champions.

"As a quarterback, Mike was actually a great thrower, but he could keep the ball anytime he wanted. One time we were playing Greenhills, and we scored I think three touchdowns in the first four or five plays we ran. It would just be an option and Mike would keep it and go all the way."

Sensibaugh would do that even when the other team had the ball. He had an instinct for interceptions, and ultimately set the Ohio State career record in that category. The record was 22, and it still stands.

He also, odd as it seems, set a *punting* record for both the school and the Rose Bowl, booting the ball an accumulated 319 yards on the fine day in Pasadena when the Buckeyes clinched the 1968 national championship. Of course, one of his kicks was returned 80 yards by O.J. Simpson for a Southern California touchdown; but Sensibaugh made up for that at the goal line, late in the game. On consecutive plays from the 3, the Trojans sent Simpson in Sensibaugh's direction and the minister's son was there to arrest him.

Before the famous game, he hadn't even been certain he would play on defense. Lou Holtz was his secondary coach, and Holtz complained that on one particular game film he couldn't find the Mill Creek kid. Prior to that, Sensibaugh had received plenty of attention as one of the Super Sophomores, or Baby Bucks, as he and his celebrated classmates were called. But he was stressing over a second-year slump as the Rose Bowl approached, and the anxiety only deepened when Hugh Sensibaugh's rapidly growing Lockland Christian Church drummed up enough money to send the whole family to California for the game. It turned out to be quite a time.

The Buckeyes went back to the Rose Bowl when Sensibaugh, Tatum, Brockington, and Stillwagon were Super Seniors and All-Americans—and they'd lost only twice: that 1971 Rose Bowl and the 1969 Michigan game. Along with Kern, Jan White, Doug Adams, Bruce Jankowski, et al, the erstwhile Baby Bucks would be generally embraced as the best class in OSU history.

For their parts, Brockington, Tatum and Sensibaugh were far from finished, proceeding on to become outstanding NFL players. As a 5-11, 190-pound free safety for the Chiefs and later the Cardinals, Sensibaugh picked off 27 pro passes. Then, after eight good years, he retired in St. Louis to build swimming pools in the summer and bird-hunt the rest of the year.

In his absence, his profile has faded some in Cincinnati. He was, however, a member of the first class of five football players (along with Socko Wiethe, Jim Bolger, Dave Foley, and Greg Stemrick) elected to the LaRosa's Hall of Fame in 1975. There are those who remember. His old high school coach is one.

"I've been doing this for forty-eight years," said Hubbard, back in Lockland as principal and football coach after ten job changes, "and Mike Sensibaugh is actually the greatest high school athlete I have personally known. I really don't think there's been a better athlete to come out of Cincinnati. He could do everything."

Hayes, for another, recognized as much when Sensibaugh was running the Lockland option as a super sophomore—four years in advance of becoming a Super Sophomore.

Greg Stemrick

Lincoln Heights cornerback class of 1970

70

IN THE MATTER OF GREG STEMRICK, WE WISH NOT TO REWRITE HISTORY BUT MAYBE TO CUT AND PASTE IT A BIT, DO A LITTLE CONSTRUCTIVE REARRANGING.

His mainstream legacy, unfortunately, revolves around his 1983 arrest for possession of cocaine and the four-game NFL suspension it led to, which in turn led to the premature end of his career. After a season in the World Football League, Stemrick had put in eight solid years with the Houston Oilers, five of them as a starting cornerback, one of them resulting in a Pro Bowl selection.

Then, in January of 1983, the Houston police were monitoring a private club called the Sportsman's Lodge for possible drug activity, and out walked Stemrick with a couple grams of the wrong stuff. After pleading no contest to the charges, he was placed on five years' probation, reprimanded by the league and waived by the Oilers, who at the time were coached by Ed Biles of Reading. Stemrick caught on with New Orleans for the rest of the year, then faded into forgettability.

As far as Cincinnati was concerned, part of that

had to do with the fact that he'd played college ball far away at Colorado State, where he first led the team in receiving then became an All-WAC defensive back. But the hometown obscurity no doubt derived, in larger part, from having been a sporting hero at a high school that ceased to exist the day he graduated.

In the fall of 1970, Lincoln Heights would be merged into the Princeton school district. It was a melancholy, inevitable development for a school that had plenty to be proud of. Lincoln Heights was an undersized, all-black public district previously known as Lockland Wayne. Wayne had been an athletics powerhouse in the days of Ray Tomlin, Tony Yates and his older brother Fletcher, winning state basketball championships in 1952 and 1955.

Consequently, Stemrick and his skillful classmates were well aware that their senior year would be a soulful swan song for the little school. And they responded with soaring voices.

First came an unspectacular football season in which Stemrick, equally dynamic on both offense and defense, was named a Hamilton County Conference all-star. Then the poetry poured out.

Under coach John Hillard, the basketball Tigers made it all the way to the Class A state tournament, reporting to St. John Arena with the worst record among the eight quarterfinalists. Not a problem. In the finals, they encountered Sebring McKinley and used a full-court press to construct a tidy lead. The deficit closed in the final minutes, but when Lincoln Heights' final basketball game had ended, the moribund school was champion of Ohio. The boys were allowed to keep their uniforms as souvenirs.

Stemrick, a three-year starter at guard—he had been to the state semifinals as a sophomore in 1968—was not a leading scorer for Lincoln Heights but made the all-tournament team for everything else that he brought. Hillard, in fact, singled out the Stork, as they called him—it gives you an idea of how he was built back then—for his defensive work on Sebring star Greg Wilson. "Stemrick," the coach told the assembled reporters, "is one of the best athletes I've ever seen."

That assessment would be borne out in the spring, when the Tigers' baseball team took up where the cagers had left off. Stemrick was an ace, undefeated pitcher, and at the district tournament in Dayton he produced a no-hitter. The next day, the district track meet was held in Cincinnati. He won three events.

The baseball team kept moving along, and in the state semifinals Stemrick took over late for the save. In the finals against Pettisville, he went the distance for a 5-3 victory and another improbable, theatrical state championship. Even at that, Stemrick wasn't quite finished. There was still a state title to be won in the 880-yard relay.

All in all, it was an historic stretch that didn't go unnoticed five years later, when Buddy LaRosa's High School Sports Hall of Fame was established. In its inaugural class, Stemrick was the youngest member inducted, taking his place alongside Jim Bolger, Mike Sensibaugh, Dave Foley, Socko Wiethe, and Tony Trabert.

It's where he's best remembered.

He was called a "diamond in the rough"—cut by Houston, picked up by the WFL Chicago Fire where his work got him a second chance in Houston. And in 1980 he was in the Pro Bowl.

THE Townsends

Mike and Willie (and Payton)

Hamilton Garfield DB, receiver class of 1970, 19

70

THE TOWNSENDS WERE STAIR-STEP BOYS, A YEAR APART, PAYTON, JR., THE FIRST (HE GOT THE HEIGHT), THEN WILLIE, THEN MIKE. PAPA TOWNSEND HAD BEEN AN ARMY ATHLETE— basketball, baseball, track, a little football, whatever—and so the gene pool wasn't long in manifesting itself. Like everybody else in Hamilton before them, they began with pick-up games on a neighborhood playground that had a basketball court, and beside it, a grassy field whose perimeters were pavement and a building wall.

Willie and Mike most often found themselves on the field, trying not to get bounced off the wall. Payton, at 6-8, hung out on the court, looking down on the mere mortals who congregated there. Willie and Mike, both basketball naturals, felt like they could do the court anytime; they preferred the more dedicated physicality of football, where they were both wide receivers.

By the time they reached high school, their staggered ages were a trial to their basketball coach who could only imagine the three of them as seniors together. He considered them *his*, telling the football coach, Lou Florio, "I let you borrow 'em for a couple of months, Lou, but they're really basketball players."

They were, too. As it was, Payton and Willie—and Clint Spearman, a tough kid who'd go on to play football at Michigan—took Garfield to the state title game in 1968 where the Griffins were leading a heavily favored Columbus East team by five points until Payton fouled out. Mike could play, as well, and his junior and senior teams went to the district finals.

So Payton, Garfield's top career scorer, went on to Southwestern Louisiana University and a pro basketball stint and Willie headed off to Notre Dame to play football, leaving Mike with a brace of recruiters from all over the country. Some of them wanted him to play basketball and some wanted him for football. Even he was confused. He tried to get some advice from the family but Payton said he should play basketball, Willie said he should play football, and his parents said he should play whatever he wanted.

So he did the smartest thing. He chose the sport he loved best, which was football, and he chose a school for purely academics. *If I don't get my studies*, he said to himself, *I don't go there*. There might have been a little Coach Florio in the decision-making process, because Lou always said books went further than the football.

"If you've got an education," he told his boys, "your career doesn't stop when the ball does."

So Mike's choice was Purdue and computer sciences. "You'll start as a sophomore," the coach told him, "and you'll see your brother on the field every year." Mike heads off for Lou's office and tells him it's Purdue. "Can we do the paperwork, Coach?" And the coach says he'll call Purdue and have them send it.

A couple of days later, Mike walks in the house after track practice and there's an envelope from Purdue on the table.

Then he hears his mom's voice. "Mike, the coach is here."

Man, he hand-delivered it, Mike thinks. But when he walks into the kitchen, Brian Boulac, the Notre Dame recruiting coach, is sitting there.

"The dude says, 'I had a premonition you were going somewhere else.' And now he's done sold my mom. 'You need *both* your sons at Notre Dame,' he tells her. So Coach Boulac wants me to go to Notre Dame, and now my mom wants me to go to Notre Dame. I can see I'm going to Notre Dame. I ask about computer sciences as a major. By the time I arrive, he says, they'll get it upgraded to a major."

So not only does Mike go to Notre Dame, become an All-American defensive back who still holds the school record for interceptions in a season (13), and help the Irish win a national title, he also gets computer sciences upgraded to a major.

Mike was converted to DB, and in practice sometimes found himself going one-on-one with Willie at receiver. The coach, Ara Parseghian, watched from his tower, commanding the field via megaphone.

"The Townsend brothers!" he'd announce through the megaphone. "What have we *today*?"

Which stirred the brothers to unbrotherly passion in beating each other.

Playing varsity basketball at Notre Dame (along with Willie), leading the nation with interceptions in 1972, being named defensive captain and a consensus All-American—none of these was Mike's favorite moment. There were two of them, actually, and they came back to back. The first was when Notre Dame beat a good Southern Cal team at home after the previous year's disastrous USC loss.

In 1972, even with Mike's two interceptions, Anthony Davis scored six times and USC beat Notre Dame 45-23. That might have been his *worst* moment. "Not a pretty sight," he sighed.

So the pressure was on the Irish in 1973, and Mike and his teammates felt it. There were signs everywhere, reading, *Oh, God in heaven, don't let Davis score seven*. There were no other topics in South Bend the week of the USC game but USC and Davis.

So here's the moment: Notre Dame had new turf that year, it had been raining, and the guys decided to go out before their last practice before the game and have a sliding contest. "We decided we'd just christen our field," Mike said. "Man, you could really slide when that thing was wet. We had a big offensive tackle who went 45 yards on his big ole butt. All that unbelievable tension? It was gone. Coaches came out, looked around, and said, 'Y'awl crazy or what? This is the biggest game of the year.' Yeah, we said, and now we're ready for it."

Davis got a score but the Irish got the win—23-14—which led to Mike's *next* great moment: the Sugar Bowl, Number 3 Notre Dame vs. Number 1 Alabama, both unbeaten.

After seven lead changes and two minutes left in the game, the Irish clung precariously to a 24-23 lead, backed up on their own goal line, third-and-9.

"We felt strong," said Mike. "And here's our attitude. Parseghian calls a pass play to the tight end coming across. The QB, Tom Clements, says, 'You want a first down, Coach, or a TD?' Parseghian slaps him on the head and says, 'Just throw the ball.'"

On third-and-8 from his own end zone, Clements throws for the first down and Notre Dame runs out the clock for a National Championship. Many still call it the greatest game in ND history.

"Forever and a day," says Mike. "That's how long I'll remember those two games..."

Time magazine called him the pick of the pros. "Always there at the right time and place," it wrote. He was a 4th round selection of Minnesota in the 1974 draft but opted to play in the World Football League, then returned to the NFL and played with the Vikings and the Giants. He soon discovered the passion he'd had in the college game was no longer the same. He heard the voice of his old Hamilton coach,

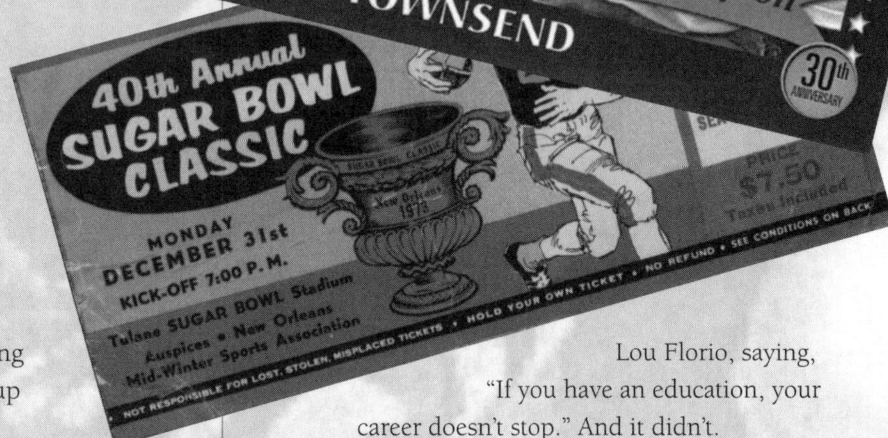

Lou Florio, saying, "If you have an education, your career doesn't stop." And it didn't.

"God had given me some skills and I had maximized them. And so I moved on. The image of my time playing ball stays with me, though, a great joy, one that I share with my brothers and my children...."

Dwayne Woodruff

New Richmond | running back/db | class of 1975

75

DWAYNE WOODRUFF LIVED IN A TRAILER IN THE VILLAGE WITH HIS MOTHER, AND HE MADE STRAIGHT A'S, AND HE PLAYED BOTH WAYS FOR THE NEW RICHMOND LIONS. MOST OF THE LIONS DID.

He was the fastest athlete in the Clermont County League, as he proved during the track season, and a large reason why New Richmond's football team dominated it in 1974. Coach Ron Bird's men didn't lose a league game, and wouldn't have lost any at all if several touchdowns hadn't been called back at Hillsboro. Bird recalls about 250 yards in penalties that night, and scores wiped out because, as the referee told him, "Coach, he's blocking both knees."

The CCL was sort of an out-of-the-way conference, and one that as a result didn't produce many football scholarships. Woodruff came by his accidentally. The Hillsboro coach had sent a tape on one of his players to Virginia Military, and one of the VMI assistants happened to notice the fast kid for New Richmond who played running back and corner.

Then the assistant took a job at the university of Louisville, and offered Woodruff, and good things happened. Four years later, he was drafted in the sixth round by the Pittsburgh Steelers, the defending and soon repeating Super Bowl champions. Beginning in 1981, Woodruff—who for a while there was regarded as the fastest player in the NFL—held down left cornerback in Pittsburgh for eight consecutive seasons.

In only his second year as a starter, he was named the Steelers' Most Valuable Player. That season, and four others, he led his proud team in interceptions. Also that season, Woodruff spent his Sunday nights and most of his Mondays back in New Richmond, visiting his mother as she suffered from stomach cancer.

Shortly thereafter, he enrolled in law school at Duquesne University in Pittsburgh, studying full-time even as he ran his career interception total to 37. He earned his law degree in 1988, and for the last three years of his career served as both the Steelers' captain and a practicing attorney.

In 1990, Woodruff retired from football and became a founding partner of a Pittsburgh law firm. In 2005, he led all candidates in the general election for judge of the Allegheny County Court of Common Pleas.

Meanwhile, after a few more floods in New Richmond, the old trailer disappeared from the village. What remains of Woodruff's time there is a college scholarship he established at the high school. He was surely grateful for his.

In 1983, **Harlon Barnett** delivered what was considered to be the key play of Princeton's 1983 state-championship season, hitting D'Juan Francisco so hard that he forced a fumble and preserved the Vikings' 28-21 victory over Moeller in the first round of the playoffs. Later, as a senior safety at Michigan State, Barnett was a first-team All-American for a Spartan squad that led the Big Ten in total defense. He was drafted by the Cleveland Browns and subsequently started 28 games at safety for the New England Patriots. Barnett took up coaching at the conclusion of his seven-year NFL career, and was in charge of the defensive backs at the University of Cincinnati until he moved with his boss, Mark Dantonio, to Michigan State, of course . . . Moeller's **Vada Murray** snatched a remarkable 13 interceptions in 1985, part of a school-record 21 for his All-American career. His baker's-dozen haul came in handy during the Crusaders' last state-championship season. Murray was named for former Reds star Vada Pinson, and in that regard it's poetic that he ended up playing the football equivalent of center field. He was Michigan's starting free safety for three seasons, and a Rose Bowl champion as a sophomore. After football, he became an Ann Arbor police officer . . . As a senior quarterback at CAPE, **David Pool's** job wasn't particularly hard. It involved handing the ball quite a bit to Carlos Snow, who was then a sophomore running back. But Pool had other talents. Tennessee determined that, at 5-9, he fit best at defensive back, which was where he played after transferring to Carson-Newman. Then, after torching the NFL combine with a 4.37-second 40-yard dash, he played five seasons of DB with the Bills, Patriots and Jets . . . **Neal Craig** had just graduated from Taft High School and embarked on his sociology degree at Fisk University when the Bengals set up shop in Cincinnati. Fisk, a historically black college, no longer fields a football team, but it served Craig's purposes just fine—got him drafted, in fact, in 1971, by the hometown team whose path he hadn't crossed. But it wasn't his own unfamiliarity with the Bengals that troubled him; it was everybody else's. "When we go out to Los Angeles or New York, people say, 'You play for the Cincinnati who?' " the strong safety lamented in 1973, after the Bengals, at 10-4, had qualified solidly for the divisional playoffs. "So I've decided we're the Cincinnati Who. We don't have the national reputation we deserve. People still think of us as an expansion team. Some think we're the Cincinnati Bingos." Craig then went out against the Miami Dolphins and did his best to carve out an appropriate reputation, intercepting one of Bob Griese's passes and taking it 45 yards for a touchdown to cut Miami's lead to 21-16 just before halftime. But that was as close as the Bengals got, and as close as Craig got to a reputation of his own. In the best secondary the local team ever put together, he was somewhat overshadowed by teammates Ken Riley, Lemar Parrish and Tommy Casanova. Even so, Craig's career lasted six years, and in none of them did he fail to intercept a pass. The balls he caught, however, don't compare in number to those corralled by his son, Cornell Craig, who, after going to high school in Louisville, set most of the pass-receiving records at Southern Illinois University and in 1999 was Division I-AA Player of the Year . . . Coming out of Colerain in 2006, **Eugene Clifford** was the top-rated safety in America, a tall, instinctive, playmaking All-American recruited by every college that thought it had a chance to get him. The cousin of former Eagles and Steelers running back Duce Staley, Clifford was the rare high school athlete who could dominate games from the secondary. He was so roundly coveted that not even Ohio State could be certain he'd sign. He did, only to transfer to Tennessee State in the summer of 2008 . . . **Rodney Heath** was not like that. Heath was lacking in size—only 5-9, 170 pounds all grown up—and Western Hills was by no means a football power. But Heath, raised in Northside, had learned toughness from his father, a police officer on the Bond Hill beat, and he was resourceful enough as a defensive back that the *Cincinnati Post* named him its local Prep Player of the Year for 1992. All of that set him up at the University of Minnesota, where he started every game his last two seasons and returned more punts than any other player in Gophers history. He was, of course, undrafted. And of course undaunted. Heath played two seasons in the Professional Indoor Football League, then delivered his tape to the Bengals, who kept him around for three years and started him for two at cornerback. He actually led the team in interceptions in 1999, returning one for a touchdown at Pittsburgh in a one-touchdown victory. After a complete tear of his hamstring, Heath was limited to just one more game with the Atlanta Falcons, and to a message. "Most of them didn't really know me," he said of the young crowd he once addressed at Western Hills. "They saw my picture in the school probably. I wanted to let them know they could make it, that you can defy the odds. I told them I was just like them." Only smaller, in many cases.

Cincinnati's
ALL-TIME PRO TEAM

OFFENSE

Quarterback

Roger Staubach, Purcell (Dallas)
Hall of Fame, MVP, six Pro Bowls, two Super Bowl championships

George Ratterman
St. Xavier (Buffalo, New York Yankees, Cleveland)
Led league in completion percentage, TD passes

Bob Hoernschemeyer, Elder (Chicago Rockets, Brooklyn Dodgers, Chicago Hornets)
All-around back threw over 700 passes for 42 TDs

Arguable: Steve Tensi, Elder (San Diego, Denver)

Running back

Bob Hoernschemeyer
Elder (Brooklyn Dodgers, Chicago Hornets, Detroit)
Two Pro Bowls, "best third-down back in pro football"

Ray Nolting, Hughes (Chicago)
Three-time All-Pro, key member of Backfield of the Century

Cid Edwards,
Taft (St. Louis Cardinals, San Diego)
Rugged blocker, nearly 4,500 yards rushing and receiving

Arguable: Marc Edwards, Norwood (San Francisco, Cleveland, New England, Jacksonville); Breezy Reid, Hamilton (Green Bay)

Wide receiver

Cris Carter
Middletown (Philadelphia, Minnesota)
Retired as No. 2 all-time in receptions and TDs, eight Pro Bowls

Dick Gordon, Walnut Hills (Chicago)
Led league in receptions, two Pro Bowls

Tom Waddle, Moeller (Chicago)
Led Bears in receptions, All-Madden team

Milt Stegall
Roger Bacon (Winnipeg Blue Bombers)
All-time CFL leader in TD catches

Arguable: Steve Junker, Elder (Detroit, Washington); Jim O'Brien, Aiken (Baltimore)

Tight end

Don Hasselbeck
LaSalle (New England, Oakland)
18 career TDs, Super Bowl champion

Tony Hunter
Moeller (Buffalo, Los Angeles Rams)
1,500 receiving yards

Arguable: Eric Kattus, Colerain (Cincinnati); Steve Junker, Elder (Detroit, Washington); Brent Celek, LaSalle (Philadelphia)

Offensive line

T: **John Jackson**, Woodward (Pittsburgh)
Highest-paid lineman in NFL, 7 playoff seasons

T: **Rich Michael**, Hamilton (Houston)
Two-time Pro Bowler

T: **Dave Foley**
Roger Bacon (New York Jets, Buffalo)
Pro Bowler was part of Electric Company that blocked for O.J. Simpson

G: **Bill Feldhaus**, Hughes (Detroit)
First local lineman in pros, one of first players to wear hinged knee guard

G: **Dave Lafary**, LaSalle (New Orleans)
Versatile nine-year veteran

C: **Steve Sylvester**, Moeller (Oakland)
Three-time Super Bowl champ

Arguable (offensive line): Dan James, Elder (Pittsburgh); Socko Wiethe, Roger Bacon (Detroit); Bob Fry, Elder (Los Angeles Rams, Dallas); Tom Luken, LaSalle (Philadelphia)

Hoernschemeyer

DEFENSE

Defensive line

E: **John Martinkovic**
Hamilton Badin (Green Bay)
Three-time Pro Bowler, Packers Hall of Fame
E: **Steve Niehaus**
NFC Defensive Rookie of Year, undermined by injuries
T: **Dana Stubblefield**
Taylor (San Francisco, Washington)
Three-time All-Pro, 15 sacks in season

T: **Walter Johnson**, Taft (Cleveland)
Three Pro Bowls, thirteen-year career

Arguable: Abdul Salaam (Larry Faulk), Woodward (New York Jets); Melvin Lunsford, Lockland (New England); Bill Feldhaus, Hughes (Detroit); Vaughn Booker, Taft (Kansas City, Green Bay, Cincinnati)

Linebacker

Hacksaw Reynolds
Western Hills (Los Angeles Rams, San Francisco)
Two Pro Bowls, two Super Bowl championships, twelve years as starter
Socko Wiethe, Roger Bacon (Detroit)
Two-time all-pro, credited as first linebacker to blitz
Dixon Edwards, Aiken (Dallas)
Three Super Bowl rings, six-year starter
Bob Crable, Moeller (New York Jets)
Stardom undercut by bad knees

Arguable: Antwan Peek, Woodward (Houston, Cleveland); Lemar Marshall, St. Xavier (Washington, Cincinnati)

Defensive back

Dwayne Woodruff
New Richmond (Pittsburgh)
Steelers MVP, fastest man in NFL, Super Bowl champ
Mike Sensibaugh
Lockland (Kansas City, St. Louis Cardinals)
27 career interceptions
Greg Stemrick, Lincoln Heights (Houston)
Pro Bowl cornerback
Todd Bell, Middletown (Chicago)
Pro Bowl safety
Carlton Gray, Forest Park
(Seattle, Indianapolis, New York Giants, Kansas City)
Started for four teams
Ahmed Plummer, Wyoming (San Francisco)
First-round draft choice had fast start until slowed by injuries

Arguable: Vinnie Clark, CAPE (Green Bay, Atlanta, Jacksonville); Harlon Barnett, Princeton (Cleveland, New England, Minnesota)

SPECIAL TEAMS

PK: **Jim O'Brien**, Aiken (Baltimore)
Famous field goal won Super Bowl V
P: **Bob Hoernschemeyer**
Elder (Chicago Rockets, Chicago Hornets, Detroit)
Averaged 41.9 yards, also returned kickoffs and punts
KR: **Al Nelson**, Taft (Philadelphia)
2,625 career yards, NFL's top two longest returns of missed field goals
PR: **Kirk Springs**, Woodward (New York Jets)
Led AFC, two game-winning TD returns
Special Mention: Ike Reese, Aiken (Philadelphia, Atlanta); Alex Bannister, Hughes (Seattle)
Both players made Pro Bowl for special teams coverage

Arguable: B.J. Sander, Roger Bacon (Green Bay); Ron Carpenter, Princeton (New York Jets); Dick Gordon, Walnut Hills (Chicago); Jeff Hill, Mount Healthy (Cincinnati); Rocky Boiman, St. Xavier (Tennessee, Indianapolis); B.J. Askew, Colerain (New York Jets, Tampa Bay); Troy Evans, Lakota (Houston Texans)

Socko Wiethe

Hamilton: The Original Tough House

In the parish schools of Hamilton at mid-century, the University of Notre Dame University loomed as a beacon of Aristotelian virtue. Sister Blandine, a short bowling ball of a nun, made the kids pray their rosaries every Friday to help Notre Dame win on Saturday.

Some of the kids didn't even know what Notre Dame was.

"Is Notre Dame a *country*?" one of the boys was heard whispering to a classmate.

Later, they understood that it was a shining place on a hill where great men played football and the grass was thick and the sun was always shining. They thought it was the only place in America where college football was played, which, if true, meant there would have been no opponents, but grade school logic often lacks perfection.

They massacred the fight song and sang:

Cheer, cheer for old Notre Dame
You take the Notre, we'll take the dame . . .

The public school kids learned their football on the sandlots; the Catholic kids, quicker organized, went from sandlot to parish teams, little moons in their precise orbits around the larger body of Hamilton Catholic High. The high school—across the street from Hamilton Public—contained no more than 250 boys, presided over by the Marianist brothers.

There was only one woman in the building, a gentle young secretary who tore up the demerit slips handed out by the brothers. In the overheated landscape of the stag and the boar, this pale creature and her shoulder-length auburn hair stood out ethereally, something in the manner of Venus in the famous painting, as if she had blown in off the Miami and was standing demurely on her scalloped sea-shell in the middle of the school office.

There *were* girls across the street at Hamilton High, but the brothers had painted the lower halves of all the classroom windows facing that way, so that even *those* girls—so near, yet so far— were mostly out of sight. The *other* sex was perceived as a kind of rare species, something on the order of the Vancouver Marmot, perhaps, or one of those rare flowers from the rainforests of Sumatra, and the boys' knowledge of them matched what they knew about marmots and rainforests.

The Brothers dealt out a rough frontier justice, and it was not unusual for a truant to be pitched down the interior stairs by one of them. As the truants had already learned football by playing tackle in the stone-filled back alleys and being bounced off garage doors, the stair was merely another infraction without a flag.

In the early 1950s, the Catholic boys practiced beside the public stadium—the Hamilton schools maintaining an odd symbiotic relationship in which the two parts, like the moons of Mars, were intimately connected yet each barely acknowledged the existence of the other.

The Catholic kids drove to practice in an old green bus where they ran plays in what was actually a parking lot. The trolley company used it to dump cinders from the stoves that heated the cars, or so the Catholic kids heard. The lot was vacant in the summer and grass had managed to struggle fitfully up through the cinders.

One of the Catholic kids described it this way: "You'd practice, then spend half an hour picking cinders out of your pants. Once **Bennie Reins** got tackled and when he got up his nose was full of cinders. The public school lockers were nearby and **George Molinsky** stole a Big Blue jersey. Their coach came over and snatched the jersey off George. Didn't even look at our coaches, just walked up to George and said, 'Gimme that,' and walked off. George had to practice in just his shoulder pads. No jersey. By the time practice was over, George was covered in cinders. He looked like he had been pulled out of a fireplace . . . ."

That was **Tony Lamke**, a freshman halfback in the fall of 1952, so dimuitive that when the newspaper photographer showed up, Big Jim Mense picked him up and sat him on his shoulder, as if he were a parakeet.

Lamke got even by going off and becoming a good little halfback on a not-so-

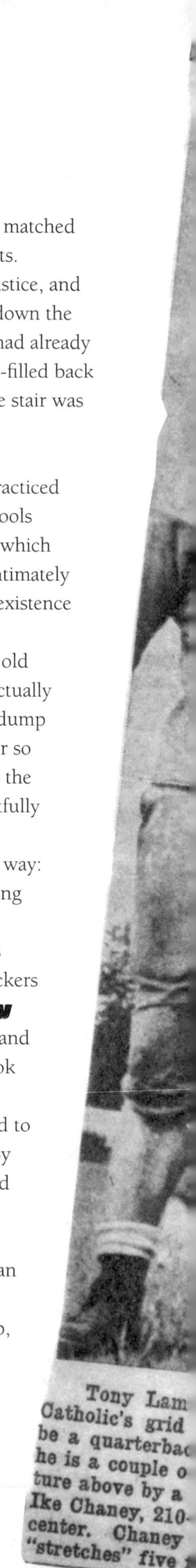

ighty Mite And Giants

—Journal-News Staff Photo

nd freshman, is a candidate for Hamilton
year. He isn't sure whether he wants t
k, center or end—that depends on how bi
om now. Tony is being supported in the pi
nts by his standards. On the left is Captai
kle, and at the right, Jim Mense, 218-pour
nse are both six-footers while Lam

good Wilmington College team. (His coach there was an ex-Chicago Bear fullback with an ego the size of the woodshed his players perpetually lived in. He brought his bulldog to practice and the dog chased the slow linemen through windsprints, nipping at their dragging backsides.) Then Lamke became legendary in Clinton County by building the first football program at Clinton-Massie High in a cornfield where the turf, put down with a grain drill, caught on fire when an opposing coach inadvertently dropped his cigarette on it. Lamke had surprising teams known for always being smart and aggressive, which everyone back in Hamilton recognized as old Second Ward athletic traits.

That was, after all, where most of Lamke's survival skills had been learned. Sometime just after the war, the Hamilton grade school games had been moved down to the Community Center, across the street from the dump. The dump sat beside the river where burning garbage mingled with the omnipresent smells of sweat, liniment, and unwashed tee-shirts, overhanging the field with a funky bouquet that marked the poor territory of the Second Ward.

The Second Ward kids hated the kids from places like St. Veronica's because St. Veronica had bigger numbers on its jerseys and shoulder pads that made them look wide as a barn door. In truth, the Second Ward kids hated most everybody because they were at the bottom end of the social scale and the town dumped its garbage on them. (They never referred to the other teams by name. They just called them "the rest of the goddam town.") One day the wind blew the smell of garbage across their houses, the next day soot from the factories fell in the backyards, turning the underwear on the clotheslines gray, and women were out in force sweeping ashes off the front porch.

There was one advantage, though. The Second Ward kids tended to be good marksmen, having learned their craft by plugging the beagle-sized rats that frolicked in the refuse.

A couple of years ago, Lamke, who had played for St. Joe's, had his hand X-rayed for some minor surgery and the doctor asked him when he'd broken it.

"Those sons-of-bitches!" Lamke said, suddenly

remembering a game from more than a half century before when a St. Veronica's lineman stomped on his hand.

Lamke had played in the famous Snow Bowl game when the great blizzard of 1950 fell upon Hamilton as the parish teams were playing their regular Saturday morning games.

"Everything disappeared," Lamke said. "The yard markers, the goal posts, the out-of-bounds line—even some of my teammates. We ran a sweep and I discovered I'd run onto Garden Avenue. There was one ref, an old guy—he must have nearly 40—and he never noticed. We won, I think, but I don't know how. No one could see anything. No one knew anything . . ."

SO HERE'S THE THESIS: maybe places themselves have DNA. Or perhaps there was just something in the water. What eveybody knew, though, was this: Hamilton was a tough house. Toughness defined it: fire, epidemic, flood, Depression, the war, various cultural disintegrations, whatever.

The city managed to survive most if it, and through it all, Hamilton guys would knock your hat off. Maybe they'd been tempered in the foundries. What were **T-Bone Malone's** two-a-days under the hill compared to the foundries? The Badin practice field cooled down in a few weeks. The heat of the foundry floor was a lifetime.

A hundred years ago Hamilton called itself the greatest manufacturing town of its size in the world. It might have been, too. Say it wasn't and prepare to defend yourself. (Back then, they called Cincinnati "Hamilton's backyard," and only half in jest.) The industries were made, for the most part, by German immigrants and their capacity for discipline and hard work. "Stout, severe men in three-piece broadcloth suits as heavy and solid as flatiron," wrote Alan Natali. "Men of a faintly patrician air, chins fleshy, thick mustaches drooping over set eyes, lips speaking determination and money."

It was *their* sons who gravitated to the playing fields, along with the Irish, the Polish, the African-Americans—the usual disenfranchised rabble yearning to breeze free. Hamilton High coach **Lou Florio** said his boys got their size from their German ancestry. "The Lindenwald Effect," he called it, for the neighborhood a lot of the big kids came out of. They already understood discipline and hard work. Perfect for a regimented sport like football. A *factory* sport, you might say.

Whatever it was, athletics helped define—and redeem—the place for half a century or more. For a time, *all* the coaches had winning records. There was **Dana King**, emerging out of the primordial gridiron mist and winning 105 games before he hung up his clipboard in 1945. He had only one losing season—his first—and his 1929 10-0 team outscored the opposition 332-19 and proclaimed itself state champions. (King's job, it seemed, was to make The Depression iconic to his schedule.) In one mid-1920s stretch, the Big Blue went 35-3-1. "The Old Master," they called him.

He left Hamilton in 1931 to coach the University of Cincinnati—which had only two winning seasons since 1914—and in his four years there went 25-10-1. But Hamilton—and its sons—understood the long odds. Even as UC had just witnessed the best freshman class in school history, the old master knew that anything might happen.

He smiled a smile that the Hamilton paper described as "more deceptive than a quadruple pass executed with bean bags during an eclipse of the moon." And then King said, "If they come out for varsity next year, we may go places. However, I'm not anticipating anything. They might get hit by automobiles in the meantime." It was perhaps that old Hamilton notion of disaster, always lurking around the next corner.

While King was away, **Ray Tilton** won 60 games at Hamilton, with bragging rights to Ohio titles in 1935 and 1939, and ushered in Hamilton's first widely recognized football heroes in the animated persons of **Harold Stapleton** and **Frank Clair**.

Tilton's 1935 boys opened with Cincinnati Automotive Trades School and beat them 80-0 (quarterback **Louis Beers** scored eight TDs), then went through the rest of the season in the manner of a medieval plague. The only close game was

Middletown. With five minutes left, halfback Stapleton took a reverse over Clair's tackle position for 71 yards and the winning TD, his 20th. It was the last game of the year, played before 6,000 in Miami University's stadium, and with the win the Big Black and Blue had

"The Hamilton Express" was one of the early area boys to make a splash on the national scene.

registered seven shutouts, scoring 319 points while giving up only nine. Beers's eight scores in the opener was a record that stood for nearly forty years, and he's *still* tied for first in Ohio (with four others). By most measures, it was one of the all-time great area teams.

Stapleton and Clair were both All-State in 1935, the second and third boys from the Cincinnati area to make the new statewide all-star teams chosen by the two newspaper wire services. (First was **Emerson Wendt**, a Middletown fullback and Middie captain who had made the first team in 1934.) Of the first two dozen All-Staters from the area, half were Hamilton players, and another six from Middletown. Inconclusive, yes, but the early lists still suggested it was probably best not to schedule the lunch bucket kids from the industrial towns as your homecoming opponent.

A few years earlier, Hamilton Catholic had produced **Bob Wilke**, who by 1936 was a 158-pound three-year halfback at Notre Dame. He scored twice against Army—Grantland Rice called him "the human quarterhorse"—and was the leading rusher as the Irish finished Number 8 in the country.

The Wilkes had quite an athletic pedigree. Bob's brother, Harry, had a cup of coffee with the Chicago Cubs back in 1927, then opened Wilke's Cafe. It began as a corner grocery store, then Harry converted a couple of rooms into a bar, and before long, the bar and cafe won out over the groceries.

Harry's boy, **Cliff Wilke**, a big, shifty halfback who weighed over 200 pounds—another Hamilton All-Stater, in 1945—followed Uncle Bob to Notre Dame where he played halfback and fullback on the freshman squad but had such a good time in South Bend that he misplaced his school books and Frank Leahy took his scholarship away.

So Cliff transferred to Xavier University and found himself playing on a good Musketeer team with his old Hamilton Catholic teammate, **John Martinkovic**, a cantankerous, elk-sized lineman whom Cliff recalled as knocking down opposing players then chortling over the fallen remains.

"'I'm going duckhunting,' he says. "The duck they shot couldn't have looked worse than John. And I stayed up half the night putting ice on his chin so he could go *duckhunting*..."

ANOTHER HAMILTON THESIS: a slug in the mouth plus stitches plus nonchalance and

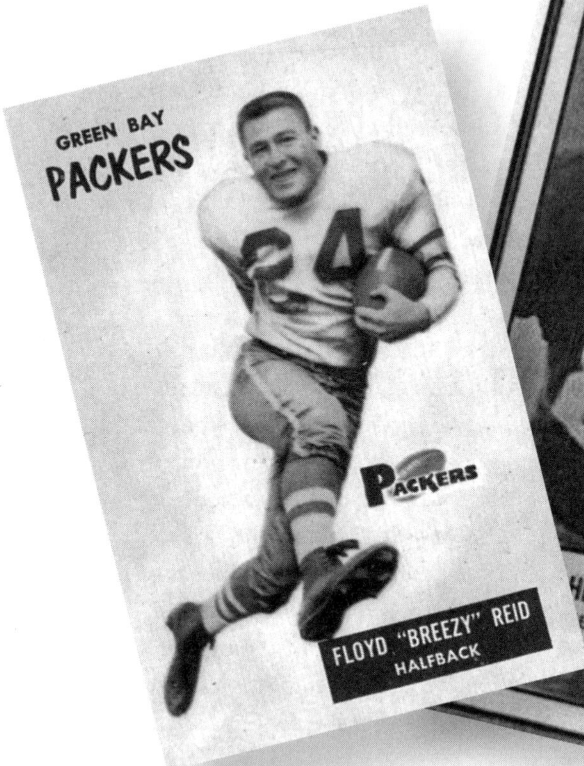

"I liked to bang people around," Martinkovic said, rather modestly, as if banging people around were merely an essential craft one learned growing up in Hamilton, which in a way, it was. It happened both ways, of course, and the sport was constructed in such a manner that one took almost as much pride in *absorbing* a good hit as handing one out. There was the time in Green Bay, for instance, when John got elbowed in the mouth.

"It was in 1953 and we were playing the Colts," he said. "Their fullback knocked me half out. The trainer said, 'Your lip looks like it could use nine or ten stitches, John.' He poked around in his bag for some anesthetic but he couldn't find any. So he just pulls out a needle and thread, sews me up. 'Does that hurt?' he says. 'A little bit,' I says. And I go back in."

The rest of the story belongs to John's wife, Clare. "After the game," she says, "we go to this bar on the bay. His lip is swollen out to here, he's drinking beer, and it's running down his chin. So most of the night I'm either up with the baby or putting ice on John's lip. About daybreak, I hear a car horn toot outside, and John is *leaving*.

"What're you doing?' I ask.

While at Miami, Boxcar ran a 9.7 hundred against the wind, they said. At right, the '46 HHS banquet. Bailey and Nuxhall were teammates—two All-State fullbacks for the price of one.

beer equals duckhunting. **Floyd (Little Breezy) Reid**, a Hamilton High halfback and John's Packer teammate, had his own lip story. *His* scar was given to him by none other than Concrete Charley Bednarik, the ferocious Eagle All-Pro for whom the adjective "bone-jarring" was invented. Reid, like John, got himself sewn up and returned to the fray.

"Bednarik thought I was getting too many yards," Reid shrugged.

Little Breezy was

the youngest of three boys, all of whom played for the University of Georgia. Ernie, the oldest (Big Breezy), was a suitcase athlete and seemed to have played at several colleges. Bernie was Georgia's co-captain in 1948, "a squat, workmanlike guard holding up the Georgia forewall."

Little Breezy went south when someone on the Georgia staff said to Bernie, "You got any more brothers?" And Bernie said, "Well, we got a little one. He seems to be a running back . . . ."

Bernie and Floyd—by this time he was about 190 pounds—played together at least that year, when Georgia tied Maryland in the Gator Bowl.

Bernie was drafted by San Francisco but that was too far to move and he ended up as a longtime scout for Denver. Little Breezy spent seven years in Green Bay. He even participated in one of the game's early holdouts. He demanded $100 more a game, and the Packers liked him so much they gave it to him.

In all of this we hear a certain voice, such as Cliff Wilke's when the big running back chooses not to talk of his touchdowns but says instead, "I knocked a lot of people about." It was the picture of the legendary **Boxcar Bailey** at linebacker, whacking runners and driving them over the little fence that circumscribed Garfield Stadium. (Remembered best as a big fullback with sub-10 second speed, he could hurt people on either side of the ball, and his brusing manner was coveted by Woody Hayes, then coaching Miami. The story in Hamilton was that after Boxcar's vandalizing performance in the North-South All-Star Game, Hayes showered with Boxcar, then spirited him off on a fishing trip, to keep him away from the other recruiters.)

Boxcar had an older teammate, **Joe Nuxhall**, another All-State fullback, and he liked contact, too. He made the All-Elbow Team when he was 16, playing Shop League basketball with the older guys, and learned football on the Hamilton sandlots where he was once stomped in the head by **Snip Huey**, a tough kid who happened to be wearing Australian lumberjack boots, the kind with the long spikes.

Hamilton Joe liked to tell of playing with a broken nose and in the 1946 Middletown game—an atonal moment if ever there was one—he got knocked into the tuba section of the Middletown band. Most of the time, though, he was the knocker, not the knockee, a trait that carried over into his pro baseball days.

The hardest hit T-Bone Malone ever saw—in the entire half century he played and coached—was delivered by his old Catholic teammate, **Jim Mense**. "We were playing Springfield Catholic and on a kickoff," Malone said, "some kid tried to block him. Jim ran completely *through* him and treaded over his body."

It helped that Mense was another of those large Hamilton kids. He was near 220 before he left high school, an All-Ohio defensive center. In the North-South High School All-Star Game of 1952, Mense blocked a punt, and the resulting two-point safety was the difference in the game.

Here's one definition of tough: In 1951, when Hamilton squared off against Middletown in the usual season-ending brawl, the local newspaper ran a related item. "**Don Brockman**," it read, "made a quick recovery from a gunshot wound in the foot and played good ball for The Blue." Even *weaponry* wasn't effective against the Hamilton guys.

It was the kind of Hamilton football that inspired **Harry Phillips** to say, upon being asked why he liked being a football player, "You walk out on that field on Friday nights and look up in the stands and there are whole gobs of people. Then you see the band coming around the corner a hundred strong, and you could hear them all over town. It was a beautiful sight. I usually left home at 5 p.m.for the game. I'd walk from Second Ward all the way to the stadium. People would holler at you from their cars. They knew who you were. They'd say, 'Hey, good luck!' You were proud to be a Big Blue football player."

In the 1950s, the Hamilton guys were recruited from all directions. West Point sent a coach out to recruit Mense and Malone. Mense wanted to go to Michigan, and Malone's parents badgered him about about how far away from home West Point was. Mense didn't get to Michigan, either. His mother, a devout Catholic, demanded that he play for Notre Dame, which he did, and magnificently. Irish coach Terry Brennan said his mid-1950s teams were built around Mense, his big center, and the Heisman Trophy "Golden Boy," Paul Hornung. Mense played in the 1956 College All-Star Game, and was drafted in 1956 by Green Bay. When he heard what the money was, he came back to Hamilton where he could actually make some.

The University of Wisconsin recruited Malone, too. He arrived at the Madison train station at 5 a.m. in the morning and the Wisconsin head coach—a former Ohioan named Ivy Williamson who was from a little pimple of a place outside of Toledo called Prairie Depot and had been captain of Michigan's 1932 national champion team—took Malone out on the lake for his first boat ride. Williamson told him he'd get a scholarship and live in a downtown hotel where he could work banquets for spending money. Malone was flattered by all the attention, but Wisconsin,like West Point, was a long way from home.

UC called and so did Xavier and the University of Dayton. UD was where his teammates John and Claude Chaney played. **The Chaney boys** were an entire backfield, and Frank Leahy said Claude could have been the next Johnny Lattner, the Heisman halfback who held Notre Dame's all-purpose yardage record for a quarter of a century.

In high school, Claude was known for running through the fences that surrrounded many of the football fields. Claude thought he ran faster with his eyes closed, so when he got into the open field, he shut his eyes. Thus with his speed and power, Claude menaced not only the opposition but the maintenance staff, as well. Somehow, though, Claude spurned Leahy and Notre Dame for the bright lights of UD.

Brother Ike was recruited heavily by Sid Gillman at UC. "Yeah," Malone said, "Gillman bought him a whole new wardrobe. I'd go over to Ike's house and store-bought clothes would be all over his room. Ike was older than the rest of us, though, and got drafted, so Gillman lost Ike *and* the wardrobe . . . ."

In Malone's mind was always this image of Cliff Wilke. It came from a photograph hanging in the cafe. As a kid, Malone sat in the back and did his homework while the old man drank beer and played cards. When the kid got tired of math problems, he wandered over and stared at the picture of Cliff running the ball. The first time he ever watched television, it was the Xavier-

Kentucky game, and there was Cliff, running the ball. And Martinkovic, toppling people over.

At Xavier, Malone had an injury-plagued career, but his 97-yard kickoff return against UC his senior year turned the game into a XU win, and he made the All-Irish/All-Catholic All-American Team. He arrived at Hamilton Catholic in 1957, just as **Lou Florio** took over across the street. Two years later, when old Hamilton High divided into Garfield and Taft, Lou went to Garfield, and while he had an assortment of players in the Big Blue tradition—for a time anyway—the handwrithing was on the wall.

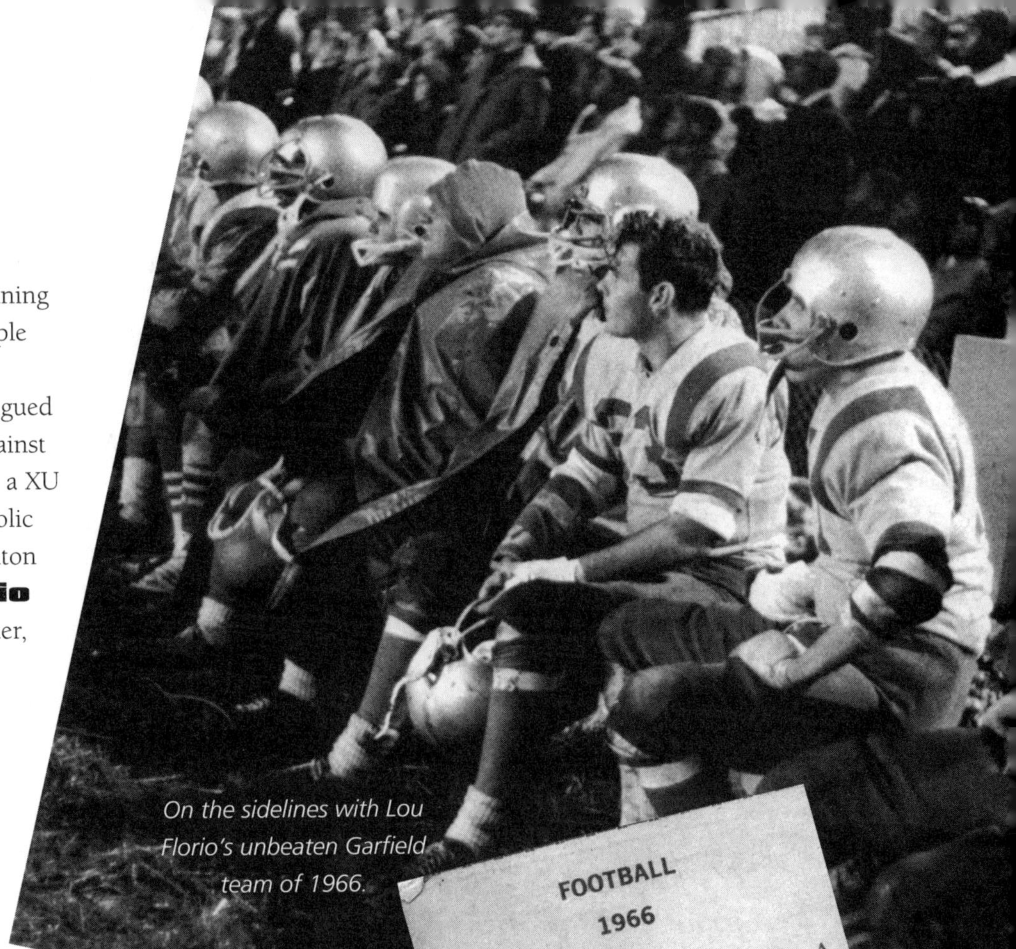

On the sidelines with Lou Florio's unbeaten Garfield team of 1966.

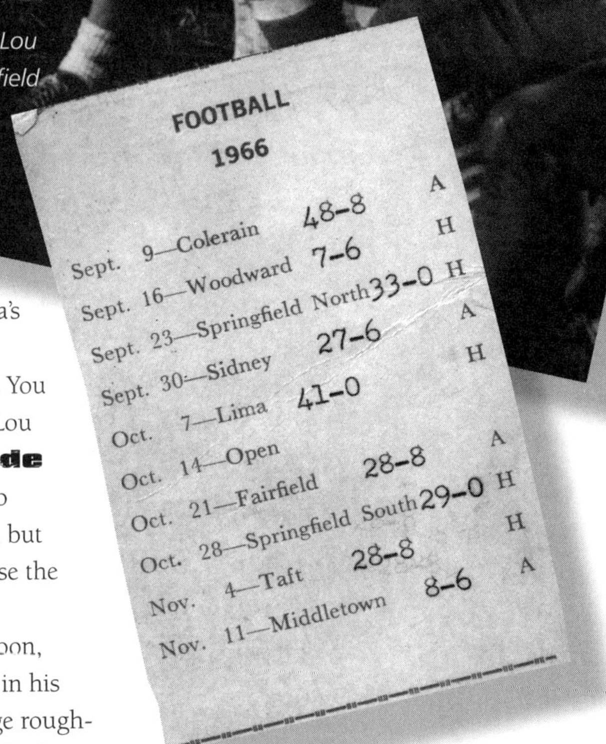

FOOTBALL
1966

Sept. 9—Colerain 48-8 A
Sept. 16—Woodward 7-6 H
Sept. 23—Springfield North 33-0 H
Sept. 30—Sidney 27-6 A
Oct. 7—Lima 41-0 H
Oct. 14—Open
Oct. 21—Fairfield 28-8 A
Oct. 28—Springfield South 29-0 H
Nov. 4—Taft 28-8 H
Nov. 11—Middletown 8-6 A

SOMETIMES HAMILTON HIGH and Garfield ran together in Lou's recollections, for he'd had so many good athletes. At Hamilton, for instance, there was **Spud Hornsby**, who many said was the best natural athlete ever to pass through the city. The Big Blue's original jock-of-all-trades, Spud—a scampering halfback—was the best player on the field when Hamilton upset a good Roger Staubach-led Purcell team and ruined its winning streak. Spud's basketball career was overshadowed by Jerry Lucas next door, but he played at UC with Oscar Robertson then tried out with the Reds where he lit up Reds pitcher Buster Freeman.

"Spud hit five straight pitches over the Crosley fence," said Lou. "So the manager, Deacon Bill McKechnie, says to Buster, 'Bear down.' And Buster says, 'I *am* bearing down.' The Reds signed Spud to a AAA contract but when it came time to leave for training, Spud never showed up. His dad said he'd gone fishing. I had to call McKechnie and tell him. He was flabbergasted. 'That boy just threw away a pro career to go fishing,' he said. Last I heard, Spud was running a marina somewhere in Florida . . . ."

And here a digression, because, well, it's another good Hamilton story. Lou was responsible for another great footballer, back in the mid-'50s, when he was Chuck Thackera's assistant at Hamilton High. You might say that Lou recruited **Clyde Murrell** to Hamilton High, but you'd have to use the term loosely.

One afternoon, Lou was sitting in his office and a large rough-hewn fellow walked in. "He needed a bath and his brogue was so thick I could barely understand him," Lou said. "He said, 'My name is Murrell and I ain't got no job and I need one.'

"I say, 'Well, this isn't an employment office,' and he says, 'I got me a boy, Clydie. You get me a job, Clydie'll play for you. He's 6-5, 250 pounds and he can play in yore backfield.'

"I say to myself, 'Well, all fathers lie about their sons

so I'll subtract ten pounds or so and a couple of inches.' But I knew this guy over at the safe company and I call over there and they say they might need a night watchman. I send Mr. Murrell over, he gets the job, and we get Clydie.

"When Clydie shows up I see that his own dad had missed Clydie by a good two inches. He weighed every bit of 280 pounds, and he was *fast*, too.

"It was at the end of summer and we start practice and Clydie gets homesick. All of the family aren't in Hamilton yet, and Clydie goes home to Kentucky. His dad had to bring him back.

"He didn't know much football, didn't even know how to get in a stance. But, my, he was something. We played him at tackle and when we got down to the goal, we ran him at fullback. He was a joy. I had him for two years, and the strongest thing I ever heard him say was 'Dadgummit.' He was a force to be reckoned with, though. He made All-State *and* All-American for me. Of course, there was only one school for him—Kentucky—and that's where he went . . . ."

One of the great—and most tragic—stories of the brief Garfield era was the story of **Raymond Pryor**, a big, quiet, polite kid who at one time lived in a Second Ward garage with no running water. He was polite, that is, everywhere but on the field. There, Lou says, "he was absolutely vicious. He played center and defensive end for me and we had to tell him over and over in practice, 'DON'T hit the quarterback.' When he forgot, we had to *replace* the quarterback. Ray didn't just want to hit you; he wanted to *bury* you."

Woody Hayes recruited him to Ohio State, and there was a Hamilton rumor that Ray had pulled a gun on Hayes. The real story, though, was this: the week before one of the Michigan games, Ray, even though he was following the instructions of his position coach, made Hayes mad, and Hayes punched Ray.

"*Nobody* punches Ray," said Lou. "So Ray punched Woody back. That evening about dark, Ray shows up at my house, distraught, and tells me what happened. The next morning, I drive to Columbus to see Woody. I explained that Ray was just following his position coach's orders. The position coach, Ernie Godfrey, was afraid to say anything. Then I say, 'You had no business hitting that kid.'

"Woody says, 'So what do you want me to do?'

"I say, 'Put him back on the team.'

"Woody says, 'Okay, but I won't apologize.'

"I didn't care whether he apologized or not. I was just thinking about Ray. He was still one of *my* kids, you see . . . ."

Ray was twice All-Big Ten, twice *Academic* All-Big Ten, and an All-American in 1966. Lou had a huge admiration for him because he completely overcame his Second Ward circumstances. There wasn't much doubt in anyone's mind that Pryor was of pro caliber, but he had no interest in pro ball.

He went to med school, then changed his mind and returned to dental school, acquired a second degree, and came back to Hamilton to practice. Not yet out of his 30s, he suffered a massive heart attack and died.

Ray's cousin, **Nate Lampley**, another Second Ward kid who got away—he's an attorney with Vorys, Sater, Seymour and Pease—remembered how everyone lived in Second Ward. "The 28th of the month comes around, you can't pay the rent, somebody offers a free month's rent, so you move. That's just what you did. We didn't think much about it. Ray's dad worked in hospital kitchens, probably never made more than $8 an hour. Ray was excessively quiet, no self-promotion, no twaddle. Remember Rosey Grier? Drop twenty pounds, lose the mustache and sideburns, and that was Ray. I thought I was a pretty good high school basketball player, but Ray would say to me, 'Your brain will outlast your jump shot.' I soon discovered that my jump shot wasn't that good anyway. It took me awhile to discover the true nature of Ray's accomplishment, though . . . ."

GARFIELD'S FIRST DECADE—THE 1960S—was a good one. Lou had **the Townsend brothers**, Mike and Willie, two-sport stars at Notre Dame; **Clint Spearman**, who was All-Big Ten at Michigan; and **Alex Davis**, a 280-pound lineman who lettered three seasons at Purdue. Davis was the mainstay on Lou's undefeated 1966 team, along with **Charley Pater**, the fullback/

linebacker. (Pater made Northwestern's first team as a freshman, but unfortunately for his coach—who discovered anew the old bromide about Jesus getting the good ones—Charley transferred to Cincinnati Bible Seminary, then earned a masters in history at Miami and became a Butler County judge.) The 1966 team's ableness was defense: the offense was usually taking over on the other side of the 50.

There was **Derek Howard**, too, class of '74, such a good athlete that Lou put him at quarterback after both regulars were injured, and Howard played there the rest of the season. "Pure athlete," Lou said. Howard's fumble recovery in the 1977 OSU-Michigan game preserved the Wolverines' 14-6 win and sent them to the Rose Bowl. Howard went twice, actually, and once to the Orange Bowl, too.

Lou had only three losing seasons at Garfield in the decade, but consider this: at old Hamilton High, there'd been but three losing seasons *in forty years*. By 1971, Florio had won 93 games. Then it took him three more years to get to 100—and that was followed by two winless ones. At one point, Hamilton had the longest losing streak in Ohio.

Lou had not suddenly become a lousy coach; the cultural circumstances had begun to intrude. Garfield's population fell almost by half. And as Lou pointed out, "We had the same schedule but not the same players. We were playing with 167-pound defensive tackles."

Industry—not only in Hamilton—was turning into the rust belt. The suburbs beckoned, at least for those who could get out, and the cities were turning against themselves. In towns such as Hamilton, the American pie now had smaller slices, if it wasn't off the table entirely.

There were many who'd never wanted Hamilton High divided. They thought that by creating schools on each side of town—tweed and cashmere on the west side, said Peter Davis in his book *Hometown*, dungarees and leather jackets on the east side—they'd merely created icons for the divide of race and class. When old Hamilton arose again in 1980 with the merger of Garfield and Taft, there was great rejoicing. And by the time the new century rolled around, **Ed Mignery**, one of Terry Malone's boys, had managed to get Hamilton into the state playoffs three times, but the Big Blue wasn't as big, and it was of a paler hue.

In that last quarter of a century, the Hamilton team to reckon

Larry Creach, muddy but unbowed, was Coach Florio's (at left) "Most Efficient Lineman" from his 1967 7-3 team.

with had been Malone's—old Hamilton Catholic had become Hamilton Badin in 1966, and T-Bone stayed so long they thought they'd just have him bronzed and stand him beside the statue of Mary in front of the school. The younger kids weren't sure whether he was a coach or a saint. Some of the older ones thought he was both, and still others thought he was neither. But in his seventeen games with Taft, Garfield, *and* Hamilton High, he got beaten once, surely occasion for sainthood.

When he retired—finally—in 2003, after forty-six years of coaching, he had a record of 360-177-8. It was the most wins in Ohio history—10th in the nation. Malone had a state title (1990), was runner-up twice (1978 and 1980), had eight unbeaten teams, and fourteen teams that lost one game.

Not bad for a guy who wasn't entirely sure he'd make it through his first season. He put nearly three dozen guys on the All-State teams, too, although you get the impression that he never had a player quite like **Doug Becker**, his fullback/linebacker from the early 1970s.

Becker loved Malone's hill, which he ran in sweltering heat wearing a weighted vest. He was 225 pounds, just over 6-0, and fast. "Once he was at a track meet with Talawanda preparing to run the 200," Malone said, "and the black kids were making fun of him, a *white* sprinter. He left everybody at the turn, and the black kid standing next to me said, 'Look at that effing white boy run!' Becker'd sprint in the hallways and belly slide through the doorways.

"He could literally take over a game, so much so that he'd shock the announcers. We were playing Dayton Carroll and he ran a kick back 95 yards and the announcer burst out, 'That's a MANCHILD!'

"Woody really wanted him at OSU, came down, and auctioned off Becker's tie in the cafeteria at lunchtime, then gave the money to the school athletic fund. Becker went up there but didn't like the place. Said in the locker room the guys wore that strange little underwear. Also Woody told him he'd play linebacker. Becker wanted to play fullback, so he went to Notre Dame and Ara Parseghian said he could play fullback. On the first day of practice, Parseghian moved him to linebacker. Woody had told him the truth, after all . . . ."

At Notre Dame, Becker played in one of the great Irish games, the 1978 Cotton Bowl rout of previously undefeated Texas, 38-10, which gave ND the national title. The Irish forced six turnovers and Becker had two of them. It was a team that featured a young Joe Montana and a handful of All-Americans, including Bob Golic and Ross Browner.

Malone had a fiery coaching style on top of a sturdy tradition built on Hamilton parishes that were little neighborhoods in themselves. Badin had been built on the west side—by a golf course, of all things—but its football maintained its old east side Hamilton Catholic roots, with a bit of ill-tempered Second Ward thrown in for good measure.

In 2008, **Jim Place** coached the Big Blue to a 7-3 season, its best in a decade, and Badin was back in the playoffs behind two first-team All-State kids, end **Scott Staarman** and a 210-pound, 6-4 quarterback named **Zach Toerner**, who led the GCL in passing with nearly 5,000 yards over the last two years.

It might not be the old days but then what was?
Hamilton is dead. Long live Hamilton.

—John Baskin, with Cathy Malone

That's Mense, Claude Chaney, and Malone in the middle of the circa 1956 Hamilton Catholic squad. (Ike Chaney is number 55). In bottom photo, it's HC at left and HHS at right, circa 1951. The gridders and coaches gather around Mayor George Ratcliffe as he proclaims "Football Week in Hamilton": coaches Jack Castignola, Mayor Bob Adams, Chuck Thackera, Byron Hollinger, Lou Florio, and Winston Metcalfe. The cheerleader, Garfield's Linda Thomas, is from the next era.

Rams

When the legendary Bron Bacevich (right) died in 1993 at age 86, ex-Moeller coach Gerry Faust finally admitted how he defensed Roger Bacon—from watching him play poker in the basement of Bacevich's Mt. Airy home. "Bron played the same way he coached," said Faust, "close to the vest. He never stayed unless he had a full house, and he always punted on fourth down. I knew how to coach against him from playing poker against him."

Coaches

Ballaban (left) and Dick Berning with their back-in-the-day St. X co-captains, Green and Boyle.

Bron Bacevich

Roger Bacon | coach | 1954-1973

54

BY THE TIME HE TOOK THE ROGER BACON JOB IN 1954, BRON BACEVICH WAS ALREADY A LEGEND IN ILLINOIS, WHERE, FOLLOWING A ROOKIE SEASON in Michigan, he had coached for twenty years, with seven undefeated teams.

In fact, that first autumn in St. Bernard, when the Spartans won only four games out of nine, would be the only losing season he would oversee in his forty-one years. By the time the winning was over and Bacevich was feted at the Cincinnati Convention Center, with Woody Hayes the featured speaker, he had piled up more victories—311—than, well, than Hayes, for one. He also had more than any other high school coach in history. He had more, in fact, than any coach of *any* kind, with four iconic exceptions. Joining Bacevich in the top five were Paul Brown, George Halas, Alonzo Stagg, and Pop Warner. That oughta tell you something.

And it's not counting the 502 victories he tacked on as a basketball coach, or the 400 in baseball.

Bacevich, widely known for his quotations, homespun or borrowed, succeeded so famously with equal parts inspiration and innovation. The popular coach made a concerted study of motivational means, hoarding pamphlets and periodicals and volumes of handy how-to wisdom and handing them out liberally. Jim Lippincott, who became the Moeller athletic director and a Bengals executive, said he once had two file cabinets filled with slogans and reading material that Bacevich had given him. Glenn Sample had a similar stash, and heaven knows who else.

Bacevich's love for the game—for all sports, in fact—may have derived from an appreciation for mere participation. He had been unable to take part in athletics until he got to North Central College in Illinois, obligated through high school to help out at his Lithuanian-born father's meat market. To Bacevich, organized sport was a veritable symbol of American privilege.

And so he thrived in it, and so did the programs

Bacevich, a legend elsewhere before he became one in Cincinnati, leads one of his early 1960s teams.

in his energetic charge. Ultimately, his stature took on national proportions. But it was on the local scale that the head Spartan was a redefining force. It was Bacevich, along with Jim McCarthy of Purcell, who put the GCL on its way to becoming Ohio's preeminent conference.

The only problem was that state championships were not in those days decided on the field. We'll introduce 1963 as an example.

That year, Bacon was coming off its second undefeated season under Bacevich, the first having occurred in 1958. For a Cincinnati school, however, going undefeated provided no assurance of a high ranking in the final state polls of the *Associated Press* and *United Press International*, which were dominated by voters from Northeast Ohio. Before the playoff system was instituted in 1972, no Southwest Ohio school was ever recognized as the best in Ohio.

In fact, during the last half of the 1950s, a period that included Roger Bacon's unblemished '58 team, no local entry even made it into the AP's *Top 10*. The streak was broken in 1960, when Purcell produced a perfect season and somehow stole into the rankings at Number 6. The polls, frankly, were a sham. Former Moeller coach Gerry Faust has expressed the unequivocal opinion that any number of McCarthy and Bacevich teams from the '50s and '60s were the best in the state.

In 1963, Roger Bacon actually had a chance to shove its prowess into the faces of the Northern critics. The Spartans' schedule included Niles McKinley, the top team in the state's highly favored region. Early in the game, the Roger Bacon quarterback separated his shoulder but played on. Later in the game, he attempted a field goal that John Kasselman, the Spartans' All-American guard, swears was good. But it wasn't called that way, and the game ended in a 0-0 tie. When the *season* ended, Bacon, sullied only by the tie, was ranked fourth by the *AP*. Niles McKinley, of course, was Number 1.

By such silliness, Bacevich never experienced the satisfaction of a state championship, mythical or otherwise. The closest he came was 1967, when his stalwart fellows, again unbeaten, were judged Number 2 by the *UPI* and Number 3 in the *AP* poll. By the time the playoff system was finally instituted in 1972, the great man was winding down his career. He retired in 1973—the year he was named National Coach of the Year—because, he said, his ailing hip hurt too much to properly demonstrate blocking techniques. Meanwhile, the local guard had already changed. Princeton and Moeller had emerged as Cincinnati's powerhouses.

But it was Bacevich who set the standard, for which he was judged by the *Cincinnati Post* as the Coach of the twentieth century. His chief challenger for that honor was Faust, who wouldn't have had it any other way. Faust has listed three principal heroes in his life—his father, Vince Lombardi, and Bron Bacevich.

Had the newspaper seen it differently, however, it

would have been forgiven by the great coach's legacy. As he once told his team, "The man who makes no mistakes lacks the boldness and the spirit of adventure."

Bacevich, in other words, wasn't afraid to lose now and then. Now and then, he actually did.

Tom Ballaban

St. Xavier coach 1953-1977

53

SEE, THE THING ABOUT THE FBI IS, YOU DON'T CALL THEM. IT'S THE OTHER WAY AROUND. IF THEY WANT. AS AN IMPATIENT YOUNG FELLOW JUST graduated from Xavier University in 1951, Tom Ballaban didn't really have a grasp of that.

He'd applied to the bureau and he hadn't heard back, so what the heck, he shot off a telegram to ol' J. Edgar Hoover requesting an answer, please. The response was on the order of "Beat it, kid."

Not knowing what else to do, he accepted a job at the downtown campus of St. Xavier High School, which he'd also graduated from. He'd played the available sports there, and after a wartime stint with the army, became quite a footballer—a Catholic All-American guard—at Xavier, which beat Arizona State to win the Salad Bowl in 1950, back before croutons were essential.

So anyway, St. X made Ballaban the basketball coach, and whaddya know, he was good at it, and liked it, and ended up coaching nearly everything at one time or another. Mostly football.

In football, the famously quotable figure won 142 games and eight GCL titles, outright or shared. He coached football at St. X long enough—twenty-seven years —that, well, two things. 1) They named the stadium after him. And 2), as only Ballaban could put it, "After thirty-seven years (counting everything), you start to *look* like a football."

Between teaching and what-all, Ballahan was actually at St. X for forty-five years, such a fixture that, as one student put it, "I thought Tom Ballaban was president of St. Xavier High School. It took me a while before I realized that he was only paid to coach football and teach us how Germany lost the war."

The long stint was attributable to the good time that

From left, it's Ballaban as the glad young warrior at Xavier University, then he's on the St. Xavier sidelines with assistant Dick Berning. The middle photograph was taken at a 1959 pep rally at St. X, and others on the St. X sidelines.

Ballahan unfailingly had (1968 was particularly pleasant, with a 9-0-1 record), whether he was teaching or coaching or playing poker with Gerry Faust, Bron Bacevich and the boys; and to his fond feeling for his workplace. "We have an ideal setting at St. X," he once said, probably at some sports banquet where he was speaking. "It's a pretty good situation with a select student body. What it means is that I've never been beaten up."

A high schooler would have been hard-pressed in that regard, however. Ballaban was tough enough to excel as an undersized blocker at Xavier U., and was drafted to play in the NFL. "I weighed 180 and played the line," he reflected years later. "I would have been a water boy in the pros, but the water boys weighed 185."

His closest brush with the big time turned out to be officiating in the Mid-American and Big Ten conferences, the effect being that he's the only person in Ohio inducted into both a coaching and officiating hall of fame.

The other effect is that it qualified Ballaban to argue with himself. For a laugh and a chicken dinner, he'd be glad to do it publicly.

Babe Bartlett

Elder coach 1927-1953

27

THE WEST SIDE OLD TIMERS—THE REALLY OLD TIMERS—SAY IT ALL STARTED WITH THE BABE. ODD THAT THE ELDER ATHLETIC MYSTIQUE would come from a St. Xavier High man, but there it was: big, handsome Walter Bartlett came from St. X, through an all-star stretch at Xavier University (he got his nickname there, being the youngest member of his class) and a brief stint of semipro football, and thence to Elder. And there The Babe remained, until a bad heart forced him into the stands.

He was only the second football coach at Elder, coached all the major sports, ran the intramural program, and taught Spanish. In all, he coached about a thousand games, and he won 577 of them, including six GCL titles in football. But it wasn't his winning percentage that was his Elder legacy (after all, he won only 16 more football games than he lost). His legacy was Elder itself; that is, Elder in its modern incarnation as a citadel of pride, tradition, and pure excellence. The Babe—having arrived so early—provided the school with its first formative definitions of itself.

Perhaps the first definition of itself was that Elder could always win. "We didn't believe another team could beat us," said Don Ruberg, who played basketball and baseball for The Babe and later coached at Elder. "You knew when Bart took the field with you as your coach that he thought he was going to beat the other guy. That made you think you *were* going to beat the other guy. I think that still permeates Elder today. Bart was the guy who started it."

He put not only attitude on the field but application. And his application was to be diligent and straight up. That was so because *he* was. He didn't swear, smoke, or drink, and if he had any beer in the refrigerator for his friends, then he bought it

He was The Babe and a Grand Old Man all at once, and before him, there wasn't much football.

somewhere out of the neighborhood, so as not to set a bad example for his boys.

He wasn't a screamer, either. The most he did was growl a bit. He didn't have to say much because he was a man who *implied* respect. Bartlett came to work in his old khakis, gray zippered sweatshirt, and baseball cap, looking, as sportswriter Bill Koch pointed out, "like a character from an old black and white sports movie."

On game days, though, he wore a suit and tie and a hat, which he used to signal plays. When he lifted his hat, Elder passed. His hat stayed mostly on his head because in those days nobody passed much. (The pass was still regarded as, well, a bit *flagrant*, the kind of gesture people might make when they didn't know any better.) So if Elder won the coin toss, The Babe would kick, and his defense took the field first because it was the defense that set the real tempo of the game. Sometimes he punted on third down to give his defense field position.

He coached the great Hoernschemeyer, who might have been the best player in the history of Cincinnati prep football, but his larger pleasure might have been coaching his own son, Jimmy, another Elder great who was a first team All-State center and went on to play at Notre Dame. The Babe won the school's first GCL title in football, and he helped institute both Elder's Thanksgiving Day series with Western Hills and the building of The Pit. He was also a father figure to several generations of Elder kids, and while he taught them winning he also taught them *how* they should win.

Elder and The Babe, as someone pointed out, was a match made in Purple Heaven. In his own painstaking way, he had laid the groundwork for one of Ohio's most enduringly competitive athletic programs. The kids might not know *him*, but they all recognized what he left them.

THE MILES OF BILES

Ed Biles was of course disappointed when, before he could even earn a letter, an injury cut short his career at Miami University. Biles had been a 12-time letterman at Reading High School—a member of a state championship baseball team in 1946 and the first Blue Devil enshrined in the school's Hall of Fame—and he had looked forward to playing for Woody Hayes, at first, and then Ara Parseghian.

But he recognized, even then, that Miami was a breeding ground for football *coaches* (his teammates included Bo Schembechler and John Pont), and *that*, thanks to the influence of esteemed Reading coach Ken Powers, was why he had taken his schooling to Oxford.

It was a good plan. While still a teenager, Biles began assisting Parseghian. By 1953, while working on his master's degree, he was an assistant coach at Woodward High. By 1954, at the age of 22, he was the Bulldogs' head coach. Then it was off to Xavier as freshman coach, and in 1961, just weeks after turning 30, he became the Musketeers' head man.

At X, Biles was the only coach who offered a scholarship to receiver Danny Abramowicz—who in 1969 led the NFL in catches—and in 1965, his Musketeers peaked at 8-2.

By the end of the decade, he had embarked on a bounce-around NFL career that finally produced a head-coaching position in 1981, with the declining Houston Oilers. It lasted just over two years.

"I've been a punching bag," Biles said at his final press conference. "I've been in the eye of the hurricane for two and a half years. I've had enough."

Except, not quite. There was some more bouncing around to do, all the way up to 2005, when H.P. Patterson, owner of the Cincinnati Marshals of the National Indoor Football League, approached him during a Bengals game and told Biles he was just the kind of guy he was looking for.

"What do I look like?" Biles replied. "A Mafia hit man or something?" He took the job, which proved to be more problematic than the one in Houston, and shorter-lived.

Counting Xavier—and not counting the Oilers, who moved to Tennessee and assumed a different name—Biles had now coached two defunct teams. Reading, however, like Miami, was still going strong.

Ron Bird

New Richmond coach 1969-2002

69

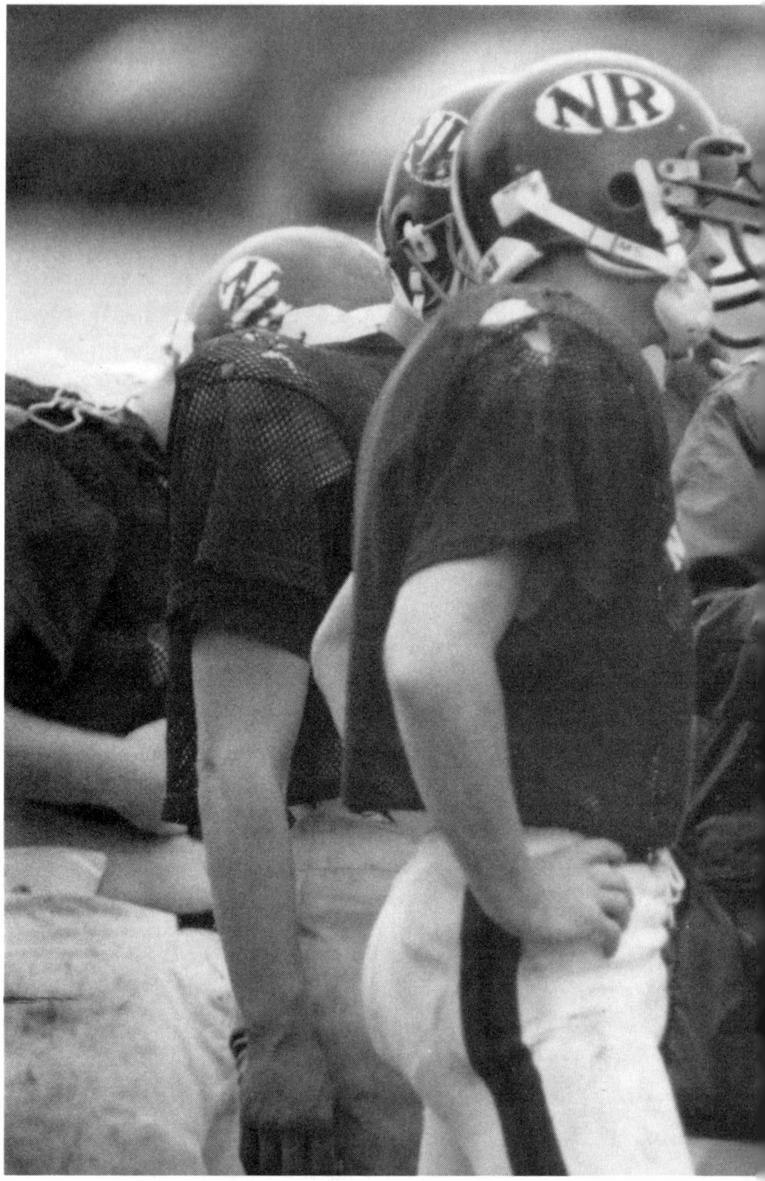

RON BIRD PLAYED DEFENSIVE END FOR BEAR BRYANT, AND YET THERE WAS LITTLE RESEMBLANCE IN PERSONAL STYLE. HE PLAYED WITH JOE NAMATH, and there was no resemblance whatsoever.

"He really is the most aw-shucks guy there ever was," said one of his former players, Jamie Corrill, who became a coach himself. "That's not an act. It might sound like a cliche, but I think that by not overcoaching, Coach Bird is really sort of a genius. He keeps it so simple, and what he does is so right."

What he did, he did at New Richmond High School for thirty-four years. What he did was win 209 games, the most in Clermont County history and twenty-third in Ohio history. Of those 209 victories, the vast majority were won with a wishbone offense. The entire majority were won without the benefit of two-a-day practices in the preseason.

What Bird did was understand his community. When he took over in 1969, New Richmond was largely agricultural, and most of the rest was hardscrabble by the river. The farm boys were needed for chores in the summer, and the Kentucky-born coach—a graduate of Holmes High School in Covington—made certain that football was not an imposition on their families.

And yet, it became a source of pride to those families nonetheless. In 1982 and again in 1991, the Lions completed their seasons undefeated. Dwayne Woodruff's team in 1974 would have been undefeated, too, if not for some creative officiating in Hillsboro. Todd Benzinger's team in 1980—one of the few that threw the ball around, given the gifts of its quarterback—would have been perfect, as well, if, in the final 7-6 loss to Williamsburg, it hadn't been too frigid and rainy for Benzinger to grip and fling the football.

It seemed that Bird was destined to coach quietly. The '82 team finished third in the regional rankings when only two made the playoffs. The '91 team finished fifth when only four qualified.

Finally, in 1999, the playoff system expanded to eight teams per region. New Richmond was the eighth. London was the first. The opening game was in London. New Richmond won. It was the first time a team from Clermont County had ever won a playoff game.

The next year, the Lions became the first team in the county to win 11 games. Two years later, Bird retired quietly.

Happy to still help in whatever way he could, he drove the bus to track meets and girls basketball games. Then, with his son as the middle-school principal, he coached the New Richmond seventh graders.

He coached them quietly. And so right, of course.

"By not overcoaching, Coach Bird is really sort of a genius."

Tom Crosby

Mariemont coach 1978-78

TOM CROSBY CAME BY HIS EXEMPLARY RECORD HONESTLY: HIS FORMATIVE YEARS WERE SPENT ON A PAIR OF BOB LEWIS'S WYOMING TEAMS IN THE LATE 1960s when the Cowboys were the area's scourge, torching the opposition so badly that whole populations hid in their basements on weekends after a date with Wyoming. A linebacker in the Cowboys' seven-diamond defense, nobody touched him. "It made me think that I was good," he said. And he was—first team All-City.

He went on to play at Ashland and got his first head coaching job at Purcell when he was just 23. The 1970s were tough years on Hackberry Street, with upstarts such as Moeller siphoning away players and creating championships elsewhere. Crosby did put a little bite into the "Assassins" in 1976 when Elder overlooked them. Trailing at the half, the Cavaliers scored twice in the fourth quarter and upset the Panthers, 19-13, and at The Pit, too.

Weary of being overmatched in the GCL, Crosby went to Mariemont as an assistant and by 1978 was head coach there, too. He was a traditional guy, not much for fads, although—shades of his old coach back at Wyoming—he'd pull something out of his coach's cap upon occasion, maybe even resurrect the seven-diamond defense. And along the way were two of the most unusual state title games on record.

He reached the ultimate game in only his third year, taking his 1980 team to the Division IV final to play Garfield Heights Trinity. Moved out of Ohio Stadium because of wet conditions—OSU wanted to save the field for the next day's OSU-Michigan game—the game was played on a local high school field, and on the same night as the much-ballyhooed season's conclusion to the popular soap opera, ***Dallas***. It was the "Who Killed J.R.?" spectacle, and people came to the stadium with portable televisions, wanting to miss none of the drama either at home (Columbus) or abroad (Dallas).

What followed was a game as suspenseful as any television production, and the fans didn't have to wait six months to learn the outcome. Mariemont fell behind but with nearly five minutes left in the game, the Warriors pulled to within five points (19-14) on a four-yard pass from quarterback Chris Bowman to tight end Greg Shelander. Garfield turned the ball over on downs, and Mariemont was in business again, quickly heading into Garfield territory where a swing pass moved the Warriors from the 35 to the five.

But with 1:25 left and in perfect position, Mariemont ran for no gain, then suffered a sack and an interception.

"Not in the cards," lamented a doleful Bowman.

It took Crosby awhile, but he brought Mariemont

back to the Big Show in 1995, which was no surprise to anyone.

The year before, the team had been bolstered by the enrollment of a tough 6-1, 210-pound linebacker named Lee Wilschevick who'd played two undefeated years at Lockland, then moved in with his father, who lived down the street from Crosby. Questions that any transfer might face were heightened by the differences between Lockland and Mariemont. Would the kid from the gritty valley school adjust to the model suburb of Mariemont?

Fortunately for Mariemont, he did, and as a junior in 1994, he helped his new team go undefeated through the regular season before suffering a second-round playoff loss. For his work, Wilschevick was Division V's Defensive Player of the Year in Ohio. As a senior, Wilschevick's presence helped the Warriors do it again; they went through the 1995 regular season as Ohio's Number 1 rated D-V school, unbeaten again. Rolling through the playoffs, the Warriors faced Lisbon David Anderson in the finals at Paul Brown Stadium in Massillon.

And this time, Mariemont appeared to be unbeatable. The Warriors led 21-7, twice stuffing Lisbon drives inside their own 5, the last one as time expired in the half. But late in the third quarter, unquenchable Lisbon was back inside the Mariemont nine. A fourth-and-one sneak appeared to fail, but the officials' spot gave Lisbon the first down by an inch, and two plays later, the game turned.

"Interesting spot," Crosby said. "But those things happen...."

The game was tied, went into overtime, and was tied again. In the second OT, Mariemont—stopped with a fourth-and-one-and-a-half near the 11—kicked a field goal for the lead. Lisbon, however, drove for a score and the 34-31 win. It was only the sixth OT game in finals history, and it tied the longest game in Ohio's championship history. The game also set a record for most points scored in a D-V final, and another for its nine combined TDs.

"You can only take so many body blows," said Wilschevick. Tug Orr, the school's all-time leading rusher, was held to 59 yards while Lisbon's All-State quarterback, Zach Williams, threw for 295 yards and three TDs. "Losing this feels like having something special stolen from you," Wilschevick said.

Still and all, Wilschevick had played four years and never lost a regular season game—40-0 (44-4 overall). He was named Ohio's Defensive Player of the Year for a second straight time, and when he graduated and his position was taken over by Matt Dunning, Dunning *also* become Ohio's Defensive Player of the Year, a near-unprecedented hat trick for Crosby and Mariemont.

Crosby by now is closing in on 200 wins, most of them at Mariemont where he has been for nearly half of the sixty years the Warriors have been playing football. He's been seven times city coach of the year, the league's coach of the year five times. He's had four teams that lost only one game, he's been in the playoffs nine times, and in the state finals twice.

Surely it's a disappointment that he hasn't won it all, but he's coached in two of the most exciting title games in Ohio's history. How many others have done as much? Since playoffs began, in all the categories other than AA or Division I, the smaller Cincinnati teams have been in the finals just ten times. And only three schools have brought back titles—Purcell, Wyoming (two), and CAPE (three). It took nearly forty years to do that. Even a less than generous fellow could see that Crosby was in elite company.

Kerry Coombs

Colerain coach 1991-2006

91

WHEN THE 2004 SEASON BEGAN, A LOT OF FOLKS, INCLUDING COACH KERRY COOMBS, BELIEVED THAT COLERAIN HAD THE BEST TEAM IN THE STATE. But that, Coombs well knew, didn't mean diddley.

For most of the previous decade, the Cardinals, with their handful of undefeated regular seasons, had been the best team in Cincinnati for sure and quite possibly Ohio. And yet, there wasn't a single state championship to show for it.

Instead, there were playoff defeats for three consecutive years to Elder, which, on the last two occasions, went on to win state. And there was the eternal hangover from 1995, when Coombs' club clobbered Brunswick in the state semifinals on Saturday, only to find out on Monday that it had been using an ineligible player all season. After the OHSAA considered the case, Colerain's record flipped from 13-0 to 0-13. There would be no title game for the Cardinals.

And there wouldn't be one in 2004 unless, after another perfect regular season, Colerain could finally beat Elder in the postseason, which it did 38-3 in the first playoff game (holding the proud and twice-defending champs to minus-22 rushing yards), and get by Moeller in the regional finals, which it did 34-6, and put away Worthington in the semis, which it did 34-3. With a 35-0 shellacking of Centerville in the mix, as well, that made the score 141-12 against some of the best teams in the state, with Canton McKinley coming up.

Coombs, a Colerain graduate himself and thoroughly possessed of the spirit, had carved out a popular tradition of standing on a bench or trunk and delivering a hoarse-throated, postgame pep talk to all the fans and parents who wished to gather 'round in the front rows. And after the McKinley game, he had to ask, “Were you nervous at the beginning? . . . Me, too!”

Understandably so. Right off the bat there was a fumble, and then another, and then another—four fumbles in six snaps, if you can believe it—and early in the second quarter the Cardinals trailed 10-6. They calmed down after that, and the final score turned out to be 50-10, the most lopsided in the history of the state championship, which tells you why a lot of people think that Colerain's 2004 team was just about the best that Ohio ever saw. Especially the defense.

That team sent five seniors to major college programs, including Coombs' son, Brayden, a defensive back. And a couple years later, their coach took the same route, accepting an assistant's position at the University of Cincinnati.

Some saw that as a peculiar move, Coombs being the local personification of a leader. He had not only built a sustainable team that carried the banner for Greater Cincinnati's public schools, but the perpetually moving coach had also brought a camaraderie to the Colerain community, enabling it to be known for something other than the big mall on the busy avenue.

He did all that not with play-calling or schematic cleverness—Colerain always ran the option, and Coombs never even attended the offensive game-plan meetings—but with organization and motivation. And good help. To wit, Coombs' offensive coordinator, Rick Haynes, was with him from the beginning. During one pregame session, the head coach yielded the floor to Haynes, who appealed to the young men that the evening's opponent might have niftier helmets and nicer cars than the Cardinals, but they didn't have *this* . . . and he reached into a cooler to pull out a cow's heart he had picked up at Stehlins Meat Market.

All the while, Coombs was smart enough to know that if you're going to make the players arrive at school by 7 a.m. every morning to watch film, you'd better get the parents on your side. He was thoughtful enough to decide that, if you're going to hold the kids responsible for lifting weights on a regular basis, it would go a long way to have all the assistant coaches in the room, too. And he was sharp enough to see that, if he could rally kids from all corners of the district, he'd have an exceptionally deep and diverse roster of athletes to work with.

In the summer of 2004, understanding that only dysfunction

Coombs was at Colerain for sixteen years and averaged a remarkable ten wins a year.

or the like could keep his talented team out of state-title contention, Coombs, Remembering the Titans, took the Cardinals to Thomas More College for a three-day summer retreat in which black players roomed with white and backs with linemen.

It certainly didn't hurt, although it's hard to say whether the bonding had as much to do with the spectacular season as the ground gaining of Mister Simpson, the quarterbacking of Dominick Goodman, or the run-stuffing of nose tackle Terrill Byrd, who was named the national Defensive Player of the Year.

At Colerain, the stars and speedsters just seemed to keep coming, the effect being that, in Coombs' sixteen seasons there, the Cardinals averaged a remarkable 10 victories. But it required an enormous store of energy on the part of the caffeinated coach, who was also a counselor and assistant principal.

To him, then, the chance to kick back and coach defensive backs at a major college, and to perhaps galvanize an entire metropolitan area as he had the northwest portion of it, sounded pretty darn good. In 2007, he showed up in Clifton with a smile and a bit of swagger.

"My first practice," he said later, "I tried to be mister cool college coach. It just didn't work. I was miserable."

By the second day, the veins in Coombs' neck had regained their familiar popping-out look. And by the end of the season, when the Bearcats led the nation in interceptions, he was feeling a *whole* lot better.

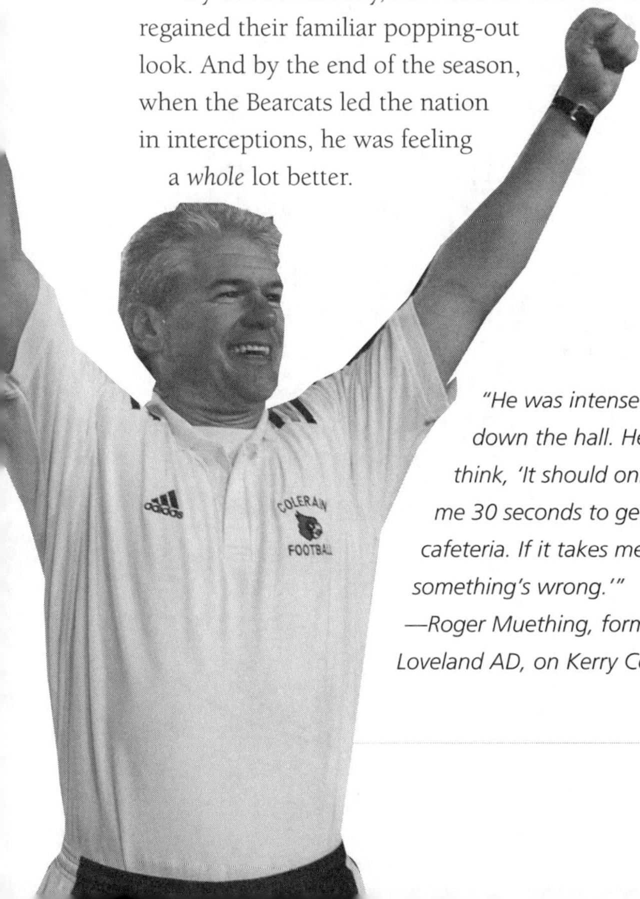

"He was intense walking down the hall. He would think, 'It should only take me 30 seconds to get to the cafeteria. If it takes me 45, something's wrong.'"
—Roger Muething, former Loveland AD, on Kerry Coombs

Tiger Ellison

Middletown coach 1945-1962

45

IT WAS ONE OF THOSE TRANSFORMING MOMENTS, SUCH AS THE WRIGHT BROTHERS STUDYING THE AERONAUTICAL PATTERNS OF BUZZARDS THEN going out and inventing flight, which in its own peculiar way, was what happened in Middletown, Ohio, in the mid-1950s.

That was when Tiger Ellison found himself on the downside of his season, on the wrong side of his gridiron ledger. "There was hell to pay," Tiger said sadly, "and we were behind in our payments." Driving morosely home one afternoon, he came upon a gang of neighborhood striplings playing *their* game of football, and he stopped to watch. As he watched the grade-schoolers, he became aware that, well, let Tiger tell it....

"The passer was a slender, willowy young man with a rubbery arm," he said. "He would scramble around big-eyed and expectant as he studied his receivers cutting downfield right or left or deep or short—according to how the defenders were covering them.

"Those youngsters were simply doing what comes natural, letting the defense determine their pass cuts:

He right, I left!
He left, I right!
He come, I go!
He go, I stay!

"Boom!" said Ellison. "There it was—THE LONESOME POLECAT!"

The next morning he unveiled his new idea to his staff.

"Absolutely crazy!" yelped Stan Lewis, his line coach.

His coaches seemed to think that Tiger had—in his own words—"slipped over the hump."

Tiger, however, was undeterred. Over the objections of staff, best friends, and even his own qualms, he installed the new offense that put on the field—for the first time—a formation whose name he borrowed from basketball: The Run and Shoot.

What he wanted to do was take his average kids and stretch the field so that their opponents, in turn, would stretch *themselves* trying to cover. Red-dogging linebackers, burned by footballs tossed in all directions, would think twice about blitzing. Gang-tackling would be more difficult.

Keep in mind, this was Woody Hayes's era. The best formation was one that functioned like a piece of earthmoving equipment. It worked in tandem with a water buffalo at fullback, a quick but sturdy halfback (accent on *sturdy*), and a quarterback who wore a crewcut, hightops, and knew his middling place in the scheme of things.

"For years," Tiger said, "we hid the football. We hid it from our opponents. We hid it from our fans. We almost hid it from ourselves. The ball was only incidental, a necessary evil...."

> "When the chips are down and there's HELL TO PAY, can you pay it?
> —Tiger Ellison.

Tiger, meanwhile, rediscovered the ball. He held it up to the light. He tossed it in the air a few times, to see if it might actually stay aloft. His motto was, "Go reckless, stay loose, and enjoy life." He sent out four-receiver sets (*four!*) who adjusted—like the striplings on the vacant lot—to whatever the defense did. Even the running back was often motioned out wide.

"Nobody could stop it," said Ellison. "We couldn't stop it *ourselves*."

In one game, Middletown scored 98 points against Portsmouth and afterward, Tiger's third-string quarterback became the top scorer in the league. The Middies

Tiger (at QB) with his 1948 Middletown staff—coaches Walker, Lewis, and Mason. The play: Gangster Pass Right.

The Big East

They were, frankly, from the wrong side of town. There are two high schools in the Forest Hills District, which straddles Beechmont Avenue, and neither—unlike Colerain or Elder from the west side (not to mention Roger Bacon, Wyoming, and St. Xavier from the central section, or Princeton, Moeller, and Reading from the northern reaches)—had a whole lot of heritage in this sort of thing.

Swimming, yes. Soccer, certainly. Cross country, to be sure. But this was football, of all sports, and this was **Anderson vs. Turpin**, of all schools, for the Division II regional championship.

To be fair, Anderson had beefed up its football program considerably under longtime coach **Vince Suriano**, who left a year too early—following the 2006 season—to accept an assistant coaching position at the College of Mount St. Joseph. Upon inheriting an unaccomplished program, Suriano had taken the Redskins to the playoffs seven times between 1992 and 2003. The trouble was, Anderson was a Division I school, which meant that its early playoff games would come against the likes of St. X or Princeton or Big Moe.

"The goal line is north and south. The cheerleaders are east and west. Please don't get the two confused."—Coach Vince Suriano, advising

So much for the season.

But in 2007, when **Jeff Giesting** took over as head coach after nineteen years as an Anderson assistant, the Redskins were reclassified as Division II. Even then—even ranked 12th in the state—they played the season in the shadow of the other Forest Hills school.

By that time, **Rob Stoll** had rebuilt Turpin into a team to be reckoned with. Five years earlier, the neighborhood rivals—both members of the Fort Ancient Valley Conference—had stopped playing each other because the Spartans had been utterly unable to compete with Anderson. But when the 2007 playoffs rolled around, Stoll's team sat undefeated and top-ranked in the region.

The two east-side squads rolled through the first couple rounds of the postseason, at which point they came, momentously, upon each other. Anderson, after losing two early non-conference games to Division I opponents, had won seven in a row but remained a considerable underdog in the biggest game of its history; and Turpin's, too. Following a weeklong tussle of yard signs and T-shirts, most of the township motored up to Princeton Viking Stadium for the Battle of Beechmont.

As expected, Turpin had the best of it for most of the night, pulling out to a 20-10 lead in the third quarter. But Anderson rallied for a touchdown to make it close. And then, with two seconds remaining in the game and the ball on the Turpin 1-yard line, the Redskins scored again—a keeper to the left by quarterback **Daniel Rod**—to make it even, 23-23.

The extra point remained. **John Howard** converted it, Turpin's fairy tale was aborted, and Anderson was in the state semifinals.

Elijah Storey, a cousin of Seattle Seahawks star Shaun Alexander, carried the ball for 209 yards that night, and he would top 200 again in the semifinal victory over Ashland.

The championship game was against Louisville, and this time it was 6-7 wide receiver **Nick Truesdell** who carried the day, with 199 total yards, as the Redskins, by a score of 31-25, brought the state football title to Anderson Township for the first time. There, the trophy would be housed three miles from the other school that could have won it just as easily.

scored 70 against Greenhills, 66 points—twice—against Hamilton Taft, and 60 against Dayton Fairview.

"We made every pass look like a run," Tiger said, "and every run look like a pass."

He counted up and found the Middies had averaged almost five TDs a game, at the rate of one TD every 10 plays for four years in a row. They punted 1.2 times a game and one of those seasons the Middies had a great punter who got to kick the ball only ten times the entire year.

It was, in fact, the beginning of the modern-day spread offense, and in all of Tiger's entire eighteen-year reign, there was only one losing season, even though it *was* made even more ignoble by the fact that it became Middletown's first losing season in thirty-eight years. Tiger's 3-7 season in 1954 was the first losing one in what might be called the modern era. Even that old Middie master, Elmo Lingrel, in all his twenty-two years at Middletown never had one. (The master went 149-32-19; his 1936 team was undefeated and unscored upon, while the opposition managed but three TDs against his 10-0 1934 team.) Losing seasons were so rare in Middletown that when they *did* occur, the locals had them appraised by the *Antiques Roadshow* staff.

Tiger, himself, acquired a 124-46-9 record, then in the mid-1960s joined the Ohio State staff, hired by Woody Hayes in a vastly prescient moment. The old Buckeye warhorse, who previously considered the aerial football as an invention of Satan, had just joined forces with the game's new Beelzebub.

Odd that a high school coach would so quickly have such an effect on the game, but word got out. Perhaps it was the new momentum in the postwar culture that required faster movement everywhere. Perhaps it was the fact that helmets were beginning to have facebars, which meant the reluctant keepers of football's conservative biases—i.e., Woody Hayes—might finally be ready to put air *under* the football, as well as in it.

Whatever it was, Tiger was at the forefront. Woody and Tiger did win a national championship, in 1968, but the pass, even in its most minimal display, was always regarded by Woody in the same way he might regard a suspicious rash. Mouse Davis used the Run and Shoot at Portland State in the 1970s, though, then took it into the CFL, and the USFL. It was the basis for Jerry Glanville's no-huddle Redgun Offense for the Houston Oilers, and, finally, it found its perfect expression in the Arena League where again Mouse Davis' name was associated with it.

Mouse, however, always gave credit where it was due. He said all he did was read Tiger's book—*Run-and-Shoot Football: Offense of the Future*. (The book, by the way, is still available somewhere online, for a mere trifle, $189, which would likely have Tiger spinning in his huddle.)

"You basically steal everything you do and then do what you do and make it your own," said Davis, with a most respectful nod to the old Middletown guru. "You never really initiate anything in football—well, you do, but it's usually the little things. What we did was very new and different to the NFL and football, and it's been a good thing, as far as I'm concerned."

Wherever Tiger is, he'd no doubt be pleased. And if he's where the Middletown folks think he is, he'll have the Big Guy in the pocket, his arm up, and at least four of the Disciples will be spread wide....

Gerry Faust

Moeller coach 1960-1980

60

FORTUNATELY FOR GERRY FAUST, AND FOR MOELLER HIGH SCHOOL, THE CREDENTIALS TO BECOME THE NEW INSTITUTION'S FIRST FOOTBALL COACH did not include sturdy legs, a silky speaking voice, or proficiency in spelling. And so it was that, at the school's first pep rally, shortly after he took the job in 1960, Faust's ungraceful gait carried him to a central spot where all could hear his raspy rallying cry for M-U-E-L-L-E-R!

Beyond that, however, the Dayton native—son of Fuzzy Faust, the estimable coach at Chaminade High School—brought along qualifications so comprehensive and cutting edge that not even he could have reasonably recognized the impact they would have, the domination they would forge, the envy they would engender, the championships they would pile up or the position to which they would take him.

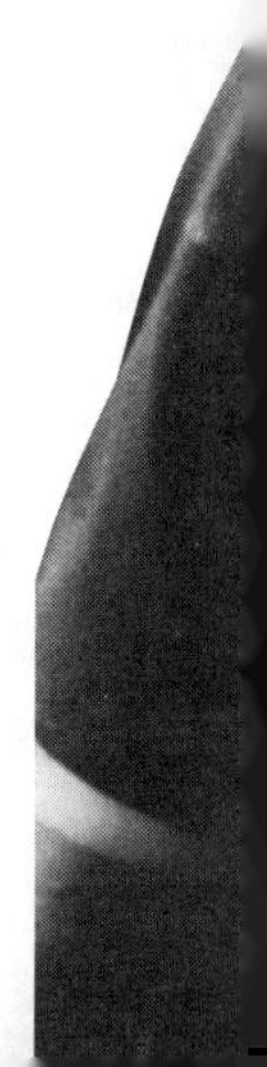

By the time he left Moeller in 1980 for the Catholic university whose fight song he used to sing while riding his bike to and from fifth-grade football practice, Faust's Crusaders had won 40 consecutive games in the Greater Cincinnati League, eight straight titles in a conference that was fast becoming the best in Ohio if not the country, five Ohio championships, four mythical national titles, and scholarships for nearly 300 players. More than a few of those young men had landed at Notre Dame, which surely played a part in Faust, to the astonishment of legions, doing the same.

The Irish were ridiculed by some for hiring a high school coach, no matter how absurdly successful. But then, Faust had never been a head coach of any kind before he started the Moeller program. That aside, it's nevertheless evident, in retrospect, that the leap required of him was practically intergalactic; that South Bend was simply too far removed from the prep scene that Faust had made-over with the Holy Steamrollers, as the Crusaders came to be called under their coach's conspicuously Catholic watch.

His eighteen-year legacy (it wasn't until 1963 that Moeller fielded a varsity team) was defined by much more than championships, or the 70 victories in his final 71 games. What Faust had done was elevate high school football.

And yet, he hadn't consciously intended that. It hadn't occurred to Faust, when he accepted the job after helping his father for two years at Chaminade, that he could hoist his suburban program to a standard previously imagined only in special places like Massillon, Ohio.

But while Fuzzy's boy was not blessed with blazing feet, he bore the gift of boundless energy and a genius for passing it along. Unpretentious and unabashed, Faust was a people coach, and the people, in turn, responded winningly to his unceasing handshakes and Hail Marys.

He somehow made the community hungry to help him. The team's first blocking sled was built by a couple of players' fathers, one a carpenter, the other a plumber. Volunteers sold ads for the annual program until it reached 200 pages. Faust's assistant coaches numbered eighteen at one point, most of them unpaid. The players were cared for by twenty-four team doctors, all of them unpaid. The result was immediate success; but nothing like it would become.

Then, in 1972, the first year of Ohio playoffs, Faust was watching Princeton High School play in the semifinals against mighty and undefeated Massillon, the team that Paul Brown made famous, the flagship program of the state's Northeast region, which had utterly monopolized the football polls that for so long had settled the matter, rendering the Southwest a

Faust, said one writer, was a master promoter whose talents generated a $1.4 million sports complex.

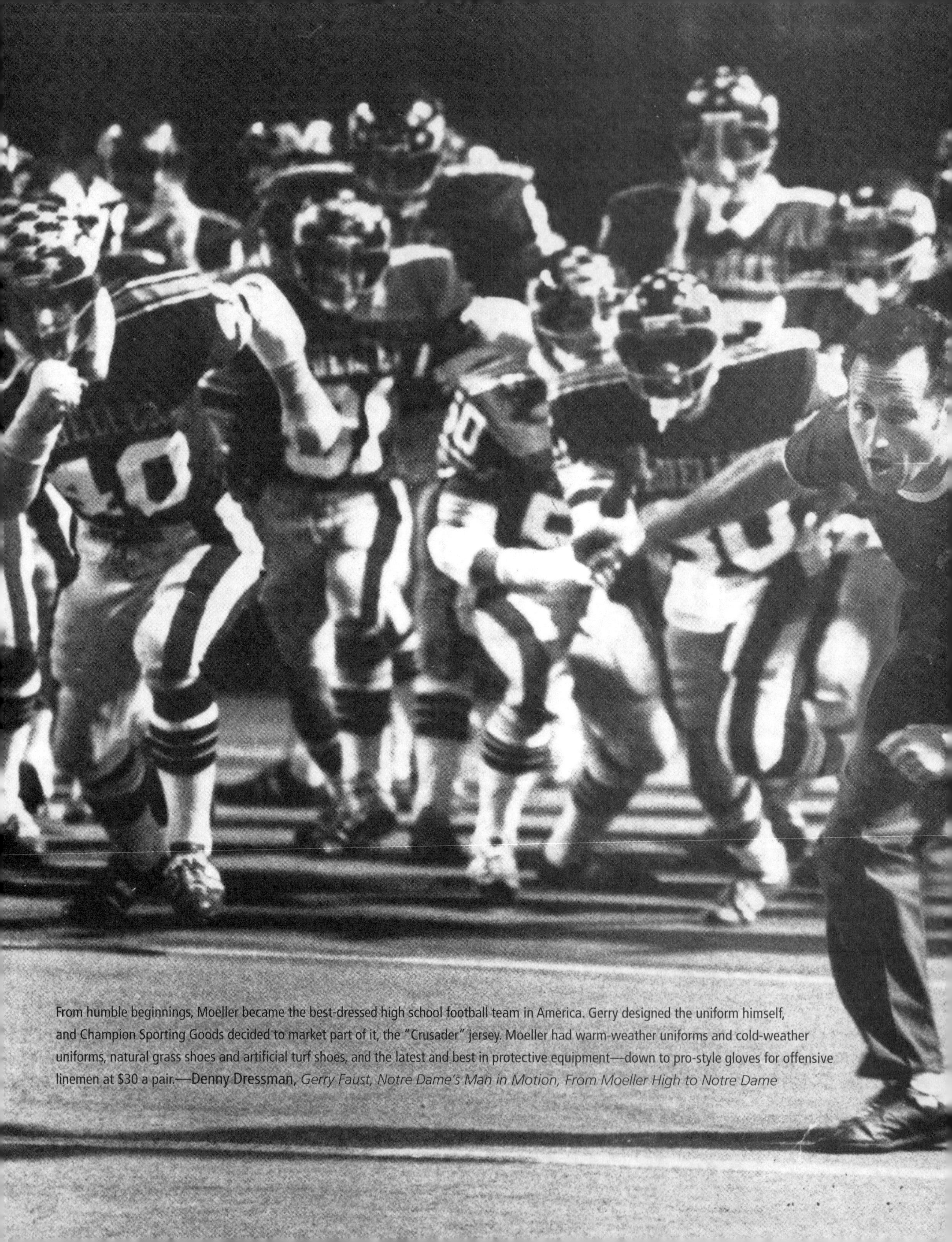

From humble beginnings, Moeller became the best-dressed high school football team in America. Gerry designed the uniform himself, and Champion Sporting Goods decided to market part of it, the "Crusader" jersey. Moeller had warm-weather uniforms and cold-weather uniforms, natural grass shoes and artificial turf shoes, and the latest and best in protective equipment—down to pro-style gloves for offensive linemen at $30 a pair.—Denny Dressman, *Gerry Faust, Notre Dame's Man in Motion, From Moeller High to Notre Dame*

provincial afterthought. Princeton won that game. To Faust, it was an epiphany.

He was sitting in the stands with his offensive line coach, Dick Baratteiri, and decided then and there—all the while underestimating his reach—that Moeller could and surely would play at the state level. "We're going to go back home and build ourselves a weight room," he told his assistant. "Because, I'll tell you what, we're going to be here from now on."

At that time, the Crusaders' weight room was still in the basement of assistant coach Bill Clark. The players worked out with sewer covers and soup cans filled with concrete. By 1972, however, school alumni were in sufficient number that their ranks included plumbers, carpenters and bricklayers, and enough of them to build a weight room in ten Saturdays.

Three years later, Lakewood St. Edward was driving toward a title-winning touchdown when Faust turned to the players on his sideline and instructed them to pray to St. Jude, the patron saint of lost causes. With less than two minutes remaining, sophomore Bob Crable fell on a St. Ed fumble and, by the score of 14-12, Moeller had its first state championship. Two years after that, it had three. Three years after *that*, it had five.

As severely as the Steamrollers laid out Ohio, they came down even heavier on out-of-state opponents. Faust sought out the best national competition available, playing powerhouses from Texas, Michigan, New York, and Pennsylvania. During his tenure, Moeller never lost to one, the closest call being a 33-13 victory over Brother Rice of Birmingham, Michigan.

Not surprisingly, the ambitious scheduling prompted questions about Moeller's perspective. Faust's methods were challenged and even resented in a manner much the same as Brown's were when he built the Massillon machine. Like Brown at the pro level, Faust, by prep standards, became an early practitioner of film study. He kept his players busy year round and saw that their other extracurricular activities didn't compromise their commitment to football. He was a tireless fundraiser. He even made his linemen take ballet lessons.

Meanwhile, he impressed upon his players Catholic theology and ritual at every turn. Prayer was a constant part of the program. His bench was virtually a Hail-Mary chorus. And every Thursday night during the season, Faust would accompany his captains up the six flights

In 1979, Penn Hills of Pittsburgh, Number 11 in the nation, played Moe in Nippert Stadium. Moeller won 30-13.

on playing big moe:
a true-life adventure

Only a power outage at Alumni Field or a bus breakdown could have saved us from Moeller, which in 1969 was in just its seventh varsity season under future Notre Dame head coach Gerry Faust. We didn't know much about this team from Cincinnati other than what we learned from game film and our coaches. By the time we discovered that this all-boys, Roman Catholic, college preparatory school prepped fast, super-sized players for Division I football, it was too late to hunt down the athletic directors or any of the other parties involved in this criminal act of scheduling.

"No one else thinks so," Coach Knowles told the *News-Journal*, "but I think we'll beat them." And we, the boys of **Wilmington High School**, believed him. I know I did, until I walked out to midfield for the coin toss and was introduced to the Crusaders' captain, Vic Koegel. He seemed to be a foot taller than I was, and about a hundred pounds heavier. The Ohio State-bound linebacker reached down to shake my hand, curls of manly golden hair glistening on his forearm. Somewhere under my helmet, the germ of trepidation stirred itself. I began to feel like the steward in charge of entertainment on the *Titanic*.

We played the game before a standing room-only crowd. Moeller brought twelve busloads of fans after requesting 2,500 pre-sale tickets. The Crusaders scored on their fourth play from the line of scrimmage when Mark Daniel, the son of Dave Daniel—an All-Ohio end at Wilmington in the 1940s—waited for our defenders to pour in on him before flipping a short pass over the middle to another Ohio State recruit, fullback Randy Keith, who carried the ball into the end zone. It was the first live screen pass I ever saw. Before the night was over, I would also see a draw play for the first time.

The score at halftime was 20-0, and Cousin Gary was unfazed. "I've got my man right where I want him," he boasted. After our first play on offense in the second half, he returned to the huddle and confessed, "I've got a new man." Faust's liberal substitution policy did not go unnoticed. "Kindness on the part of the Moeller coach prevented the score from being worse than the final 40-0," reported the *News-Journal*.

Knowles said we had received a lesson in the laws of physics. "Their line was made up of big boys with no fat. You just can't move a 230-pounder with a 150-pounder." The newspaper did not identify our teammate who said, "I feel like I faced the Green Bay Packers," but he spoke for all of us. Moeller finished 10-0 and ranked third in the final Ohio Associated Press Class AA poll behind Upper Arlington and Elyria. Seven state titles and five national championships would follow in the 1970s and '80s.

—*Michael Graham*

Captain Koegel, Ohio State-bound, through Wilmington.

of concrete steps leading to the Church of Immaculata in Mount Adams, saying a Hail Mary on every step, as the custom is. Late on Friday nights, usually alone, he returned.

Faust's piety, though, was eyed suspiciously by those who were put off by what they viewed as Moeller's excesses. Inevitably, the coach's critics condemned him for recruiting practices they presumed were illegal. Athletes came to Moeller from as far away as Northern Kentucky. The Francisco brothers, superstar running backs, moved into a house that Faust partially owned. But no violations were ever revealed, and through it all Faust never shied from pitching the school he openly loved. Part of his job at Moeller was to recruit students from parochial grade schools with a slide show and inspirational chat. Mindful that nearly 3,000 boys in Moeller's district played some form of organized football from the third grade through the eighth, he naturally mentioned the accomplishments of his widely celebrated team, though it probably wasn't necessary. So deep was the player pool, and so compelling was the prospect of wearing Moeller's colors, that an average of 220 fellows dressed every year for Faust's freshman, reserve, and varsity squads.

The result of all the above was a monstrous, pulsing organism that trampled the known parameters of high school football, a phenomenon documented by the likes of NBC, ABC, *Sports Illustrated*, *Time* and the *Wall Street Journal*. Under Faust, Moeller ripped off seven undefeated seasons. It shut out 90 opponents. And on a Friday night in 1977, when Monsignor Farrell of New York City brought its 27-game winning streak to Nippert Stadium and Tom Seaver was pitching against the Braves at Riverfront, it outdrew the Reds. It also pummeled Farrell, 30-0. And made more than $21,000 in the process.

That year, on the way to one of Big Moe's national championships, Crable, a ferocious linebacker, led a defense that gave up just 38 points all season, playing perhaps the roughest schedule in the country. It may have been Faust's best team, though some might prefer the one the year before, the first so-called national champ, led by quarterback Tim Koegel. And some might opt for Faust's farewell club, the undefeated 1980 team.

It was appropriate that Faust's final opponent would be Massillon, for the state championship, at Nippert Stadium. And that, with the superstitious coach wearing the sock with the hole in the toe and the floppy blue and gold hat that he had sported for every title game, Moeller would have its way, 30-7. The Crusaders' 33rd straight victory gave them an astonishing, eighteen-year varsity record of 174-17-2.

The next day, Faust was named as the most improbable head coach in Fighting Irish history. For years, it had been a running joke that when Faust signed his latest Moeller contract, he would say to his principal, Lawrence Krusling, "I love Moeller, but will you let me out of the contract to go to Notre Dame?"

In the beginning, it had seemed like a silly question. Things like that just didn't happen.

But then, neither did programs like Faust's.

A Faustian Chronology

1953—Future dynasty-maker Gerry Faust is recruited by Xavier, Ohio, Dayton, Harvard, and Notre Dame, where he is invited to a campus workout when such practices were legal. "Quarterbacks over here!" a coach yelled. There were nineteen quarterbacks in line, including Len Dawson and Paul Hornung.

"Holy Mackerel!" he said. "What am I doing here?" When his turn came, he said to the coach, "Sir, you don't really want to see me throw."

He became, instead, a quarterback at Dayton, then was offered a job in the Canadian Football League. He chose coaching instead, and two years later he was at Moeller.

1960—Gerry Faust starts the Moeller program with a freshman team. Though the school colors are blue and gold, the Crusaders dress in black jerseys and pants donated by the University of Cincinnati. Moeller's first varsity season in 1963 produces a 9-1 record.

In Moeller High's formative season, players not only wear Bearcat hand-me-downs but old helmets bought from the University of Dayton at two bucks each.

1974—Moeller footballers begin first ballet class, to the chagrin of manly players who previously thought a grand jeté was a European import. By 1980, a hundred players are participating in the classes, the choreographer, Jack Louiso, could predict, with 80 percent accuracy, the next season's starters, and Woody Hayes tried to hire him. Said Louisa, "I only work for one coach."

Late 1970s—"Gerry Faust is, all at once, all of the time, a devoted son, true friend, thoughtful husband, concerned father, and an uncommonly devout Catholic. He is not afraid to hug his father, kiss his mother, and tell them 'I love you' whenever they might meet; he sends his wife thank-you notes for all she does; and he never forgets to write to his friends on every occasion of personal importance to them. Always his cards and letters are inscribed 'JMJ' for Jesus, Mary, and Joseph, a carryover from his grade school days; always they end with 'God Bless You.' Gerry begins every day with early morning Mass wherever he is—and did so even while honeymooning in Miami Beach. And he spends every day thinking football, even during the annual family vacation. His world is a hundred yards long, with a goal post at one end and an altar at the other."

—Denny Dressman, *Gerry Faust, Notre Dame's Man in Motion, From Moeller High to Notre Dame*

1980—Gerry Faust, the man who built Moeller into Big Moe, leaves for a larger parish—Notre Dame—thereby exchanging America's top high school program for America's most famous collegiate one. He says he has dreamed of this day while riding his bike to and from CYO practice in the fifth grade and that Notre Dame was the only place that could tear him away from Moeller. After five largely unfortunate years in the bigger big time, Faust is excommunicated, ending up in that Protestant purgatory, Akron.

Ben Hubbard

Seven Mile to Lockland coach 1960–

60

SOMETIMES AN INTRODUCTION IS ALL IT TAKES. GROWING UP ON A NEW MIAMI FARM, SIXTH-GRADER BEN HUBBARD STAYED AFTER SCHOOL AND hung around so often watching his brother practice football with the junior high team that the coaches gave him some equipment and let him practice, too. Since he couldn't play in the school games, it was football in its purest form. There was nothing else but the game, perfect training for a boy who would grow up to spend his entire life in it.

When Hubbard was old enough, he played guard and linebacker for Seven Mile, one of the dozen or more small places that played football in pre-consolidation Butler County. Then he received a football education playing Air Force service ball, making the All-Air Force Team. He played a year at Miami, too, before lean finances propelled him into a teaching job—back at Seven Mile—where he was also a football assistant.

It would be the first stop on a peripatetic career that would take Hubbard through a Cook's tour of southwestern Ohio coaching jobs and a varied lifetime of football that even retirement couldn't quell. He was the gridiron equivalent of the western figure riding into troubled towns to restore order and a decent offense.

He started the modern-day program at Blanchester, returned to Seven Mile (he says he was "traded"), coached at Talawanda and Lockland, helped put Colerain on the path to its later glory, and won a state title at Fairfield.

Over time, he evolved a small handful of principles, one of them being that every coach should have the opportunity to start a program. (Note: "opportunity" may also be read as "affliction.") Hubbard's first shot at managing from the turf up occurred at Blanchester, where football was such an alien concept that not only had no one *played* the game before, many of them had never *seen* a game. First, he had to teach them how to dress, for the pads were mysterious, particularly the

Hubbard: A Cook's tour of southwestern Ohio coaching jobs and a varied lifetime of football.

tailbone protectors on the old-school hip pads, which most of them—as teenagers overly concerned with their tender selves—thought went in *front*.

Blan scrimmaged Mason that year, another new program, and Hubbard thought it was probably the worst scrimmage in the history of prep football. Neither team's players knew quite what to do, and the coaches were all over the field, trying to show them. At some point, Hubbard looked up to discover that the benches of both teams had cleared and the players were embroiled in a gigantic fistfight.

"We put both teams on the same sideline," Hubbard said, "which wasn't smart. But you could tell the players had no experience. They all had their helmets off swinging at each other. Anyone who's ever played knows that in a football fight you keep your helmet on."

Three stops later, Hubbard found himself at Lockland, the smallest football school in the area but the one with the best stadium. There, Hubbard's teams competed regularly against much larger schools: Princeton, Anderson, and Norwood. His kids were tough, though, and they played hard for him. There might be about a hundred boys in the student body, and he'd have seventy or eighty of them on the team. Melvin Lunsford and Mike Sensibaugh, both of whom would go on to the NFL, played for Hubbard.

Hubbard is fond of the 1960s and 1970s, an era he recalls as a more collegial time. Coaches, even competing ones, tended to share information. Trying to figure out Bob Lewis's seven-diamond defense at Wyoming gave many coaches problems. But when Hubbard asked Lewis about it, Lewis not only explained it but gave Hubbard a book and a film on the defense.

"At least then I knew how and why I got beat," Hubbard said ruefully.

In the mid-1970s, Colerain came knocking. Hubbard wondered about giving up a successful tenure at Lockland to attempt yet another program-building. That was what he did, though, and his first year, one of his assistants pointed out the arm on one of his sophomore kids. The kid was Tim Clifford, and by the fourth game, Clifford was the starting quarterback, the kind of instinctive player who made things happen.

A basic football rule is: Do not roll out and throw the ball across the field, for only bad things happen. In one game, however, Clifford rolled out, threw across

the field, and hit receiver Jeff Krouse in the end zone. And he threw the ball *underhanded*. The resurgence in Colerain football may have begun with that single play.

There was another memorable Colerain game, at Fairfield. Being near where Hubbard grew up, his old classmates were members of Fairfield's chain gang. When Fairfield ran out to a 21-8 lead, the gang was in high gloating mode. Then with 1:18 left, fourth and eight on his own 8, Clifford began to move Colerain miraculously downfield, scoring in 35 seconds.

On the first play after the kickoff, Hubbard blitzed. He told his nose guard to stick his helmet where the ball was going. The kid did just as he was told and—classic moment—hit the back and quarterback at the handoff,

Hubbard and defensive end Steve Speh.

the ball shot back into the end zone, and Colerain recovered for the winning TD. On the sidelines, Hubbard's chain gang buddies collapsed in disbelief.

He would, of course, coach Fairfield next. Once again, he found himself at the helm of a program that needed to turn upfield, and in one of the toughest leagues in the state, the Greater Miami Conference. He began by beating Badin, Fairfield's longtime nemesis, and concluded by winning a state title.

Going into the 1986 season, Hubbard had a lot of players back from a playoff team. A regular season win over Princeton was key, and although no one expected Fairfield to advance past its first-round opponent, Milford, Fairfield upset a good Dayton Dunbar team, 19-9, beat Worthington 17-14 on a late field goal, and ended up in the title game against seemingly invincible Lakewood St. Edward.

The conventional wisdom then was that the parochial school always won. But led by quarterback Scott Hormann, who accounted for all three Fairfield scores—one TD run and two TD passes to John Pfeifer, his best friend and next-door neighbor—Fairfield beat both conventional wisdom and St. Ed in a 21-20 come-from-behind win.

The newspapers called Fairfield's win "improbable." Hubbard liked that. To him, football was all about converting the improbable into the probable. His entire career, it might be said, was such a journey. So it was entirely in keeping that he would spend a year coaching a Finnish pro team, the Helsinki Wolverines. Maybe Finland was a reaction to spending his life within twenty miles of Seven Mile. Just one more improbable.

The football was good in Finland, the game basically the same, although each team was allowed to have only three American players. The Americans had to wear large A's on the back of their helmets, which Hubbard thought served as targets for the locals while allowing referees to ignore late hits and other infractions. Still, he liked Finland enough to coach there twice.

Always, though, there was an abiding fondness for the smaller schools. He thought it took more creativity to coach smaller. At Fairfield and Colerain, the coach managed a *program*. At New Miami, for instance, the coach managed *players*—and did some of his own janitorial work. He didn't always have athletes at every position, either.

The challenge, he said, is to hide one's own weakness (bad players) while trying for an edge on the opposition (finding out where he's hiding *his* bad players).

In 2008, he had 184 wins—well over 200, if his wins in Finland were counted—and went into the Ohio Football Coaches' Hall of Fame. For most coaches, that would be a career. So where is Hubbard? Back at Lockland, with his Panthers looking for the playoffs again.

And since Hubbard is immune to retirement, you might look for him sometime soon at a school near you. If it's small enough, or aswim in the gridiron doldrums, or in need of a bit of grid-lift, Hubbard's your man.

The Jones boys

Middletown players/coaches 1904

04

Howard Jones and his brother, Tad Albert Dwight Jones, were both from Excello when Excello was a place one could actually be from, and both played at Middletown High at the dawn of local football. The Middies were coached by a Yale man, Bill Oglesby, '02, a hometown boy who had been so inspired by reading Frank Merriwell that he left the banks of the Great Miami and headed east, only to learn, sadly, that his gridiron abilities wouldn't take him past the Yale freshman team. He was better at baseball where he *did* make the varsity and in time returned to Middletown only to find that the Middie boys had no coach, no substitutes, and certainly, no advantage. It was a situation ready-made for a Yale man.

So the local boys went to work for Mr. Oglesby, finishing the season with ten players and 143 points to the opponents' 22—most of those in their only losing game.

"They played football the way I learned it at Yale," Mr. Oglesby said at the end of the season, "and their opponents *didn't* play it that way."

He also said, "my two halfbacks were honeys," meaning none other than the Jones brothers, who played both ways, of course, equally good on defense. Mr. Oglesby could spot only one flaw about them: They were thinking of going off to *Princeton*.

Mr. Oglesby, as he put it, "talked Yale to them," and they saw the folly of their ways. Later, he would say, proudly, "I look upon them as my gift to my school." And with good reason.

The Jones boys, Tad and Howard: Excellence from Excello.

The brothers never played in a losing college game; their record was 28-0-2, the Yalies claimed three straight national titles, and Tad was named Walter Camp's All-American quarterback in 1907—the second bonafide All-American from Ohio (*see page 90*). Howard labored more obscurely at end, and while Tad went on to a successful coaching career at his alma mater, Howard was the real coach in the family.

Each of them had a straightforward way with words, and each was idealistic, serious, and somewhat square. Tad was known for telling his charges, "Gentlemen, you are going out to play football against Harvard. Never again in your life will you do anything so important." Howard, talking to his boys, was a bit more blunt: "Lick a man," he said, "and hold your position."

Howard coached Ohio State for a year (he was 6-1-3 in 1910), but his real accomplishments happened at Southern California where in sixteen seasons he went 116-36-13, coaching USC to seven conference titles, five Rose Bowl wins, and two national championships (1931 and 1932, while four of his other teams ended up on one national title list or another). His 1931 come-from-behind win over Notre Dame is still considered a classic.

Down 14-0 in the fourth quarter, USC won 16-14. MGM filmed the game, then rushed it to Loew's State Theatre, the premier LA movie house, and the film—first time a football game had been presented as a full-length feature—broke all the theatre's records.

Spartan and work-obsessed, Jones thought of little else but football. "I prohibit the boys from hanging around poolrooms," he said, "because the air in such places is usually bad."

He also thought pool didn't afford enough exercise, he was suspicious of dancing (a boy could become heated then cool off too fast, he explained), and he disliked profanity (his libertine exclamation was, "Dadburnit!"). His most profligate habits were chain-smoking and putting his players' names on gambling chips, which he used to move around and devise new formations (red chips for linemen, blue for backfield, white for opponents).

He was open-minded and versatile, even though he wasn't regarded as a grand innovator. Howard liked his linemen to have once played in the backfield, he wanted his quarterback to be a multiple threat, and he was a firm proponent of playing clean—almost to a fault. Playing Stanford once, Jones learned that Stanford's All-American running back, Bobby Grayson, had an injured knee. He told his players not to hit Grayson's bad leg, and they didn't.

It was something that might have come straight from Frank Merriwell. There was always that somewhat mystic Yale connection. The Merriwell creator once said that he chose the name this way: "Frank for frankness, merry for a happy disposition, well for health and abounding vitality." Their old Middie coach, Oglesby, had been introduced to Merriwell and Yale and, in return, he had introduced the Jones brothers to Yale. From then on, their game was truly one of abounding vitality.

Bob Lewis

Wyoming coach 1956-1978

56

After a while it got so absurd that Bob Lewis would actually try to let the other team score. Score once, anyway. That was after the 1962 season in which his Wyoming Cowboys didn't give up a single stinkin' point.

The collective score that year was Wyoming 446, Everybody Else 0. And toward the end of it, the boys in blue were so consumed with the pristine point total that, well, Lewis didn't like it. So he decided that, the next year, unless the first game was surprisingly close, he'd see if he could let a touchdown sneak in to take the pressure off. The first game wasn't surprisingly close. None of them was.

There was also 1959, when opponents totaled a whopping six points against Wyoming's famous seven-diamond defense, which featured only four players,

Big Red's Last Hurrah

It was the last game for that Hughes High institution, Mr. Big Red Schoolhouse himself, Red Krueck, one year shy of three decades at Hughes. The game that Friday night in 1945 was an institution, too—the 25th conflict between Hughes and arch-rival Withrow.

And *that* institution was about to inspire another, the big pre-Withrow bonfire rally at Hughes. It was the game Red had been both anticipating and fearing. The anticipation because he had a new stratagem up his sleeve, the fear because, well, it was his last game.

The crowd was estimated at 15,000 as the Big Red "battled its way across the green turf like an orchestra playing in perfect harmony, the sound of their music drowning out the feeble roars of the hapless Tigers." And when the mixed metaphors had subsided, the Big Red had won one for Red, 21-7.

Said the reporters from the yearbook staff, "Every trick that the master mentor had in his repertoire came out that night. And Red Krueck had wrought a miracle. In one week, he had given his team an entirely new set of plays, every one attesting to the genius of their inventor."

In two years, Coach Krueck would be dead, at 52, of a failed heart. It seemed that he had given it to Hughes, and there wasn't much of it left.

configured like a sparkling gem, behind the line of scrimmage. And there was the disaster of 1964, when the bad guys got *14!* Of course, those were both undefeated seasons. In Lewis' twenty-three years at Wyoming, there were 11 undefeated seasons. And 21 losses.

Mind you, Wyoming was no juggernaut when Lewis, a native of Portsmouth, arrived from Marysville, Ohio, in 1956. There was a *long* tradition, the program having started in 1919, and there was an undefeated, unscored-on team in 1941 (182-0).

To this day, Wyoming ranks third all-time in Ohio in winning percentage, behind only Moeller and Massillon. But the Cowboys hadn't won a conference championship, or even beaten Lockland, in fifteen years. That changed immediately.

The new coach was a Marine sergeant in sneakers. Said Bob Goodridge, quarterback and star of the historic '62 team, "We used to drill and drill and drill until the boredom became intolerable."

If winning was also boring, then the Cowboys must have been out of their skulls with the old ennui. Under Lewis, there were streaks of 43, 27, 24 . . .

Of course, things being how they were in those days, none of this early winning resulted in a wire service state championship, or anything close. When the Ohio playoffs were instituted in 1972, Wyoming suddenly became a contender. In 1977, it won the AA title.

But a strange thing happened in '78. The defending state champs were 10-0, with an average score of 39-5. They were Number 1 in both the state polls. At that time, however, only one team from each region advanced to the tournament. Wyoming had the second-highest Harbin total in all of Ohio. Unfortunately, the highest belonged to Hamilton Badin, which played in the same region. Badin won the playoff spot by .12.

What made it even harder for Lewis and his team to take was the fact that, had all the season's games been included in the computer rankings, they would have finished higher than Badin. The difference was in the points Wyoming was awarded for beating Western Hills. The Cowboys did not receive the extra value that should have been theirs by virtue of Western Hills beating Elder, because that game occurred on Thanksgiving Day, after the playoffs had been set. Even so, a representative from the state called Lewis to congratulate him for making the playoffs, not realizing that Taft had beaten Hughes, which padded Badin's point total just enough for the Rams to overtake Wyoming.

The whole process soured Lewis so profoundly that he promptly left Wyoming—left Ohio—and accepted a job at Conner High School in Boone County, Kentucky.

Five years later, he won a Kentucky state championship with Conner.

KLONNE'S CRUSADE

In his first year as Moeller head coach in 1982—a season removed from Gerry Faust's last before leaving for Notre Dame (Ted Bacigalupo was the man in between)—**Steve Klonne** went undefeated, beat Massillon for the state championship and brought home a *national* championship in the process. In his fourth season, Klonne led the Crusaders to their last state title, taking the measure of Canton McKinley in the final. What happened after 1985 was that the rules were changed and parochial schools were no longer permitted to play student-athletes who lived outside the parish boundaries. The two events—Moeller's last state title and the downsizing of the player pool—were no doubt closely related.

And yet, somehow, after 19 remarkable years, Klonne's performance wasn't satisfactory to Big Moe's administration. His 169-48 record wasn't satisfactory. His two state championships, his five title-game appearances, his nine GCL crowns, all unsatisfactory.

Klonne, a St. Xavier graduate, had come to Moeller in 1978 as one of Faust's assistants, and was soon promoted to defensive coordinator. As a head coach, he pulled within six victories of overtaking Faust, a point he reached in 2000, when the Crusaders were 9-1 during the regular season but lost to Fairfield in the first round of the playoffs. A few months later, Klonne was told that he could coach at Moeller for only one more year.

First, he said he would. Then he changed his mind. He took an assistant's job at McNicholas, and in 2005, at age 59, Klonne became the Rockets' head coach. A couple years later, Moeller fired his replacement, Bob Crable.

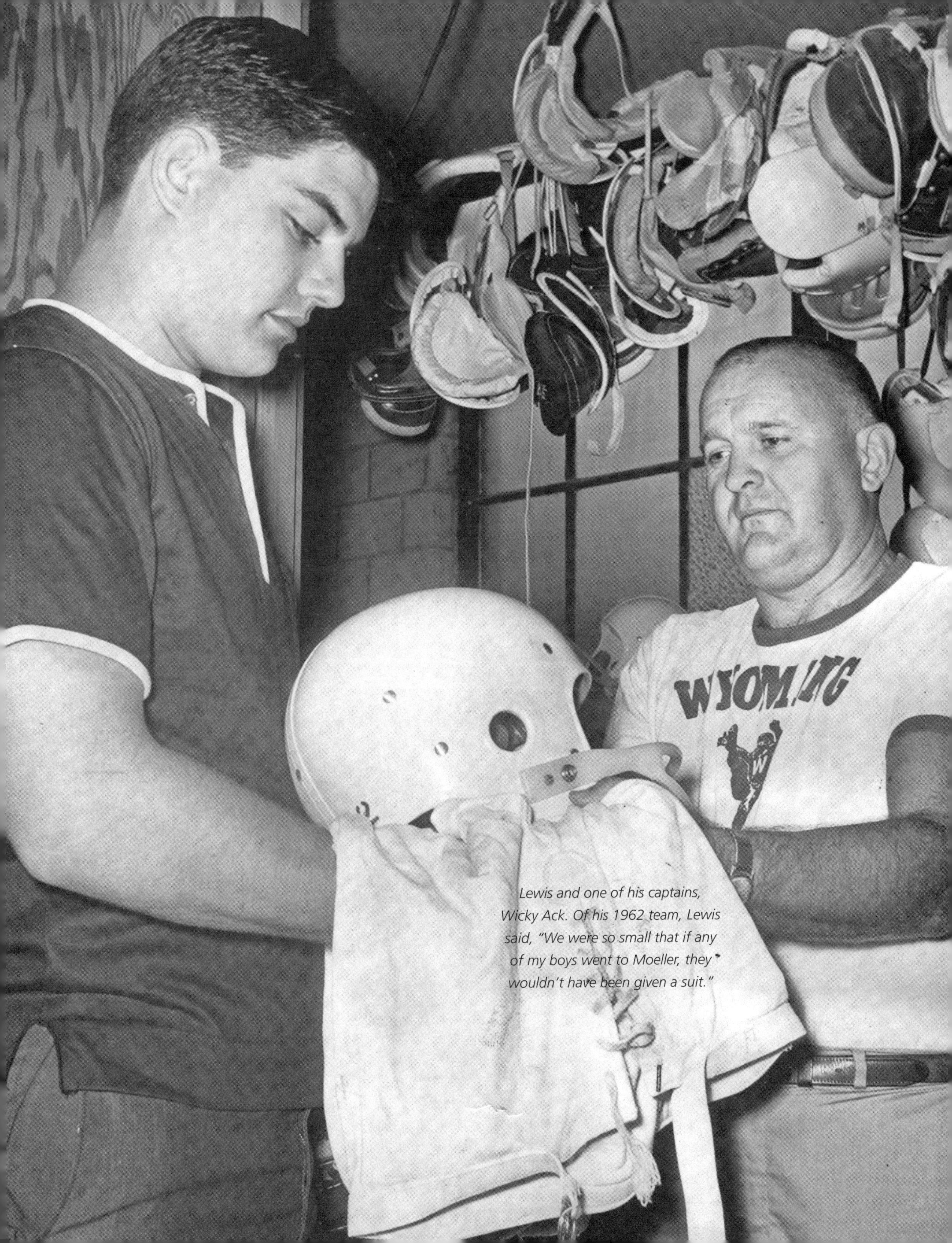

Lewis and one of his captains, Wicky Ack. Of his 1962 team, Lewis said, "We were so small that if any of my boys went to Moeller, they wouldn't have been given a suit."

Tom Lichtenberg

Mason, etcetera back/coach 1962-62

SCRATCH THE SURFACE OF A GUY WHO IS PART OF TODAY'S "OLD MASON" AND YOU'LL PROBABLY FIND HIS ROOTS ARE IN THE VALLEY. IN THE '50S AND '60S, families were leaving the Mill Creek Valley and turning the farming community of Mason into a commuter village. The promised land of home ownership was in Mason, and they commuted downhill to jobs at Stearns & Foster, Philip Carey Manufacturing, and General Electric.

So when the Mason school reached critical mass and thoughts turned toward starting a football program, the newcomers turned to one of their own—a valley boy named Tom Lichtenberg. Tom's father, Clem, having recently joined the exodus from the valley, now lived in Mason but maintained close ties to Lockland through his bar, Lichty's.

Lichty's was what passed in those days as a sports bar. No wall-to-wall televisions but a more primitive place where men who worked all day in the plants would stop for a beer—or two—and discuss the important issues of the day, which usually involved sports. Bars like Lichty's were community anchors, sponsoring athletic teams and serving as public meeting houses where opinions, stories, exploits, and lies were served up in equal measure, all with a "whatever's said after two beers stays here" mentality.

Clem's son was well known to the valley transplants. In 1957, Tom led the Lockland Panthers to a 13-12 upset over Bob Lewis's undefeated Wyoming Cowboys. It was the last game of the season—postponed from an earlier game when flu decimated both squads—and it decided the league championship. Wyoming jumped out to a 12-0 first quarter lead, then Lichtenberg took over. His 12-yard run near the end of the half cut the lead to six. With 2:20 left in the third quarter, he took the ball over left tackle, broke to the sideline, and outran the Cowboys for an 80-yard touchdown run. He broke the tie when he faked a dive and threw a jump pass to Jack Reid for the extra point. He made both the *Enquirer* and *Post and Times Star* All-City teams, finishing second in the city in scoring with 104 points.

So, fresh out of the University of Louisville where he was a three-year letterman on three good Cardinal teams (he split time with Ernie Green, who later blocked for Jim Brown), he was called upon to start Mason's fledgling program. In 1962, only a few of the candidates had ever played the game—and it showed. There was a famous moment in which two novice coaches—Tom and the new Blanchester coach, Ben Hubbard—held what they called "the worst scrimmage in the history of prep football." The coaches didn't know enough not to put both teams on the same sideline—a kind of wildlife moment in which two elk find themselves at the same waterhole—and when a gigantic fight broke out, the players didn't know enough to keep their helmets on. Then the first home game had to be rescheduled because the field wasn't ready.

Playing mostly freshmen and sophomores, Mason took its lumps; during one three-game run, the Comets were outscored 130-0. But after a few years, Lichtenberg had taught them to block and tackle—as well as keep their helmets on—and in the first five years of the Fort Ancient Valley Conference, they ran off a 41-7-2 record and won three league championships.

His next job was Purcell in the early 1970s as the school struggled with changing demographics, and then he moved into college coaching under a former Louisville assistant, Roy Terry, then at Morehead State University. While at Morehead, he recruited Mike Marksbury of Norwood and Ron Mosley from Purcell, but his most notable recruit was a Kentucky quarterback, Phil Simms. Marksbury was a 6-2, 245-pound All-City tackle (and the Ohio shot put champion in 1973), Mosley had played for Tom at Purcell, and Simms would later take the New York Giants to a 39-20 win over Denver in Super Bowl XXI and earn MVP honors. They were Tom's first college recruits, which placed recruiting high within his skill set.

After Morehead, a surprise call came from Earle Bruce, whom he had met when Bruce was at Ohio State and recruiting Mason's big tackle, Mike Biehle. Bruce, now at Iowa State, hired Tom to coach running backs. Adding to his reputation as a first-rate recruiter, Tom brought in Dwayne Crutchfield, a crushing running back from North College Hill who became one of the school's leading all-time rushers and an NFL draft pick.

Then the marathon was on. Tom left Iowa for the head coaching job at Morehead and after two seasons, Gerry Faust, freshly departed from Moeller, called from Notre Dame. In the pre-cell phone age, Tom on the road somewhere, his wife, Sue, accepted the Notre Dame job for him. Three years later, he was back at Iowa State as assistant athletic director. As an Ohio State assistant, he recruited a pair of CAPE All-Staters, Carlos Snow and Vinnie Clark, and hired Urban Meyer as a grad assistant.

He coached briefly with Lou Holtz at Notre Dame. He followed Bruce to Northern Iowa and Colorado State, took Maine to the NCAA Division I-AA playoffs, then became head coach at Ohio University. He spent a season in Columbus semi-retired (coaching at OU supposedly does that) where he coached Worthington Middle School's team, then became offensive coordinator for Bowling Green University. Reuniting with Bruce, he coached the Iowa Barnstormers of the Arena Football League, then the Columbus Destroyers. In 2007, about to settle into a season of sun and golf in Florida, Lichtenberg went to Drake University.

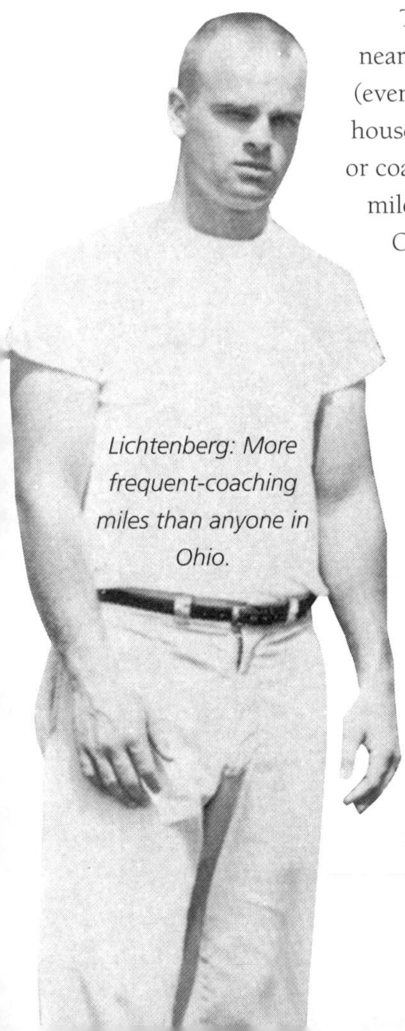

Lichtenberg: More frequent-coaching miles than anyone in Ohio.

The tally by now included nearly twenty teams, inhabiting (even if briefly) nearly forty houses, some 500 games (playing or coaching), and more coaching mileage than anyone in Southwest Ohio. His oldest son and daughter graduated in Ames, Iowa, another daughter in South Bend, one in Worthington, and the youngest son played on four high school football teams in four years, making All-State in three and being named Gatorade Player of the Year in Maine.

Tom seems to have retired, but no one is betting on it, particularly his wife, Sue, the resident real estate manager. The phone still rings, and during each of the last two years, calls have come for Tom to "play for pizza," as the coaching fraternity calls it. (It means a coaching job in Italy, and it's the first time he's turned down so many frequent coaching miles.)

At any rate, chances are good that by fall, Tom Lichtenberg will be on the sidelines—somewhere. There might even be a flag football team around that needs some help. Check the stadium nearest you.

Terry Malone

HCHS/Badin fullback/coach 1957-2003

57

WHAT HADN'T THE COACH SEEN IN ALL THAT TIME? HE'D SEEN THE HAMILTON OLD-TIMERS WHO USED FOOTBALL AS A WAY OF PLAYING THEMSELVES OUT of the old East Side, guys like Johnny Martinkovic who went to Xavier and ended up in Green Bay. Johnny didn't even know where Green Bay was, then made the Pro Bowl there. Mothers pointed Martinkovic out to their children as he ambled through town in his Green Bay jacket as if every suckling on the East Side could grow up to be the size of a redwood stump and go to the Pro Bowl.

Martinkovic was at Xavier when Kentucky played the Musketeers in 1949. They played on television and the widow down the block had the first set in the neighborhood. Terry did chores for her so she let him watch. Xavier played the Kentuckians a hard-nosed game closer than the 21-7 score, and Martinkovic dominated the line. It was XU's only loss that year, and Bear Bryant's team went on to win the Orange Bowl.

Terry's thoughts about football were mostly in present time but when he was a sophomore at Hamilton Catholic, Ed Kluska, the XU coach, saw the Rams play and told someone in the pressbox that if the Malone kid kept coming along, there might be a scholarship for him. Terry was a big boy, with some of Martinkovic's meanness. "He'd run over you," said Claude Chaney, one of Terry's teammates, a pretty fair football player himself. "You'd just have to hang onto 'im until you got 'im down."

Terry's first start was as a freshman, against Fairfield. In grade school, he'd be waiting on his bus and the Fairfield kids passed by and yelled obscenities at him. The Hamilton Catholic-Fairfield rivalry, one might say, began at the bus stop and ended up on the playing field. As a senior, he scored twice against Fairfield and both scores were called back. It didn't matter much since his early revenge came when he was on defense—and later as a coach. On the sidelines against Fairfield, he could still see himself as a schoolboy at the bus stop, the Fairfield bus trailing verbal abuse behind it like exhaust.

As a senior fullback, he weighed 190 pounds. A skinny underclassman playing defensive back remembers getting the scare of his life during practice: meeting Terry Malone in the secondary. "It was like getting run down by an ocean liner wearing a helmet," Tony Lamke recalled years later. "I was the original sacrificial Ram…."

West Point came visiting, and Terry was invited up to the University of Wisconsin where he got his first motorboat ride. Xavier had a smorgasbord with prime rib and honey ham for its recruits. Football, Terry understood, would be his vehicle, but education was his goal. Even in high school, he knew that.

In the dusty (and little-used) Hamilton Catholic library, he discovered a biography of Father Damien, a Belgian priest who spent his life ministering to a leper colony, and for a time, Terry himself considered the priesthood. If not, then surely there was a clear line of descent from priest to coach and lepers to linemen.

So under the thrall of prime rib, the Musketeers on local television, and the prospect of a Catholic education, an earnest and hopeful Terry Malone began his Xavier career. Soon, he discovered a major influence: a despot named Mick Connolly, an ex-navy veteran and former Boston College star once described by one of his players as "195 pounds of solid mouth." (Connolly said the statement wasn't true; he weighed 200 pounds.) "Blunt, abusive, or forceful assertions were a part of Connolly's style," said the *Cincinnati Post*. "If you don't get it done," Connolly told his charges, "I'm going to break your plate." He walked a marginal line between fear and respect, and the players themselves couldn't always tell the difference. One of them, smoking outside the cafeteria, saw Connolly approaching and stubbed the cigarette out in his hand.

Terry's breakout year—he'd undergone back and knee surgery—came as a junior, playing the crosstown rival Bearcats at Nippert Field. That was when he took a kickoff to the house. As he fled down the sidelines, Connolly ran down the sidelines beside him, tie flapping, screaming at him. He had to outrun both the UC defense and his own coach. The 97-yard runback turned the game for Xavier, and the Musketeers won 34-14.

"Running these goddamn sprints is the reason you

THE PATH TO MCCARTHYISM

The Hackberry Street Assassins earned their name under the stewardship of **Jim McCarthy**, an unflinching former Naval officer who had several things working in his favor. One was a depth of talent previously not seen in the Cincinnati area, which McCarthy cultivated by romancing the local parents with evening film sessions (Purcell crowds averaged about 10,000 in those heady days) and capitalized on by instituting the region's first platoon system. (Juniors played defense. Seniors played offense.)

Other advantages included four future collegiate All-Americans—quarterbacks Roger Franz and Roger Staubach, halfback Jim Bolger, and end Ron Beagle, who thought so much of Purcell that he rode his bike over from Covington, Ky., to get there. And finally, the white-haired taskmaster enjoyed the distinct benefit of following **Ed Kluska**.

For all the well-deserved credit that is heaped upon McCarthy—he was acknowledged as being the predecessor to Roger Bacon's Bron Bacevich as the coach who elevated Cincinnati football, just as Bacevich preceded Gerry Faust in that respect—it was Kluska who put Purcell on the path to local dominance. In his four years at the Eastside school, the Cavaliers lost just one measly game.

A smallish Pennsylvanian born of Polish immigrants, Kluska installed the T-formation offense that McCarthy subsequently used to such fabulous effect. In 1947, he ran the same alignment at Xavier when he was named head coach of his alma mater. There, he won three straight Ohio Intercollegiate titles, putting up a record of 27-2-1 in were able to make that run on Saturday," Connolly said to Malone as the team ran at Monday practice. Malone's kickoff return against UC was a school record, and he was an All-Irish/All-Catholic All-American that year.

The guys who remembered those Xavier days would say that Terry was "a Mick Connelly coach," and Malone never denied it. There was more than one moment of testimony to the fact. Years later, after one of Coach Malone's young charges who lived outside of town had suffered through a difficult practice, he blurted out at the supper table, "Coach Malone is as mean as that bull out yonder in the pasture!"

THERE ARE SMILES AND SMILES IN XAVIER DRESSING ROOM

—Enquirer (Heise) Photo

Coach Mick Connolly of Xavier, center, led four heroes of yesterday's rout of University of Cincinnati in V for Victory celebration in Musketeers' dressing room. Ends Steve Junker and Bob Young, at extremes, caught passes setting up two touchdowns. Second string fullback Terry Malone, second from left, came off the bench to gain crucial yardage and returned Cincinnati kickoff 95 yards to score in game's turning point in third quarter. Quarterback Roger Bertoia, second from right, scored twice and ably directed Muskies to surprising victory.

The Coach would have smiled at that. Keep the boys on their toes, was his thinking, and he had his ways. He could explode in a nuclear paroxysm and five minutes later display the peaceful countenance of a Trappist monk. Once, he threw his jaw out in a halftime tirade. At Talawanda, he destroyed a blackboard and the school sent him a bill.

A Hamilton High assistant saw The Coach scream so loudly his teeth fell into a puddle. The assistant watched him pick them up, wipe them on his pants, and put them back in his mouth. Then, he started yelling again. After the game, he walked out and shook hands, the nicest man the assistant had ever met. The assistant wondered who he had just shaken hands with—Dr. Jekyll or Coach Hyde?

The teeth were particularly terrifying to The Coach's players. If one of the players was summoned to his old office downstairs by the coal bin and he walked in to see The Coach's teeth sitting on the desk, he knew he was about to be yelled at. And that his body, scorched and withered by The Coach's invective, might be found perfectly preserved in some season yet to come. The Coach

that lustrous stretch. The first of those seasons was 1949, when the Musketeers smacked Arizona State in the Salad (now Fiesta) Bowl and Kluska got the best of it in coaching matchups against Woody Hayes (Miami) and Sid Gillman (Cincinnati), losing only to Bear Bryant at Kentucky. Bryant later called that Xavier team one of the best he'd ever seen.

The last of Kluska's consecutive conference championships came in 1951, when XU produced its first undefeated record in 50 years and the grim overseer was named Little All-America Coach of the Year. "He wouldn't smile," observed one of his players, future coaching legend Tom Ballaban, "unless the sun shined for a week and he won three games in a row." Of course, the grin, in that event, made regular appearances, depending on the sun.

and the coal bin became a kind of blue collar minotaur-and-the-labyrinth, where a confrontation with the teeth was a mark of honor. (The mythological reference to a creature who was part-man and part-bull wasn't lost on The Coach's smarter players. Over time, even his dimmer ones got a sense of the legend.)

The players who were yelled at, or had been initiated in the coal bin, learned that they were actually among the elite; they discovered that he saved his purest vitriol for those who would play for him. They began to understand that they had been witness to high drama. The problem was that The Coach was so good at it they were never sure when he was acting. (Once, after a particularly unholy tirade when only the asbestos ceiling tile had saved the rest of the student body, The Coach walked out of the locker room and said to one of his assistants, "How'd you like *that* one?")

The Coach went so long before he had a losing season that the school morphed from Hamilton Catholic to co-ed Stephen T. Badin High (and across the street,

NO PRACTICE WITH LOSING

The water stung **Ed Mignery** as he sagged against the cold tiles of the shower, but it wasn't strong enough to wash away the feeling of despair. He was exhausted and beaten by the loss against Murray State. It was his first start for Morehead State, he was only three games into his freshman season, and every day had been hard.

But none of it was as hard as losing. When he arrived on campus, he came in with half a scholarship, as if he were only half as good. Then, in the first practices, he wore a white jersey, which screamed of his lowly fourth-team status. He felt like he had just climbed out of a turnip truck, three colors removed from the Promised Land-red worn by the first team.

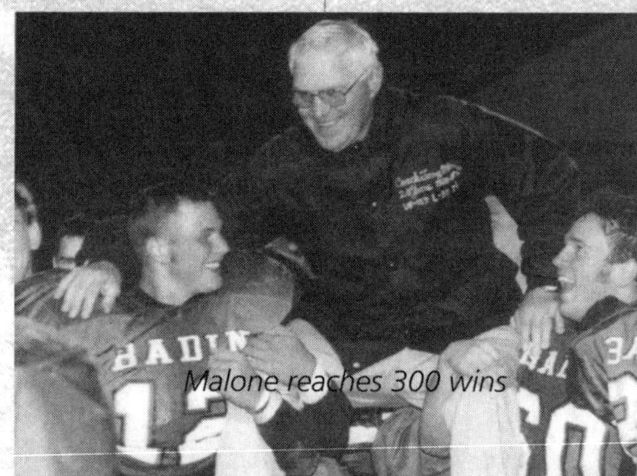

Malone reaches 300 wins

He knew he was better than this, and one thing said he would be: He had played for Papa. He still remembered Badin's night practices at Hogan Airport when the team ran the same play over and over on the dusty field, no water breaks. Then numb from repetition, they ran sprints until all the oxygen in the county disappeared and they seemed to be breathing only Papa's slander. Ed felt like he had been pushed so far inside himself that his will for the game had calcified into a spot behind his breastbone that would probably show up on an X-ray.

And that was why—by the week before Morehead's third game—he was wearing a red jersey. So he had won his colors, and his full scholarship, but Morehead had lost the game. He, personally, felt as if *he'd* lost the game, even though nothing could have been further from the truth.

In his head, he replayed his team's every movement over and over again. He remembered something Papa had always said: *If you're on that field and you don't give everything you have, then what you hold back will be lost forever.*

But he had given everything. And still they lost. He filed to the back of the team bus and collapsed into his seat. Hanging his head, he began to sob.

His coach, John Behling, noticed him and walked to the back of the bus.

"Mignery, you alright?" he said, fearing Mignery might be injured.

Ed shook his head.

"Coach, that is the first loss I've experienced in years, and I don't like this feeling," he said.

In his four years as a high school player, his team suffered only a single loss, the last game of his freshman year against Elder. Then Hamilton Catholic won thirty-two games in a row.

Mignery's pain was intense because he had no practice with losing.

He did not even have a memory of it.

—excerpted from Cathy Malone's forthcoming book on her father, T-Bone, A Life in Football. *Mignery went on to coach at Hamilton High where from 1988 through 2001 he won 77 games. He even managed to beat his old coach and Badin—once.*

An unusually calm moment on the sidelines with the usually tempestuous Malone.

Hamilton High split into Taft and Garfield, then consolidated back into Hamilton High). Two generations of players had come and gone before he had his first losing season in 1985. In the intervening time, Hawaii had become a state, there'd been five presidents, the Berlin Wall had gone up, the PC had been invented (along with Michael Jackson), women gained the vote in Switzerland, and Pie Traynor died.

When a season didn't turn out exactly right, The Coach would announce to the family that he was going into the insurance business. Then he'd say, "Maybe one more year," while the kids went into laughing fits.

Before The Coach retired in 2003, he had won a state title (1990), been runner-up twice (1978 and 1980), and been to the final four on five other occasions. He had six perfect teams that never got a chance at a state title because Ohio did not have playoffs until 1972. Once the playoffs started, he went sixteen times.

Most of what got him there was Basic Malone: the 37 Slant, what The Coach called a "bludgeon" play, four yards and a cloud of Woody Hayes twenty times a game. He had about nine running plays, the same number of passing plays, a handful of formations, and his boys just beat other teams to death.

"He would run the off-tackle and the sweep almost identical," said Jerry Scrivner, a Hamilton High assistant. "On the off-tackle, the end would block down on the tackle. On the sweep, the end would slide off the tackle and pick up the linebacker. It would look like the off-tackle was going to close down and it would be a sweep. Then you'd think it was going to be the sweep and it would be the off-tackle. Then if you would play it right he'd throw a pass to the back side.

"We knew it was coming. You'd have your kids coached, but they'd get confused. It was hard to get a handle on it. It was a true *offense*..."

The bludgeon, you might say, was his bread-and-batter play. Like Woody's OSU offense, the opposition knew what was coming. Unlike Woody, Malone did it to everybody for nearly five decades. The 37 Slant was so habitual, Malone's Bishop Avenue mailman used it.

The Coach's 100th win was against—who else?—Fairfield. So was his 200th. His old resentment, harbored long ago at the bus stop, continued unabated. In the late 1960s, the rivalry was so intense the workers at Fisher Body bet thousands of dollars on the game.

"Old man Riegert grabbed me when we were coming out of the locker room," remembered The Coach's son, John Malone (one of three Malone boys to quarterback Badin) "and he said, 'You better do well. I bet twenty grand on this game.'"

There was a bit of the old Catholic antipathy, as well. In the 1976 game, when John was a freshman, coming in for the injured regular, a fish sailed into the huddle.

"Don't worry, Malone," one of the linemen said, "we got ya covered."

The Coach, meanwhile, did his part. "They're calling me and saying things like, 'Malone, we're going to whip your ass this week!'" he'd tell his players—despite the fact the Malone number was unlisted. "I hope they're not right," he'd say, hanging his head, dolefully. Some-

THE YEAR THE WEATHER WON

In 1932, the Battle of Price Hill took place at Redland (later known as Crosley) Field, when the Thanksgiving Day temperatures would have really frozen your bird. It was zero degrees overnight, and Western Hills coach **Arch McCartney** was up early and off to the hardware store where he bought two tinners' stoves and a supply of charcoal. When he arrived at the game, he performed what may have been the most charitable act of the entire West High/Elder series: he took one of his stoves over to the Elder coach, **Walter "Babe" Bartlett**.

At timeouts, both teams forewent the water bucket and sent out the stove. It didn't help much but it provided some comic relief: Elder back Carl Williams burned out the seat of his football pants (new meaning for the term "burner"). The cold was so rigorous the keys froze on the WH band instruments, but there was still music in Western hearts; the Mustangs won 29-13. Then victor and vanquished alike raced homeward because, as everyone knows, home is where the heat is.

times he sang the Fairfield fight song during practices.

When Badin played Fairfield, the players kept their helmets on, even leaving the field. That wasn't anything new. They had learned to keep their helmets on around The Coach, too. He had a way of getting their attention by whacking them in the head with his clipboard.

In the old days, The Coach might scrimmage with his boys. Tommy Pate remembers him running. No helmet, legs up high. "Damn it, guys," he'd say, "if *I* can do it..."

Sometimes, when the Rams practiced at the old airport, they stayed after dark and parents turned on their car lights so the kids could finish practice.

In late October of 2003, Badin beat North College Hill 45-7, for Malone's 360th win, and then he left. "I'm tired of making game plans," he said. He was the winningest high school coach in Ohio history and only nine coaches in the entire country had more wins.

He'd be canonized by now but his miracles weren't posthumous. He was doing miracles in the mid-1960s when he coached Badin to a 33-game winning streak. Besides, he swears a bit—that turns heads in any celestial choir—but what's a man to do? First, it was all those hard-headed East Side kids he had to teach the 37 Slant to and now all these years later he's having to teach his daughter the same play because she's writing a book about him and never paid any attention before. (The kid is one serious student, though, and she approaches her book the way he approached his games, which means she may have The Coach—and half his players—running The Hill before *her* game is over.)

The Coach is a faithful man, even with all the aggravation, found every Sunday morning in his pew at St. Ann's where he's been since the ark came up the Miami and his first pair of offensive tackles disembarked. Since the head slap is frowned upon by the modern church, he sometimes whacks his former assistant Dean Smith in the head with the offertory. Just to keep him on his toes, he'd say.

He's like a visiting bishop at Badin games in the autumn, up in the stands where he can barely see the game, surrounded as he is by old acolytes who come by for the customary laying on of hands. They feel safer these days, for The Coach has mellowed, if ever so slightly, and there's not a clipboard in sight.

Pat Mancuso

Princeton coach 1960-1996

60

IT WASN'T THE MERGER THAT MADE THE PRINCETON HIGH SCHOOL FOOTBALL TEAM SUCH A WONDERFUL THING. BUT, TO A GREAT EXTENT, IT WAS THE football team that made something wonderful of the merger, and of Princeton High School.

By 1970, Pat Mancuso had been on the job ten years as Princeton's detailed, spit-polished head coach. They were good years, establishing a fast tradition for a suburban school that had been created in 1955 by consolidating eight small neighborhood districts. It wasn't long at all before Mancuso made Princeton a force in local football, winning the Hamilton County League in his first season and doing it three more times before the Vikings became a charter member of the Greater Miami Conference in 1967.

They carried over their success to the GMC, and then, after winning the league's first two titles, their prospects were suddenly amplified. The Mill Creek community of Lincoln Heights was placed in the Princeton district, and Mancuso understood immediately that things would be different from that moment on. The superintendent, Robert Lucas, suspected it as well and said as much to Mancuso, adding that he wasn't expecting Princeton to be *Massillon*, as far as football went, but at least a program of some local repute. Mancuso could relate well to that perspective, having grown up in Northeast Ohio—Leetonia, to be precise—watching and admiring the likes of Massillon and Canton McKinley. In fact, his personal ambition, as Princeton's coach, was for things to go well enough that he could return to a better position somewhere up there.

What he did, upon receiving the word about Lincoln Heights, was *make sure* that things went well. There was certainly no inherent guarantee to that effect. When Princeton's parameters were first mapped out, the territory had straddled and conspicuously left out the nation's largest all-black city.

Lincoln Heights was a poor, proud and resourceful

Mancuso will be forever known as the coach who showed the South that it could compete with the North, and then some.

school district with a long-standing excellence in athletics. But there was a clear commentary in the original consolidation that left it separate from Princeton, and painfully unequal. While Princeton was supported by a per capita tax assessment of $32,000 per pupil, Lincoln Heights got along as best it could on $7,000 a kid.

So delicate was the federally imposed merger that it was agreed to keep the Lincoln Heights students in their existing building for the first three years. The two student bodies would come together only for special classes and extracurricular activities.

Mancuso and The Coach

And the first activity was football. Practice for football begins during the summer, and to prepare for it in 1970, Mancuso made countless trips to the unfamiliar tract just added to his jurisdiction. His mission was to get to know his new players and vice versa; to clear safe passage through the racial divides that had separated the two schools. The exercise so resembled the much-later movie, *Remember the Titans*, that when it came out, the Princeton team was invited to watch it together. For Mancuso, it was like reliving the assimilation of Lincoln Heights.

Years later, after Princeton had become broadly recognized as one of the most progressive and effective high schools in Ohio, the district superintendent remarked that its greatest facilitator had been Pat Mancuso. To those who question the connection between football and education, the coach had demonstrated, to the grandest degree, what a team can do for a school.

Thanks largely to him, the transition was more than smooth. On all levels—social, educational, athletic—it was stunning.

To this day, local coaches and historians credit Princeton for debunking the fable that for so many years had defined Ohio high school football. For as long as state championships were decided by wire services, few, even in Southern Ohio, disputed that the seat of power lay in Northern Ohio. When the tournaments were finally established in 1972, it was fully expected that the schools up there—led, of course by mighty Massillon—would formalize their claim.

That initial year of playoffs left Princeton as the first regional champion of the Southwest, its reward being a trip to Ohio Stadium to play Massillon, of all teams, in the state semifinals. The only perceptible advantage for the Sharonville school was in the reconnaissance area; one of the Northeast writers phoned Mancuso complaining that he couldn't find Princeton on the map.

The Vikings were officially designated as the home team, which meant that they could occupy the spacious Ohio State locker room. But when they arrived, Massillon was already in it. Rather than acquiesce and accept the cramped quarters set aside for the visitors—which Massillon coach Bob Cummings urged him to do—Mancuso insisted upon receiving his team's full and roomy rights.

The tournament officials went along, Massillon moved, and Princeton had scored a moral victory before the game even started. When it *ended*, the scoreboard declared a whole new order, by the score of 17-14.

Mancuso's men would subsequently lose the championship game to Warren Western Reserve, but by that time hope was already coursing through Cincinnati's veins. Gerry Faust, for one, had seen the Princeton-Massillon game and been moved by the possibilities it introduced. Three years later, Moeller would bring the first big-school title to Southwest Ohio.

With that, Cincinnati schools would take off on a streak of six consecutive championships, five of them by Moeller. The Crusaders' reign was interrupted only in 1978, by an undefeated Princeton team led by 5-9, 167-pound running back Ken Roundtree, who personally scored more touchdowns (13) than the Vikings surrendered all season (11).

On the many occasions that Moeller won state, its toughest opponent along the way was typically Princeton. Theirs was a neighborhood rivalry of regional eminence and national implications.

Over a period of thirteen years, Southwest schools would bring back eleven Division I (or AAA) titles. Of those, three would belong to Mancuso's program.

Princeton's championships were spread evenly over 10 seasons, with no single class or player taking part in more than one. It was the sort of sustainable standard that screams of great coaching.

Mancuso provided that beyond dispute. Under his gentlemanly stewardship, the Vikings never suffered a losing record. They cobbled together six undefeated regular seasons and, incredibly, won the GMC in the first nineteen years of its existence; twenty-three of the first twenty-five. In all, Mancuso coached on Chester Road for thirty-seven years, compiling an enviable ledger of 305-76-11, the victory total (323, counting his early wins at Leetonia) surpassing all others in Ohio history, to that point.

Not surprisingly, he was presented numerous opportunities in the collegiate ranks, turning down offers to work on Bo Schembechler's staff at Michigan and Earle Bruce's at Ohio State.

It would have been wonderful, no doubt, to coach bigger, faster players in bigger, louder stadiums. But as a paragon of perspective, Mancuso understood that even at such colossal institutions, with such remarkable resources, he could not possibly accomplish anything as wonderful as what he had at Princeton High School.

Tom O'Brien

St. Xavier coach 1967-67

TOM O'BRIEN NEVER PLANNED ON COACHING. GROWING UP IN THE BOND HILL NEIGHBORHOOD AS THE OLDEST OF THE SIX O'BRIEN KIDS, HE bedeviled his parents with pudding fights in the kitchen and sneaking out of the house after lights-out (usually caught in the process by Muskie, the family boxer named for the Xavier Musketeers).

Earning tuition money selling programs at XU football games and caddying, he was soon a player himself, leading all St. Xavier High tacklers from his end position, as well as making All-GCL. He was good enough, too, for a spot on the Naval Academy's team, and he made the All-East team in 1970.

The Border Wars: Princeton-Moe, 1965-2004

To hear the stories—the legend—you'd think that Moeller and Princeton played each other every year, back to back, end of the season, with all of the marbles and most of the world's precious gems at stake.

It wasn't quite like that. Five times, though, it *did* happen that way, more or less, beginning in 1980, which was the first time such a thing *could* begin, because it was the first time more than one team from each of Ohio's four regions was permitted to play for the state championship.

By then, though, the rivalry had already leapt out of the landscape. So we need to do some backing up. To 1972, when the playoffs were initiated after a long history of wire-service championships that favored the Northern schools to an utterly ridiculous degree.

Initially, and for quite a while, it was Moeller that dominated the competitions between the two powers of the state, city and metropolitan area's northern suburbs, both schools prospering from the population infusion that followed the completion and linking of the community's three major interstates, I's 75, 71 and 275. They actually began to play each other in 1965, when both were still in swaddling clothes. It was the season opener. Moeller won, 14-0, and would achieve a similar result in 14 of the first 17 engagements, at which time the regularly scheduled game, which had been moved to the end of the season, was briefly discontinued.

But back to '72. Moeller had won the previous five meetings, and would win the next five, but the significance of the '72 game was vastly enhanced. It put Princeton in the playoffs, which is to say the state semifinals, against mighty Massillon, and all Moeller coach Gerry Faust could do was watch enviously as Pat Mancuso's team pulled off what must still be considered as the greatest upset in Ohio playoff history, 17-14. The Vikings would be routed in the state championship game by Warren Western Reverse, but their mark had been made, and Faust had taken note. He had identified both the challenge and the challenger.

Faust & Mancuso: war lords.

It was tacitly declared, at that moment, that the war was on; it was schoolo-a-schoolo.

"It came down to us and Moeller," recalled Mancuso. "And you had to beat them."

The rivalry was lit by mutual ambition and fanned by familiarity. Neighborhood students who rode buses to Moeller actually got on them at Princeton's campus in Sharonville.

"There was a real, real good relationship between Princeton and Moeller students," Mancuso added, "because at that time the Catholic schools could only draw students from parishes within their district, and Princeton was one of them. So our kids knew the Moeller kids real well, and there was great respect for one another. There was always that great rivalry.

"When we first started playing, we always played at our field. There were many Friday nights when I-75 was almost blocked because of the cars parked on it; because people could see from there. There were no bushes obscuring the field, and the stadium was sold out. If they didn't watch from the highway, people would go to the reserve baseball field and guys would climb up the backstop to watch the game."

It was compelling theatre at least most of the time. In 1977, when the Holy Steamrollers—behind All-American linebacker Bob Crable, All-American defensive back (and future major-league pitcher) Bill Long, junior tight end Tony Hunter (a future Ohio Lineman of the Year), and sophomore running back Eric Ellington (a future Ohio Player of the Year)—won their third straight state and second straight national championship, Moeller inflicted upon Princeton the most lopsided beating in the series' history to that point, 35-7. In 1978, the Crusaders paid for it with a 13-12 defeat that ended their 53-game, regular-season winning streak. The winning points came on a 37-yard field goal that barely cleared the goalpost and landed, rudely, in the Moeller band.

That season, Princeton went on to claim its first state championship, making four in a row for the interstate corridor. Two years later —after Moeller had won its sixth state and fourth national title—the streak was extended to six.

As the premier program in the country, Moeller generally had its way against the big public school. But there's no doubt that Princeton's speed and fundamental soundness raised the Crusaders' standard, just as Moeller's methodical excellence—not to mention its *size*—did for the Vikings. "We didn't know kids grew that big," Mancuso observed, remembering, in particular, an All-American lineman and future pro from 1970. "(Steve) Sylvester and those kids, they looked *gigantic*.

"Absolutely, Moeller made us better. In order for us to get to where we wanted to go, we had to get to their level. Gerry and I always talked about this, and Steve Klonne talked about it when he was there. We always felt that the winner of our game could be the state champion. The years we beat them and went on to win state, *they* could have won it without a doubt."

Had the Big Game been moved earlier to the end of the regular-season schedule, it would have effectively served as a first-round playoff match. With the switch occurring as it did in 1980, it coincided with Ohio's expansion of the postseason pool to eight teams. That meant two could qualify from each region. In the Southwest region, that pretty much meant Moeller and Princeton—even if they had just *played*.

And so, in Faust's last time around before proceeding on to Notre Dame, Moeller won a 14-13 thriller to finish the regular season, then regrouped to take on Mancuso's team again the following week. The second time, the outcome was a more comfortable 28-3, which was roughly the same margin by which the Steamrollers, paced by All-American fullback Mark Brooks, steamrolled Massillon (30-7) for the state championship.

Big Moe kept winning the Princeton games through the regular-season finale of 1983, when, with a powerhouse lineup led by Mark Kamphaus (quarterback), Tom Waddle (receiver), Byron Larkin (defensive back, All-American, MVP) and D'Juan Francisco (running back, All-American, Cincinnati Player of the Year), the Crusaders prevailed 28-21. Trouble was, they had to play Princeton again a week later, and find yet another way to contain PHS quarterback Michael Taylor, later of Michigan. They couldn't. In the rematch, the victory was the Vikings', by the very same score. Safety Harlon Barnett, headed for Michigan State and the NFL, arranged it with a jarring, fumble-forcing tackle on Francisco.

Princeton, following form, went on to win state, outclassing Akron Garfield 24-6. With that, the two

The Sheehan Definition

After thirteen years as an assistant coach (Roger Bacon, Covington, Aiken) and about half a dozen applying for head-coaching positions, **Steve Sheehan** finally got one in 1982. It was a different sort, involving a new City of Cincinnati public school specializing in physical education. Sheehan, confident in both himself and the situation, promised his bosses at CAPE that he would win a small-school state championship in five years.

He was wrong.

It took four.

It also took superstars Carlos Snow and Vinnie Clark; but it was Sheehan who did the building from scratch, and it was Sheehan who made good on his guarantee, leading the Crusaders to an undefeated season in 1985.

CAPE had a fan base of a couple of hundred, no field, and an attitude of, as one player said, "us against the world—the other team, their fans, and sometimes the officials."

Cincinnati schools had combined to play in nine consecutive Ohio title games (1975-'83), triumphant in all but one. And on it went. Over 13 years ('75-'87, when the Vikings won their third championship), Moeller and Princeton totaled 10 state titles—with another brought home by Fairfield, a nearby and familiar opponent of Princeton's in the Greater Miami Conference. In the first 22 years after the playoffs began in 1972, the Crusaders and Vikes reached 16 Division I championship games, winning 10 (Moeller seven, Princeton three).

It was after the dramatic events of '83 that Mancuso and Klonne—who actually replaced Ted Bacigalupo, who head-coached Moeller for just a single season after Faust left (one in which the Montgomery school was shut out by Canton McKinley in the state championship game, 13-0)—decided maybe things had gotten just a bit too intense, and maybe everybody ought to just take a little break. So there was no Princeton-Moeller game in 1984. Or in 1985, when the Crusaders, given another title shot against Canton McKinley, made the most of it, 35-11.

In the absence of the Big Game, public protests were overwhelming. It was consequently restored in 1986. Princeton responded with its most resounding victory of the series, 45-21; but it was Fairfield's year. The Vikings' year came next.

In 1987, the trophy awarded the victor of the suburban set-to was named King of the Block and taken home by Princeton, which beat Moe twice in a row for the first time and won state for the third. It was, to this day, the last Ohio championship claimed by either institution. Princeton would lose to St. Ignatius in 1988. Moeller would lose to St. Ignatius in 1989. Princeton would lose to Warren Harding in 1990—all three by a touchdown.

The raucous rivalry began to fade after 1993, when Moeller turned back the Vikings, 20-7, to end the regular season, then nipped them by a field goal two weeks later in the regional finals, only to lose again to St. Ignatius in the championship game. After that, the two schools stopped meeting in the postseason. After 2004, they stopped meeting at all.

By then, out-of-state clashes and day-long classics had become the fashion, occupying the slots in the schedules that used to be reserved for out-of-conference affairs with old acquaintances. This time, there was no discernible clamor over what had become of Princeton-Moeller.

The Big Game had been reduced to legend and would in turn be magnified by the same, eligible now for exaggeration and wistful thinking. Dormant and more historic by the month, the rivalry, it seemed, took on greater proportion than ever.

The school, which drew students from across the city, had a small student body, as well, and fought stereotypes of being "Jock Tech" throughout its short existence (although some 60-65 percent of its students went on to college).

Dominant at the Division III and IV levels, CAPE followed with another title in 1986, and then—after Snow and Clark had completed their careers at Ohio State—a third in 1992.

But in the spring of 1994, CAPE was closed after a short and distinguished existence. Sheehan, CAPE's only coach, was 117-25-1, and three of his players played professionally—Clark, Snow, and David Pool. Snow, its most famous graduate, was called "the greatest high school running back Ohio has ever known," and his 7,761 prep rushing yards still ranks among the best national marks.

Addicted to challenges, Sheehan then won a league championship at Withrow and coached at Oak Hills before agreeing, in 2007, to head up the new varsity program at Clark Montessori, another City of Cincinnati public school.

Afterward, he found himself assigned to the Quantico Marine Base where he played linebacker on the Marines' last football team. Surely it was the *semper fi* experience, resembling as it does the absolute aspects of the playing field, and afterward, O'Brien returned to the Academy as line coach. There, he was responsible for bringing Cincinnati's Napoleon McCallum on board, which was one of the fortuitous historic moments in Navy recruiting.

Perhaps it was those landlocked Midwestern boys yearning for a vista not their own, but whatever it was, the Academy seemed to have a special tie to Cincinnati. O'Brien's coach, Rick Forzano (briefly a Bengals assistant) had helped recruit that most famous Cincinnati midshipman of them all, Roger Staubach, who'd won the Heisman in 1963. Then in 1967, Jeri Balsly, a 180-pound Madeira halfback with sprinter speed (he ran a 9.7 in the Middie Relays), was Navy's leading rusher.

Balsly set a precedent, too: Cincinnati kids who liked to upset Army. First, Balsly helped Navy upset unbeaten Syracuse, then—after the Midshipmen collected $6,960 for a *New York Times* ad featuring a dead mule under an RIP headstone—he gained 109 yards while "running like a berserk billiard ball and making a shambles of Army's vaunted defense."

Navy 19, Army 14.

O'Brien's 1970 team wasn't that good, but again it saved its best for last, and again it upset Army. Again it was a Cincinnati kid doing most of the damage. This time, it was a former Boy Scout and Wyoming High quarterback named Mark Schickner, a three-sport star (football, basketball, and baseball) who, as a Wyoming senior, captained all three teams. The 6-2, 186-pound Schickner had forfeited football in 1969 for basketball at Navy (he lettered as a forward), but returned to play safety and led Navy's come-from-behind win with four interceptions—a record still unbeaten in Navy's archives.

"A one-man main feature show," newspaper headlines blared, with accompanying photos of a happy Schickner with his fifth pick of the afternoon—the game ball he'd grabbed before racing off to the locker room.

Navy 11, Army 7.

(Footnote: There was another good Cincinnati kid on that 1970 team—Mick Barr, who led Navy in receiving in both 1970 and 1969. He had been called "one of the best athletes ever at Mason High," a receiver with great hands on teams that didn't throw much.)

O'Brien—called by his boss, George Welsh, "the best line coach in college football"—stayed with Welsh through lengthy stints at both Navy and Virginia, and his first head coaching job didn't come until late 1996, at Boston College. There, he observed his old Academy origins by running every noon (rain or shine), referring to wake-up calls as reveille, and peppering his pep talks with tales of military derring-do.

He became the first coach since the 1920s to lead Boston to eight consecutive winning seasons. He went 5-3 against Notre Dame; his 2005 senior class won 35 games, the most in BC's modern history; and he took BC to six straight bowl wins—the longest active bowl streak in the country—before leaving for N.C. State at the end of 2006.

To finish O'Brien's last season, the Eagles won a 25-24 squeaker over—you guessed it—Navy, BC being coached by Frank Spaziani, O'Brien's defensive coordinator and an old Navy man himself.

At one time, the Navy job was the one O'Brien really coveted. When he didn't get it, he thought maybe he'd never become a head coach. He did, though. And in ten years at BC, he never lost to his old alma mater.

As he moved on, there was only one small lingering regret: "I don't want to be the head coach at Navy anymore, but I'd like to be the head coach in the Army-Navy game. Just one time. Give me *one* shot...."

O'Brien: "I thought I'd rather coach than work for a living."

X marked his spot

There was no way that **Steve Rasso** could quip and cut-up and generally entertain like Tom Ballaban, his predecessor as head coach at St. Xavier High School. His only chance was to *outlast* him.

That was a long, tall order, but Rasso, in the end, was able to call Ballaban's quarter of a century and raise him one year. From 1978 to 2003, he also raised the St. X program to the edge of where *his* successor, Steve Specht, finally took it two years later, and again two years *after that*—the state championship.

"St. X has come a long way," said former Moeller coach Steve Klonne upon Rasso's retirement. "His last seven or eight seasons were as good as anybody. From 1992 to about 1999, they were the team to beat in the city."

It wasn't always that way at the big school on North Bend Road. For quite a while, St. X, outclassed by the likes of Moeller and Elder, was more or less the competitive partner of LaSalle, the *other* school on North Bend Road. As it happened, Rasso actually coached the Lancers for seven years before he was fired. It marked the first time he had been out of a coaching job since he stopped playing.

His last uniformed gig was at the University of Cincinnati, where he arrived under unusual circumstances. Rasso grew up in Niagara Falls, N.Y., and loved football so dearly that he, along with a couple accomplices, decided not to graduate after four years in order to have another season on the field.

But over the summer, New York instituted the policy that four years was the limit for athletic participation. It happened that another high school teammate, Jim Leo—who would play in the NFL—had accepted a scholarship to the University of Cincinnati, and with respect to his friends he arranged for two of them to come to UC for a visit with coach George Blackburn. Blackburn watched them all play basketball, then offered scholarships to Rasso and his pal.

A running back and defensive back, Rasso acquitted himself well enough at UC to be drafted by the Detroit Lions; but alas, they cut him. So did the Minnesota Vikings. He was about to give the Buffalo Bills a try when it dawned on him that it was time to get on with coaching.

His fiancée, Sally Carmosino, was a West Side girl; so Cincinnati it had to be. Actually, there was a year in Cleveland first, *then* Cincinnati. Elder. Rasso was a defensive assistant for the Panthers. Then, as a head coach for the first time, he started the program at Covington Catholic in Northern Kentucky.

He also coached Mariemont for a season but yearned to return to the GCL. LaSalle was a challenge that he gladly took on, posting a 47-31-3 record in seven years. His dismissal in 1975 was sudden and stunning.

But it made him available to St. X after Ballaban retired. Over the next 26 years, Rasso quietly won 189 games—103 more than he lost with the Bombers—to drive his career total for Hamilton County to 249, second only to Pat Mancuso.

Three times in Rasso's last dozen autumns, the humble New Yorker took St. Xavier as far as the Ohio championship game. Unfortunately, he never won it.

But then, neither did Ballaban.

Rasso: putting St. Xavier on the map.

It was **Ken Powers** whose fine example encouraged one of his players at Reading High School, Ed Biles, to become a football coach. It was Powers who persuaded Woody Hayes to take a look at an unimposing halfback named Jim Herbstreit. And it was Powers who, when he arrived at Reading in 1928, and in fraternal cahoots with **Herald "Rick" Roettger** of Lockland, started and orchestrated such a respected and amicable neighborhood rivalry that players from the two Mill Creek schools would trudge back home together, in their uniforms, after their annual Thanksgiving morning tussles. "It was a brutal rivalry," said Herbstreit, "and they were like brothers. And that was the way it was." In Roettger's last gobbler game, played in 1953, Lockland showed up as the underdog and trounced the Blue Devils, 42-7, as a going-away gift for the retiring coach, who in his 36 years at the little school had guided the Panthers to two undefeated seasons and 14 Millcreek Valley League titles. Lockland's historic stadium, a landmark of high school athletics in Southwest Ohio, was later renamed in his honor. It was only fitting that, in 1976, Powers and Roettger were inducted together into the second class of LaRosa's Greater Cincinnati High School Hall of Fame . . . In 1928, **Arch McCartney**, a graduate of Hughes and onetime assistant coach there to Red Krueck, started the football program at the new Western Hills High School. McCartney remained at West High, as either athletic director or a coach of any number of sports, and often both, until 1955. What that means is that he beat Elder on a fairly regular basis, beginning in 1931 at Redland Field, 6-0—winning the game on a pass, no less—a favor that would not be returned until 1935. McCartney, for whom the Western Hills baseball field is named, was a second-year inductee of the LaRosa's Hall of Fame, along with Powers and Roettger . . . **Joe Clark** had a pretty good idea from the beginning that he would succeed at Indian Hill. Well, maybe not the *very* beginning. That was when the Youngstown native, a World War II submarine veteran—accustomed to surfacing from way down under, which would come in handy—showed up to check out the woodsy school and circumstances and noticed, in addition to the telling total of four victories over the previous three seasons, that there was no seven-man blocking sled for the practice field. He mentioned it. When he reported for full-time duty in the summer of 1959, there was the blocking sled. With community support such as that, Clark led the Braves to the top of the hill in no time. By 1962, they were 9-1. The next season was their first of three (1963, 1968, 1970) that would go by without a defeat. After an 8-1-1 performance in 1975, Clark accepted a coaching position at LaSalle. He would later be elected to the Ohio High School Coaches Hall of Fame . . . There are coaching luminaries in St. Xavier's long football history, including the likes of Tom Ballaban and Steve Rasso. But none could bring home a state championship (although Rasso got his team to the finals three times) until **Steve Specht** did it in 2005, with a perfect season capped by a tense upstate triumph over Massillon. Specht was a St. X captain back in 1985, and a captain, also—in baseball, too—at Earlham College, where he majored in English Literature. He is a thoughtful, thorough coach whose meticulous approach to his job seems to fit well with the scholarly students who attend the high-achieving, boys-only private institution on North Bend Road. Specht's style fits so well, in fact, that two years after winning the school's first state football title, the Bombers tacked on another one. The second was perhaps even more impressive, entailing another undefeated autumn, this time in the context of a

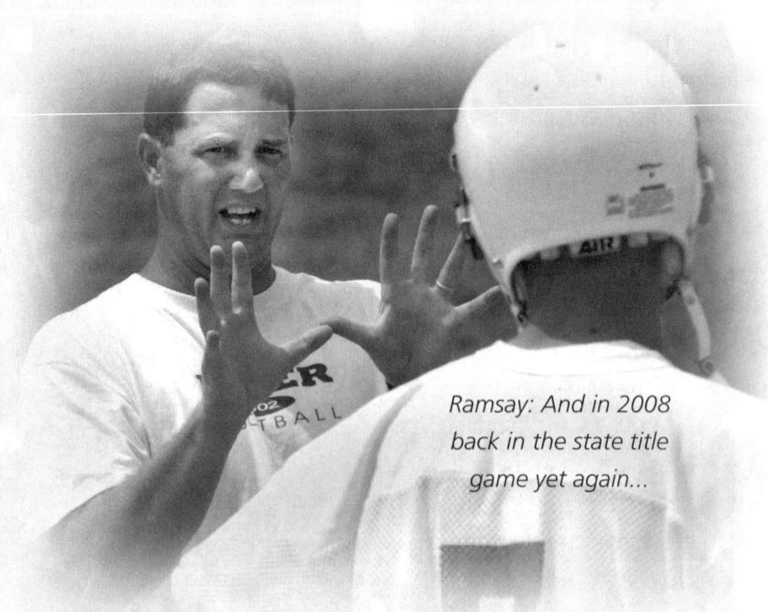

Ramsay: And in 2008 back in the state title game yet again...

FROM THE HILLS TO HOLLYWOOD

Before "the nice Jewish girl from Cincinnati," Theodosia Goodman, became filmdom's first sex symbol, her early practice involved the Walnut Hills football squad where her infatuation with a gridiron star is believed to be the only recorded example—certainly the first—in which vamping actually won a football game.

Theodosia, a.k.a. **Theda Bara**, put the word "vamp" into the dictionary, of course, but that was some time after the 1903 Walnut Hills season during which its star back injured his arm, causing the whole school to mourn Walnut Hills' chances in its next game. The back, however, played injured and scored the winning TD.

Vamping for dear old Walnut Hills

"You were wonderful!" Theodosia said afterward.

"Don't you know why?" he asked.

"No, why?"

"On account of you," he answered.

"You wonderful boy!" she said. "And you must have suffered so much!"

"Aw, no," he said, "it didn't hurt at all—not at all."

The pain, one supposes, was relegated largely to the dialogue, although it was reported by Ms. Goodman herself, returning to Cincinnati fourteen years later, after she had become one of the most famous actresses of the silent screen (where snappy dialogue was usually held to a minimum).

Smoky-eyed and exotic, she had left the Walnut Hills drama club for a couple of years at the University of Cincinnati, then was remade by press agentry into an Arab princess who wore heavy indigo makeup and became Hollywood's first *femme fatale*.

And to think, it was prompted—in small part, anyway—by a Walnut Hills jock who had a hand (perhaps an arm) in the creation of a legend.

national schedule that may have been the toughest in America. In the early stages of the 2007 season, St. X had to battle through without the services of its marquee tailback, Darius Ashley, whose worth was put on spectacular display in the state championship game against Mentor. The effect was a 27-0 shutout, and a ringing testimonial to a coach who was assuming his place in the local pantheon . . . And the same for **Doug Ramsey**. Like Specht at St. X, Ramsey walked into a steep, strong tradition at Elder. His predecessors as head coach included Babe Bartlett and the man who, in 1988, gave Ramsey his first job in the GCL, **Tom Grippa**. A fancier of passing, Grippa was the coach who restored the purple tradition that Bartlett had built in the first half of the century. When he accepted the Elder job in 1987, the Panthers were coming off back-to-back-to-back losing seasons. But over Grippa's ten years in Price Hill, they went 84-23, with two undefeated regular seasons (1989 and 1991) and five GCL championships—nearly half of the dozen that Elder had claimed by that time. When Grippa, with Ramsey freshly hired at his side, engineered a league title in 1988, it was the Panthers' first in 16 years. The regional championship they won in 1996 was the school's first ever. At the end of that fine season, however, Grippa unexpectedly picked up and moved to Fairfield, where he again inherited a program with a recent history of losing. Again, he rebuilt the tradition. Then, in 2003, the former Reading star set himself for one more high hurdle, returning to the GCL in an attempt to bring LaSalle—where he had learned the coaching trade as an assistant under **Ray Heidorn**—up to speed with the rest of the league. By that time, his erstwhile offensive coordinator had taken Elder to the summit of not only the great conference but also the great state. Ramsey, like Grippa (and Ed Biles) a product of Reading High School (he had quarterbacked and assistant-coached there), had replaced his mentor at Elder in 1997, and five

Dick Kerin, first season at Aiken, 1963

years later had overseen an upset of Warren Harding for the Panthers' first championship of all Ohio. And then it happened again in 2003, when Elder, routing Lakewood St. Edward, joined Moeller, Canton McKinley and Cleveland St. Ignatius as the only D-I schools in Ohio to win consecutive state titles. Between them, Ramsey and Specht—Elder and St. Xavier—hoarded four state championships over a six-year period, with one in between from Colerain, yet another large school in Cincinnati's western half . . . **Dick Kerin** never coached the great teams. Not that they were bad. At Greenhills, he won a Hamilton County Suburban League championship. At Aiken, he started the program that ultimately sent Jim O'Brien, Dixon Edwards and Ike Reese to the NFL. The Mount Vernon, Ohio, native was also one of the area's most accomplished wrestling coaches. His biggest victory, however, was World War II. Kerin was a Marine who watched the American flag go up on Iwo Jima, then, a couple weeks later, took a bullet that entered through his arm and left through his back. He won two Purple Hearts. And, in spite of leading teams that were seldom if ever advantaged, he won the unanimous respect of his peers in Southwest Ohio, who borrow his name for the coaching clinic they put on every year. . . . Night high school football in Hamilton began during the Depression when city and school officials allied themselves and put up a $2,400 lighting system. It was September 15, 1934, **Ray Tilton's** first year as coach, and the new system illuminated Athletic Field with some extra shine spilling over on the city. In Tilton's eight years, Hamilton went 60-10-4, with bragging rights to two state titles. Tilton's fullback, **Frank Clair**, also began his career under the lights, going from Hamilton to Ohio State where from 1938-1940 he was quarterback Don Scott's favorite receiver. After a brief layover with the Washington Redskins, he got down to business—as a coach—in the Canadian Football League. There, he was known as "The Professor" for his unparalled ability to spot and develop talent. He took the Toronto Argonauts to two Grey Cup titles in the early 1950s, then transformed the Ottawa Rough Riders from a struggling franchise to CFL powerhouse in the 1960s and 1970s. When he left the game, his name was plastered all over the CFL record book: his teams had made the playoffs in 17 of his 19 seasons, gone to the conference final 12 times, and appeared in the Grey Cup six times, winning five. He was a shoo-in for the Canadian Football Hall of Fame and Lansdowne Park in Ottawa was renamed after him. Which wasn't bad for a Hamilton kid who began playing football just as they brought electricity in. . . . About the same time and just up the road a ways—long before **Weeb Ewbank** won the two most important games played in the NFL, he developed his coaching chops at McGuffey High, a little demonstration school run by Miami University's School of Education. There were only about sixty boys enrolled, and while it almost always played against larger schools, Weeb—named by his baby brother who couldn't pronounce his given name, which was "Wilbur"—won 70 and lost only 21. His McGuffey Green Devils went unbeaten in 1936, 1937, and 1940. At one time they had a winning streak of 21 games, outscoring opponents 270-0. He spent thirteen formative seasons there, coaching both at McGuffey and his alma mater, Miami, where he'd once been the quarterback. When he moved on, he did so with a vengeance, coaching the Baltimore Colts to a 23-17 NFL championship over the New York Giants in 1958 in what has been called "the greatest game in history." It went into sudden death overtime and marked the rise of what had been a backwater sport into a mainstream popularity. Then in 1969, Weeb's Joe Namath-led Jets won Super Bowl III over heavily-favored Baltimore, a game that gave the upstart AFL parity with the established NFL graybeards. Once again, the game had been redefined dramatically. And even after he was voted into the Pro Football Hall of Fame, he said his 1940 McGuffey High team—which won the Little Southwestern League title with wins over the much larger schools of Fairfield, North College Hill, and Norwood—was the most dominant team he'd ever coached. He retired to Oxford where his visitors gazed upon the famous mementoes from the great Colts and Jets teams. But there was also a photograph of his McGuffey Green Devils. "No matter where I went afterward," the Oxford don said, "there was still a bit of McGuffey in me." . . . And, finally, the quintessential coaching quote from Deer Park High's **Bob Hollifield**, two-time coach of the year, who suffered a heart attack and thought he had died and gone to heaven. "I looked around," he said, "and I saw a lot of coaches and teachers but no administrators. That's when I knew it had to be heaven . . . ."

It was mid-October of 1998 when Roger Bacon's **B.J. Sander** stepped purposefully away from the spot where his holder set up at midfield, strode into the football, and whacked it deep and true with his left foot, straight toward the crossbar in Centerville, Ohio, where the flags atop the goal posts stood objectively still. When the ball clipped the crossbar and skidded over, giving the Spartans a 10-0 lead over Kettering Alter late in the first quarter, Sander had broken the Ohio high school record with a 60-yard field goal. He was, of course, first-team All-State; and yet, placekicking was not what he did best—at least, according to Ohio State. After first winning the job as the Buckeyes' punter, then losing it to a teammate (Andy Groom) who went on to become an All-American, Sander got it back again and went Groom one better. He won the Ray Guy Award as the nation's best punter. That led to a third-round draft selection by the Green Bay Packers in 2004, which didn't work out particularly well. Nor did his field-goal record last forever: Kevin Harper of Mentor topped it in 2007 with a 61-yard monster. Nevertheless, let the record show that Sander was the most accomplished all-around kicker in Cincinnati history . . . **Kevin Kerr**, however, was not far behind; and frankly can't be denied as a pure field-goal kicker. Kerr was actually a stellar kickball player as a kid, and became so enthused about the art of kicking a ball that he set his mind on becoming St. Xavier's placekicker. His father turned some pipes into a backyard goalpost, with 50 yards of grass to work with. By the time he was a freshman, Kevin had the job. By the time he was a senior in 1998, he was so extraordinary that he was named GCL Player of the Year and the *Cincinnati Post's* Offensive Player of the Year for the entire city. Both of those selections were heartily endorsed by Elder coach Doug Ramsey, whose Panthers were almost single-footedly defeated by St. Xavier's sweet-kicking Bomber. Kerr scored 14 of St. X's points in that 26-21 victory. "He did so many things that changed our game," said Ramsey. "Not only as far as field position was concerned, but also from a morale standpoint. All his kickoffs were in the end zone, so we started from our 20 seven times. His punts made us start on the 2 once and the 10 another time." In the season's final game, Kerr set an Ohio championship-game record with a stirring 56-yard field goal against Canton McKinley. He finished his career third in national high school history in field goals, with 36. Kerr then proceeded to break Ohio University's career record for field goals. For all of the above, he was the kicker named on the *Cincinnati Post's* all-century team . . . Among the many people who failed to fully appreciate **Kirk Springs** over his football career, Cliff Branch is not included. Branch was a quicksilver receiver for the Los Angeles Raiders in 1982, when the Raiders were playing Springs' New York Jets in the second round of the playoffs. (The Jets had blasted the Bengals the week before.) Springs was in the game as an extra defensive back at the time, and it happened that he intersected simultaneously with both Branch and the ball, whereupon Springs laid out the former and sent the latter looping into the air for an easy interception that made a major difference in a 17-14 victory. As the New York defense danced off the field, linebacker Greg Buttle was heard to say, "What a great hit!"—which is of course the highest praise a linebacker can give. Springs' greatest value, however, came on most of the special teams, through not only his conspicuous hitting but also the returning of punts and kickoffs. In 1984, he placed in the top ten in the league in both categories. He had started returning punts only the season before, finishing second in the league and enjoying his few minutes of fame when, with just over two minutes remaining in a tight Monday Night game against New Orleans, he returned one 76 yards for the winning touchdown. It was certainly more than the Jets had bargained for when they signed him as a free agent out of Miami, where he was twice All-MAC and once honorable mention All-American. That followed a three-sport career at Woodward that failed to attract the usual Big Ten suitors—which, ironically, considered themselves special teams . . . There were reasons upon reasons why, in 2007, the University of Cincinnati broke through as a Top 20 football team. There was the new coach, Brian Kelly, and the quarterback, Ben Mauk, and in the same sentence there was the punter,

B.J. Sander

The KICK of his LIFe

We were playing Loveland, they were 8-2 that year and we were 0-10. And we scored with four minutes left to make it 10-7. Had everything going for us. So I told our kicker, Brisbon, 'Onside kick, all right? Onside kick.'

And he said: 'Okay, Coach.'

And I told the special team: 'Okay, White Team, onside kick,' and they went out.

I grabbed Brisbon again and I said: 'Make it a good one, okay, kid? Ten yards on the nose.'

And he said: 'Right, Coach.'

'Go call it in the huddle out there,' I said, and he ran out and did: 'Onside kick, left.'

So they line up and call: 'Shift!' And all our men go left and Brisbon kicks the ball deep to inside the one.

To the right.

To the fastest high hurdle man in the county.

He told me after the game that all he could think while he was waiting for the ball to come down was the headline: *Ninety-nine Yard Kick Return Caps Victory*. Because all our guys were hunting like chickens for grain, looking for the ball way over on the other side of the field.

Willie, my assistant then, he's got his arms spread out yellin': 'What's he doin'? What's he doin'?' But me, I couldn't speak, just 'Awwwwk awwwwwk.'

I thought I had a heart attack, I mean it, I'm not kidding. There was a real sharp pain in my heart, it doubled me over, you can see it in the game films, I'm bent over sayin': 'Call a doctor, call the police, get me an ambulance.'

And I see this kid run by. Brisbon followed the ball and somehow he managed to get clipped and the play got called back.

I ran out, they coulda called a penalty on me, but I was crazy, I grabbed his jersey and picked him right up and screamed at him: 'Whatwereyoudoin? Whatwereyoudoin? It was supposed to be an onside kick!'

'I forgot,' he said.

'You forgot!' I said.

'I'm sorry, Coach,' he said. 'But it was the best kick of my life, did you see it? All the way to the one!'

I went back to the sidelines and Willie said: 'What did he say?'

'He forgot,' I said, 'and he said not to get upset because it was the best kick of his life.'

—Norwood coach Don Rahe, who celebrated the Bill Brisbon Memorial Onside Kick annually in team practice, as quoted by Bob McKay, *Ohio magazine*, September 1982

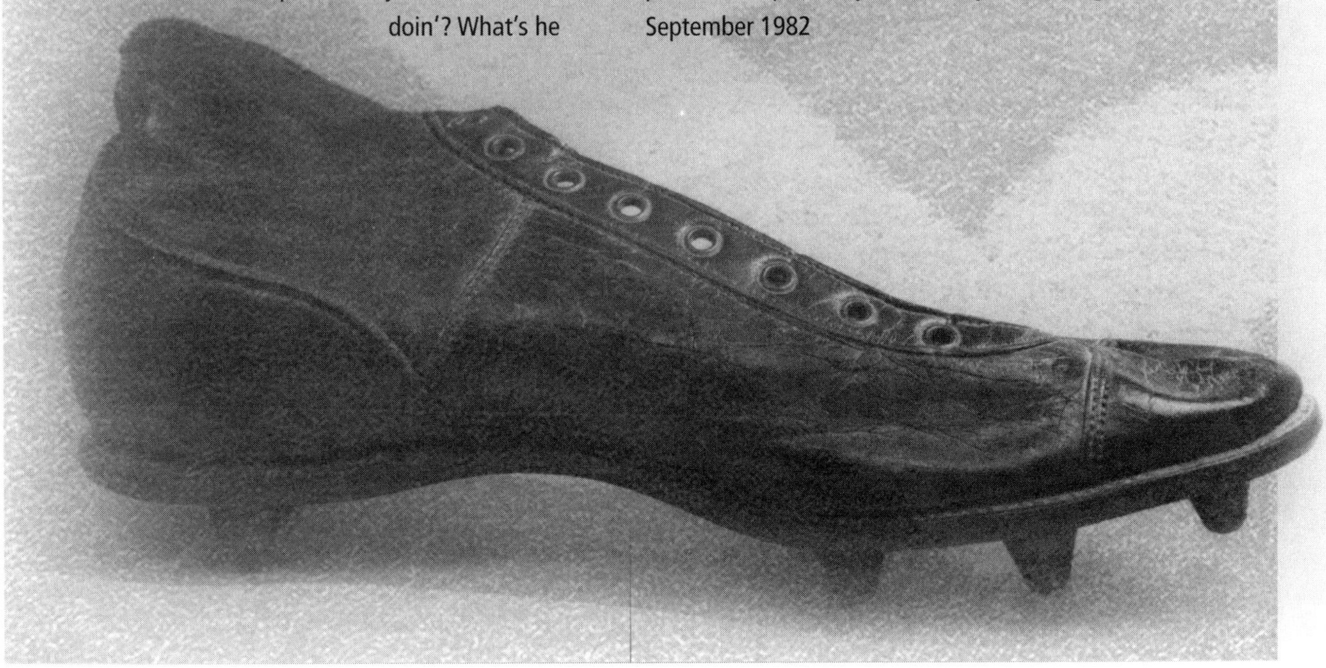

Kevin Huber. A three-time All-GCL selection at McNicholas High School, Huber had not fulfilled his collegiate potential until he attended a punting camp after his sophomore season and returned to school to lead the nation with an unlikely 46.9-yard average. As fabulous as that was, it told only part of the tale. Huber placed more than a third of his punts inside the opponent's 20-yard line, and twice stopped his boot on the 1. He was, of course, a first-team All-American. To boot, he repeated the honor in 2008 . . . At Hughes High School, where in 1996 he was scarcely noted as an honorable mention all-area player, and at Eastern Kentucky, where he was recognized as a Division I-AA All-American, **Alex Bannister's** purpose was to avoid contact, more or less. He was a lanky (6-5, 207—less in high school), deluxe pass-catcher, as a Colonel producing a very major 71 catches for 1,122 yards and a dozen touchdowns his senior year. It's not every year that EKU places a player in the NFL draft, but Bannister so stood out that he went to the Seattle Seahawks in the fifth round of 2001. On the West Coast, he floundered as a wide receiver—he just wasn't wide—instead making his mark by making marks on other people. As a special teams cover guy, Bannister became so exceptional that in 2003 he was noted to the ultimate extent, earning a place on the NFL's All-Pro team. . . During school ceremonies in 1992, the shoe of CAPE placekicker **Robert Allen** was retired and placed in a case with the school's Division IV state championship trophy (its third title). Allen's 40-yard field goal—longest in school history—helped CAPE to a 17-16 win over Warren John F. Kennedy in Massillon. He also kicked one against Wyoming in the first-round game for a 9-7 win. Allen was bemused. "I've never heard of a foot being retired," he said . . . At Princeton High in the early 1970s, **Tom Klaban** was so bad at swimming, his coach kindly sent him over to the football team; maybe his kick would be more effective through air than water. Still, in the *Cincinnati Post's* kicking contest held at Nippert Stadium, Klaban placed only fifth. His history suggested that he might be best as a long distance man—when he was 12, his family escaped from Czechoslovakia, then passed through an Italian refugee camp with brief sojourns in Germany and Canada before settling in Cincinnati. The good thing about such journeys, however, was that it made almost any destination seem possible. So Klaban asked Woody Hayes about playing for Ohio State as a walk-on. He was called "spindly and splay-footed," but every day he hopped on first one leg, then the other, up and down the Ohio Stadium steps, building his strength, which he demonstrated in the 1974 Michigan game by kicking field goals of 47, 45, 43, and 25 yards and winning the game almost single-footedly. It was an interesting transformation: the kid who in high school couldn't swim the water had just demonstrated that in college he could walk on it. It was one of the most significant player afternoons in the rivalry's history. He kicked OSU into the Rose Bowl, as well. He wasn't even on scholarship, either, a problem Woody immediately repaired just after giving Klaban the game ball. (Woody called it "the greatest kicking game I've ever seen.") Klaban's grandmother, still in Czechoslovakia, took his newspaper clippings to the authorities and told them she wanted to see her grandson in the Rose Bowl. She had her visa in two days, watching Klaban kick the Bucks into a late 17-10 lead against USC. Unfortunately, USC scored even later, somebody made a near-impossible catch for the two-point conversion, and OSU lost 18-17. Still, she couldn't have seen anything like it in Prague. For the year, Klaban converted 52 of 53 extra points and nine of twelve field goals—most of them against Michigan. He even outscored Mr. Heisman, Archie Griffin, that season. His 52 PATs still ranks Number 5 in OSU's record book. His afternoon against Michigan, though, is someplace else—in the heart of every diehard Bucks fan . . .

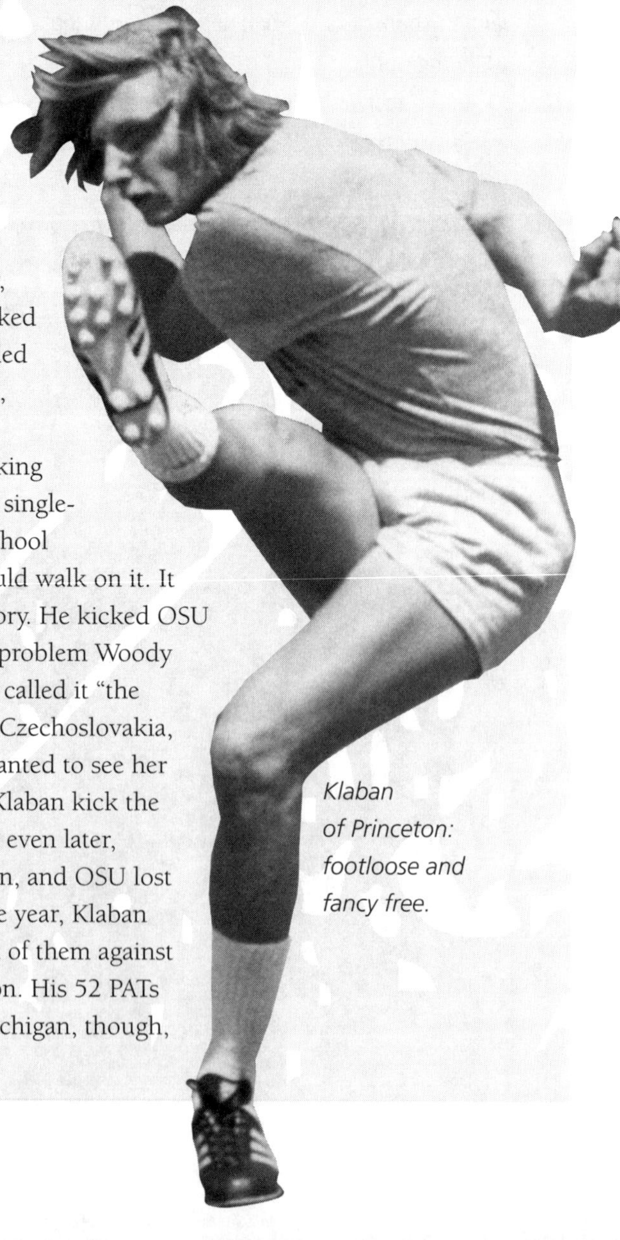

Klaban of Princeton: footloose and fancy free.

A Special (Teams) Moment

He might not have been a legend himself, but you could say he started one. **Barry Cromer**, a walk-on from Cincinnati Country Day, was the contain man that unearthly 1982 afternoon in Berkeley as Stanford—holding a 20-19 lead after a Mark Harmon field goal—kicked off to Cal. "This is one of the great finishes," said the announcer, noting the eight seconds left on the clock. "Only a miracle can save the Bears."

But first things first. How did an undersized kid from CCD end up in front of 75,662 people, playing in one of football's oldest rivalries? It was mostly Harvard's fault, actually. Cromer, a 175-pound fullback/linebacker, was finishing up his expansive prep athletic career—12 letters, captain of five different teams—and thinking he was good enough to play in the Ivy League. Which was when Harvard told him he was too small.

So he headed the *other* way, all the way to Stanford, where he spent the autumn of his freshman year watching, unimpressed, the Cardinal defense and thinking, *I can play here*. He walked on at spring practice, and he was right: he made the team. He was a nonscholarship player, though, and not even on the traveling squad until one weekend early in the 1982 season when Stanford flew east to play vaunted Ohio State before what would be a then-record Ohio Stadium crowd of terminally inflamed Buckeyes.

Then with 1:50 left, John Elway took Stanford 80 yards for a 23-20 upset—and the kid from CCD had played a first-rate game on special teams. Harvard had sent him west, then Ohio State had gotten him a scholarship.

Which brings us back, finally, to the "Big Game in Berkeley." As Stanford kicked off—eight seconds left, remember—even the most disappointed Cal supporter was certain that Cal had lost, even while begrudgingly understanding the game had been a classic.

The kick was a squib to Cal's Kevin Moen, a former option QB, and just as Cromer hit him, Moen lateraled. Cromer slipped past Moen, nearly fell, and recovered just in time to see a second lateral.

What is this, Cromer thinks, *rugby?*

The third Cal guy, running back Dwight Garner, went down, Cromer jumped on the pile, and the nearest ref blew a whistle. But in the last-second chaos, no one seemed to hear it. Garner, who contended his knee never touched the ground, shovel-passed the ball from underneath what appeared to be most of the Stanford team to yet *another* teammate. By this time, the Stanford band was on the field, along with extra players from both teams, but after two more laterals—*five* in all—and a runover trombone player, Moen—the original receiver who had somehow ended up with the ball *again*—scored the impossible winning points. ("It appeared to me," said a spectator afterward, "that the weakest part of the Stanford defense was the woodwinds.")

A quarter of a century later, across most of the country, you could hear Cromer's eyeballs roll. "One of the laterals was a forward lateral, then the guy was down, *and* there should have been a penalty before the ball was even kicked . . . ."

The loss meant Elway would not see a bowl game until he got to the pros, and Barry Cromer would forever be identified with "the wildest kickoff return in history." He finished as Stanford's special teams captain and went on to med school where he found his calling in orthopedics. Today he's part of the El Paso Orthopedic Surgery Group, one of the largest in the southwest. It's a perfect, if unintended, synergy between a defensive player and the damage he once caused.

Dr. Cromer started out in primary care but preferred what he calls the nuts-and-bolts aspects of orthopedics. "It's the closest thing to construction work," he says. "And you get to use drills and hammers . . . ."

Spoken like a true special teams man.

His Eminence

It was a lesser observation for the year 1974, but only because it was a quieter one. **Howard Wirtz**, the only Cincinnatian to ever officiate a Rose Bowl game, retired that year after a half-century of the best view in the house. Wirtz did his Queen City turf work by spending a dozen years calling the traditional Elder-Western Hills Turkey Day game, moving on to Xavier University and the college scene where he became the premier Big Ten referee.

He was called "aloof, dictatorial, and magnificent on the field," but his fellow refs bowed to his consummate knowledge, calling him "His Eminence." ABC-TV executive Roone Arledge asked Wirtz to wear a white hat so cameramen could immediately spot the referee, and the hat became standard gear the next season.

He never played the game himself, something he called an asset. "I never got emotionally involved over a game," he said. "I was only concerned with how it was played." He was involved emotionally only with the atmosphere itself. "I don't think there is anything more wonderful," he said, "than a college town the night before a big game . . . ."

Elder kicker Mike Riga demonstrates the footwork that led him to eight school records, including a 55.2-yard kickoff average in 2002 and a 41-yard field goal at St. Ignatius that kept the Panthers on the road to their first state title.

Hiawatha Francisco was D'Juan's big brother, both All-Americans for Moeller where their brotherly attributes were a plague on the GCL's best defenses.

Photo credits

Photographs not otherwise listed are from the extensive picture archives of the *Cincinnati Enquirer*, with special assistance from Michael Perry; Michael McCarter, the Director of Visuals; and archivist Jeff Seuss. Every effort has been made to correctly identify both content and owner of each photograph reproduced herein; please notify publishers of any omissions or inaccuracies.

Preliminaries
ix—Joe Thesing, Elder High School; xvi-xxv—courtesy Archives and Rare Books Library, University of Cincinnati.

Quarterbacks
2—Staubach at Navy, courtesy U.S. Naval Academy; 9—Elder medal, Orange Frazer Press; 11—Carvitti, Chris Smith for Orange Frazer Press; tickets and team photograph, Elder High School; 12-13—Poland by Chris Smith for Orange Frazer Press; 16—Murray, courtesy Archives and Rare Books Library, University of Cincinnati; 18—background drawing from Ellison's original book, *Run and Shoot Football: Offense of the Future*, in the Orange Frazer library; 19—Freddie Ratterman, courtesy Archives and Rare Books Library, University of Cincinnati; 21—the younger Ratterman, courtesy Archives and Rare Books Library, University of Cincinnati; 24—Redrow, courtesy Wilmington College; 26-27—Selcer photographs, Elder High School; 27—Rubin, courtesy Archives and Rare Books Library, University of Cincinnati; 32—young Staubach, courtesy Archives and Rare Books Library, University of Cincinnati; 35—Tensi, Elder High School; Bibent, courtesy Archives and Rare Books Library, University of Cincinnati; 37—the young Zimmer, courtesy Archives and Rare Books Library, University of Cincinnati; 38-39—Western Hills lettermen, courtesy Archives and Rare Books Library, University of Cincinnati; 40—Franz, courtesy Archives and Rare Books Library, University of Cincinnati.

Running backs
44—Barkley, courtesy Archives and Rare Books Library, University of Cincinnati; 45—Bolger, courtesy Archives and Rare Books Library, University of Cincinnati; 52-53—*Columbus Dispatch*; 58, Key, courtesy Archives and Rare Books Library, University of Cincinnati; 63—Bentley, courtesy Archives and Rare Books Library, University of Cincinnati; 65—Mason pictures, courtesy Archives and Rare Books Library, University of Cincinnati; 66-67—courtesy Archives and Rare Books Library, University of Cincinnati; 68—Minor, courtesy Wilmington College; 71—the Roeckers, courtesy Xavier University; 71—background action, courtesy Archives and Rare Books Library, University of Cincinnati; 73—Pete Rose, courtesy Archives and Rare Books Library, University of Cincinnati; 74—LIFE, from the Orange Frazer library; 79—Walter Johnson card, Michael O'Bryant; 80-81—Otis Williams, courtesy Archives and Rare Books Library, University of Cincinnati; 82—the Charms, courtesy Archives and Rare Books Library, University of Cincinnati; 84-85—courtesy Archives and Rare Books Library, University of Cincinnati.

Fullbacks
86—Roger Bacon action, courtesy Archives and Rare Books Library, University of Cincinnati; 87, Walnut Hills action, courtesy Archives and Rare Books Library, University of Cincinnati; 88, Boxcar Bailey, thanks to Miami University and Mike Pearson; 89, Boxcar, courtesy Archives and Rare Books Library, University of Cincinnati; 90, drawing of Butterworth, courtesy Archives and Rare Books Library, University of Cincinnati; 90-91, drawing of game at League Park, courtesy Archives and Rare Books Library, University of Cincinnati; 95, Nolting, courtesy Archives and Rare Books Library, University of Cincinnati; 96-97, Hamilton team, courtesy Archives and Rare Books Library, University of Cincinnati; 99, Parker, courtesy Archives and Rare Books Library, University of Cincinnati; 101, Shuttlesworth, courtesy Archives and Rare Books Library, University of Cincinnati; 103, "The Sheik," Elder High School.

Ends and receivers
111—Purcell, courtesy Archives and Rare Books Library, University of Cincinnati; 114—Beagle, courtesy U.S. Naval Academy; 117,

Hasselbeck—courtesy Archives and Rare Books Library, University of Cincinnati; 121, Joslin, courtesy Archives and Rare Books Library, University of Cincinnati; 123—Kelly, Elder; 125—O'Brien, courtesy Archives and Rare Books Library, University of Cincinnati; 135—Wendt, courtesy Archives and Rare Books Library, University of Cincinnati; 138—LaSalle, courtesy Archives and Rare Books Library, University of Cincinnati; 139—The Pit, Elder High School.

Linemen
140—Anderson and team, courtesy Archives and Rare Books Library, University of Cincinnati; 141—Biehle, Miami University; 142—Koepfle, courtesy Archives and Rare Books Library, University of Cincinnati; 148—Jackson, Eastern Kentucky University; 150—Bob James, Chris Smith for Orange Frazer Press, and Dave James, Elder High School; 157—Martinkovic, courtesy Archives and Rare Books Library, University of Cincinnati; 159—Langenbeck, courtesy Archives and Rare Books Library, University of Cincinnati; 167—Sylvester, courtesy Steve Sylvester; 168—Tehan, Xavier University; 170, Socko Wiethe, courtesy Archives and Rare Books Library, University of Cincinnati; 171—Wiethe, courtesy Xavier University; 172—Wilburn, courtesy Archives and Rare Books Library, University of Cincinnati; 173—Feldhaus, courtesy Archives and Rare Books Library, University of Cincinnati; Fry, Elder High School; 175-177—Elder High School.

Linebackers
178—Pillman, Miami University; 179—Elder High School; 186—Evans, courtesy Archives and Rare Books Library, University of Cincinnati; 188—Grote, Elder High School; 196—Reynolds, courtesy Archives and Rare Books Library, University of Cincinnati; 198-199—Western Hills team, courtesy Archives and Rare Books Library, University of Cincinnati; 203—cheerleaders, courtesy Archives and Rare Books Library, University of Cincinnati.

Defensive backs
206—Goodridge, courtesy Bob Goodridge; 209—Bibent, courtesy Archives and Rare Books Library, University of Cincinnati; 212-215—courtesy Bob Goodridge; 216—Gray, courtesy Archives and Rare Books Library, University of Cincinnati; 219—Herbstreit, courtesy Archives and Rare Books Library, University of Cincinnati; 221—Sensibaught, The Ohio State University; 223—Stemrick, courtesy Archives and Rare Books Library, University of Cincinnati; 225—Townsend, courtesy Archives and Rare Books Library, University of Cincinnati; Woodruff, the Pittsburgh Steelers.

Hamilton
233—Tony Lamke; 235—Wilke, courtesy Archives and Rare Books Library, University of Cincinnati; 263—Boxcar, Miami University; football cards, courtesy Archives and Rare Books Library, University of Cincinnati; football banquet, Joe Nuxhall private collection; 239, 241, 242, 243—courtesy Linda Thomas; 243—Hamilton Catholic team, courtesy Terry Malone and Cathy.

Coaches
244—Bacevich, courtesy Archives and Rare Books Library, University of Cincinnati; 245—Ballaban and Berning, courtesy Archives and Rare Books Library, University of Cincinnati; 246-247—Roger Bacon team, courtesy Archives and Rare Books Library, University of Cincinnati; 248-249—Ballaban pictures, courtesy Archives and Rare Books Library, University of Cincinnati; 250—Bartlett, Elder High School; 258—Ellison and staff, courtesy Archives and Rare Books Library, University of Cincinnati; drawing is from Ellison's book, *Run and Shoot Football: Offense of the Future*; 272—Jones brothers, courtesy Archives and Rare Books Library, University of Cincinnati; 273—Krueck, courtesy Archives and Rare Books Library, University of Cincinnati; 277, Lichtenberg, courtesy Archives and Rare Books Library, University of Cincinnati; 279-281, courtesy Terry Malone and Cathy; 290—O'Brien, courtesy North Carolina State; 291—Rasso, courtesy Archives and Rare Books Library, University of Cincinnati; 292—Ramsey, Elder High School; 293—Theda Bara, Orange Frazer library; 294—Kerin, courtesy Archives and Rare Books Library, University of Cincinnati: 98—Klaban, *The Columbus Dispatch*.

Young Brinkmeyer of Woodward in a 1930s practice session.

Turkey Day, 1929-1978, R.I.P.

It was the nearest thing to a Cincinnati bowl game, and it had everything: great athletes, spirited encounters, standing room only crowds, atmosphere—a neighborhood turf war fought every Thanksgiving over a hundred-yard strip of crabgrass. There was never a better way to spend the day, even if only half the crowd could *really* be thankful, for there was always next Thanksgiving when you might be again.

The rivalry wasn't even strictly *seasonal*, for the players in those days lived in Price Hill and Covedale, played baseball together during the summer, and had known each other forever. Whatever the season, **The Game** always lay out in front of them, possible vindication for any number of other athletic failures—no matter *what* field of play—and it was surely the capstone of any Elder or Western Hills football season.

So people went to mass, the game began at 10 a.m., finished up at noon, there was a little lunch, then folks were off to the early afternoon UC-Miami game, followed by the turkey. The next day, the Christmas season officially began. When was life ever better?

Over the years, The Game was played all over town: at The Pit, of course, on West High's field, old Crosley Field, Nippert Stadium, Xavier University's Corcoran Field, Trechter Stadium, and it ended up on the Riverfront. The first game was played on old Redland Field, Crosley's West Side predecessor. It came in 1929, a month after the stock market crash. Elder, roused by the St. Joseph Orphanage band, beat Western Hills, 12-0, but the rivalry stayed game-for-game until 1950.

In 1952, Western Hills scored two late touchdowns to ruin Babe Bartlett's final game of coaching. Defensive end Russ Nixon, who would go on to manage the Cincinnati Reds, blocked a punt on the Elder 6-yard line. The punt was by Dick Selcer, the Elder All-Stater who would become an NFL coach.

In 1958, a scrappy West High halfback named Pete Rose caught a touchdown pass to give his team the lead, and Western Hills won 31-14. Thereafter, Elder put the series in a stranglehold, although Pete's brother, Dave Rose, broke a string of five straight Elder shutouts by running back a kickoff for 85 yards and a score.

He averted the shutout, but not the outcome: Elder ran off 20 straight victories before West High won the tradition's final installment.

That came in 1978, because the Ohio High School Athletic Association expanded its playoff format: Elder would now have a good chance of getting into the playoffs and playoff games would conflict with the Turkey Day classic. So there would be no old Turkey Day neighborhood skirmish but there would be a new tradition: Panthers in the state playoffs.

The Lord giveth.

The Lord taketh away.

The final game was held in a suitable venue for such an institution: Riverfront Stadium. For the first time in memory, things looked good for West High; the Mustangs were 7-1-1, had shut out seven of their opponents, and won the Public High School League championship for the first time in twenty years.

Ray Bachus, the Elder coach, was 11 years old when he saw his first Thanksgiving Day game in 1958. He remembered nostalgically a fistfight in the stands and went on to become an All-City Elder lineman. He would not remember the 1978 game quite so sentimentally for Elder lost, 6-0, so overcome by West's defense that the Panthers didn't pick up a single first down.

Bachus *did* remember the ride home, up Elberon Avenue where every stop seemed populated by hordes of West High fans, hooting victory. The West win also meant it kept the revolving trophy permanently, a last bit of West Side irony: Elder had won 35 of the Thanksgiving games, lost 13, tied once, and Western Hills got the trophy.

The truth was, it was a *city* trophy and *everybody* lost: The Game had lasted for half a century and in all the Queen City's spirited crosstown rivalries since, there's been nothing quite like it.

Arnold Franklin was Princeton's All-American tight end/linebacker in 1981, when he was considered the best high school player in America.

Index

1891 Hughes defeats Woodward on October 30, creating the oldest current rivalry in Ohio high school football. The teams met twice more before the season ended with Woodward winning both games. The rivalry, sixth oldest nationally, predates Massillon Washington–Canton McKinley by two years.

1893 Frank Butterworth, born in Maineville (he moved East after his father was elected to Congress), is recognized as an All-American—most likely Ohio's first—as he shines at fullback and heads a Yale defense that allows only 12 points all season. The next year, he was on the receiving end when Harvard unveiled the notorious "flying wedge."

1924 At the famous Chariots of Fire games in Paris, DeHart Hubbard wins the long jump and becomes the first African-American to bring home an Olympic gold medal. Hubbard's football interests had been thwarted when public-school officials removed him from the Walnut Hills roster for vague reasons of eligibility.

1932 John Anderson, a strongboy lineman from Hughes, wins a gold medal in Los Angeles and sets an Olympic record in the discus.

1932 Howard Jones of Middletown, overshadowed by his brother, Tad, as a player—an All-American quarterback at Yale— fashions his lasting legacy as a head coach. His Southern Californians claim their second straight national championship. He also won five Rose Bowls.

1940 Hughes grad Ray Nolting, three-time MVP of the Chicago Bears, plays his typically prominent role in Chicago's famous 73-0 thrashing of the Washington Redskins for the NFL championship. Nolting, who later coached at the University of Cincinnati, led the Bears that season in total yards and interceptions.

Hoernschemeyer

1944 A future Hamilton High School fullback, Joe Nuxhall, debuts for the Cincinnati Reds at age 15, making him the youngest major-leaguer of the modern era.

1953 Bob Hoernschemeyer of the Detroit Lions, the pride of Elder High, becomes the second leading rusher (behind Steve Van Buren) in professional football history.

1954 Two-way end Ron Beagle of Purcell, a sharp-looking Midshipman, wins the Maxwell Trophy as the best player in college football.

1958 Starting with a formation he calls "the lonesome polecat"—with the quarterback under center and everybody else spread across the field—Middletown coach Glenn "Tiger" Ellison creates a wide-open offense utilizing four wide receivers and frequent forward passes. Ellison later authored an influential book on his innovative air attack, which evolved into the pro-style run-and-shoot.

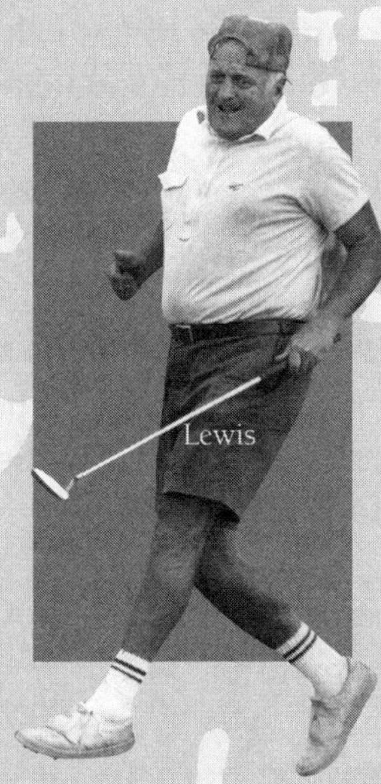
Lewis

1960s

1962 Wyoming High School, coached by Bob Lewis, completes its ten-game schedule without surrendering a single point, while scoring 446. In the AP poll dominated by Northern Ohio interests, the Cowboys are not ranked in the top ten.

1963 Purcell grad Roger Staubach, playing for Navy, wins the Heisman Trophy, which the wife of the Academy publicist stores in the trunk of her car. It makes for unusual trips to the supermarket. "I'd tell the bag boys," said the publicist's wife, "'to put the groceries in there, right next to the Heisman Trophy.'"

1969 Jack Reynolds of Western Hills earns himself a permanent nickname by using a hacksaw to cut through an abandoned Chevrolet Bel Air at the University of Tennessee.

1970s

1972 Ohio finally institutes a playoff system, and the first—and perhaps still greatest—upset is registered by Princeton High in the opening (semifinal) round. In a jolt to the pride and tradition of Northern Ohio, the Vikings knock off mighty Massillon, the mythical powerhouse that for decades had dominated the wire-service rankings that determined the state champions.

1973 The great Bron Bacevich retires from Roger Bacon with 311 victories, more (at the time) than any other high school coach in history.

1975 In a playoff game against Minnesota, Staubach, now the quarterbacking icon of the Dallas Cowboys, heaves a winning, 50-yard touchdown pass to Drew Pearson with time running out. "I just closed my eyes and said a Hail Mary," allows the former altar boy. This is widely reported as the origin of the Hail Mary pass.

1976 Moeller High School, coached by Gerry Faust and quarterbacked by Tim Koegel, wins its second straight state championship and its first of five national titles in a seven-year period.

1980s

1977 The Greater Catholic League celebrates a half century of existence. The organization of Catholic boys high schools known for its tenaciousness in both classroom and on the playing field has been called by recruiters, "the best high school football league in the Midwest, and one of the best in the nation." Every year, more than a dozen league players receive Division I rides and its athletes have turned up in every major conference in America.

1980 Faust departs Moeller for a larger parish—Notre Dame—thereby exchanging America's top high school program for its most famous collegiate one. After five largely unfortunate years in the bigger big time, Faust is banished, ending up in that Protestant purgatory, Akron.

1981 Arnold Franklin, a tight end and linebacker from Princeton, is named national Player of the Year.

1982 Steve Klonne is *USA Today's* national high school coach of the year after his Moeller team was named the national champions. Klonne, who won state titles in 1982 and 1985, would be pushed out in 2001 with a record of 169-48, and six wins shy of Gerry Faust's Moeller total.

1984 Milford product Napoleon McCallum, in the continuing tradition of Cincinnatians doing stellar service at the Naval Academy, sets a collegiate record for all-purpose yards.

1985 Former Western Hills halfback Pete Rose, a key member of the last West High team to beat Elder in twenty years (1958 to 1978), surpasses Ty Cobb to become baseball's all-time hit king.

1985 Staubach, having retired as the NFL's highest-rated passer, is inducted into the Pro Football Hall of Fame in Canton, Ohio.

1989 The *Enquirer* calls national scoring record by Carlos Snow the achievement of the decade on the local prep scene: 105 rushing TDs (108 overall) in four years. He rushed for 7,587 yards, averaging more than than 10 yards every time he got the ball, and led CAPE to a Division IV title in 1985 and a Division III one in 1986. ("Two in the Shoe," said CAPE AD Cindy Windburn before the second title.)

1990s

1991 Roger Bacon coaching legend Bron Bacevich is inducted into the National High School Sports Hall of Fame. National Coach of the Year in 1973, his Roger Bacon teams won seven league titles. Bacevich, who as a lad missed out on sports because of having to work in his father's meat market, finally got to play at North Central College where he starred at quarterback, playmaking guard, and shortstop. When he retired in 1974 he said it was because of his bad hip, which didn't allow him to demonstrate proper blocking techniques.

1992 Former Princeton running back Markus Thomas becomes Division I-AA's all-time leading rusher. He also sets an NCAA record for yards-per-carry, at 6.57.

1997 Dana Stubblefield, a large lineman out of Taylor High School, is named NFL Defensive Player of the Year.

1998 Jason Bainum closes out his illustrious Williamsburg career as the all-time leading rusher in Ohio high school history.

1998 Woodward grad John Jackson, a longtime Pittsburgh Steeler, signs a six-year contract with San Diego for $26.55 million, making him the richest lineman in NFL history. A few months later, Cris Carter of Middletown signs with Minnesota for four years and $23.5 million, becoming the highest-paid wide receiver in the league. He's also the most acrobatic and sure-handed.

2001 A crowd of 47,743, the biggest ever for an Ohio playoff game, gathers at Paul Brown Stadium for a doubleheader matching the best of the city's public and Catholic schools: Colerain vs. Elder and Princeton vs. St. Xavier. Winners are Elder, St. X and the marching bands. The Bengals had tried to prevent the bands from performing at halftime for fear they would damage the grass of the playing field.

2003 Hamilton Badin legend Terry Malone retires with a coaching record of 360-177-8. His victory total is the highest in Ohio prep history.

2004 Michael Larkin, Miami University's senior wide receiver from St. Xavier High, sets an NCAA record for consecutive games (48) with at least one reception.

2008 Milt Stegall of Roger Bacon, already the Canadian Football League's all-time leader in touchdown catches, becomes the CFL record-holder in receiving yards.

2009 On New Year's Day, Tony Pike, a lanky quarterback from Reading High, leads the University of Cincinnati into the Orange Bowl, the first BCS bowl game in school history. Also starring for the Big East champs are receiver Dominick Goodman and defensive tackle Terrill Byrd (both from Colerain), offensive lineman Trevor Canfield (Western Hills), defensive back Brandon Underwood (Hamilton) and All-American punter Kevin Huber (McNicholas).

Stegall

In 1994, two Cincinnatians made Parade magazine's annual All-American team, Mario Strayhan, a defensive back from Princeton, and Cincinnati Country Day's 6-1, 215-pound Andre Barkley (at left), one of the most sought after running backs in the country, even though he played for a Division IV school. Barkley was also the Ohio champion in the 100 meters (10.6) and a second team All-City basketball guard. He led Cincinnati runners in 1993 with 2,067 yards, averaging 10 yards a carry, and was called the most-heralded breakaway running back since CAPE's Carlos Snow in 1986.

author bios

The highlight of **Lonnie Wheeler's** football career occurred in the finals of the fifth-grade gym class tournament. His team led by a touchdown—*his* touchdown—with the clock speeding toward arithmetic. The other guys had the ball at around midfield, and as they huddled, the teacher informed them that time remained for only one more play. So, arms around shoulders, they leaned close, studied the situation with diligence, then broke purposefully toward the line of scrimmage. It was then that the captain announced, "We'll punt." The smug young scribe fairly giggled with glee.

Mike O'Bryant played on Mason High's first football team where his prowess at defensive back was such that he was quickly moved to offense. His finest moment came as a senior, after his 70-yard scoring scamper—*Wing Right, Right 22*—in the season opener was called back. Two plays later, he did it again, this time for 50 yards and a righteous score. Mason was 9-1 that year, and O'Bryant graduated after winning the league in the 100y, 220y, and 440y dashes (although not in the same year). He had a brief fling at running back with the semipro Cincinnati Blue Devils but doesn't remember much about it as beer was served on the sidelines. O'Bryant coached at Purcell with Tom Lichtenberg, then coached at Mason for twenty years.

John Baskin was the first player from his high school in upstate South Carolina to make the varsity of a college team, a gratuitous and little-known fact he earned largely by default—and the fact that Hillcrest High's stellar fullback, Baskin's classmate, became so homesick he left his Wingate College camp where he was contending for a starting position, took a bus back to Greenville, then walked twelve miles home carrying two suitcases. Baskin's finest moments seemed to occur in either spring practice or twenty years later in the annual Mars Hill College varsity-alumni game where he played two quarters and was awarded the only athletic trophy of his life, which, he later learned, was awarded to anyone who was 40 years old and dumb enough to suit up against the varsity.

Jacket photographs—From back jacket, far left, at top: Jim O'Brien (88), Aiken High; Jim Herbstreit (45), Reading High; and Barry Larkin, Moeller. Bottom: Kyle Rudolph (9), Elder High; Connor Smith, Colerain; and Mike Healey, St. Xavier. Front jacket: Extreme top, Bron Bacevich's Roger Bacon squad, circa 1960. Portraits are Cris Carter, Middletown; Carlos Snow, CAPE; Roger Staubach, Purcell High; Bob Hoernschemeyer, Elder High; and Kerry Coombs, Colerain. At bottom, left corner, Napoleon McCallum, Milford High; and at bottom right, underneath the swash, Gerry Faust of Moeller excoriates Eric Ellington. Inside rear flap, The Pit, Elder High.

At top—The cheerleader is Marcia McCalla of Mariemont, cheering for Ohio State at the OSU-Northwestern game in 1964.